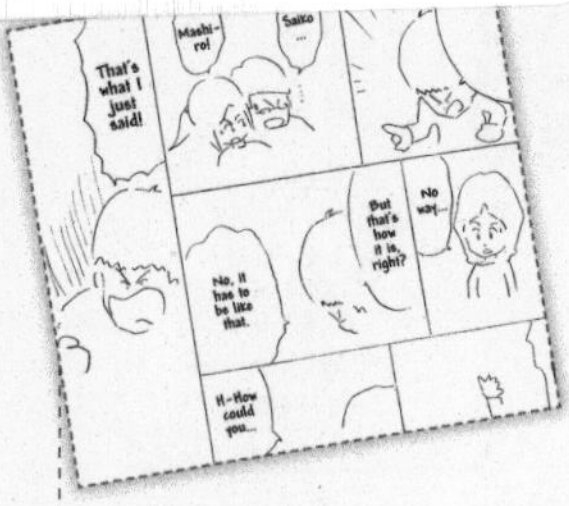
Saiko ...
Mashi-ro!
That's what I just said!
No way...
But that's how it is, right?
No, it has to be like that.
H-How could you...

Sometimes I can't decide on the dialogue, so I just draw the speech balloons and put it off until later. But often I'll end up erasing the balloon and then my editor will tell me my writing doesn't make any sense at all.

—Tsugumi Ohba

I like mechanical pencils, but I'm all about the traditional ones. But I really like Pop-A-Point Pencils too.

—Takeshi Obata

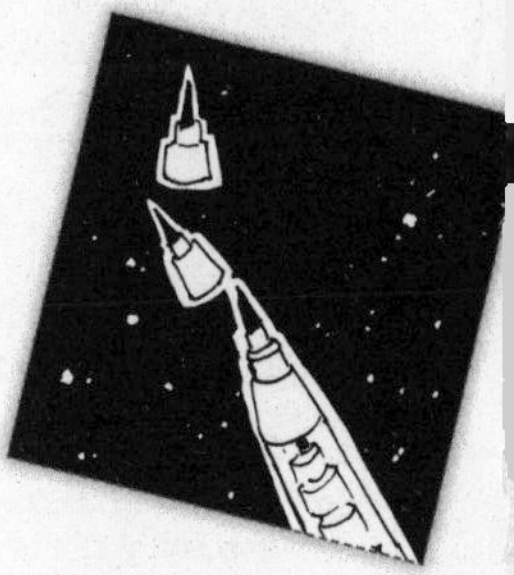

Tsugumi Ohba

Born in Tokyo, Tsugumi Ohba is the author of the hit series *Death Note*. His current series *Bakuman。* is serialized in *Weekly Shonen Jump*.

Takeshi Obata

Takeshi Obata was born in 1969 in Niigata, Japan, and is the artist of the wildly popular SHONEN JUMP title *Hikaru no Go*, which won the 2003 Tezuka Osamu Cultural Prize: Shinsei "New Hope" award and the 2000 Shogakukan Manga award. Obata is also the artist of *Arabian Majin Bokentan Lamp Lamp*, *Ayatsuri Sakon*, *Cyborg Jichan G.*, and the smash hit manga *Death Note*. His current series *Bakuman。* is serialized in *Weekly Shonen Jump*.

BAKUMAN。

Volume 12

SHONEN JUMP Manga Edition

Story by **TSUGUMI OHBA**
Art by **TAKESHI OBATA**

Translation | **Tetsuichiro Miyaki**
English Adaptation | **Julie Lutz**
Touch-up Art & Lettering | **James Gaubatz**
Design | **Fawn Lau**
Editor | **Alexis Kirsch**

Published by VIZ Media, LLC
P.O. Box 77010
San Francisco, CA 94107

10 9 8 7 6 5 4 3 2 1
First printing, July 2012

VIZ
MEDIA
www.viz.com

SHONEN
JUMP
www.shonenjump.com

BAKUMAN。

12

ARTIST and MANGA ARTIST

STORY BY
TSUGUMI OHBA

ART BY
TAKESHI OBATA

SHONENJUMP MANGA

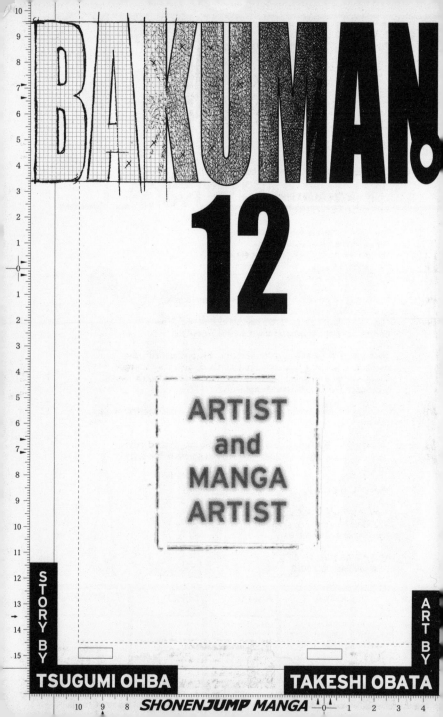

UMAN。 バクマン。 vol. 12

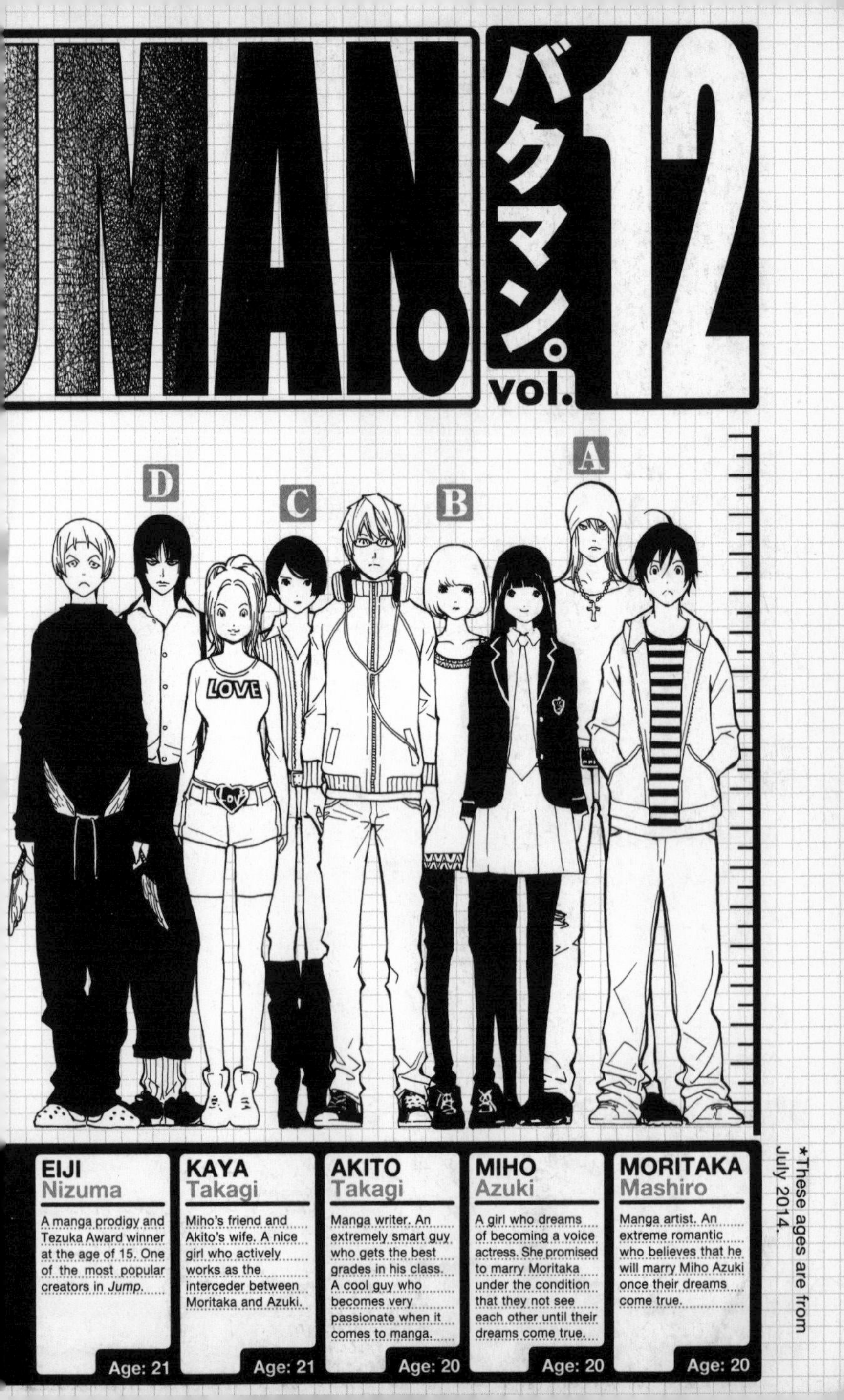

A
B
C
D

EIJI
Nizuma

A manga prodigy and Tezuka Award winner at the age of 15. One of the most popular creators in *Jump*.

Age: 21

KAYA
Takagi

Miho's friend and Akito's wife. A nice girl who actively works as the interceder between Moritaka and Azuki.

Age: 21

AKITO
Takagi

Manga writer. An extremely smart guy who gets the best grades in his class. A cool guy who becomes very passionate when it comes to manga.

Age: 20

MIHO
Azuki

A girl who dreams of becoming a voice actress. She promised to marry Moritaka under the condition that they not see each other until their dreams come true.

Age: 20

MORITAKA
Mashiro

Manga artist. An extreme romantic who believes that he will marry Miho Azuki once their dreams come true.

Age: 20

*These ages are from July 2014.

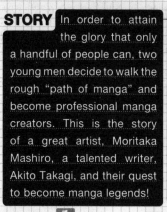

STORY In order to attain the glory that only a handful of people can, two young men decide to walk the rough "path of manga" and become professional manga creators. This is the story of a great artist, Moritaka Mashiro, a talented writer, Akito Takagi, and their quest to become manga legends!

6
1
4
5
2
I
L
G
J
E
H
K
7
3
8
F

WEEKLY SHONEN JUMP Editorial Department

1. Editor in Chief Sasaki
2. Deputy Editor in Chief Heishi
3. Soichi Aida
4. Yujiro Hattori
5. Akira Hattori
6. Koji Yoshida
7. Goro Miura
8. Masakazu Yamahisa

The MANGA ARTISTS and ASSISTANTS

- A SHINTA FUKUDA
- B KO AOKI
- C AIKO IWASE
- D KAZUYA HIRAMARU
- E RYU SHIZUKA
- F NATSUMI KATO
- G YASUOKA
- H SHOYO TAKAHAMA
- I TAKURO NAKAI
- J SHUICHI MORIYA
- K SHUN SHIRATORI
- L ICHIRIKI ORIHARA

vol. BAKUMAN。
12
CONTENTS

(ARTIST AND)
(MANGA ARTIST)

EIGHT YEARS AGO
YAKUSA CITY
MEIYO MUNICI
MURMUR
MURMUR
MURMUR
AIKO, THE RESULTS FOR THE TEST ARE OUT! YOU'RE IN SECOND PLACE.
I'M IN 11TH...
1st Year Achievement Test Re
Top 20 Students
1 Akito Takagi 496
2 Aiko Iwase 48
3 Seiji Jinb
4 Miki S
JINBO MUST HAVE GOTTEN FIRST PLACE...
!
Top
1 Akito Ta
2 Aiko Iwa
AKITO TAKAGI IS IN CLASS 1. I THINK HE'S FROM MEISO ELEMENTARY.
JINBO, YOU STUDIED SO HARD BUT ONLY LANDED IN THIRD?
TH-THAT'S CAUSE I DIDN'T STUDY AT ALL!
LIAR. YOU STUDY FOUR HOURS WITH A TUTOR EVERY DAY AND ALL DAY ON WEEKENDS. PRESSURE'S ON WHEN YOUR PARENTS ARE DOCTORS.
I DON'T WANNA BE A DOCTOR! THAT'S WHY I'M AT A PUBLIC SCHOOL!
MORE LIKE YOU DIDN'T MAKE IT INTO A PRIVATE ONE!
UGH, I HATE IT WHEN PEOPLE STUDY AND DENY IT.
...
CHAPTER 98 HANDSHAKE AND REVISION

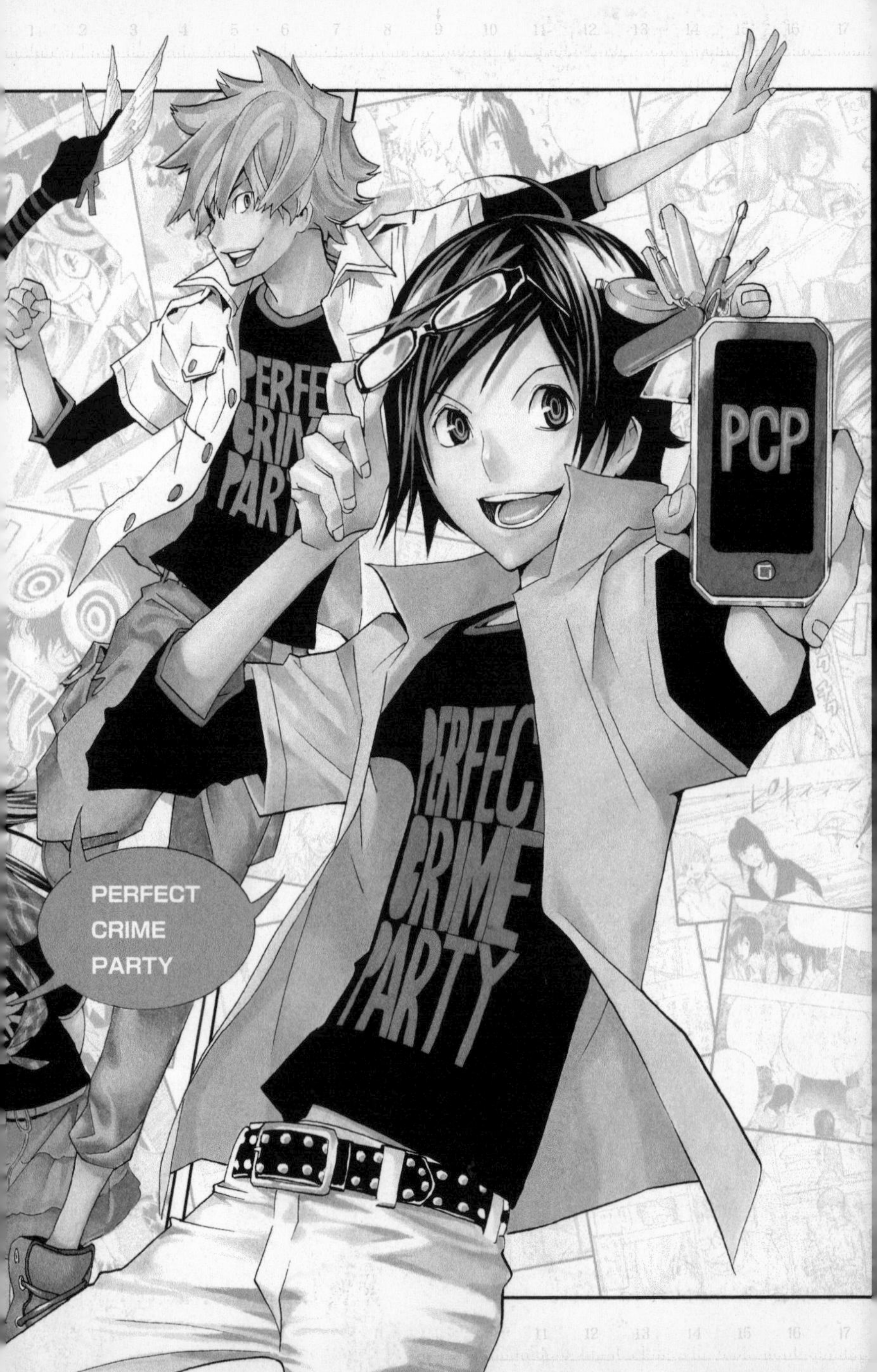
PCP
PERFECT
CRIME
PARTY

CHAPTER 98 HANDSHAKE AND REVISION

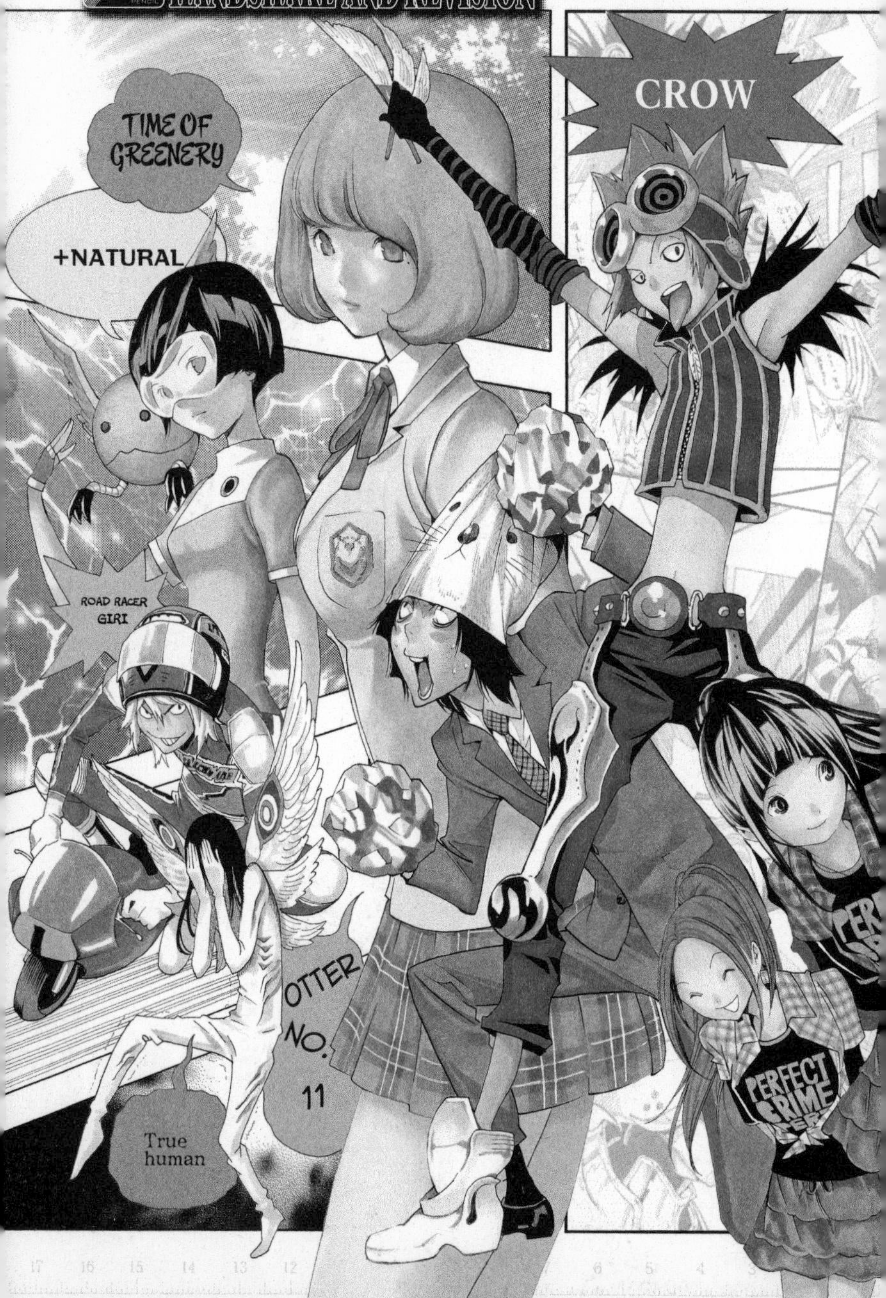
CROW
TIME OF GREENERY
+NATURAL
ROAD RACER GIRI
OTTER NO. 11
True human

BAKUMAN。

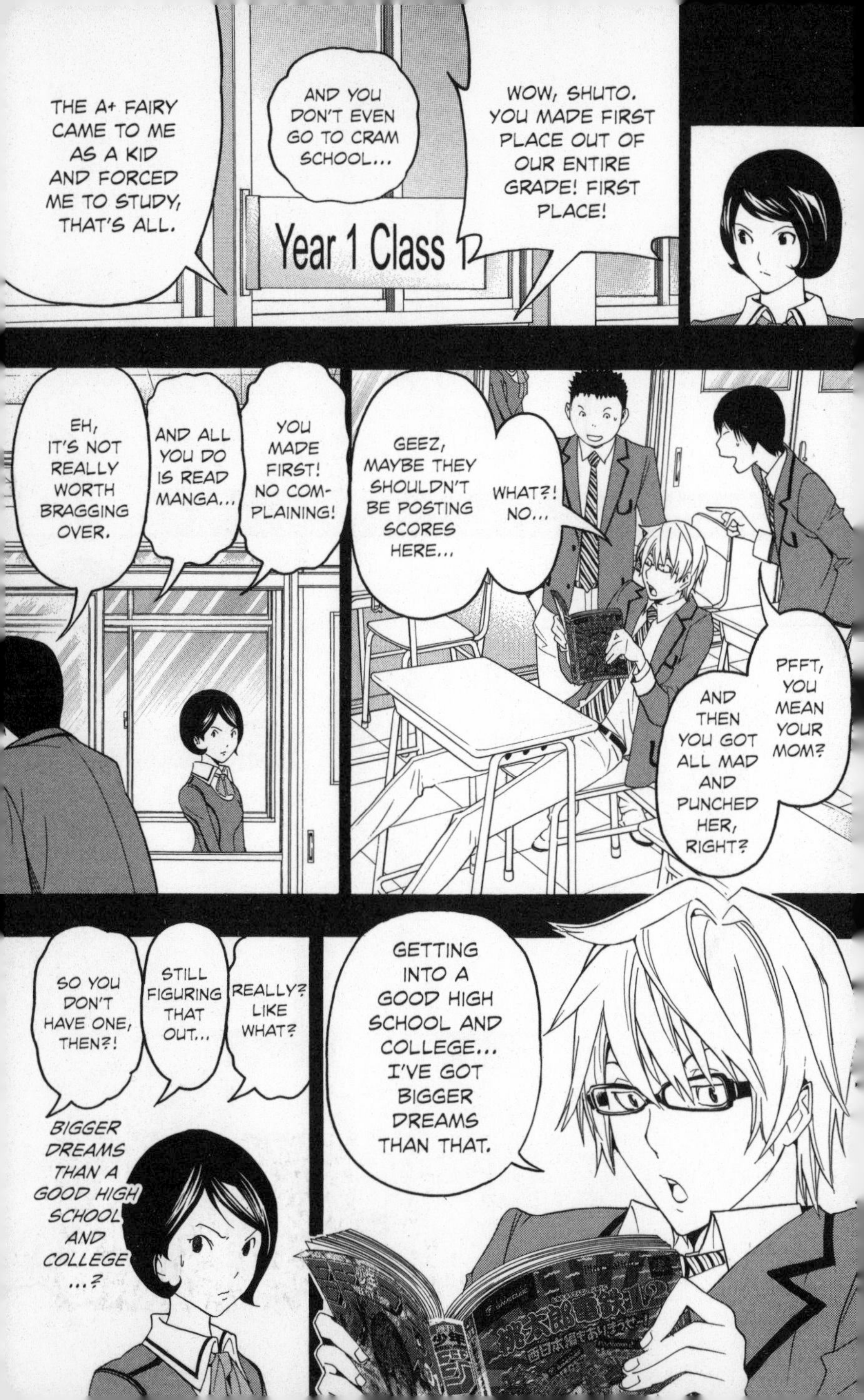
WOW, SHUTO. YOU MADE FIRST PLACE OUT OF OUR ENTIRE GRADE! FIRST PLACE!
AND YOU DON'T EVEN GO TO CRAM SCHOOL...
THE A+ FAIRY CAME TO ME AS A KID AND FORCED ME TO STUDY, THAT'S ALL.
Year 1 Class 1
WHAT?! NO...
GEEZ, MAYBE THEY SHOULDN'T BE POSTING SCORES HERE...
PFFT, YOU MEAN YOUR MOM?
AND THEN YOU GOT ALL MAD AND PUNCHED HER, RIGHT?
YOU MADE FIRST! NO COM-PLAINING!
AND ALL YOU DO IS READ MANGA...
EH, IT'S NOT REALLY WORTH BRAGGING OVER.
GETTING INTO A GOOD HIGH SCHOOL AND COLLEGE... I'VE GOT BIGGER DREAMS THAN THAT.
REALLY? LIKE WHAT?
STILL FIGURING THAT OUT...
SO YOU DON'T HAVE ONE, THEN?!
BIGGER DREAMS THAN A GOOD HIGH SCHOOL AND COLLEGE...?

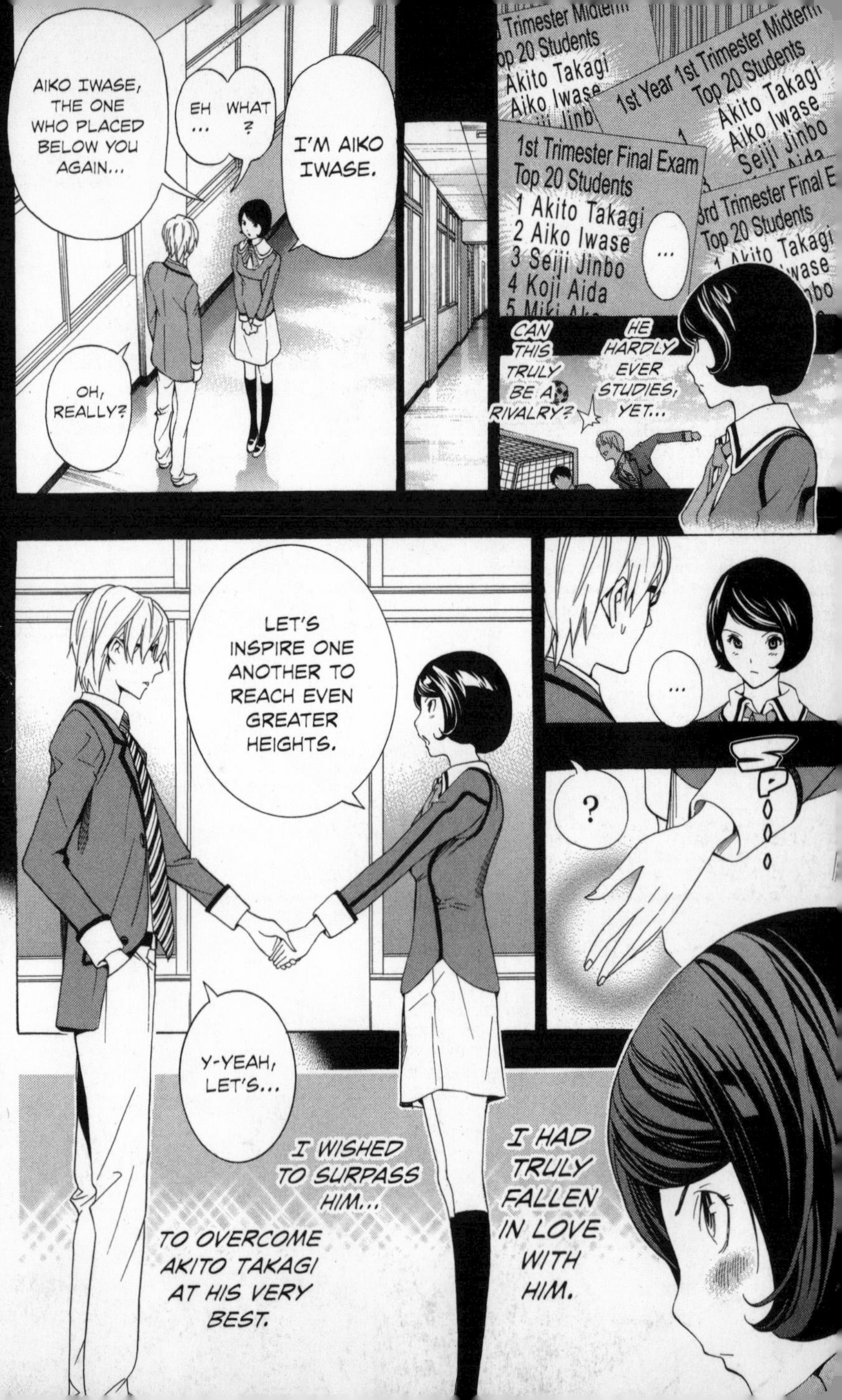
1st Year 1st Trimester Midterm
Top 20 Students
Akito Takagi
Aiko Iwase
Seiji Jinbo
1st Trimester Final Exam
Top 20 Students
1 Akito Takagi
2 Aiko Iwase
3 Seiji Jinbo
4 Koji Aida
Top 20 Students
...
HE HARDLY EVER STUDIES, YET...
CAN THIS TRULY BE A RIVALRY?
I'M AIKO IWASE.
EH ... WHAT ?
AIKO IWASE, THE ONE WHO PLACED BELOW YOU AGAIN...
OH, REALLY?
...
?
SPOOO
I HAD TRULY FALLEN IN LOVE WITH HIM.
LET'S INSPIRE ONE ANOTHER TO REACH EVEN GREATER HEIGHTS.
Y-YEAH, LET'S...
I WISHED TO SURPASS HIM...
TO OVERCOME AKITO TAKAGI AT HIS VERY BEST.

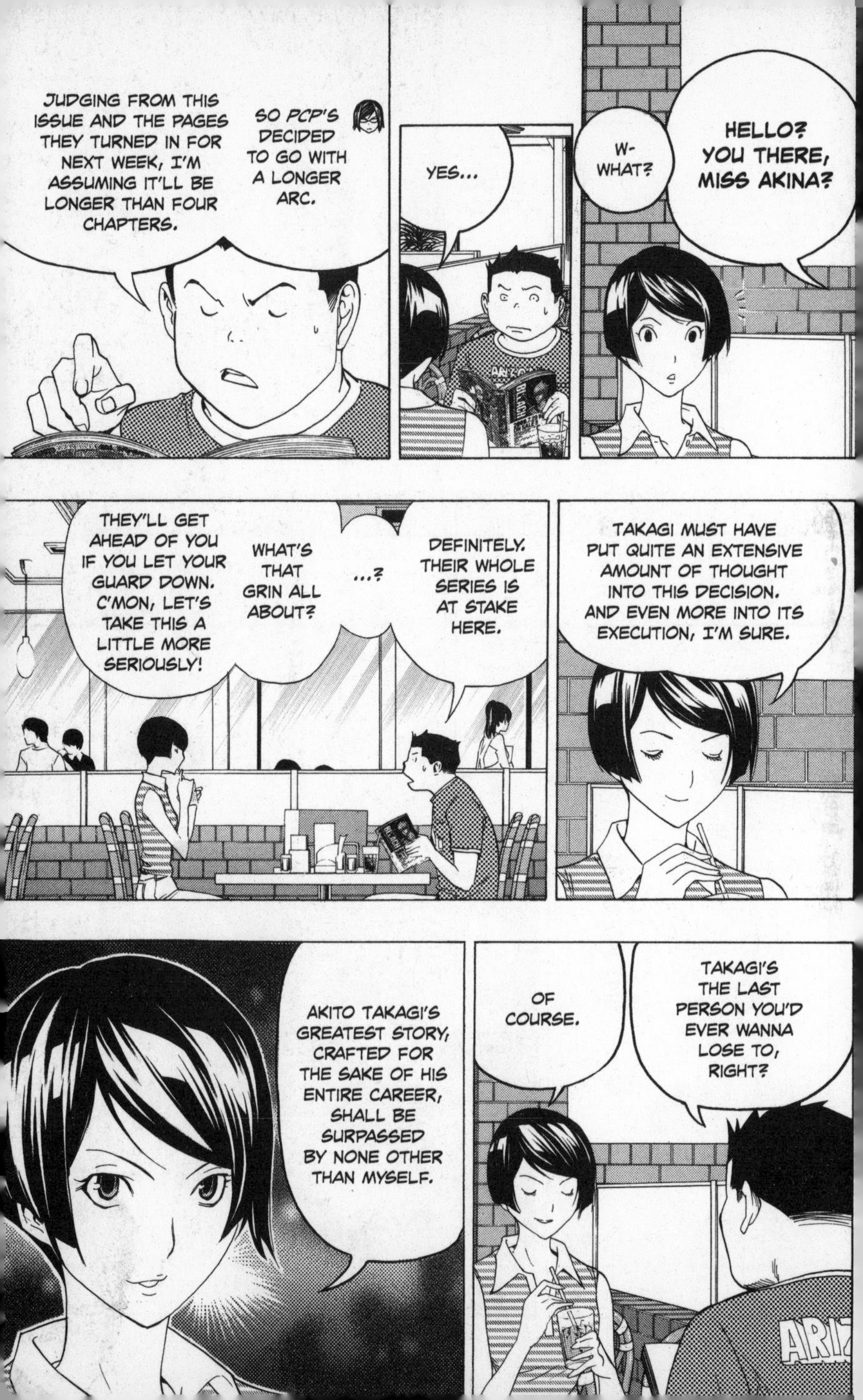
HELLO? YOU THERE, MISS AKINA?
W-WHAT?
YES...
SO *PCP'S* DECIDED TO GO WITH A LONGER ARC.
JUDGING FROM THIS ISSUE AND THE PAGES THEY TURNED IN FOR NEXT WEEK, I'M ASSUMING IT'LL BE LONGER THAN FOUR CHAPTERS.
TAKAGI MUST HAVE PUT QUITE AN EXTENSIVE AMOUNT OF THOUGHT INTO THIS DECISION. AND EVEN MORE INTO ITS EXECUTION, I'M SURE.
DEFINITELY. THEIR WHOLE SERIES IS AT STAKE HERE.
...?
WHAT'S THAT GRIN ALL ABOUT?
THEY'LL GET AHEAD OF YOU IF YOU LET YOUR GUARD DOWN. C'MON, LET'S TAKE THIS A LITTLE MORE SERIOUSLY!
TAKAGI'S THE LAST PERSON YOU'D EVER WANNA LOSE TO, RIGHT?
OF COURSE.
AKITO TAKAGI'S GREATEST STORY, CRAFTED FOR THE SAKE OF HIS ENTIRE CAREER, SHALL BE SURPASSED BY NONE OTHER THAN MYSELF.

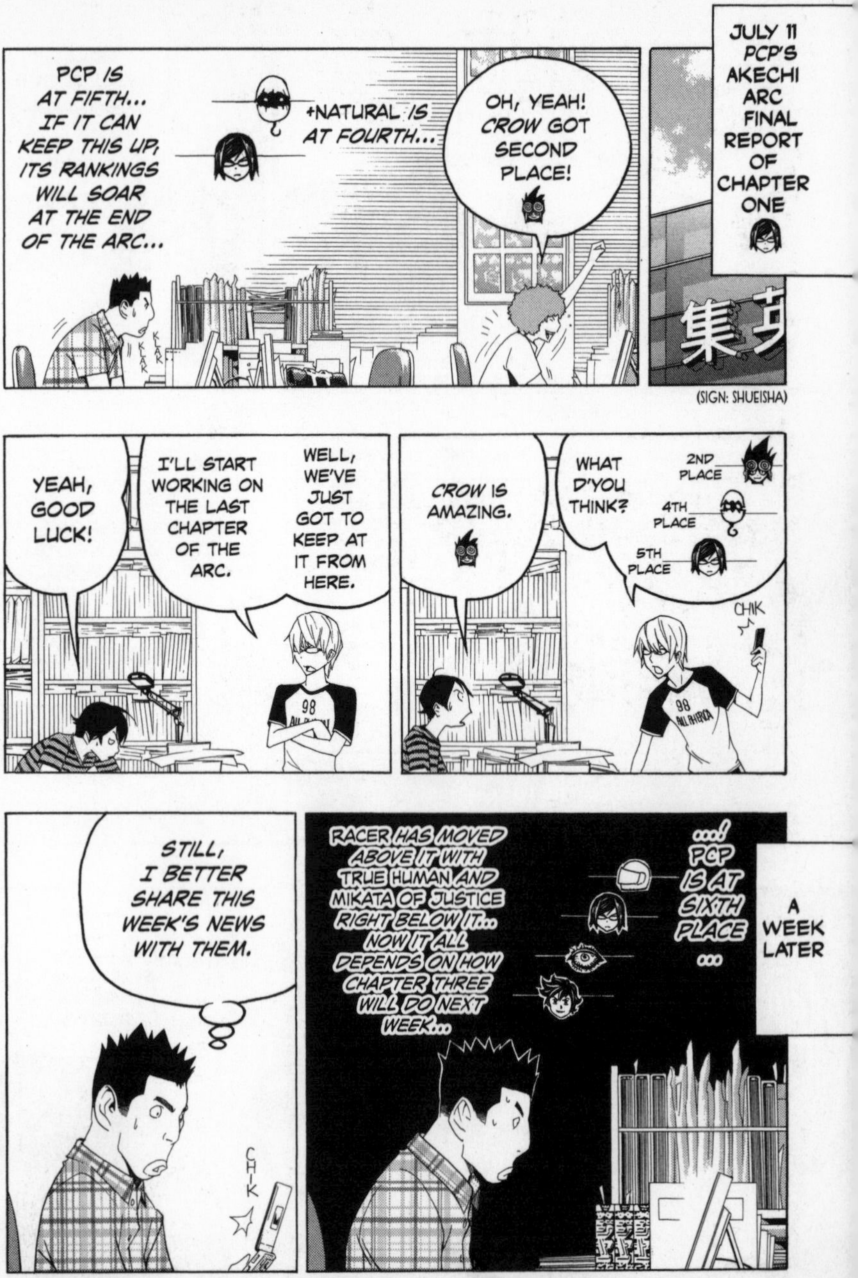
JULY 11 PCP'S AKECHI ARC FINAL REPORT OF CHAPTER ONE
集英
(SIGN: SHUEISHA)
OH, YEAH! CROW GOT SECOND PLACE!
+NATURAL IS AT FOURTH...
PCP IS AT FIFTH... IF IT CAN KEEP THIS UP, ITS RANKINGS WILL SOAR AT THE END OF THE ARC...
KLAK KLAK
WHAT D'YOU THINK?
2ND PLACE
4TH PLACE
5TH PLACE
CHIK
CROW IS AMAZING.
WELL, WE'VE JUST GOT TO KEEP AT IT FROM HERE.
I'LL START WORKING ON THE LAST CHAPTER OF THE ARC.
YEAH, GOOD LUCK!
A WEEK LATER
...! PCP IS AT SIXTH PLACE...
RACER HAS MOVED ABOVE IT WITH TRUE HUMAN AND MIKATA OF JUSTICE RIGHT BELOW IT... NOW IT ALL DEPENDS ON HOW CHAPTER THREE WILL DO NEXT WEEK...
STILL, I BETTER SHARE THIS WEEK'S NEWS WITH THEM.
CHIK

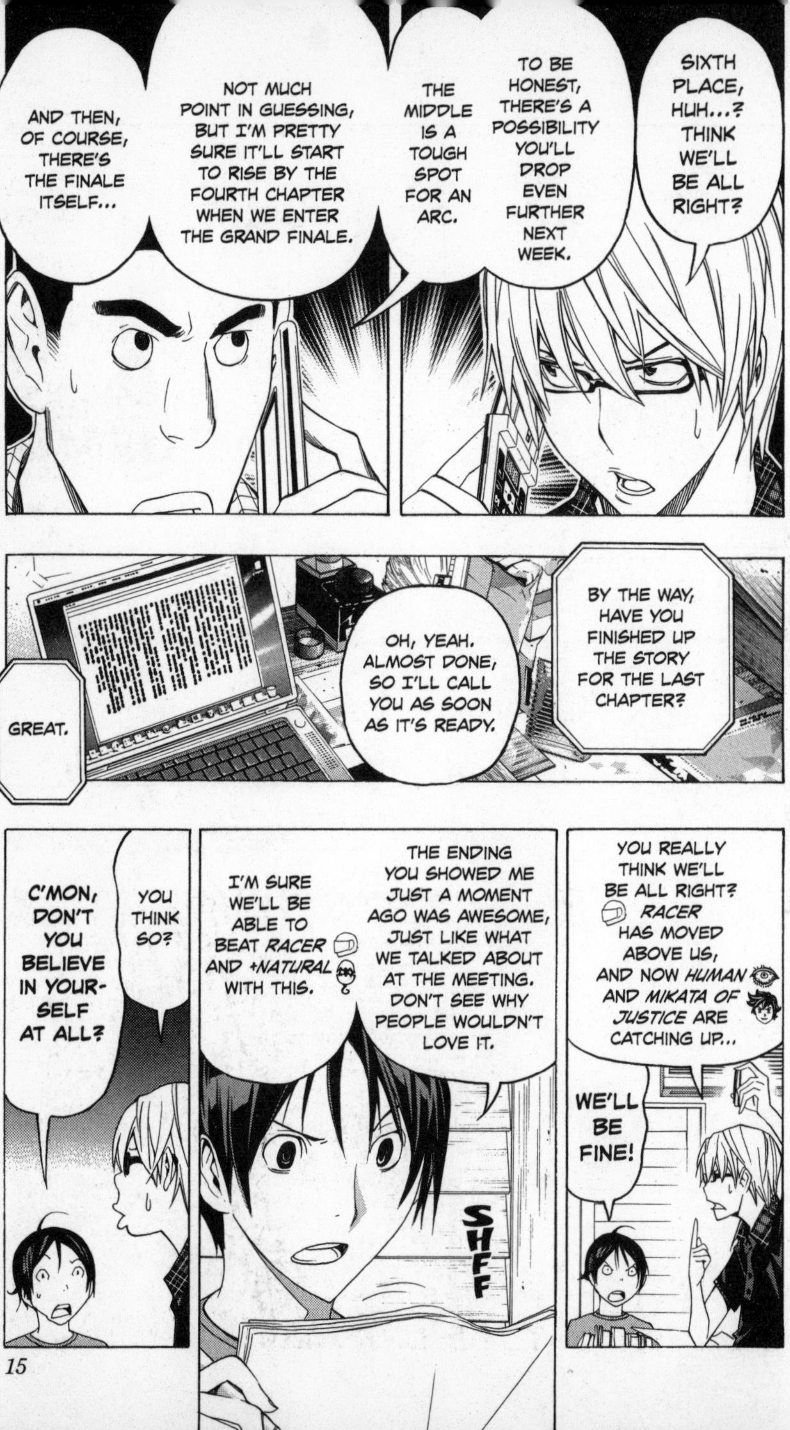
SIXTH PLACE, HUH...? THINK WE'LL BE ALL RIGHT?
TO BE HONEST, THERE'S A POSSIBILITY YOU'LL DROP EVEN FURTHER NEXT WEEK.
THE MIDDLE IS A TOUGH SPOT FOR AN ARC.
NOT MUCH POINT IN GUESSING, BUT I'M PRETTY SURE IT'LL START TO RISE BY THE FOURTH CHAPTER WHEN WE ENTER THE GRAND FINALE.
AND THEN, OF COURSE, THERE'S THE FINALE ITSELF...
BY THE WAY, HAVE YOU FINISHED UP THE STORY FOR THE LAST CHAPTER?
OH, YEAH. ALMOST DONE, SO I'LL CALL YOU AS SOON AS IT'S READY.
GREAT.
YOU REALLY THINK WE'LL BE ALL RIGHT? RACER HAS MOVED ABOVE US, AND NOW HUMAN AND MIKATA OF JUSTICE ARE CATCHING UP...
WE'LL BE FINE!
THE ENDING YOU SHOWED ME JUST A MOMENT AGO WAS AWESOME, JUST LIKE WHAT WE TALKED ABOUT AT THE MEETING. DON'T SEE WHY PEOPLE WOULDN'T LOVE IT.
I'M SURE WE'LL BE ABLE TO BEAT RACER AND +NATURAL WITH THIS.
SHFF
YOU THINK SO?
C'MON, DON'T YOU BELIEVE IN YOURSELF AT ALL?

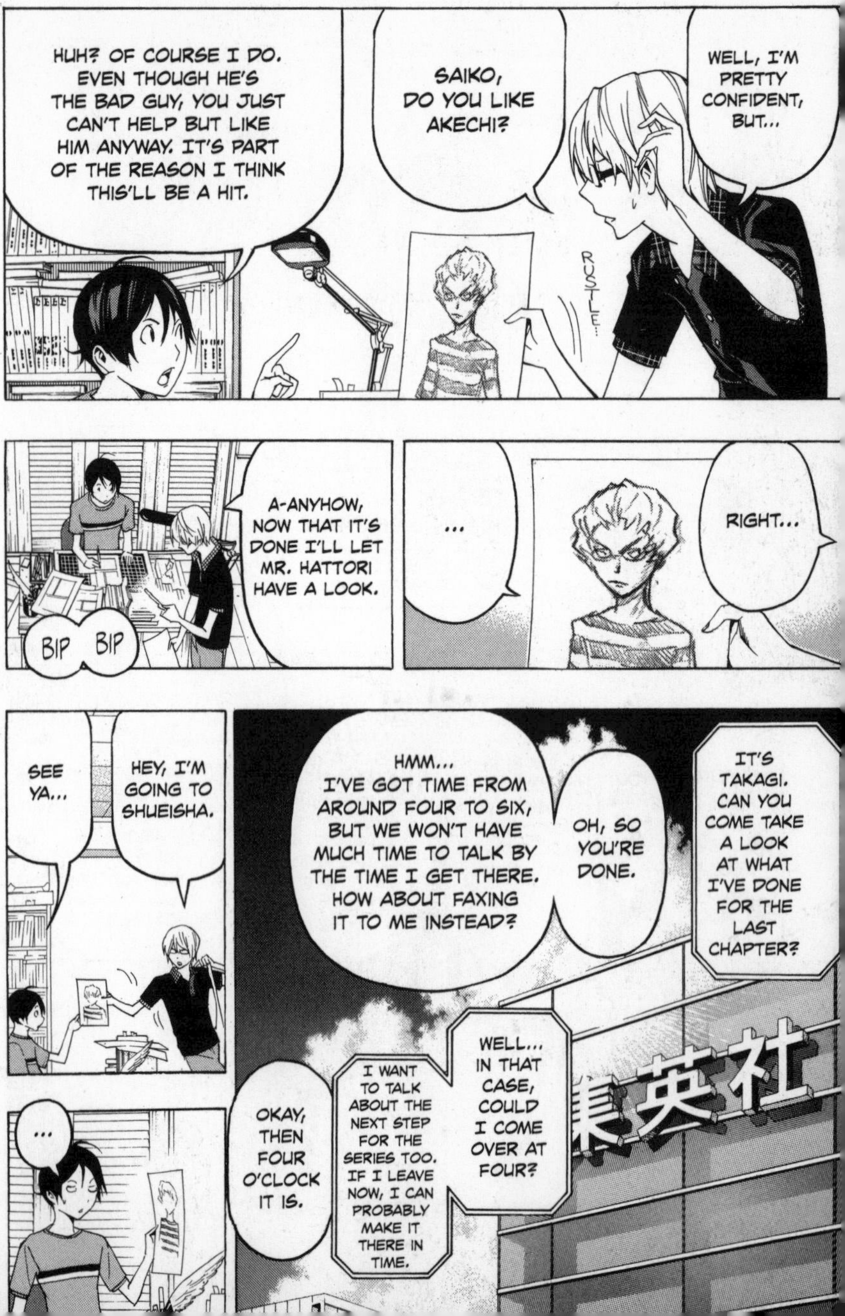
WELL, I'M PRETTY CONFIDENT, BUT...
SAIKO, DO YOU LIKE AKECHI?
RUSTLE...
HUH? OF COURSE I DO. EVEN THOUGH HE'S THE BAD GUY, YOU JUST CAN'T HELP BUT LIKE HIM ANYWAY. IT'S PART OF THE REASON I THINK THIS'LL BE A HIT.
RIGHT...
...
A-ANYHOW, NOW THAT IT'S DONE I'LL LET MR. HATTORI HAVE A LOOK.
BIP BIP
IT'S TAKAGI. CAN YOU COME TAKE A LOOK AT WHAT I'VE DONE FOR THE LAST CHAPTER?
OH, SO YOU'RE DONE.
HMM... I'VE GOT TIME FROM AROUND FOUR TO SIX, BUT WE WON'T HAVE MUCH TIME TO TALK BY THE TIME I GET THERE. HOW ABOUT FAXING IT TO ME INSTEAD?
WELL... IN THAT CASE, COULD I COME OVER AT FOUR?
I WANT TO TALK ABOUT THE NEXT STEP FOR THE SERIES TOO. IF I LEAVE NOW, I CAN PROBABLY MAKE IT THERE IN TIME.
OKAY, THEN FOUR O'CLOCK IT IS.
HEY, I'M GOING TO SHUEISHA.
SEE YA...
...

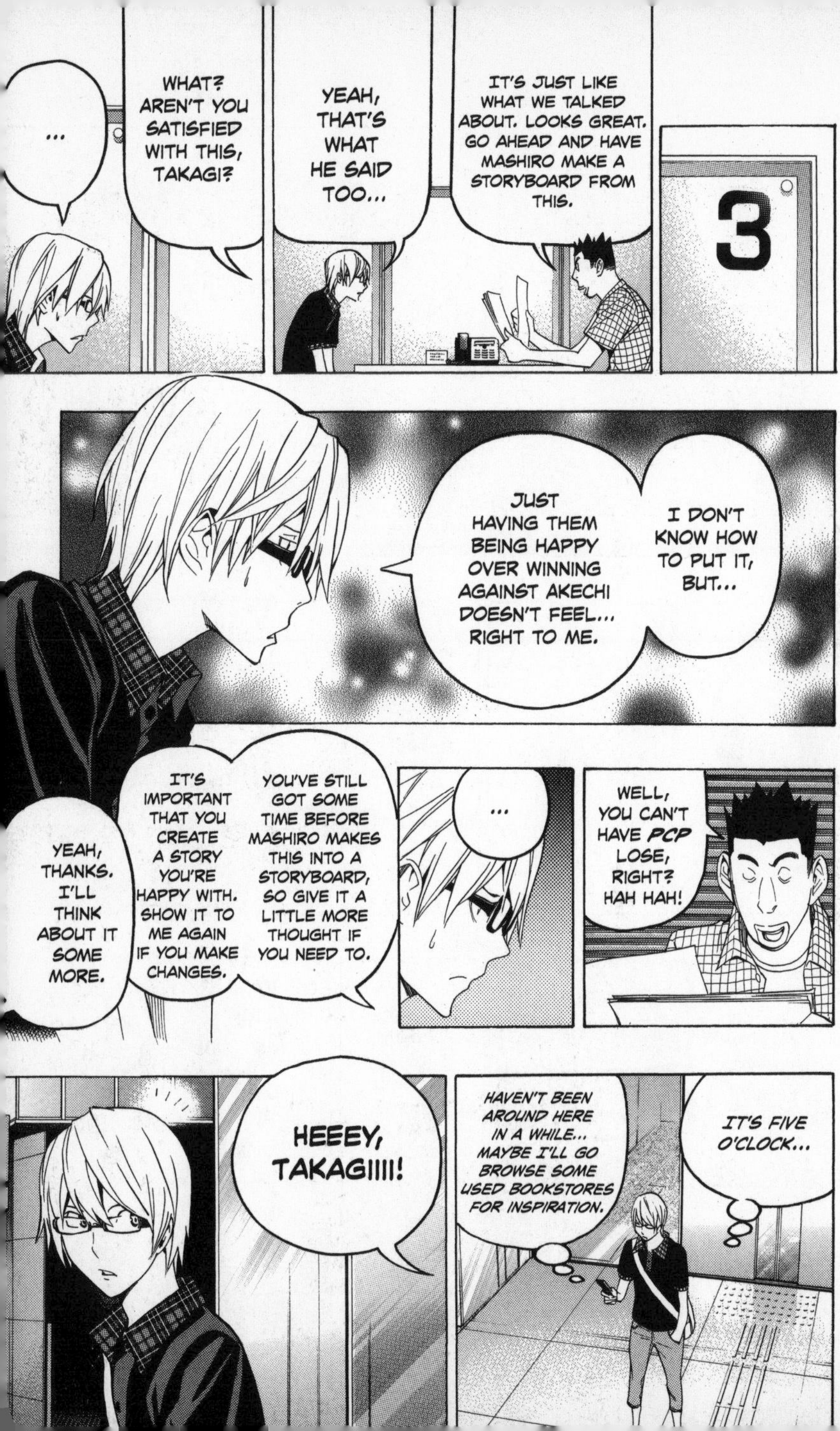
3
IT'S JUST LIKE WHAT WE TALKED ABOUT. LOOKS GREAT. GO AHEAD AND HAVE MASHIRO MAKE A STORYBOARD FROM THIS.
YEAH, THAT'S WHAT HE SAID TOO...
WHAT? AREN'T YOU SATISFIED WITH THIS, TAKAGI?
...
I DON'T KNOW HOW TO PUT IT, BUT...
JUST HAVING THEM BEING HAPPY OVER WINNING AGAINST AKECHI DOESN'T FEEL... RIGHT TO ME.
WELL, YOU CAN'T HAVE PCP LOSE, RIGHT? HAH HAH!
...
YOU'VE STILL GOT SOME TIME BEFORE MASHIRO MAKES THIS INTO A STORYBOARD, SO GIVE IT A LITTLE MORE THOUGHT IF YOU NEED TO.
IT'S IMPORTANT THAT YOU CREATE A STORY YOU'RE HAPPY WITH. SHOW IT TO ME AGAIN IF YOU MAKE CHANGES.
YEAH, THANKS. I'LL THINK ABOUT IT SOME MORE.
IT'S FIVE O'CLOCK...
HAVEN'T BEEN AROUND HERE IN A WHILE... MAYBE I'LL GO BROWSE SOME USED BOOKSTORES FOR INSPIRATION.
HEEEY, TAKAGIIIII!

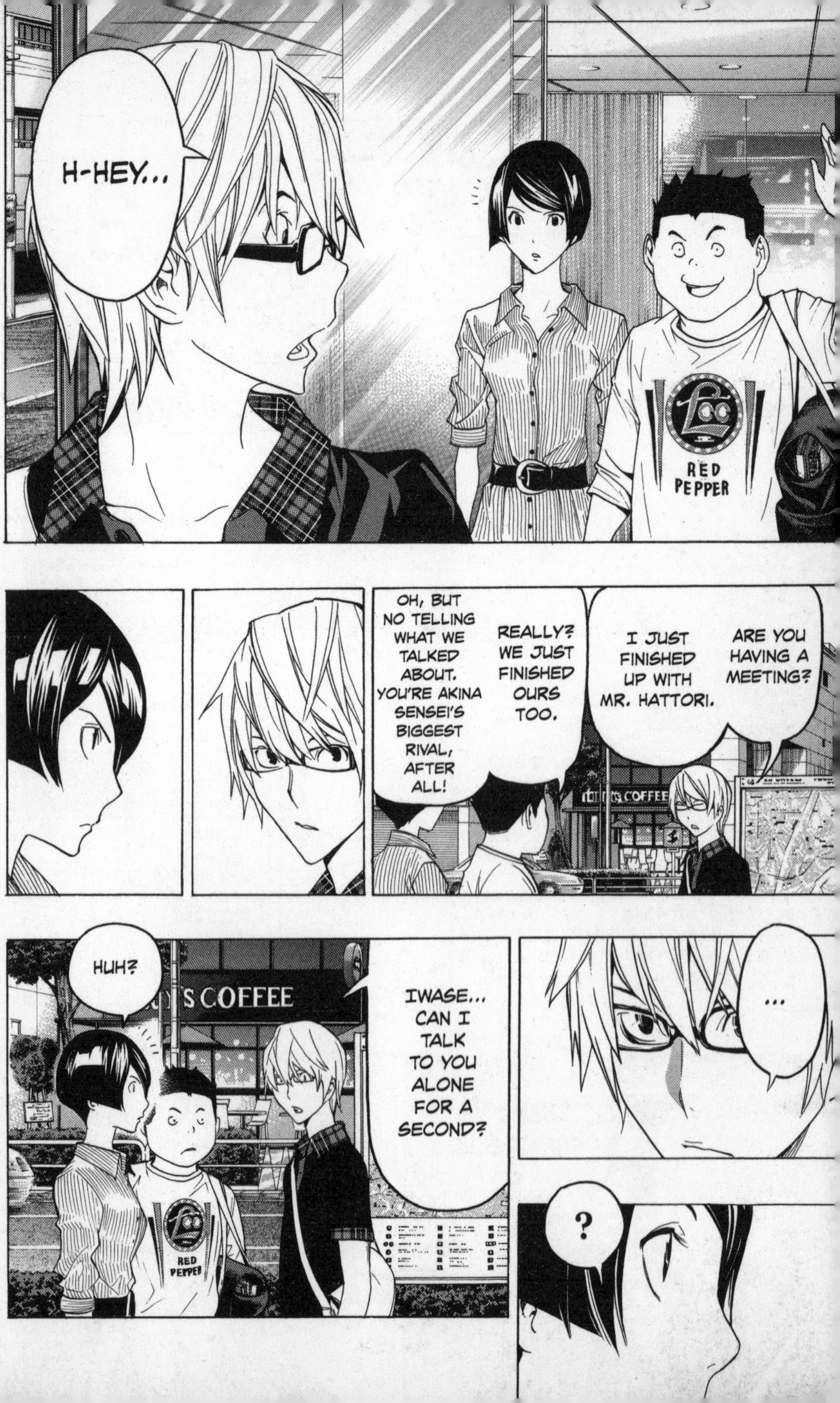
H-HEY...
RED PEPPER
ARE YOU HAVING A MEETING?
I JUST FINISHED UP WITH MR. HATTORI.
REALLY? WE JUST FINISHED OURS TOO.
OH, BUT NO TELLING WHAT WE TALKED ABOUT. YOU'RE AKINA SENSEI'S BIGGEST RIVAL, AFTER ALL!
...
?
IWASE... CAN I TALK TO YOU ALONE FOR A SECOND?
HUH?

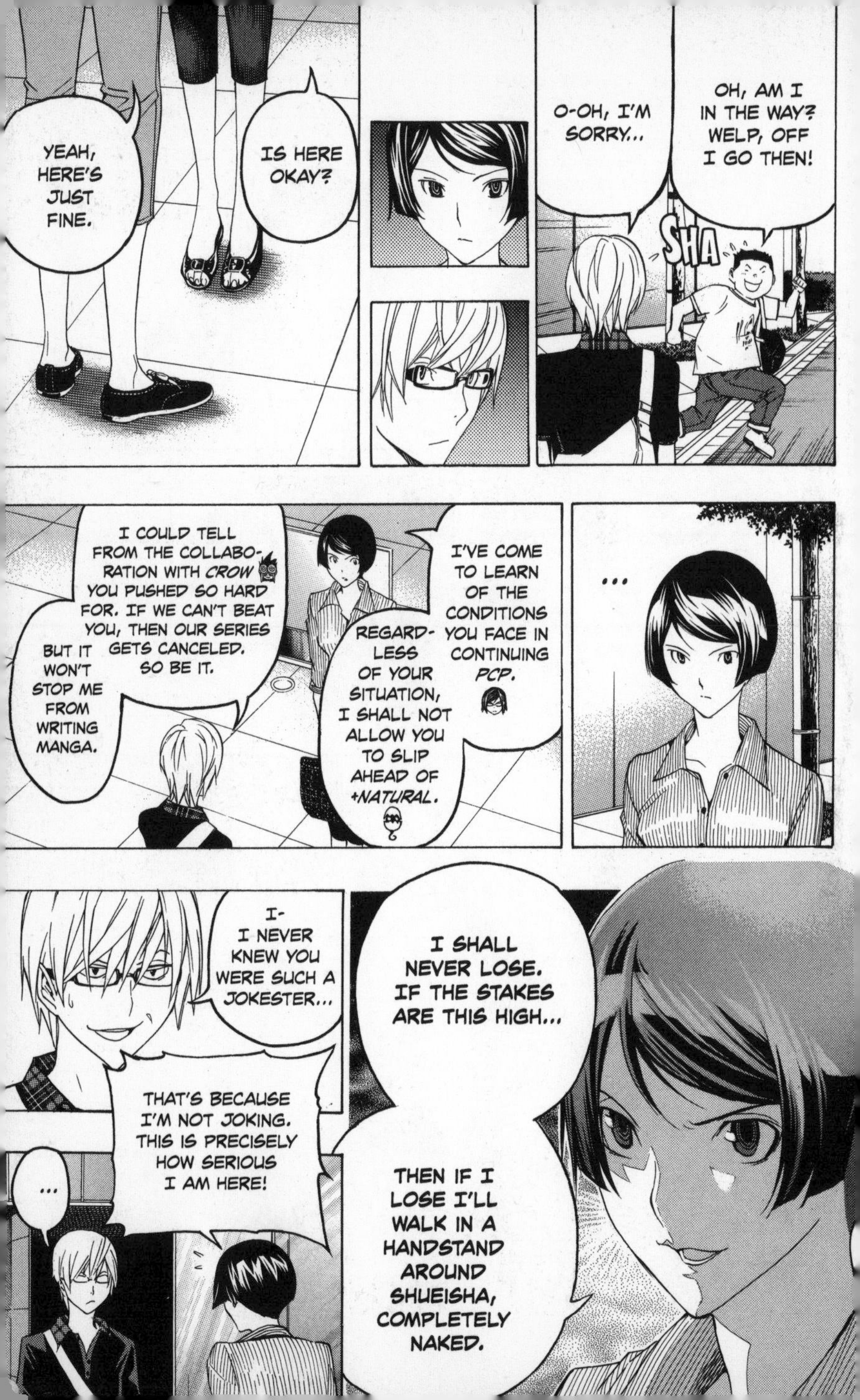
OH, AM I IN THE WAY? WELP, OFF I GO THEN!
O-OH, I'M SORRY...
SHA
IS HERE OKAY?
YEAH, HERE'S JUST FINE.
...
I'VE COME TO LEARN OF THE CONDITIONS YOU FACE IN CONTINUING PCP.
REGARDLESS OF YOUR SITUATION, I SHALL NOT ALLOW YOU TO SLIP AHEAD OF +NATURAL.
I COULD TELL FROM THE COLLABORATION WITH CROW YOU PUSHED SO HARD FOR. IF WE CAN'T BEAT YOU, THEN OUR SERIES GETS CANCELED. SO BE IT.
BUT IT WON'T STOP ME FROM WRITING MANGA.
I SHALL NEVER LOSE. IF THE STAKES ARE THIS HIGH...
THEN IF I LOSE I'LL WALK IN A HANDSTAND AROUND SHUEISHA, COMPLETELY NAKED.
I- I NEVER KNEW YOU WERE SUCH A JOKESTER...
THAT'S BECAUSE I'M NOT JOKING. THIS IS PRECISELY HOW SERIOUS I AM HERE!
...

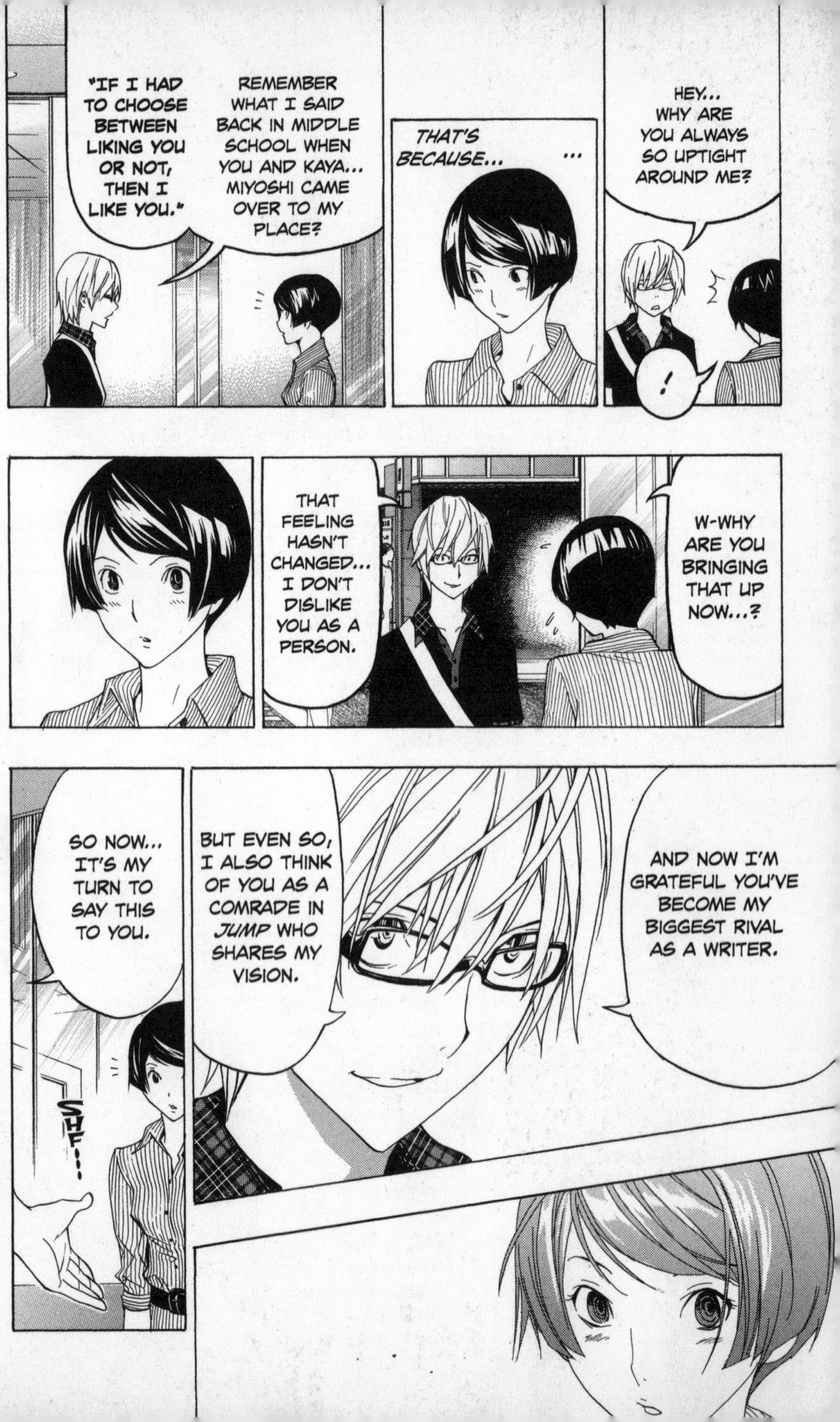
HEY... WHY ARE YOU ALWAYS SO UPTIGHT AROUND ME?
!
THAT'S BECAUSE...
...
REMEMBER WHAT I SAID BACK IN MIDDLE SCHOOL WHEN YOU AND KAYA... MIYOSHI CAME OVER TO MY PLACE?
"IF I HAD TO CHOOSE BETWEEN LIKING YOU OR NOT, THEN I LIKE YOU."
W-WHY ARE YOU BRINGING THAT UP NOW...?
THAT FEELING HASN'T CHANGED... I DON'T DISLIKE YOU AS A PERSON.
BUT EVEN SO, I ALSO THINK OF YOU AS A COMRADE IN *JUMP* WHO SHARES MY VISION.
AND NOW I'M GRATEFUL YOU'VE BECOME MY BIGGEST RIVAL AS A WRITER.
SO NOW... IT'S MY TURN TO SAY THIS TO YOU.
SHF...

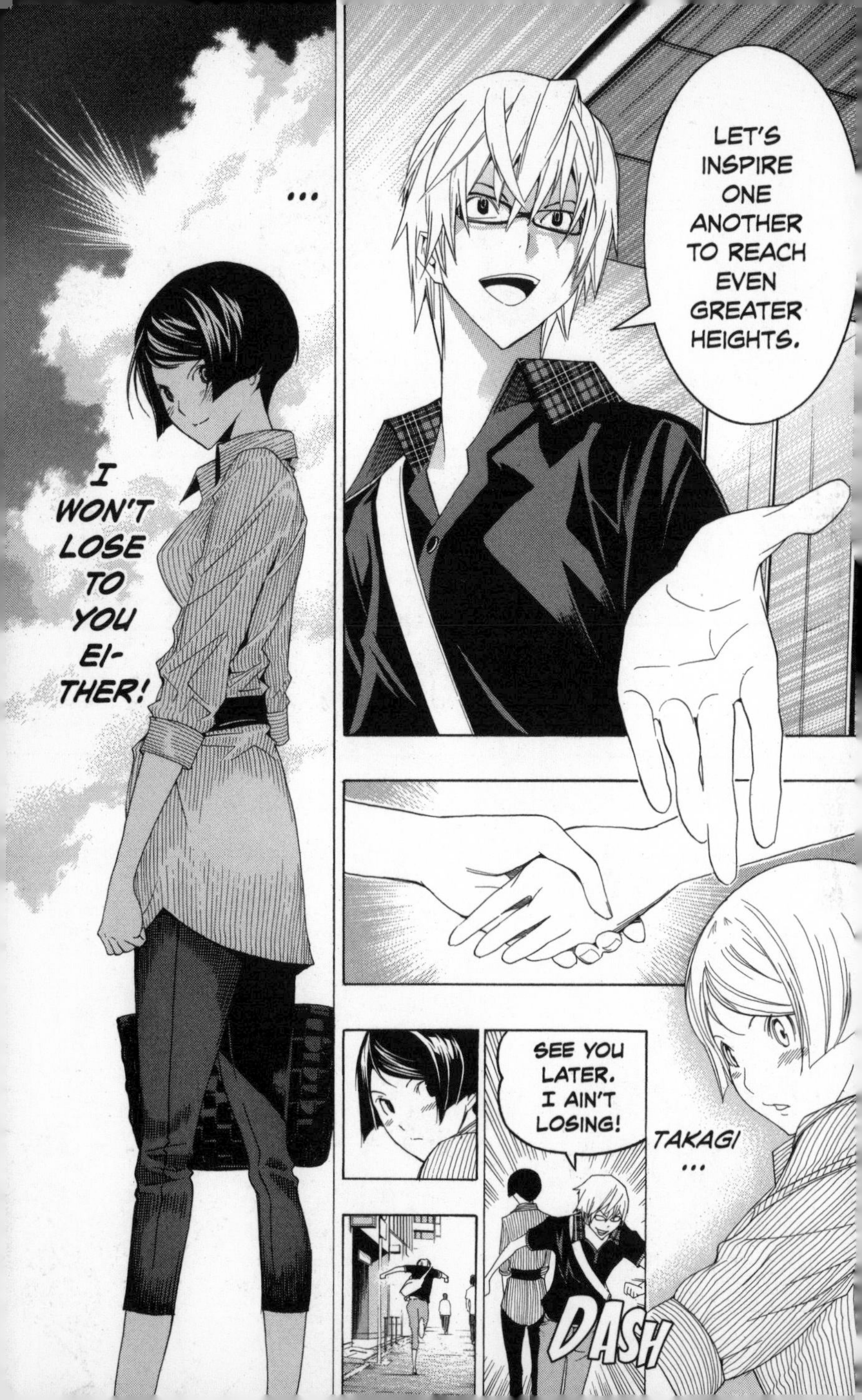
LET'S INSPIRE ONE ANOTHER TO REACH EVEN GREATER HEIGHTS.
SEE YOU LATER. I AIN'T LOSING!
TAKAGI ...
DASH
...
I WON'T LOSE TO YOU EI-THER!

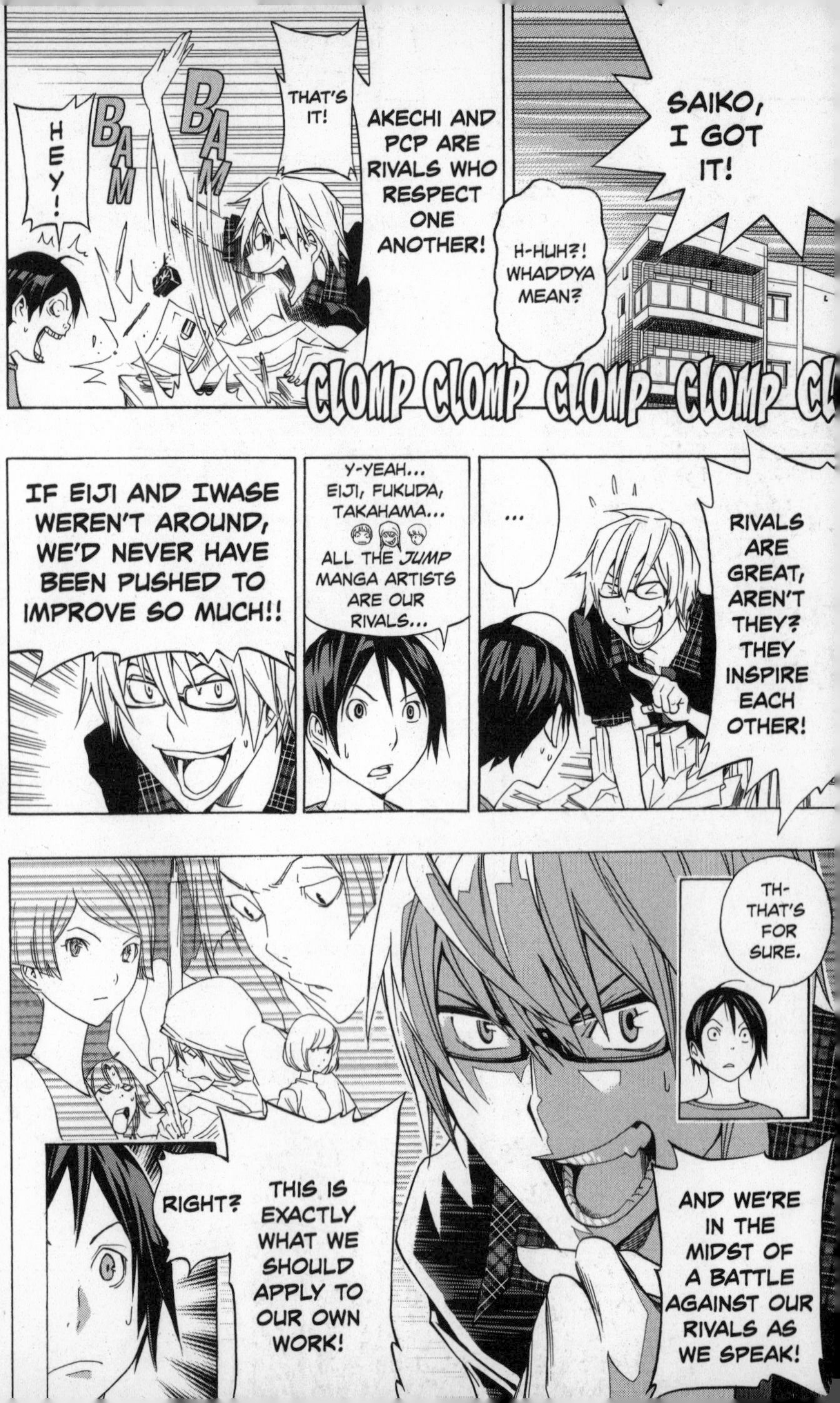
SAIKO, I GOT IT!
H-HUH?! WHADDYA MEAN?
CLOMP CLOMP CLOMP CLOMP CL
THAT'S IT!
AKECHI AND PCP ARE RIVALS WHO RESPECT ONE ANOTHER!
BAM
BAM
HEY!
RIVALS ARE GREAT, AREN'T THEY? THEY INSPIRE EACH OTHER!
...
Y-YEAH... EIJI, FUKUDA, TAKAHAMA...
ALL THE *JUMP* MANGA ARTISTS ARE OUR RIVALS...
IF EIJI AND IWASE WEREN'T AROUND, WE'D NEVER HAVE BEEN PUSHED TO IMPROVE SO MUCH!!
TH-THAT'S FOR SURE.
AND WE'RE IN THE MIDST OF A BATTLE AGAINST OUR RIVALS AS WE SPEAK!
THIS IS EXACTLY WHAT WE SHOULD APPLY TO OUR OWN WORK!
RIGHT?

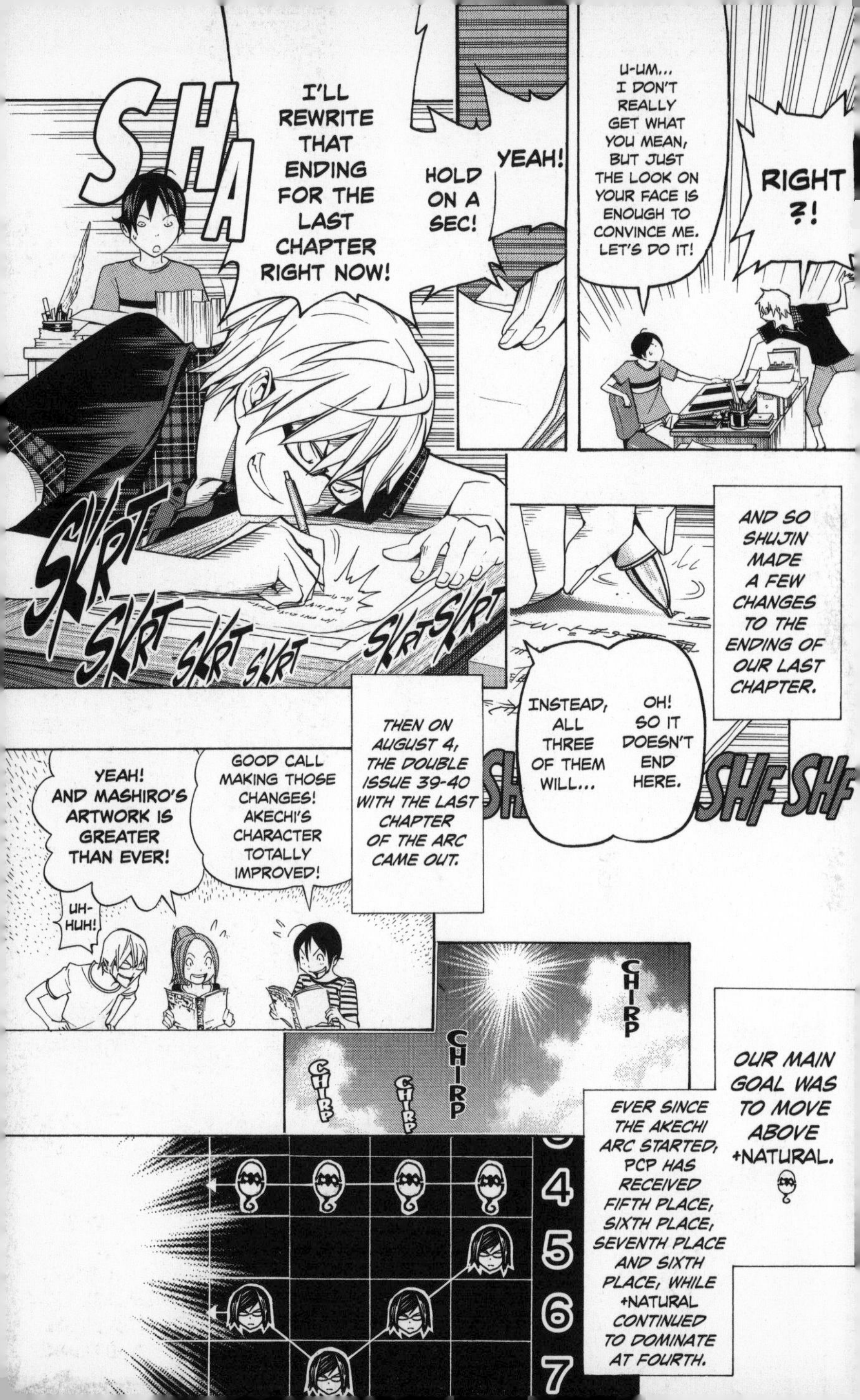
RIGHT?!
U-UM... I DON'T REALLY GET WHAT YOU MEAN, BUT JUST THE LOOK ON YOUR FACE IS ENOUGH TO CONVINCE ME. LET'S DO IT!
YEAH!
HOLD ON A SEC!
I'LL REWRITE THAT ENDING FOR THE LAST CHAPTER RIGHT NOW!
SHA
SKRT SKRT SKRT SKRT SKRT SKRT
AND SO SHUJIN MADE A FEW CHANGES TO THE ENDING OF OUR LAST CHAPTER.
OH! SO IT DOESN'T END HERE.
INSTEAD, ALL THREE OF THEM WILL...
SHF SHF SHF
THEN ON AUGUST 4, THE DOUBLE ISSUE 39-40 WITH THE LAST CHAPTER OF THE ARC CAME OUT.
GOOD CALL MAKING THOSE CHANGES! AKECHI'S CHARACTER TOTALLY IMPROVED!
YEAH! AND MASHIRO'S ARTWORK IS GREATER THAN EVER!
UH-HUH!
CHIRP
CHIRP
CHIRP
CHIRP
OUR MAIN GOAL WAS TO MOVE ABOVE +NATURAL.
EVER SINCE THE AKECHI ARC STARTED, PCP HAS RECEIVED FIFTH PLACE, SIXTH PLACE, SEVENTH PLACE AND SIXTH PLACE, WHILE +NATURAL CONTINUED TO DOMINATE AT FOURTH.
4
5
6
7

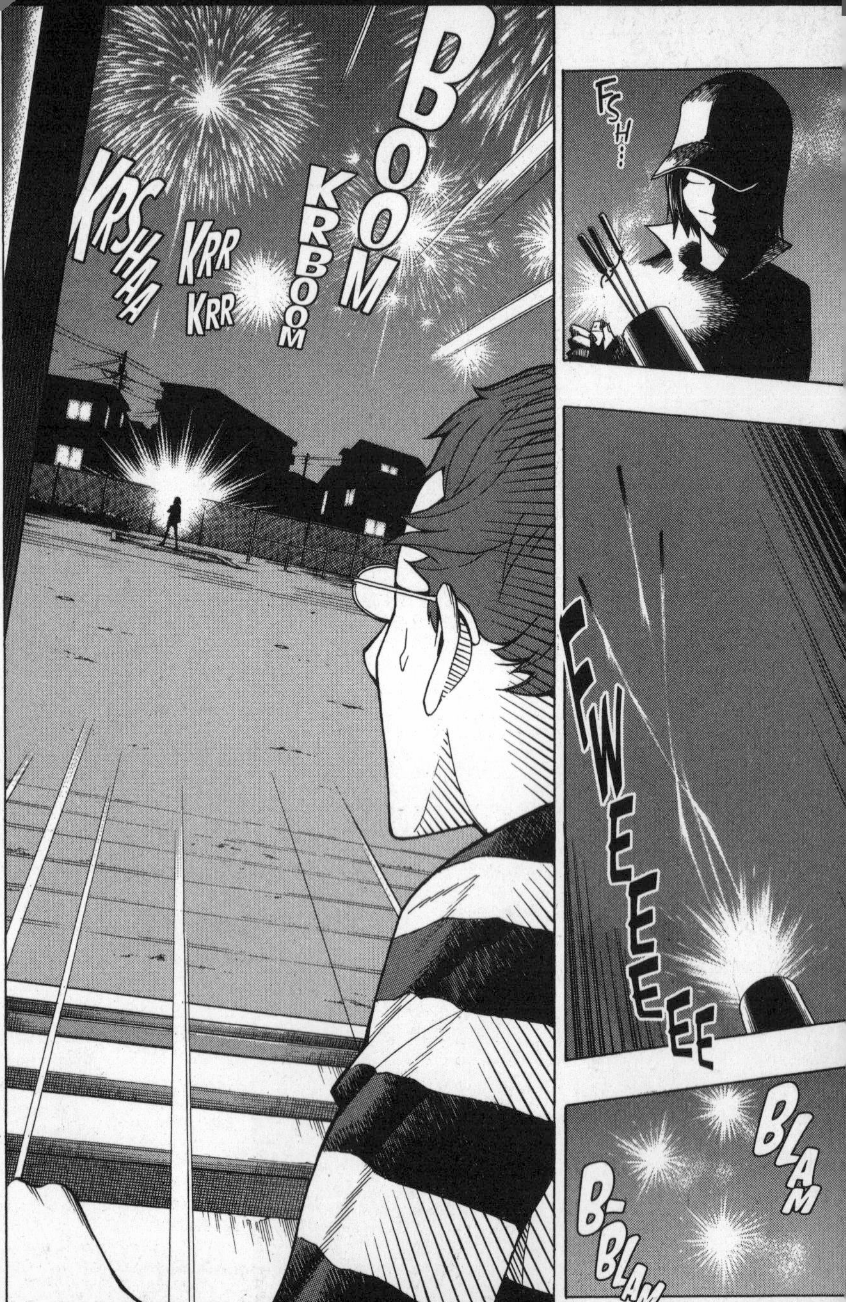
FSH...
FWEEEEEE
BLAM
B-BLAM
BOOM
KRBOOM
KRR
KRR
KRSHAA

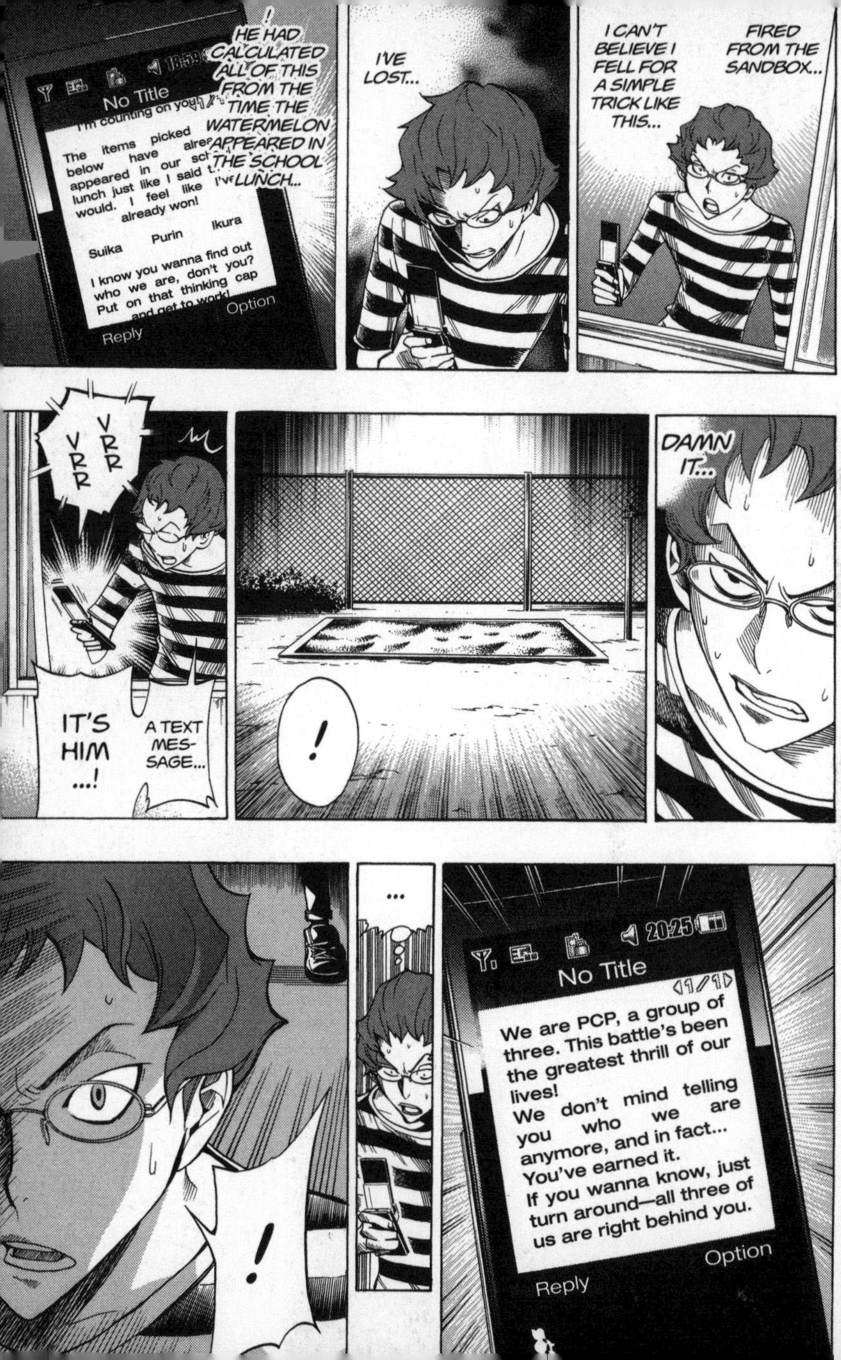
FIRED FROM THE SANDBOX...
I CAN'T BELIEVE I FELL FOR A SIMPLE TRICK LIKE THIS...
I'VE LOST...
! HE HAD CALCULATED ALL OF THIS FROM THE TIME THE WATERMELON APPEARED IN THE SCHOOL LUNCH...
No Title
Suika Purin Ikura
I know you wanna find out who we are, don't you? Put on that thinking cap
Option
Reply
DAMN IT...
!
VRR VRR
A TEXT MES-SAGE...
IT'S HIM ...!
20:25
No Title
1/1
We are PCP, a group of three. This battle's been the greatest thrill of our lives!
We don't mind telling you who we are anymore, and in fact...
You've earned it.
If you wanna know, just turn around—all three of us are right behind you.
Option
Reply
...
!

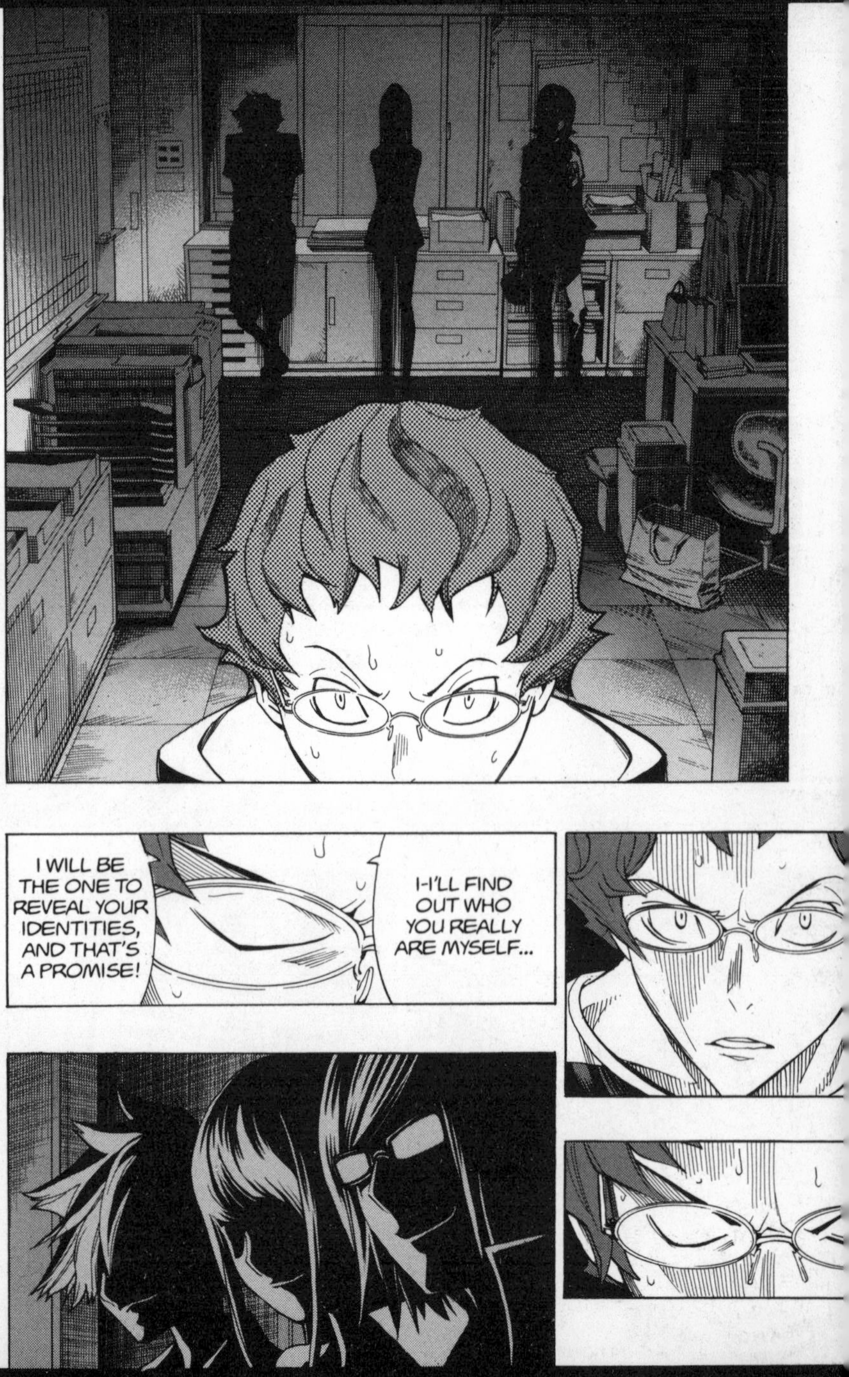
I-I'LL FIND OUT WHO YOU REALLY ARE MYSELF...
I WILL BE THE ONE TO REVEAL YOUR IDENTITIES, AND THAT'S A PROMISE!

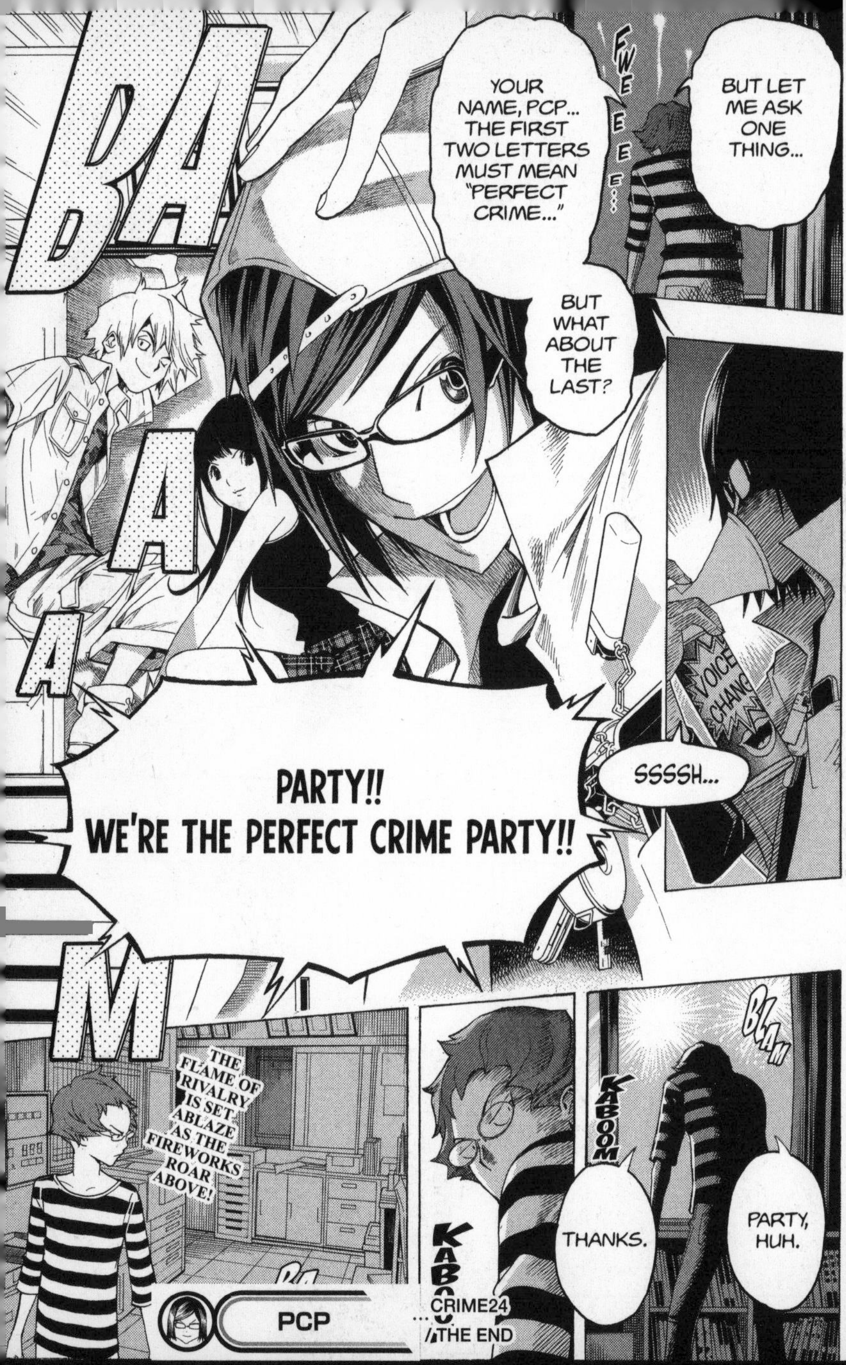
BUT LET ME ASK ONE THING...
FWEEEE...
YOUR NAME, PCP... THE FIRST TWO LETTERS MUST MEAN "PERFECT CRIME..."
BUT WHAT ABOUT THE LAST?
VOICE CHANG
SSSSH...
BA
A
A
M
PARTY!! WE'RE THE PERFECT CRIME PARTY!!
BLAM
KABOOM
PARTY, HUH.
THANKS.
KABOO
THE FLAME OF RIVALRY IS SET ABLAZE AS THE FIREWORKS ROAR ABOVE!
PCP
...CRIME24 / THE END

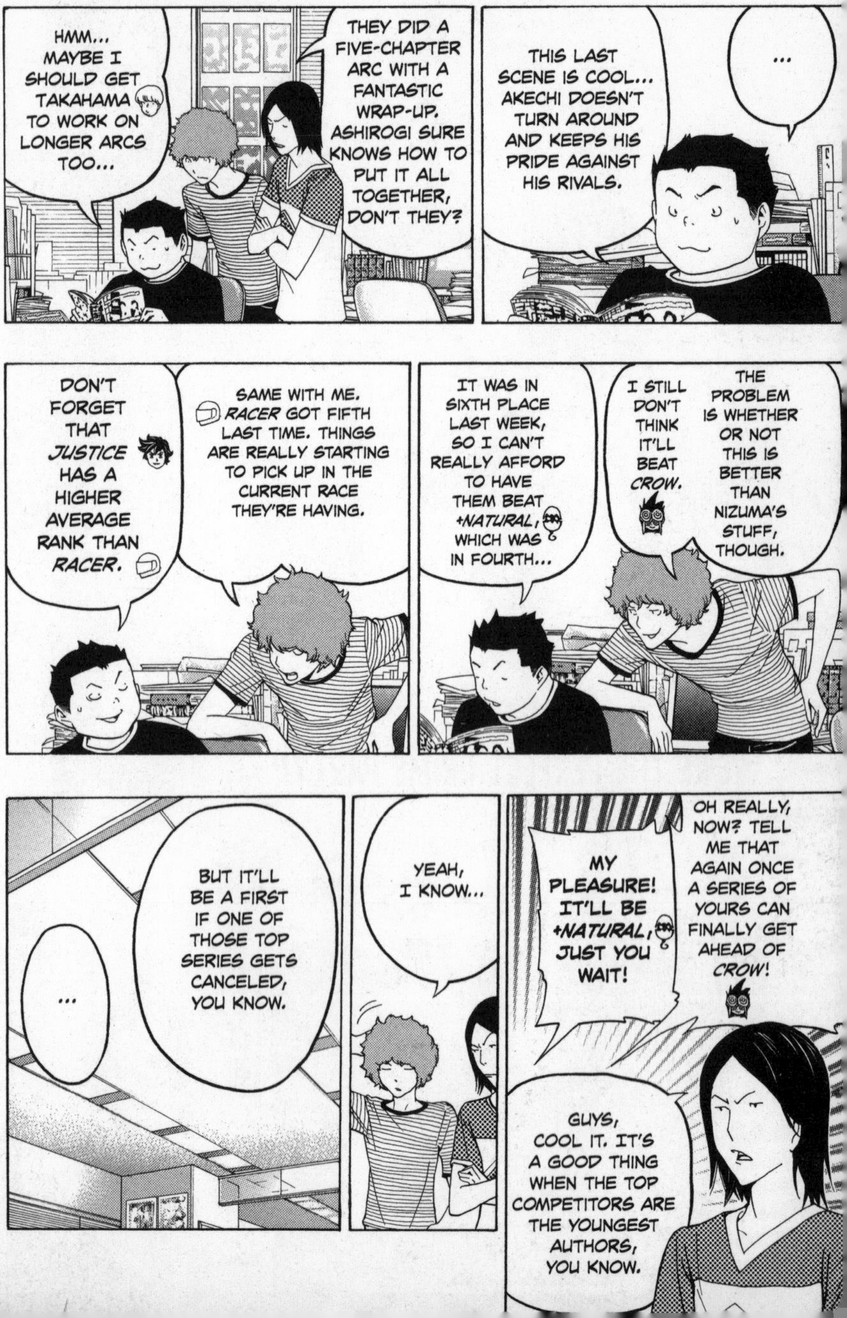
...
THIS LAST SCENE IS COOL... AKECHI DOESN'T TURN AROUND AND KEEPS HIS PRIDE AGAINST HIS RIVALS.
THEY DID A FIVE-CHAPTER ARC WITH A FANTASTIC WRAP-UP. ASHIROGI SURE KNOWS HOW TO PUT IT ALL TOGETHER, DON'T THEY?
HMM... MAYBE I SHOULD GET TAKAHAMA TO WORK ON LONGER ARCS TOO...
THE PROBLEM IS WHETHER OR NOT THIS IS BETTER THAN NIZUMA'S STUFF, THOUGH.
I STILL DON'T THINK IT'LL BEAT *CROW*.
IT WAS IN SIXTH PLACE LAST WEEK, SO I CAN'T REALLY AFFORD TO HAVE THEM BEAT *+NATURAL*, WHICH WAS IN FOURTH...
SAME WITH ME. *RACER* GOT FIFTH LAST TIME. THINGS ARE REALLY STARTING TO PICK UP IN THE CURRENT RACE THEY'RE HAVING.
DON'T FORGET THAT *JUSTICE* HAS A HIGHER AVERAGE RANK THAN *RACER*.
OH REALLY, NOW? TELL ME THAT AGAIN ONCE A SERIES OF YOURS CAN FINALLY GET AHEAD OF *CROW*!
MY PLEASURE! IT'LL BE *+NATURAL*, JUST YOU WAIT!
GUYS, COOL IT. IT'S A GOOD THING WHEN THE TOP COMPETITORS ARE THE YOUNGEST AUTHORS, YOU KNOW.
YEAH, I KNOW...
BUT IT'LL BE A FIRST IF ONE OF THOSE TOP SERIES GETS CANCELED, YOU KNOW.
...

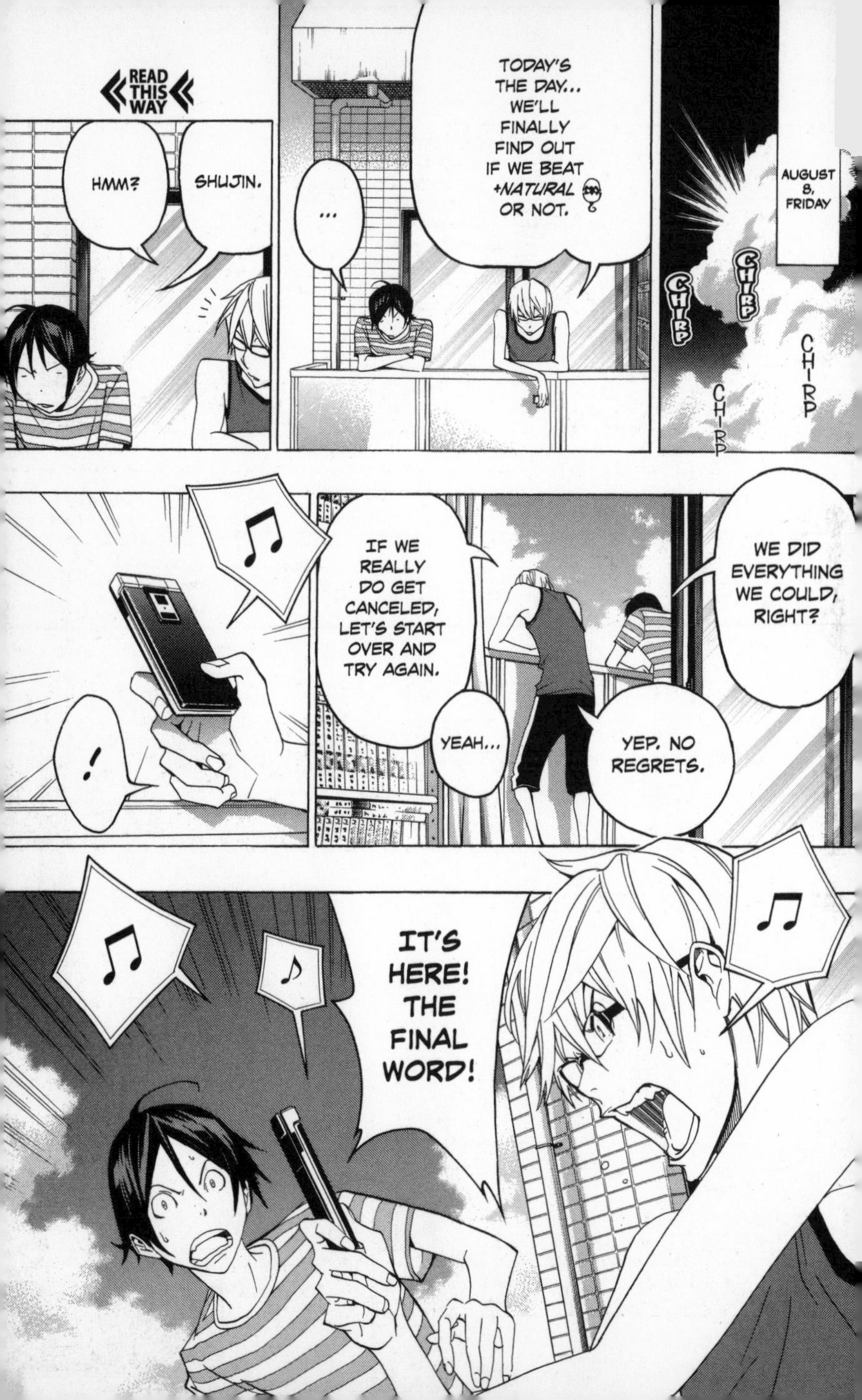
READ THIS WAY
AUGUST 8, FRIDAY
CHIRP
CHIRP
CHIRP
CHIRP
TODAY'S THE DAY... WE'LL FINALLY FIND OUT IF WE BEAT +NATURAL OR NOT.
...
SHUJIN.
HMM?
WE DID EVERYTHING WE COULD, RIGHT?
IF WE REALLY DO GET CANCELED, LET'S START OVER AND TRY AGAIN.
YEP. NO REGRETS.
YEAH...
!
IT'S HERE! THE FINAL WORD!

OHBA'S STORYBOARD

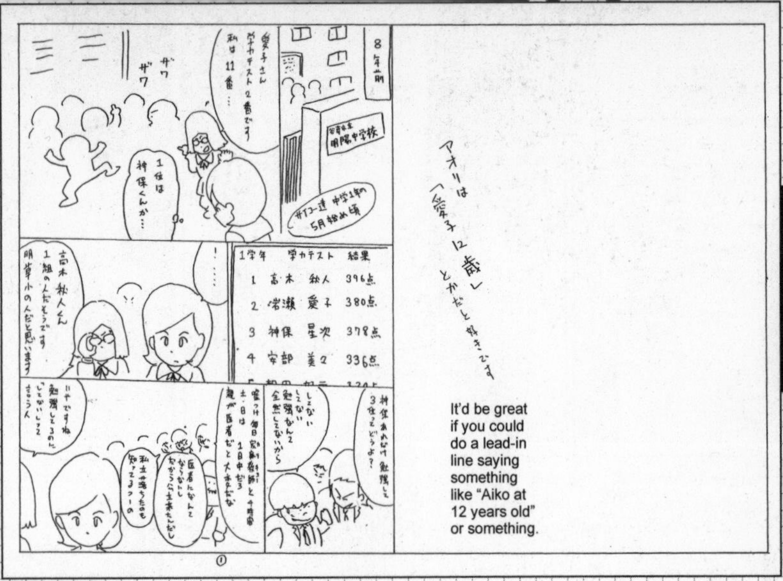
8年前
明陽中学校
サイコー達 中学1年の 5月始め頃
愛子さん 学力テスト2番です
私は11番…
1位は 神保くんか…
ザワ ザワ
1学年 学力テスト 結果
1 高木 秋人 396点
2 岩瀬 愛子 380点
3 神保 星次 378点
4 安部 美々 336点
高木秋人くん 1組の人だそうです 明草小の人だと思います
しょうがない 勉強なんて 全然してないから
アオリは「愛子12歳」とかだと好きです

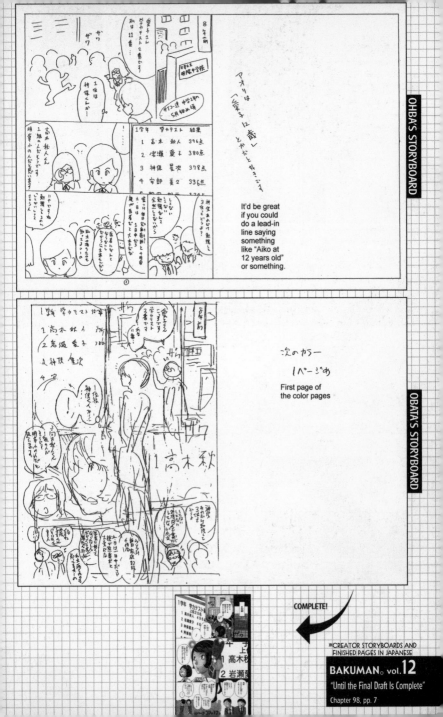

It'd be great if you could do a lead-in line saying something like "Aiko at 12 years old" or something.

OBATA'S STORYBOARD

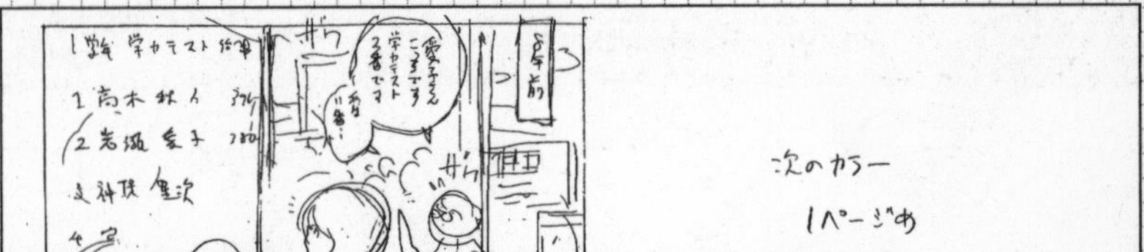
1 高木秋
次のカラー 1ページめ

First page of the color pages

COMPLETE!

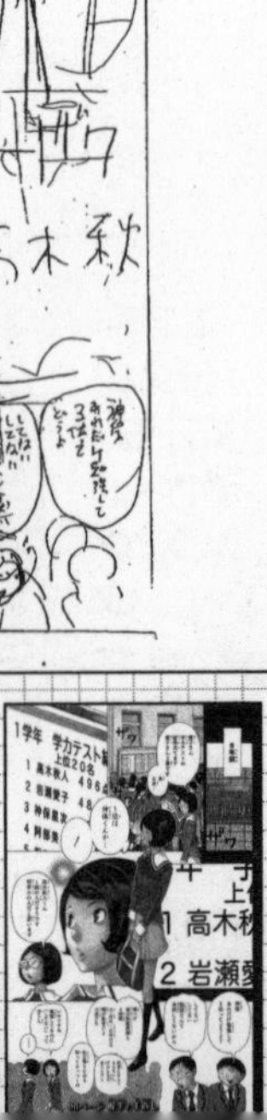

※CREATOR STORYBOARDS AND FINISHED PAGES IN JAPANESE

BAKUMAN。vol.12

"Until the Final Draft Is Complete"

Chapter 98, pp. 7

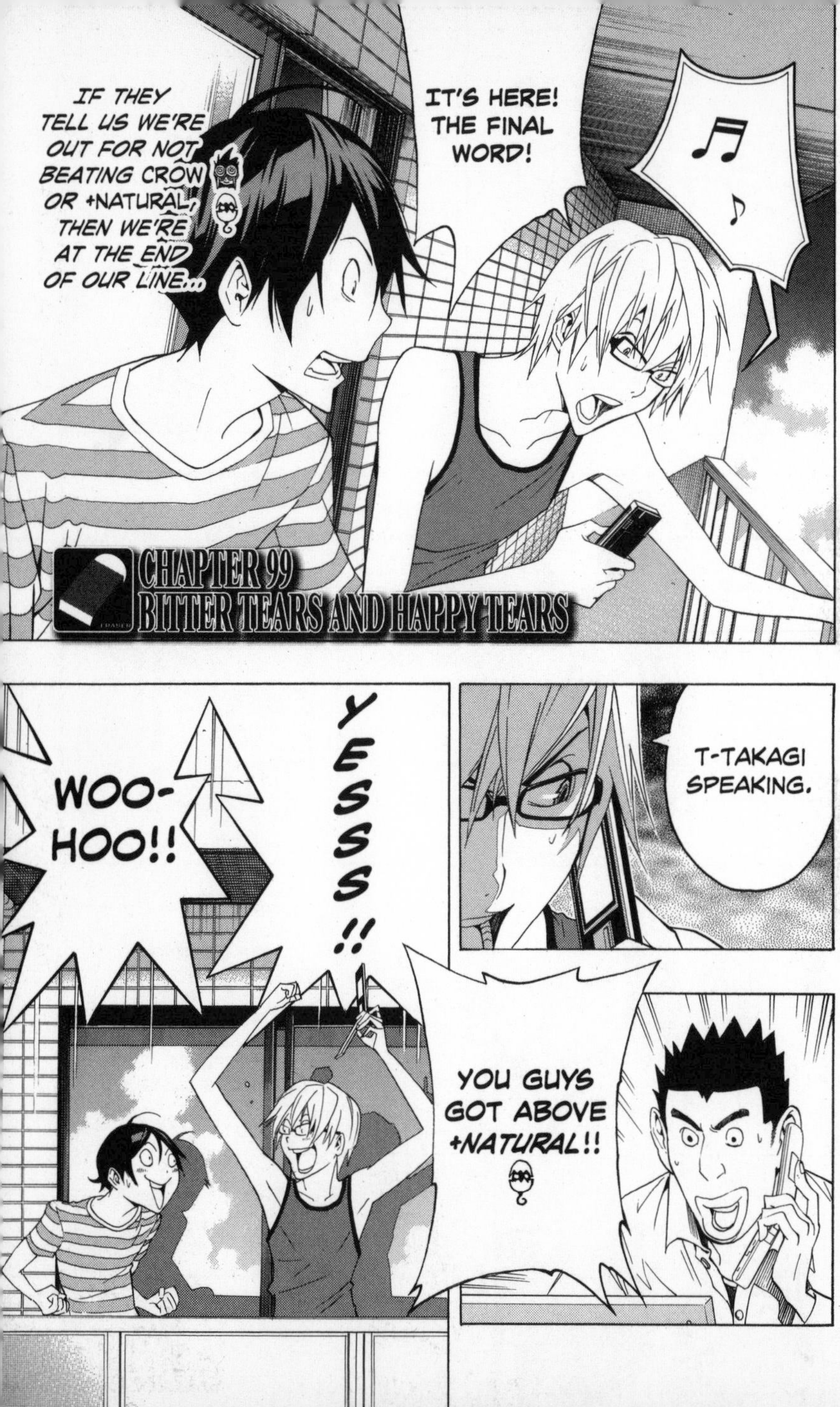
♫ ♪
IT'S HERE! THE FINAL WORD!
IF THEY TELL US WE'RE OUT FOR NOT BEATING CROW OR +NATURAL, THEN WE'RE AT THE END OF OUR LINE...
CHAPTER 99
BITTER TEARS AND HAPPY TEARS
T-TAKAGI SPEAKING.
YOU GUYS GOT ABOVE +NATURAL!!
YESSS!!
WOO-HOO!!

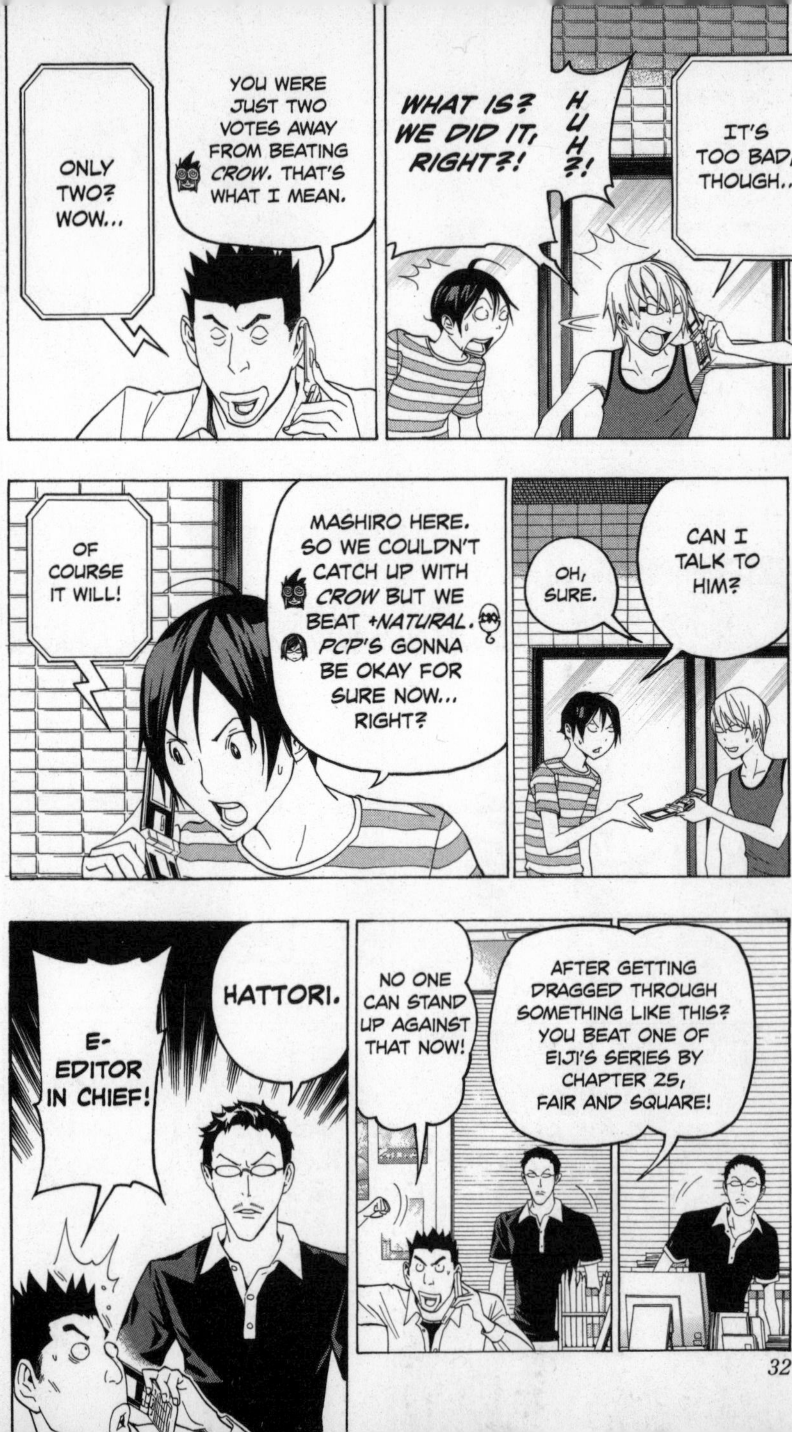

IT'S TOO BAD, THOUGH...
HUH?!
WHAT IS? WE DID IT, RIGHT?!
YOU WERE JUST TWO VOTES AWAY FROM BEATING *CROW*. THAT'S WHAT I MEAN.
ONLY TWO? WOW...
CAN I TALK TO HIM?
OH, SURE.
MASHIRO HERE. SO WE COULDN'T CATCH UP WITH *CROW* BUT WE BEAT *+NATURAL*. *PCP*'S GONNA BE OKAY FOR SURE NOW... RIGHT?
OF COURSE IT WILL!
AFTER GETTING DRAGGED THROUGH SOMETHING LIKE THIS? YOU BEAT ONE OF EIJI'S SERIES BY CHAPTER 25, FAIR AND SQUARE!
NO ONE CAN STAND UP AGAINST THAT NOW!
HATTORI.
E-EDITOR IN CHIEF!

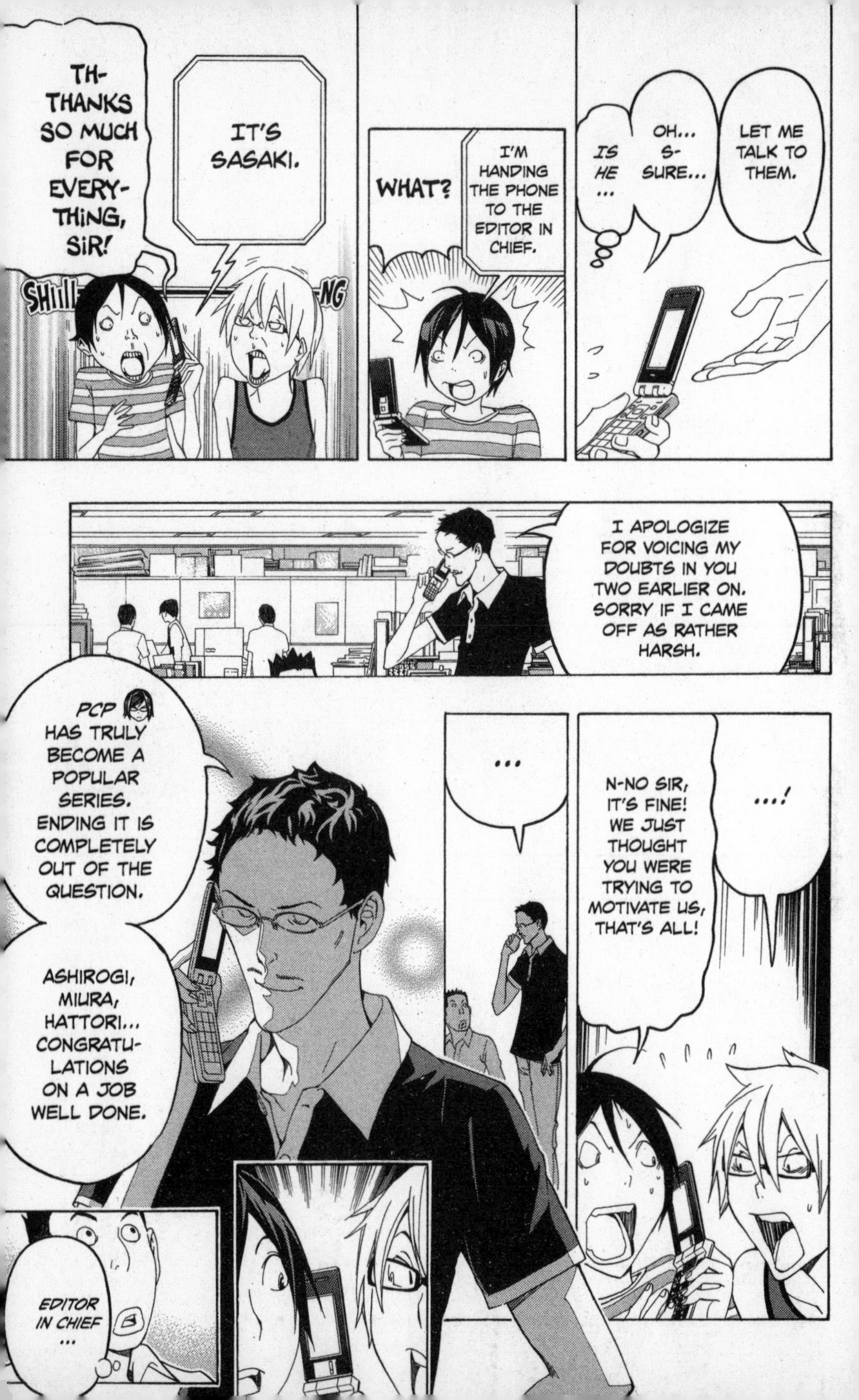
LET ME TALK TO THEM.
OH... S-SURE...
IS HE ...
I'M HANDING THE PHONE TO THE EDITOR IN CHIEF.
WHAT?
IT'S SASAKI.
TH-THANKS SO MUCH FOR EVERYTHING, SIR!
I APOLOGIZE FOR VOICING MY DOUBTS IN YOU TWO EARLIER ON. SORRY IF I CAME OFF AS RATHER HARSH.
...!
N-NO SIR, IT'S FINE! WE JUST THOUGHT YOU WERE TRYING TO MOTIVATE US, THAT'S ALL!
...
PCP HAS TRULY BECOME A POPULAR SERIES. ENDING IT IS COMPLETELY OUT OF THE QUESTION.
ASHIROGI, MIURA, HATTORI... CONGRATULATIONS ON A JOB WELL DONE.
EDITOR IN CHIEF ...

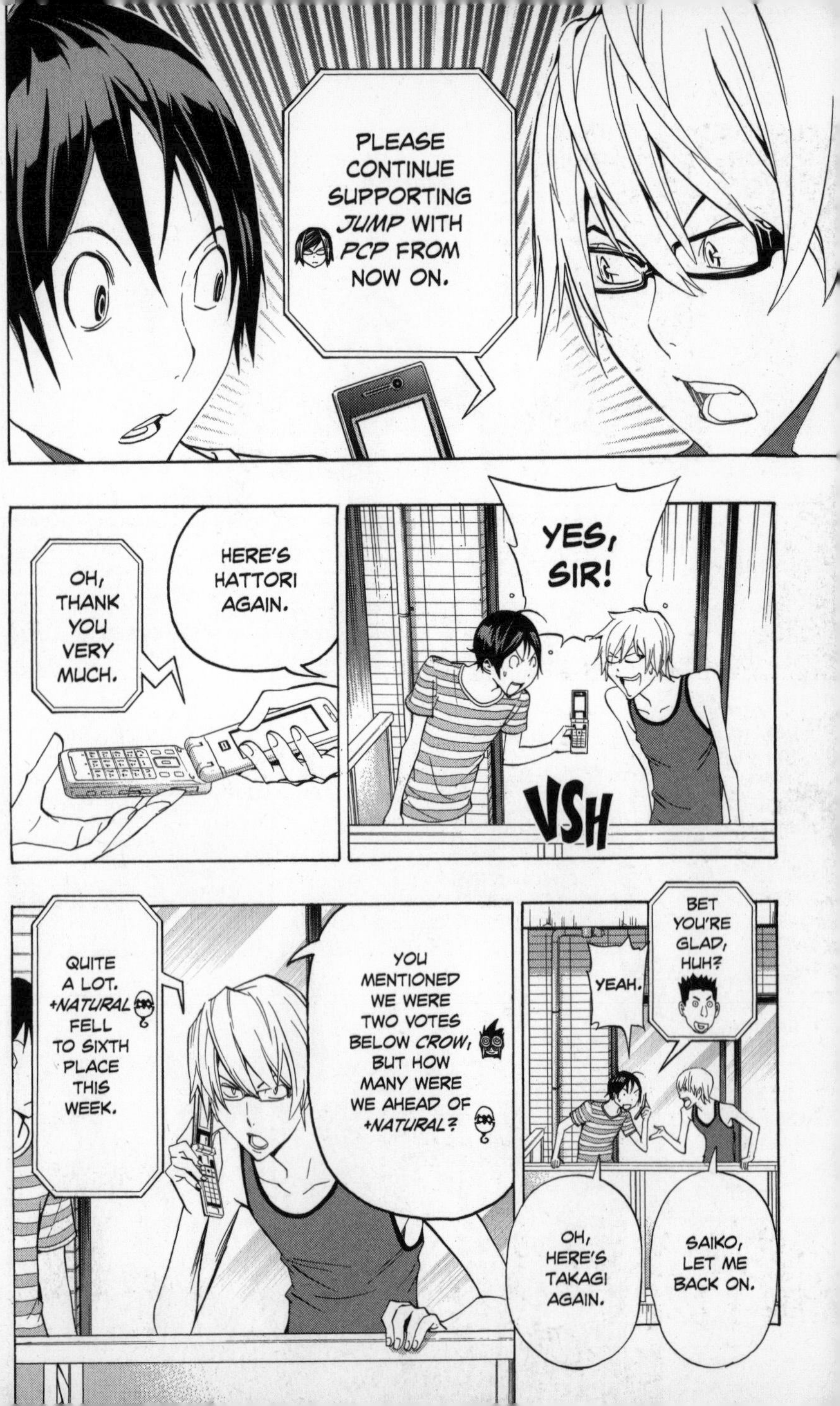
PLEASE CONTINUE SUPPORTING *JUMP* WITH *PCP* FROM NOW ON.
YES, SIR!
VSH
HERE'S HATTORI AGAIN.
OH, THANK YOU VERY MUCH.
BET YOU'RE GLAD, HUH?
YEAH.
SAIKO, LET ME BACK ON.
OH, HERE'S TAKAGI AGAIN.
YOU MENTIONED WE WERE TWO VOTES BELOW *CROW*, BUT HOW MANY WERE WE AHEAD OF *+NATURAL*?
QUITE A LOT. *+NATURAL* FELL TO SIXTH PLACE THIS WEEK.

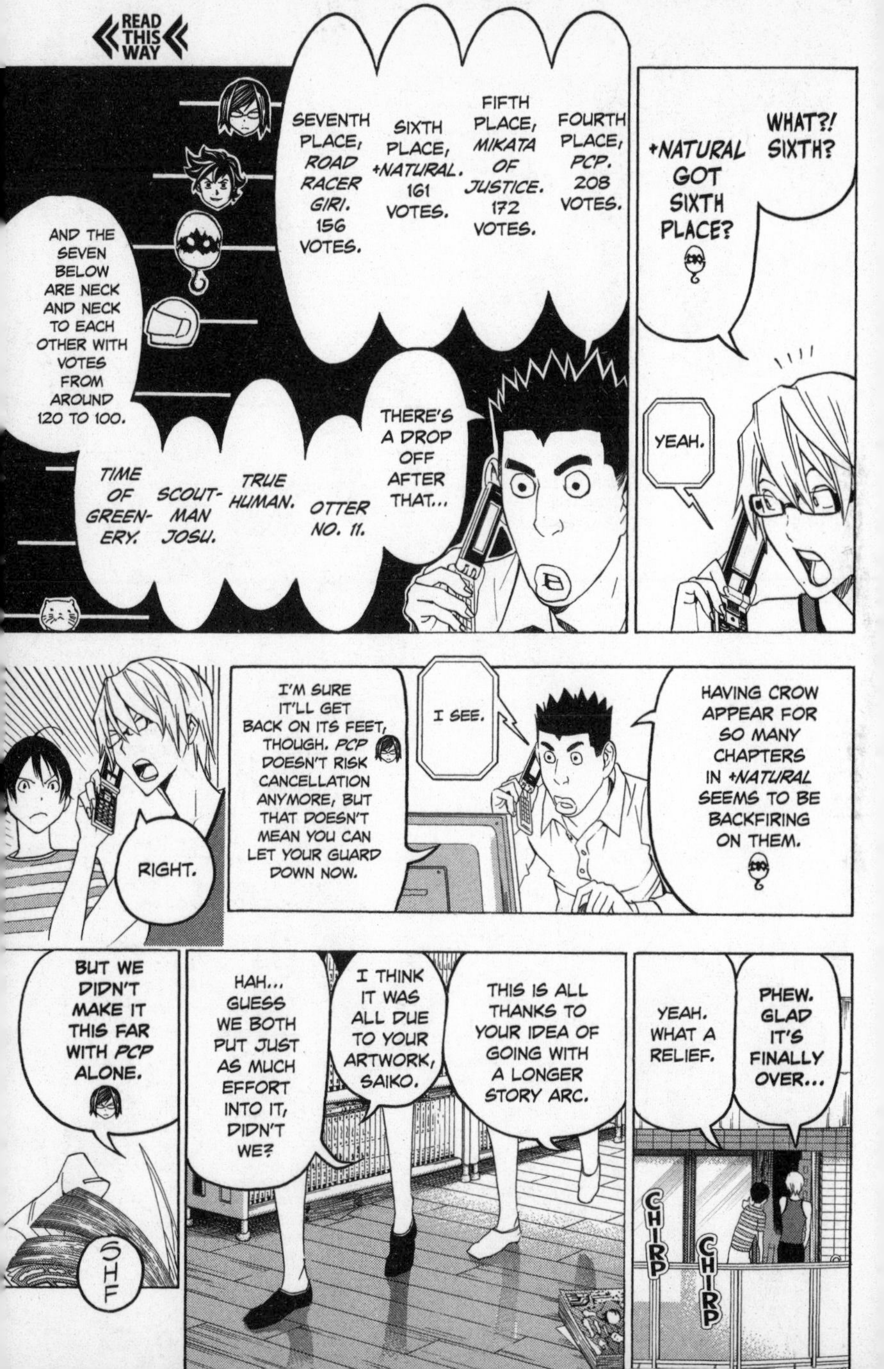
READ THIS WAY
WHAT?! SIXTH?
+NATURAL GOT SIXTH PLACE?
YEAH.
FOURTH PLACE, PCP. 208 VOTES.
FIFTH PLACE, MIKATA OF JUSTICE. 172 VOTES.
SIXTH PLACE, +NATURAL. 161 VOTES.
SEVENTH PLACE, ROAD RACER GIRI. 156 VOTES.
THERE'S A DROP OFF AFTER THAT...
OTTER NO. 11.
TRUE HUMAN.
SCOUT-MAN JOSU.
TIME OF GREENERY.
AND THE SEVEN BELOW ARE NECK AND NECK TO EACH OTHER WITH VOTES FROM AROUND 120 TO 100.
HAVING CROW APPEAR FOR SO MANY CHAPTERS IN +NATURAL SEEMS TO BE BACKFIRING ON THEM.
I SEE.
I'M SURE IT'LL GET BACK ON ITS FEET, THOUGH. PCP DOESN'T RISK CANCELLATION ANYMORE, BUT THAT DOESN'T MEAN YOU CAN LET YOUR GUARD DOWN NOW.
RIGHT.
PHEW. GLAD IT'S FINALLY OVER...
YEAH. WHAT A RELIEF.
CHIRP
CHIRP
CHIRP
THIS IS ALL THANKS TO YOUR IDEA OF GOING WITH A LONGER STORY ARC.
I THINK IT WAS ALL DUE TO YOUR ARTWORK, SAIKO.
HAH... GUESS WE BOTH PUT JUST AS MUCH EFFORT INTO IT, DIDN'T WE?
BUT WE DIDN'T MAKE IT THIS FAR WITH PCP ALONE.
SHF

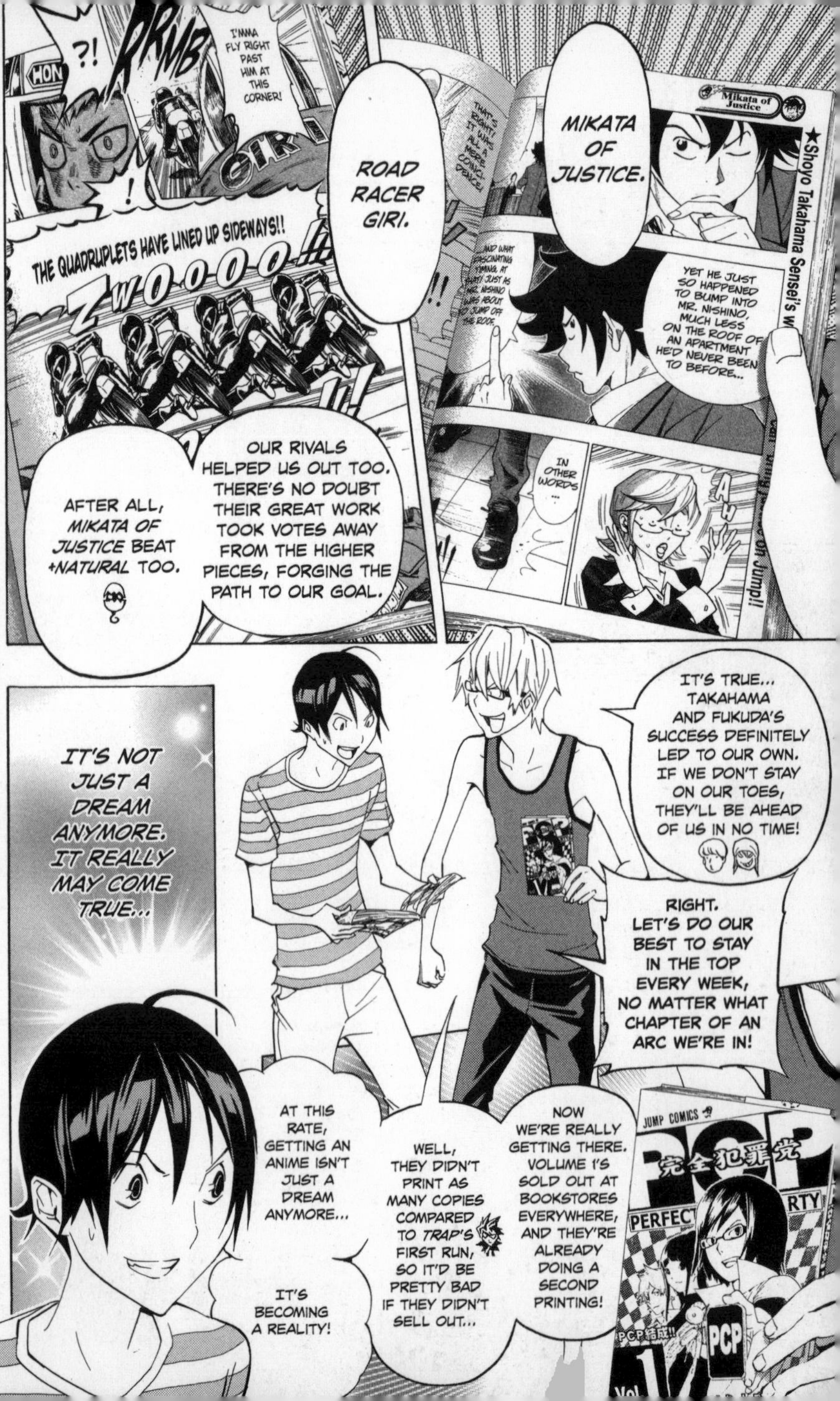
MIKATA OF JUSTICE.
Mikata of Justice
★Shoyo Takahama Sensei's w
YET HE JUST SO HAPPENED TO BUMP INTO MR. NISHINO, MUCH LESS ON THE ROOF OF AN APARTMENT HE'D NEVER BEEN TO BEFORE...
...AND WHAT FASCINATING TIMING, AT THAT! JUST AS MR. NISHINO WAS ABOUT TO JUMP OFF THE ROOF.
AH
IN OTHER WORDS...
on Jump!!
ROAD RACER GIRI.
I'MMA FLY RIGHT PAST HIM AT THIS CORNER!
?!
!
THE QUADRUPLETS HAVE LINED UP SIDEWAYS!!
ZWOOOOO
OUR RIVALS HELPED US OUT TOO. THERE'S NO DOUBT THEIR GREAT WORK TOOK VOTES AWAY FROM THE HIGHER PIECES, FORGING THE PATH TO OUR GOAL.
AFTER ALL, MIKATA OF JUSTICE BEAT +NATURAL TOO.
IT'S TRUE... TAKAHAMA AND FUKUDA'S SUCCESS DEFINITELY LED TO OUR OWN. IF WE DON'T STAY ON OUR TOES, THEY'LL BE AHEAD OF US IN NO TIME!
RIGHT. LET'S DO OUR BEST TO STAY IN THE TOP EVERY WEEK, NO MATTER WHAT CHAPTER OF AN ARC WE'RE IN!
JUMP COMICS
完全犯罪党
PCP
NOW WE'RE REALLY GETTING THERE. VOLUME 1'S SOLD OUT AT BOOKSTORES EVERYWHERE, AND THEY'RE ALREADY DOING A SECOND PRINTING!
WELL, THEY DIDN'T PRINT AS MANY COPIES COMPARED TO TRAP'S FIRST RUN, SO IT'D BE PRETTY BAD IF THEY DIDN'T SELL OUT...
AT THIS RATE, GETTING AN ANIME ISN'T JUST A DREAM ANYMORE...
IT'S BECOMING A REALITY!
IT'S NOT JUST A DREAM ANYMORE. IT REALLY MAY COME TRUE...

READ THIS WAY

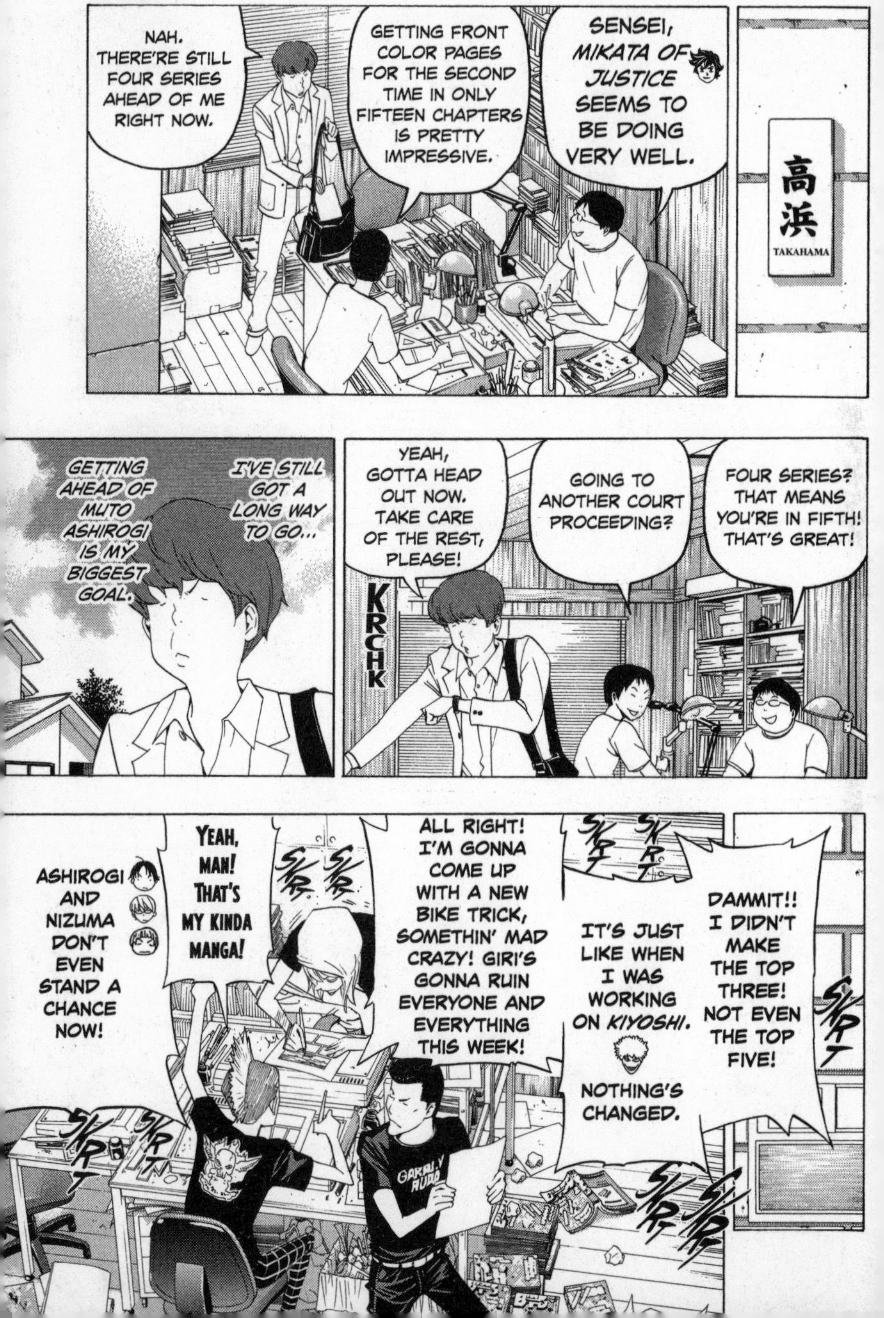
高浜
TAKAHAMA
SENSEI, MIKATA OF JUSTICE SEEMS TO BE DOING VERY WELL.
GETTING FRONT COLOR PAGES FOR THE SECOND TIME IN ONLY FIFTEEN CHAPTERS IS PRETTY IMPRESSIVE.
NAH. THERE'RE STILL FOUR SERIES AHEAD OF ME RIGHT NOW.
FOUR SERIES? THAT MEANS YOU'RE IN FIFTH! THAT'S GREAT!
GOING TO ANOTHER COURT PROCEEDING?
YEAH, GOTTA HEAD OUT NOW. TAKE CARE OF THE REST, PLEASE!
KRCHK
I'VE STILL GOT A LONG WAY TO GO...
GETTING AHEAD OF MUTO ASHIROGI IS MY BIGGEST GOAL.
DAMMIT!! I DIDN'T MAKE THE TOP THREE! NOT EVEN THE TOP FIVE!
SKRT
SKRT SKRT
IT'S JUST LIKE WHEN I WAS WORKING ON KIYOSHI.
NOTHING'S CHANGED.
SKRT SKRT
ALL RIGHT! I'M GONNA COME UP WITH A NEW BIKE TRICK, SOMETHIN' MAD CRAZY! GIRI'S GONNA RUIN EVERYONE AND EVERYTHING THIS WEEK!
SKRT SKRT
YEAH, MAN! THAT'S MY KINDA MANGA!
ASHIROGI AND NIZUMA DON'T EVEN STAND A CHANCE NOW!
SKRT SKRT

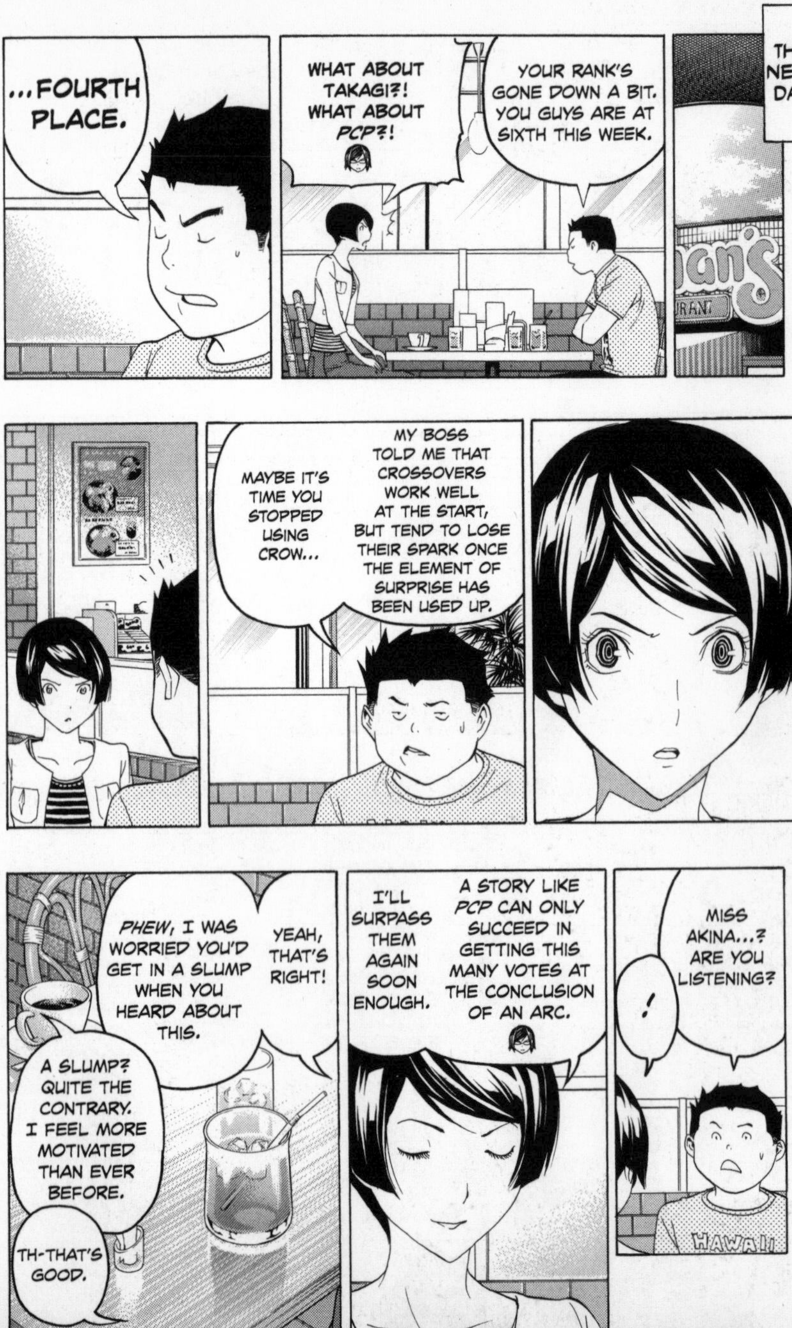
THE NEXT DAY
YOUR RANK'S GONE DOWN A BIT. YOU GUYS ARE AT SIXTH THIS WEEK.
WHAT ABOUT TAKAGI?! WHAT ABOUT PCP?!
...FOURTH PLACE.
MY BOSS TOLD ME THAT CROSSOVERS WORK WELL AT THE START, BUT TEND TO LOSE THEIR SPARK ONCE THE ELEMENT OF SURPRISE HAS BEEN USED UP.
MAYBE IT'S TIME YOU STOPPED USING CROW...
MISS AKINA...? ARE YOU LISTENING?
!
A STORY LIKE PCP CAN ONLY SUCCEED IN GETTING THIS MANY VOTES AT THE CONCLUSION OF AN ARC.
I'LL SURPASS THEM AGAIN SOON ENOUGH.
YEAH, THAT'S RIGHT!
PHEW, I WAS WORRIED YOU'D GET IN A SLUMP WHEN YOU HEARD ABOUT THIS.
A SLUMP? QUITE THE CONTRARY. I FEEL MORE MOTIVATED THAN EVER BEFORE.
TH-THAT'S GOOD.

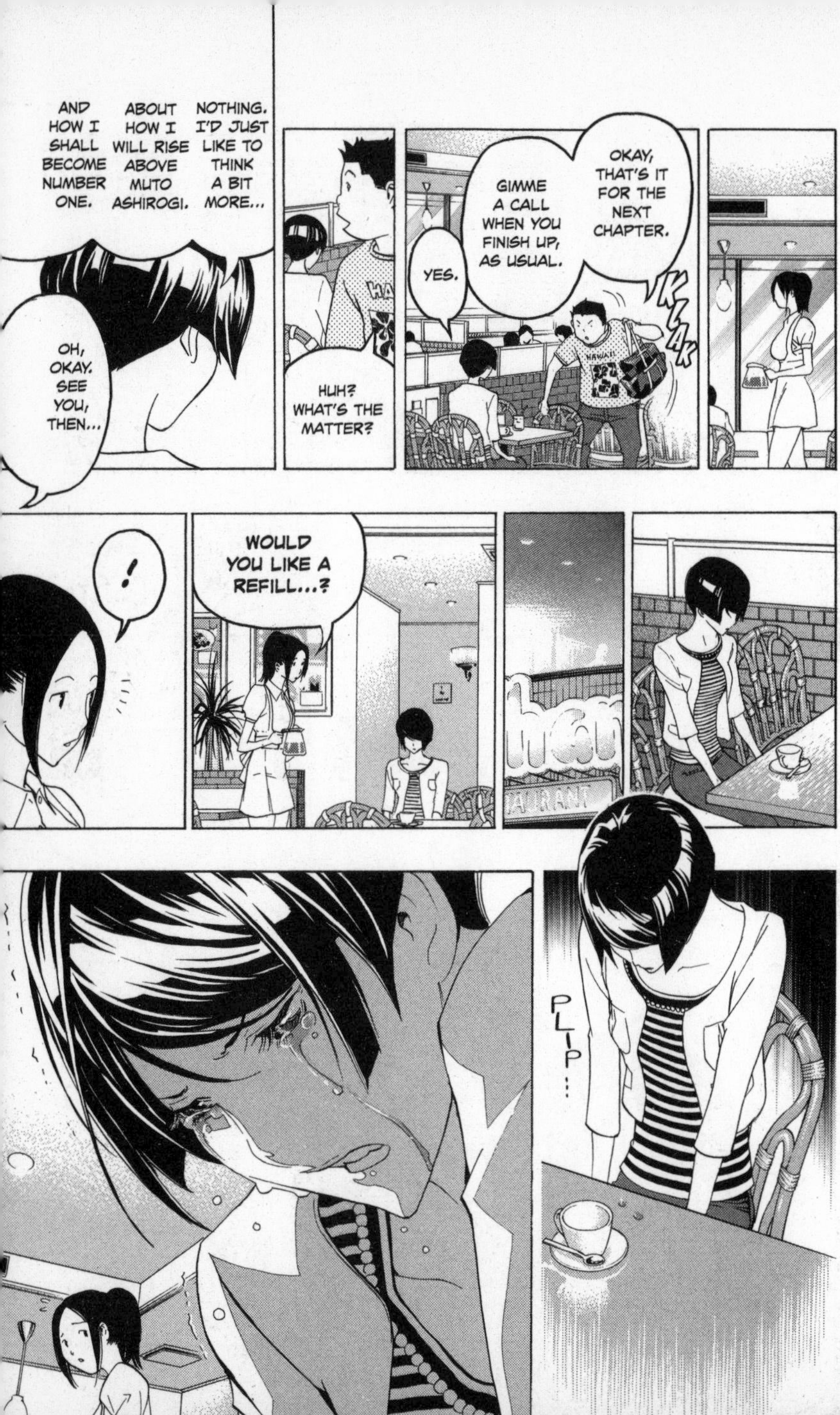
KLAK
OKAY, THAT'S IT FOR THE NEXT CHAPTER.
GIMME A CALL WHEN YOU FINISH UP, AS USUAL.
YES.
HUH? WHAT'S THE MATTER?
NOTHING. I'D JUST LIKE TO THINK A BIT MORE...
ABOUT HOW I WILL RISE ABOVE MUTO ASHIROGI.
AND HOW I SHALL BECOME NUMBER ONE.
OH, OKAY. SEE YOU, THEN...
WOULD YOU LIKE A REFILL...?
!
PLIP...

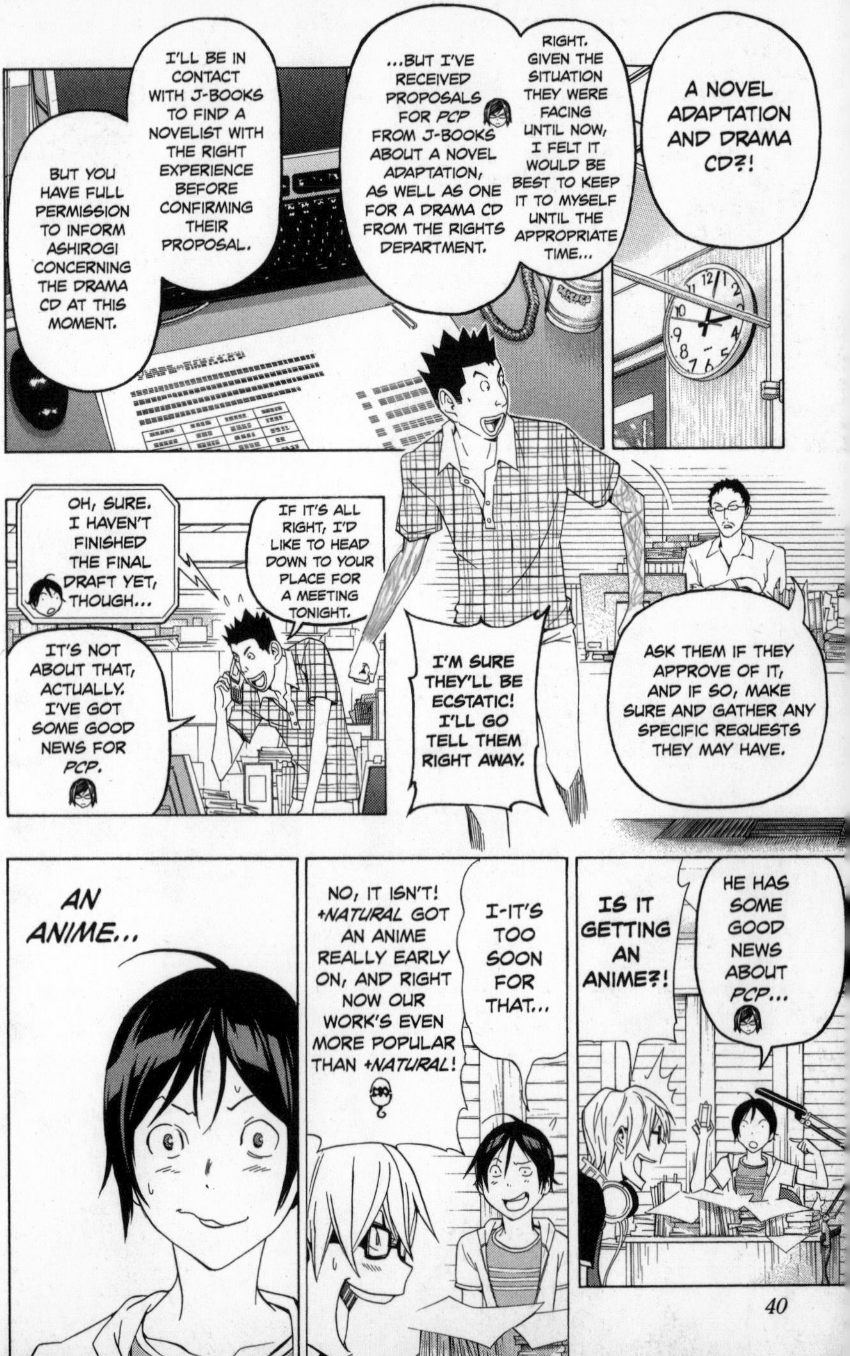
A NOVEL ADAPTATION AND DRAMA CD?!
RIGHT. GIVEN THE SITUATION THEY WERE FACING UNTIL NOW, I FELT IT WOULD BE BEST TO KEEP IT TO MYSELF UNTIL THE APPROPRIATE TIME...
...BUT I'VE RECEIVED PROPOSALS FOR *PCP* FROM J-BOOKS ABOUT A NOVEL ADAPTATION, AS WELL AS ONE FOR A DRAMA CD FROM THE RIGHTS DEPARTMENT.
I'LL BE IN CONTACT WITH J-BOOKS TO FIND A NOVELIST WITH THE RIGHT EXPERIENCE BEFORE CONFIRMING THEIR PROPOSAL.
BUT YOU HAVE FULL PERMISSION TO INFORM ASHIROGI CONCERNING THE DRAMA CD AT THIS MOMENT.
ASK THEM IF THEY APPROVE OF IT, AND IF SO, MAKE SURE AND GATHER ANY SPECIFIC REQUESTS THEY MAY HAVE.
I'M SURE THEY'LL BE ECSTATIC! I'LL GO TELL THEM RIGHT AWAY.
IF IT'S ALL RIGHT, I'D LIKE TO HEAD DOWN TO YOUR PLACE FOR A MEETING TONIGHT.
OH, SURE. I HAVEN'T FINISHED THE FINAL DRAFT YET, THOUGH...
IT'S NOT ABOUT THAT, ACTUALLY. I'VE GOT SOME GOOD NEWS FOR *PCP*.
HE HAS SOME GOOD NEWS ABOUT *PCP*...
IS IT GETTING AN ANIME?!
I-IT'S TOO SOON FOR THAT...
NO, IT ISN'T! *+NATURAL* GOT AN ANIME REALLY EARLY ON, AND RIGHT NOW OUR WORK'S EVEN MORE POPULAR THAN *+NATURAL*!
AN ANIME...

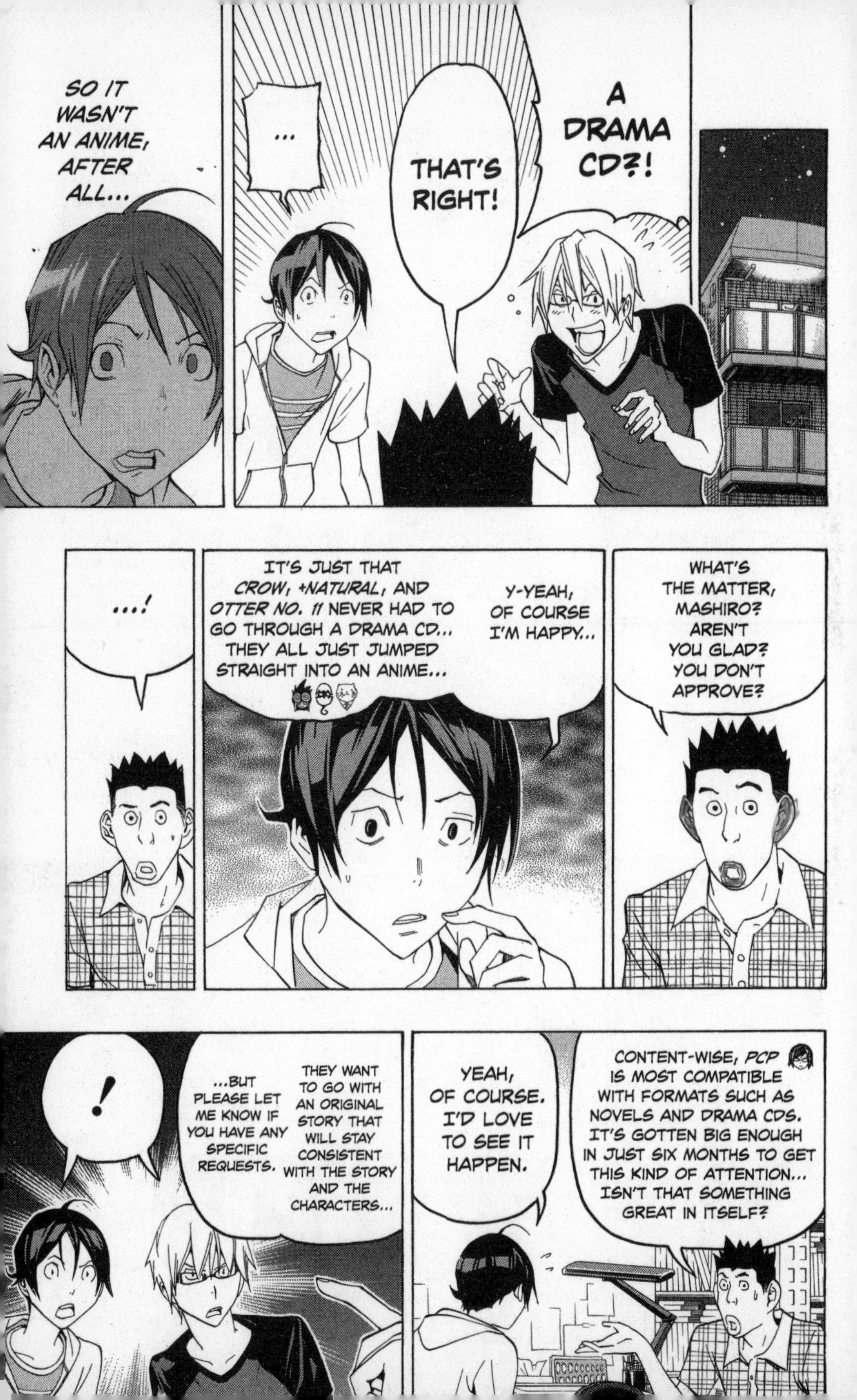

A DRAMA CD?!
THAT'S RIGHT!
...
SO IT WASN'T AN ANIME, AFTER ALL...
WHAT'S THE MATTER, MASHIRO? AREN'T YOU GLAD? YOU DON'T APPROVE?
Y-YEAH, OF COURSE I'M HAPPY...
IT'S JUST THAT *CROW*, *+NATURAL*, AND *OTTER NO. 11* NEVER HAD TO GO THROUGH A DRAMA CD... THEY ALL JUST JUMPED STRAIGHT INTO AN ANIME...
...!
CONTENT-WISE, *PCP* IS MOST COMPATIBLE WITH FORMATS SUCH AS NOVELS AND DRAMA CDS. IT'S GOTTEN BIG ENOUGH IN JUST SIX MONTHS TO GET THIS KIND OF ATTENTION... ISN'T THAT SOMETHING GREAT IN ITSELF?
YEAH, OF COURSE. I'D LOVE TO SEE IT HAPPEN.
THEY WANT TO GO WITH AN ORIGINAL STORY THAT WILL STAY CONSISTENT WITH THE STORY AND THE CHARACTERS...
...BUT PLEASE LET ME KNOW IF YOU HAVE ANY SPECIFIC REQUESTS.
!

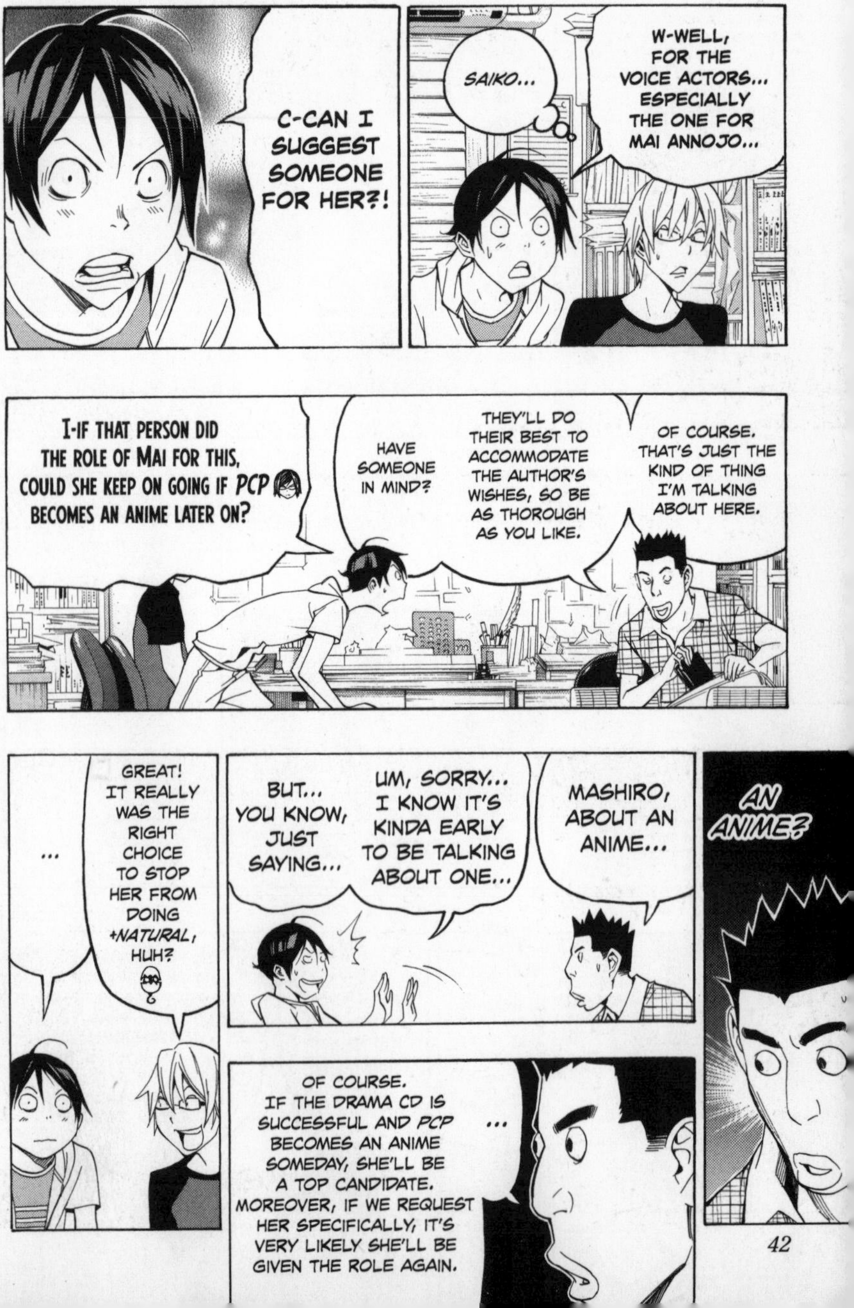
W-WELL, FOR THE VOICE ACTORS... ESPECIALLY THE ONE FOR MAI ANNOJO...
SAIKO...
C-CAN I SUGGEST SOMEONE FOR HER?!
OF COURSE. THAT'S JUST THE KIND OF THING I'M TALKING ABOUT HERE.
THEY'LL DO THEIR BEST TO ACCOMMODATE THE AUTHOR'S WISHES, SO BE AS THOROUGH AS YOU LIKE.
HAVE SOMEONE IN MIND?
I-IF THAT PERSON DID THE ROLE OF MAI FOR THIS, COULD SHE KEEP ON GOING IF PCP BECOMES AN ANIME LATER ON?
AN ANIME?
MASHIRO, ABOUT AN ANIME...
UM, SORRY... I KNOW IT'S KINDA EARLY TO BE TALKING ABOUT ONE...
BUT... YOU KNOW, JUST SAYING...
...
OF COURSE. IF THE DRAMA CD IS SUCCESSFUL AND PCP BECOMES AN ANIME SOMEDAY, SHE'LL BE A TOP CANDIDATE. MOREOVER, IF WE REQUEST HER SPECIFICALLY, IT'S VERY LIKELY SHE'LL BE GIVEN THE ROLE AGAIN.
GREAT! IT REALLY WAS THE RIGHT CHOICE TO STOP HER FROM DOING +NATURAL, HUH?
...

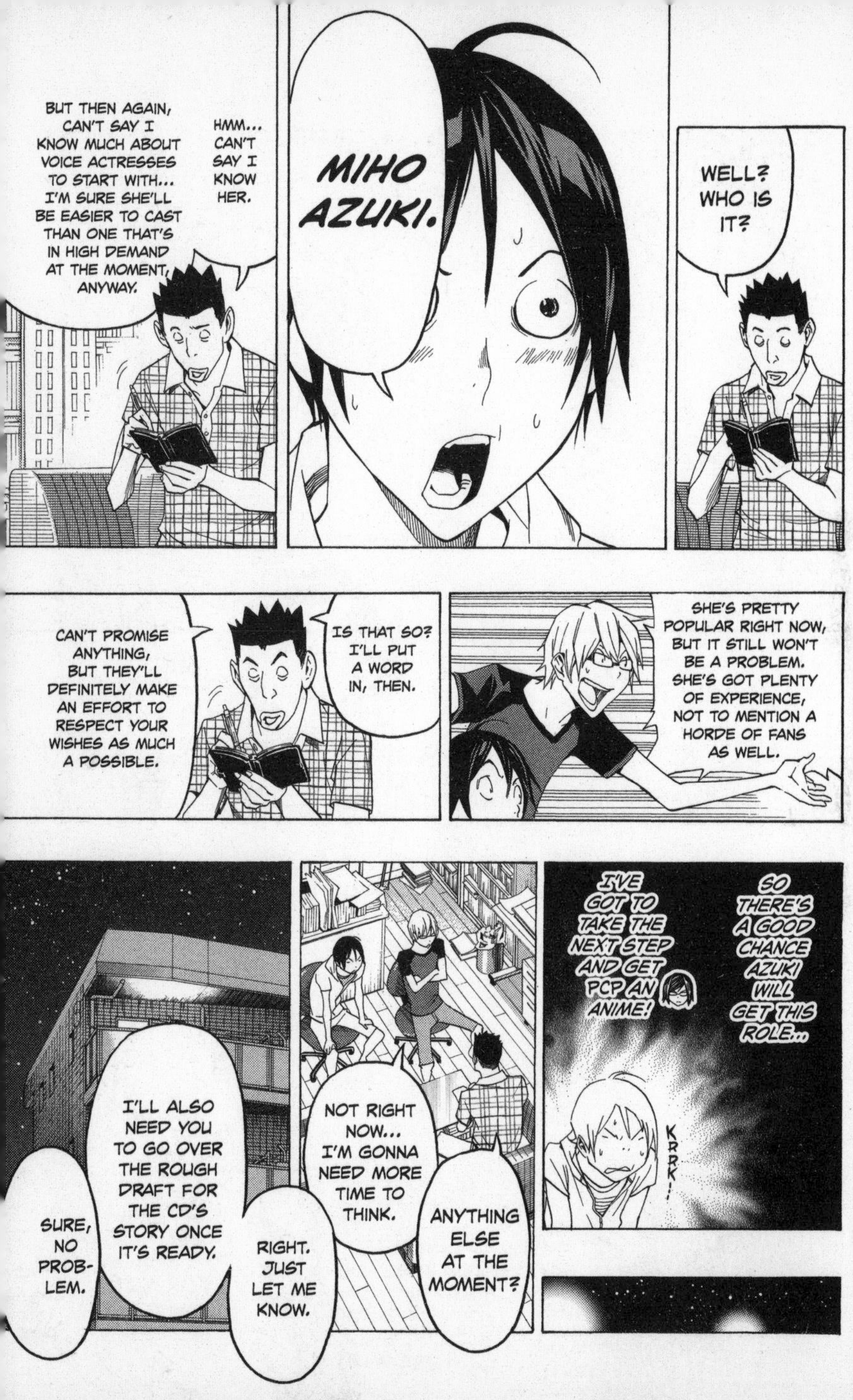
WELL? WHO IS IT?
MIHO AZUKI.
HMM... CAN'T SAY I KNOW HER.
BUT THEN AGAIN, CAN'T SAY I KNOW MUCH ABOUT VOICE ACTRESSES TO START WITH... I'M SURE SHE'LL BE EASIER TO CAST THAN ONE THAT'S IN HIGH DEMAND AT THE MOMENT, ANYWAY.
SHE'S PRETTY POPULAR RIGHT NOW, BUT IT STILL WON'T BE A PROBLEM. SHE'S GOT PLENTY OF EXPERIENCE, NOT TO MENTION A HORDE OF FANS AS WELL.
IS THAT SO? I'LL PUT A WORD IN, THEN.
CAN'T PROMISE ANYTHING, BUT THEY'LL DEFINITELY MAKE AN EFFORT TO RESPECT YOUR WISHES AS MUCH A POSSIBLE.
SO THERE'S A GOOD CHANCE AZUKI WILL GET THIS ROLE...
I'VE GOT TO TAKE THE NEXT STEP AND GET PCP AN ANIME!
KRRK!
ANYTHING ELSE AT THE MOMENT?
NOT RIGHT NOW... I'M GONNA NEED MORE TIME TO THINK.
RIGHT. JUST LET ME KNOW.
I'LL ALSO NEED YOU TO GO OVER THE ROUGH DRAFT FOR THE CD'S STORY ONCE IT'S READY.
SURE, NO PROBLEM.

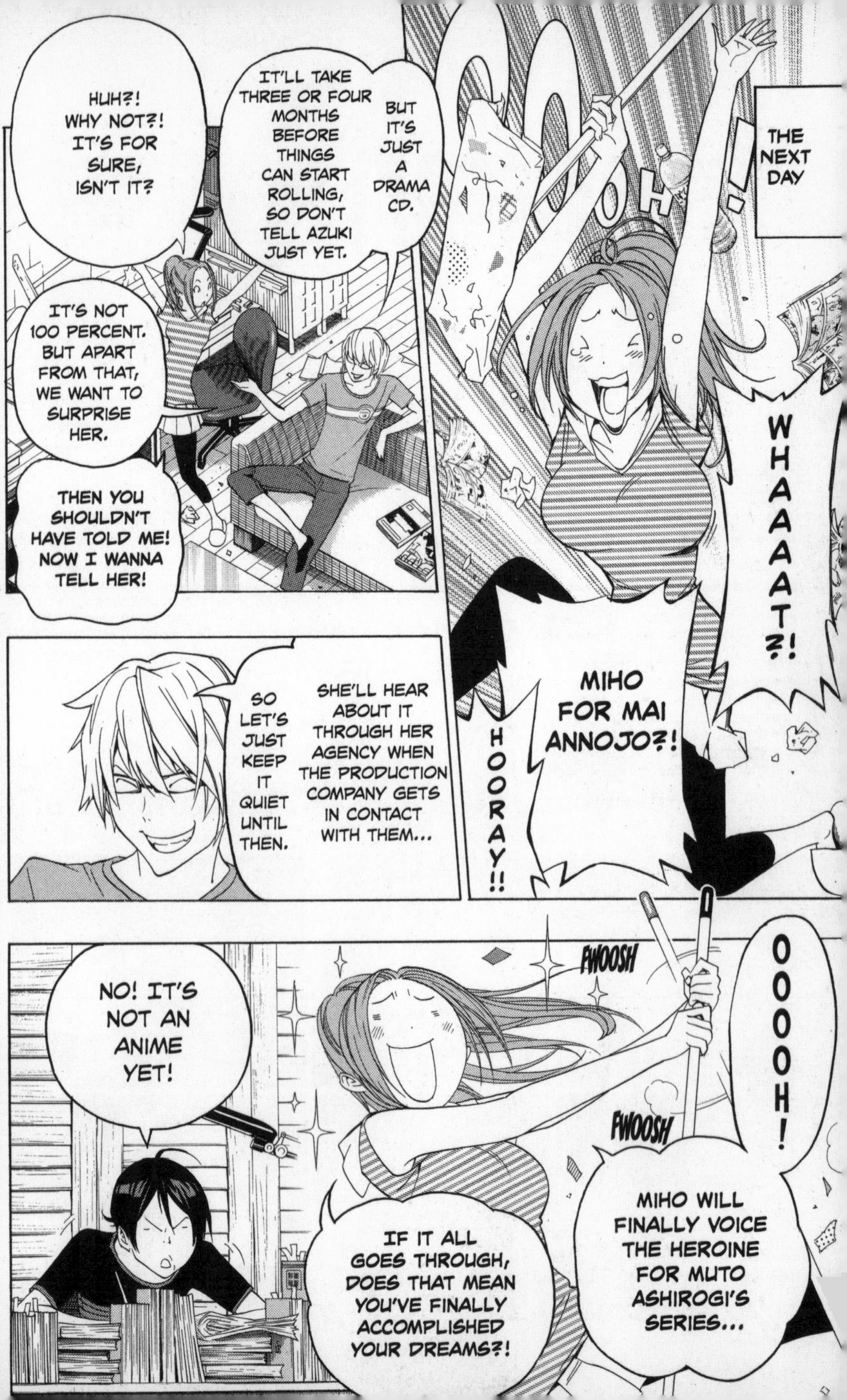
THE NEXT DAY
WHAAAAT?!
MIHO FOR MAI ANNOJO?!
HOORAY!!
BUT IT'S JUST A DRAMA CD.
IT'LL TAKE THREE OR FOUR MONTHS BEFORE THINGS CAN START ROLLING, SO DON'T TELL AZUKI JUST YET.
HUH?! WHY NOT?! IT'S FOR SURE, ISN'T IT?
IT'S NOT 100 PERCENT. BUT APART FROM THAT, WE WANT TO SURPRISE HER.
THEN YOU SHOULDN'T HAVE TOLD ME! NOW I WANNA TELL HER!
SHE'LL HEAR ABOUT IT THROUGH HER AGENCY WHEN THE PRODUCTION COMPANY GETS IN CONTACT WITH THEM...
SO LET'S JUST KEEP IT QUIET UNTIL THEN.
OOOOOH!
FWOOSH
FWOOSH
MIHO WILL FINALLY VOICE THE HEROINE FOR MUTO ASHIROGI'S SERIES...
IF IT ALL GOES THROUGH, DOES THAT MEAN YOU'VE FINALLY ACCOMPLISHED YOUR DREAMS?!
NO! IT'S NOT AN ANIME YET!

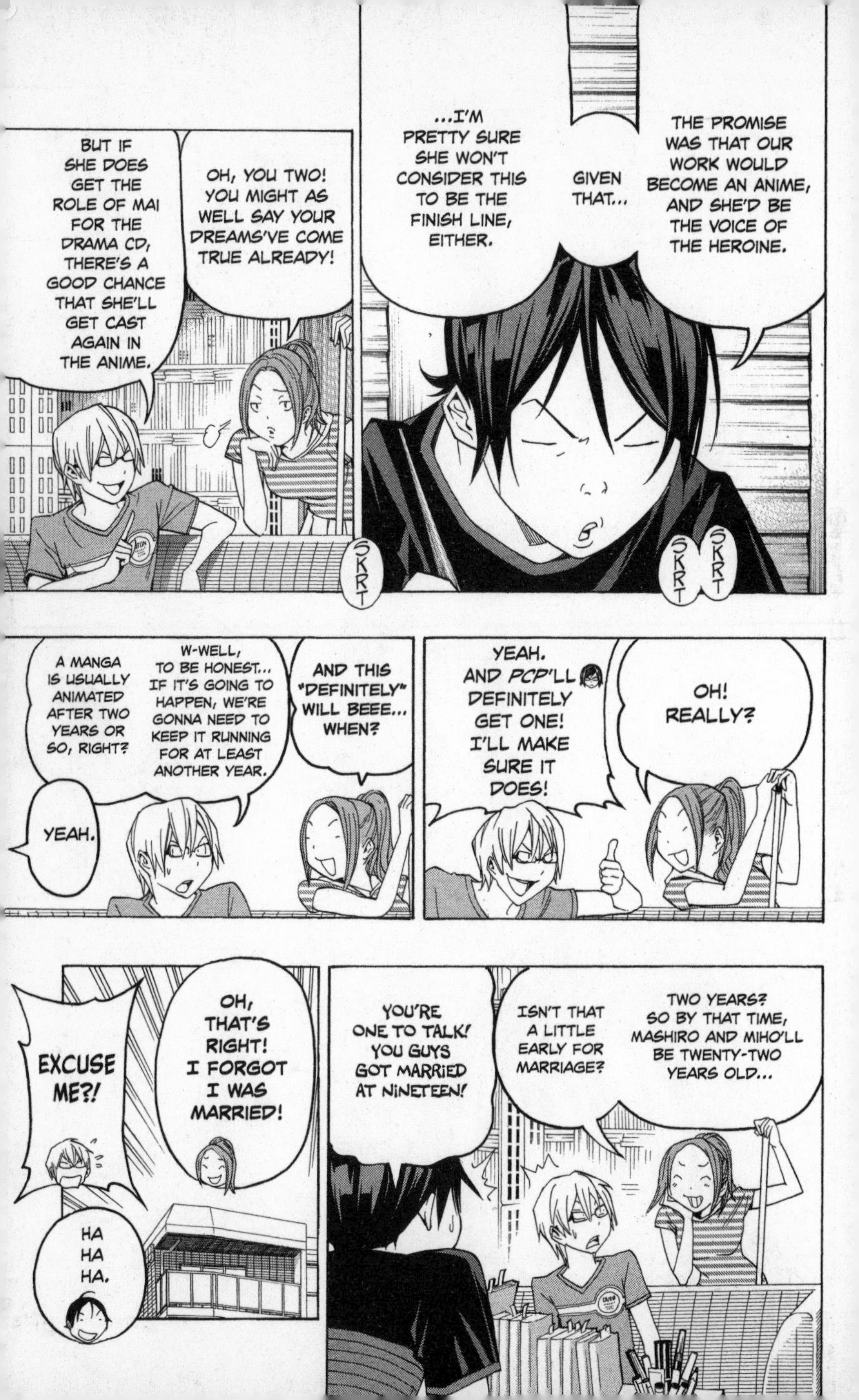
THE PROMISE WAS THAT OUR WORK WOULD BECOME AN ANIME, AND SHE'D BE THE VOICE OF THE HEROINE.
GIVEN THAT...
...I'M PRETTY SURE SHE WON'T CONSIDER THIS TO BE THE FINISH LINE, EITHER.
SKRT SKRT
SKRT
OH, YOU TWO! YOU MIGHT AS WELL SAY YOUR DREAMS'VE COME TRUE ALREADY!
BUT IF SHE DOES GET THE ROLE OF MAI FOR THE DRAMA CD, THERE'S A GOOD CHANCE THAT SHE'LL GET CAST AGAIN IN THE ANIME.
OH! REALLY?
YEAH. AND *PCP*'LL DEFINITELY GET ONE! I'LL MAKE SURE IT DOES!
AND THIS "DEFINITELY" WILL BEEE... WHEN?
W-WELL, TO BE HONEST... IF IT'S GOING TO HAPPEN, WE'RE GONNA NEED TO KEEP IT RUNNING FOR AT LEAST ANOTHER YEAR.
A MANGA IS USUALLY ANIMATED AFTER TWO YEARS OR SO, RIGHT?
YEAH.
TWO YEARS? SO BY THAT TIME, MASHIRO AND MIHO'LL BE TWENTY-TWO YEARS OLD...
ISN'T THAT A LITTLE EARLY FOR MARRIAGE?
YOU'RE ONE TO TALK! YOU GUYS GOT MARRIED AT NINETEEN!
OH, THAT'S RIGHT! I FORGOT I WAS MARRIED!
EXCUSE ME?!
HA HA HA.

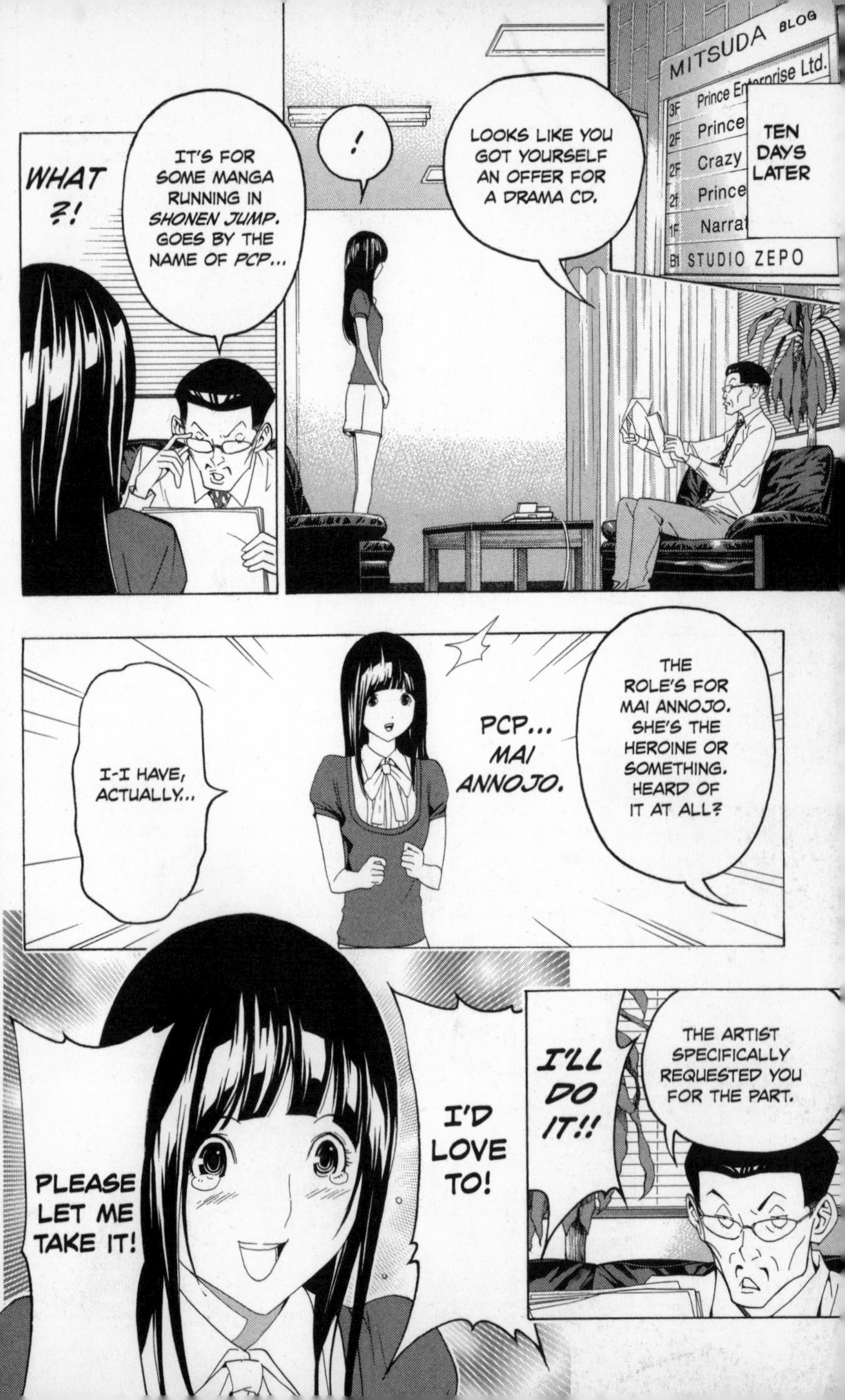
MITSUDA BLOG
Prince Enterprise Ltd.
3F Prince En
2F Prince
2F Crazy
2F Prince
1F Narrat
B1 STUDIO ZEPO
TEN DAYS LATER
LOOKS LIKE YOU GOT YOURSELF AN OFFER FOR A DRAMA CD.
!
IT'S FOR SOME MANGA RUNNING IN *SHONEN JUMP*. GOES BY THE NAME OF *PCP*...
WHAT?!
THE ROLE'S FOR MAI ANNOJO. SHE'S THE HEROINE OR SOMETHING. HEARD OF IT AT ALL?
PCP... MAI ANNOJO.
I-I HAVE, ACTUALLY...
THE ARTIST SPECIFICALLY REQUESTED YOU FOR THE PART.
I'LL DO IT!!
I'D LOVE TO!
PLEASE LET ME TAKE IT!

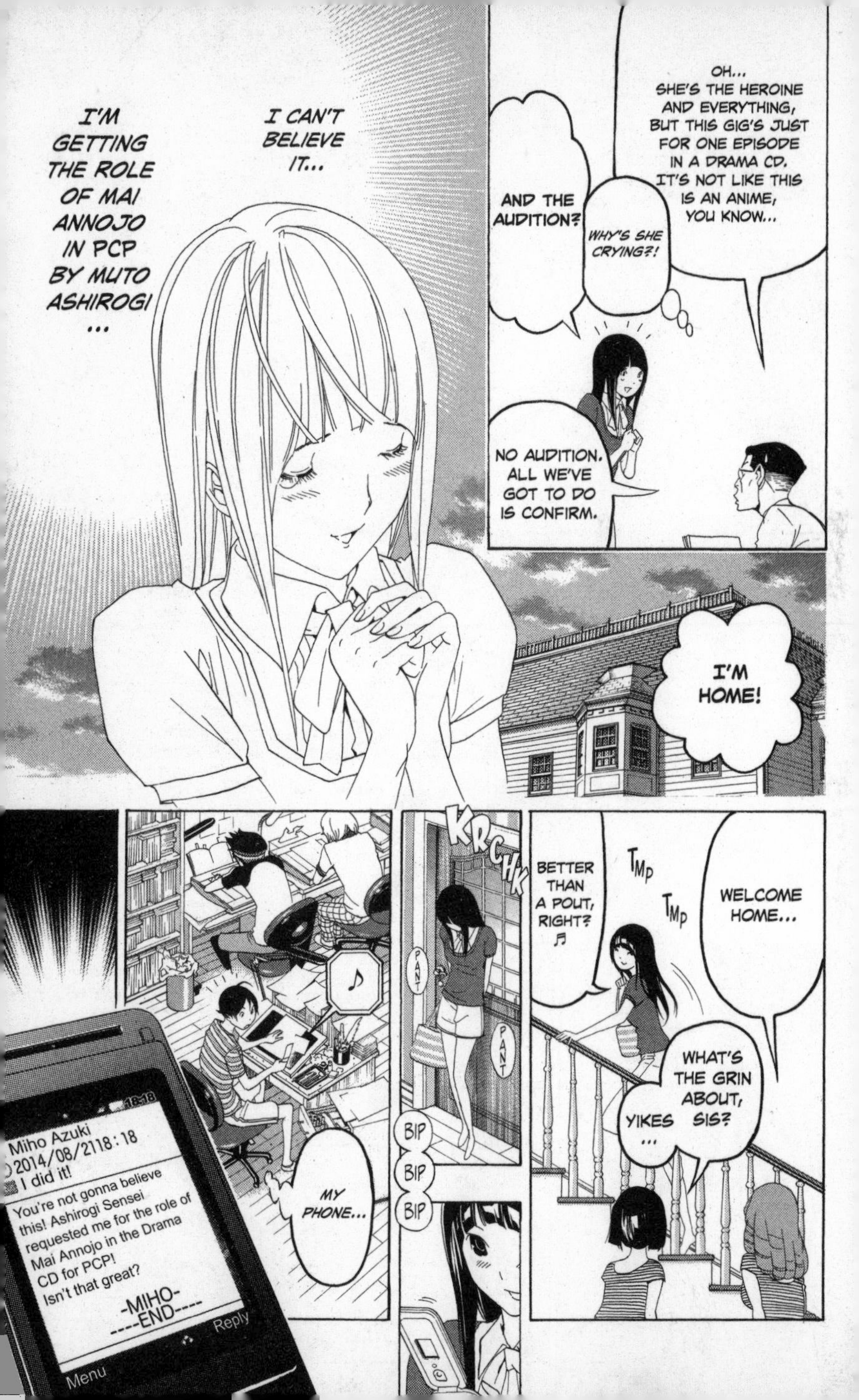
OH... SHE'S THE HEROINE AND EVERYTHING, BUT THIS GIG'S JUST FOR ONE EPISODE IN A DRAMA CD. IT'S NOT LIKE THIS IS AN ANIME, YOU KNOW...
WHY'S SHE CRYING?!
AND THE AUDITION?
NO AUDITION. ALL WE'VE GOT TO DO IS CONFIRM.
I'M HOME!
I CAN'T BELIEVE IT...
I'M GETTING THE ROLE OF MAI ANNOJO IN PCP BY MUTO ASHIROGI ...
WELCOME HOME...
TMP
TMP
BETTER THAN A POUT, RIGHT? ♬
WHAT'S THE GRIN ABOUT, SIS?
YIKES ...
KRCHK
PANT
PANT
BIP
BIP
BIP
♪
MY PHONE...
18:18
Miho Azuki
2014/08/2118 : 18
I did it!
You're not gonna believe this! Ashirogi Sensei requested me for the role of Mai Annojo in the Drama CD for PCP! Isn't that great?
-MIHO-
----END----
Reply
Menu

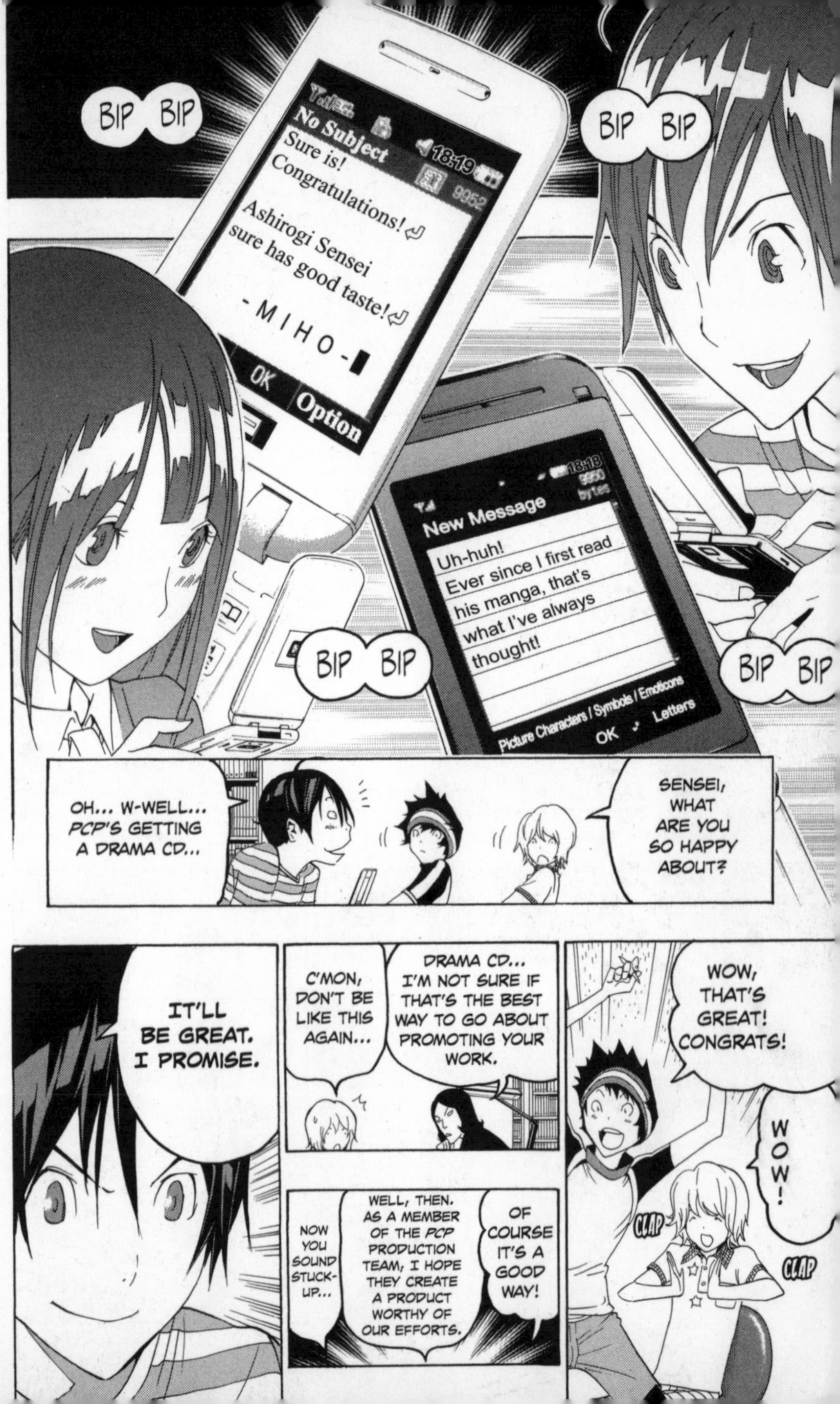
BIP BIP
BIP BIP
No Subject
18:19
9952
Sure is!
Congratulations!
Ashirogi Sensei
sure has good taste!
-MIHO-
OK
Option
18:18
New Message
Uh-huh!
Ever since I first read
his manga, that's
what I've always
thought!
Picture Characters / Symbols / Emoticons
OK
Letters
BIP BIP
BIP BIP
SENSEI, WHAT ARE YOU SO HAPPY ABOUT?
OH... W-WELL... *PCP*'S GETTING A DRAMA CD...
WOW, THAT'S GREAT! CONGRATS!
WOW!
CLAP
CLAP
DRAMA CD... I'M NOT SURE IF THAT'S THE BEST WAY TO GO ABOUT PROMOTING YOUR WORK.
C'MON, DON'T BE LIKE THIS AGAIN...
OF COURSE IT'S A GOOD WAY!
WELL, THEN. AS A MEMBER OF THE *PCP* PRODUCTION TEAM, I HOPE THEY CREATE A PRODUCT WORTHY OF OUR EFFORTS.
NOW YOU SOUND STUCK-UP...
IT'LL BE GREAT. I PROMISE.

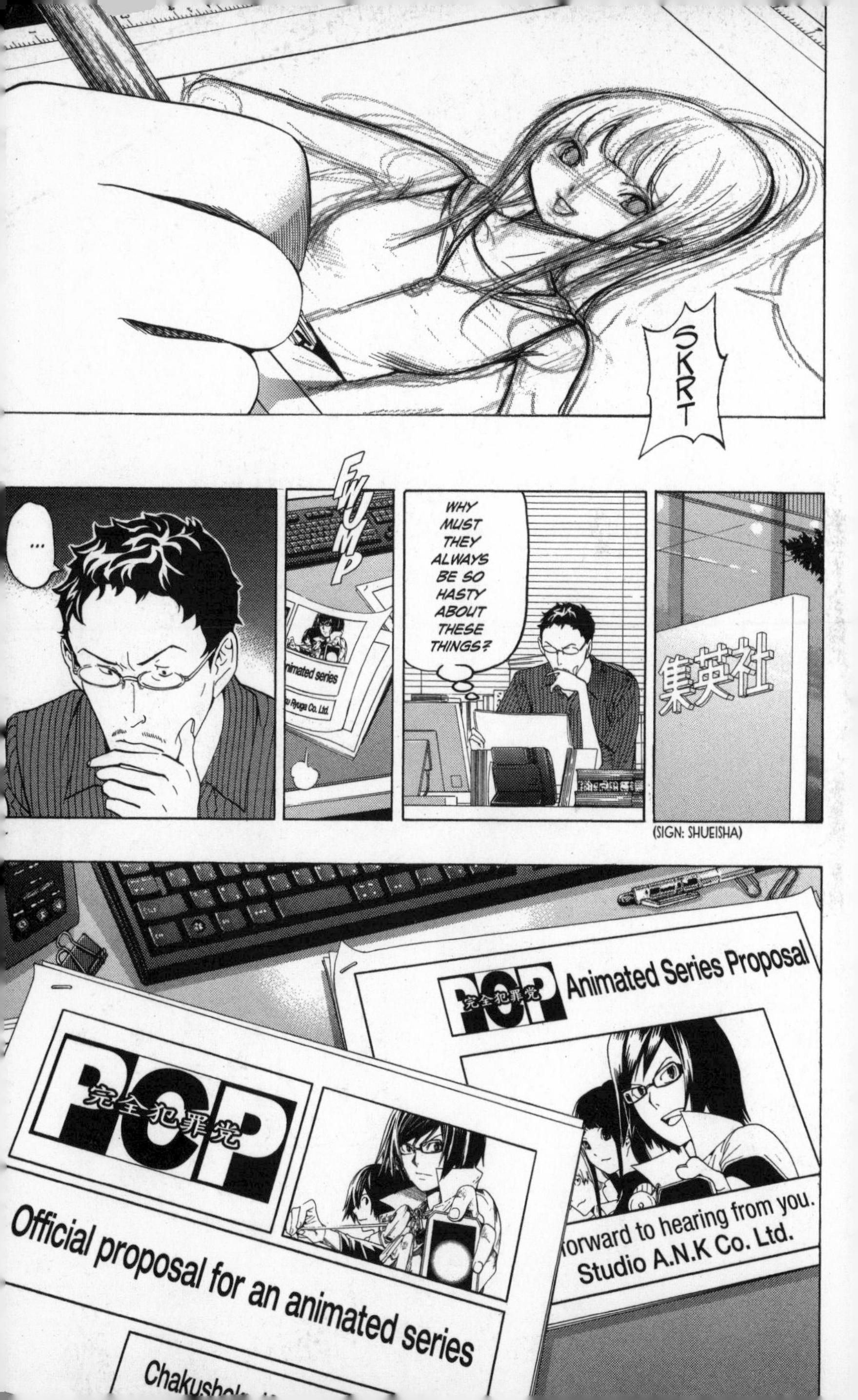
SKRT
(SIGN: SHUEISHA)
集英社
WHY MUST THEY ALWAYS BE SO HASTY ABOUT THESE THINGS?
FWUMP
...
完全犯罪党
POP Animated Series Proposal
orward to hearing from you.
Studio A.N.K Co. Ltd.
完全犯罪党
POP
Official proposal for an animated series

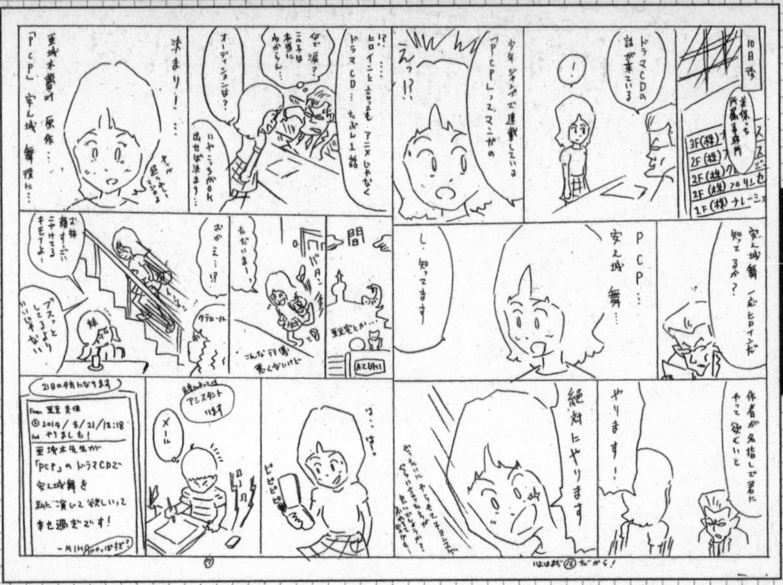
10日後
ドラマCDの話が来ている
!
少年ジャンプで連載している「PCP」ってマンガの
えっ!?
安え城舞 一応ヒロインだ 知ってるか?
PCP…安え城 舞…
し、知ってます
作者が名指しで君にやって欲しいと
やります!
絶対にヤります
!?……ヒロインと言っても アニメじゃなく ドラマCD… ちょい1話
何で涙? この子は本当にわからん…
オーディションは?
いや こっちがOK出せば決まり…
決まり!…
亜城木夢叶 原作…「PCP」安え城 舞役に…
ただいまー!
おかえ…!?
お姉 顔すごいニヤけてるキモイよ
ブスッとしてるよりいいじゃない
21日の夕方になります
From 亜豆美保
2014/3/21/18:18
Sub やりました!
亜城木先生が「PCP」のドラマCDで安え城舞を私に演じて欲しいって 超興奮です!
—MIHO

OHBA'S STORYBOARD

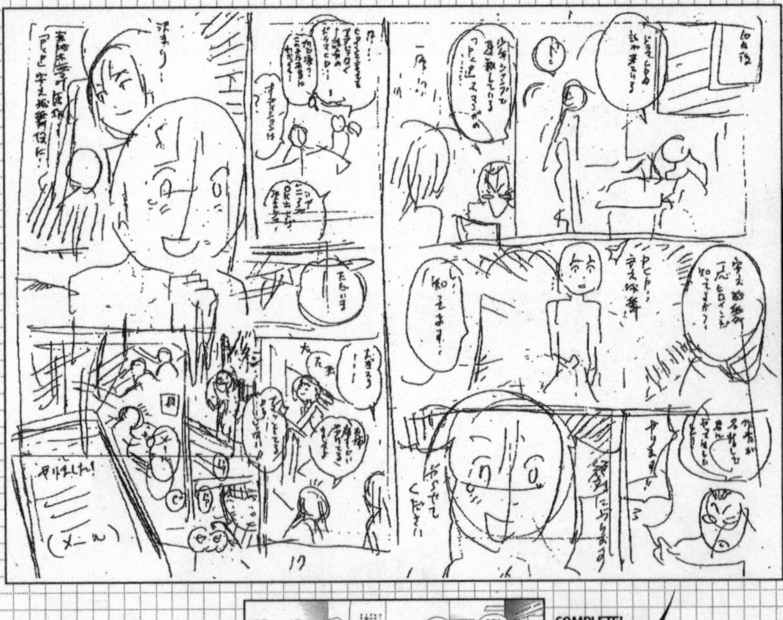
やりました!
(メール)

OBATA'S STORYBOARD

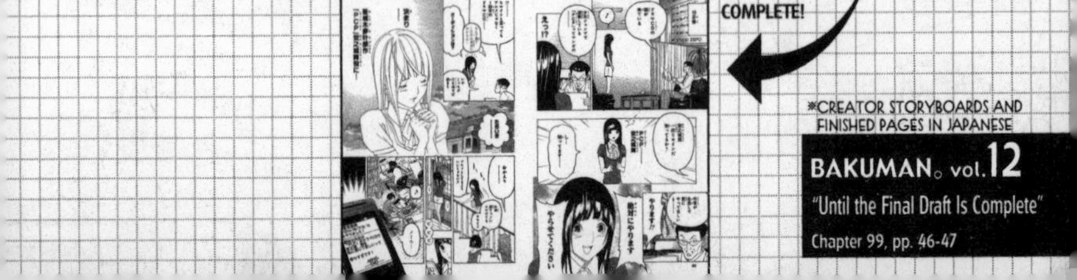

COMPLETE!

※CREATOR STORYBOARDS AND FINISHED PAGES IN JAPANESE

BAKUMAN。 vol.12

"Until the Final Draft Is Complete"

Chapter 99, pp. 46-47

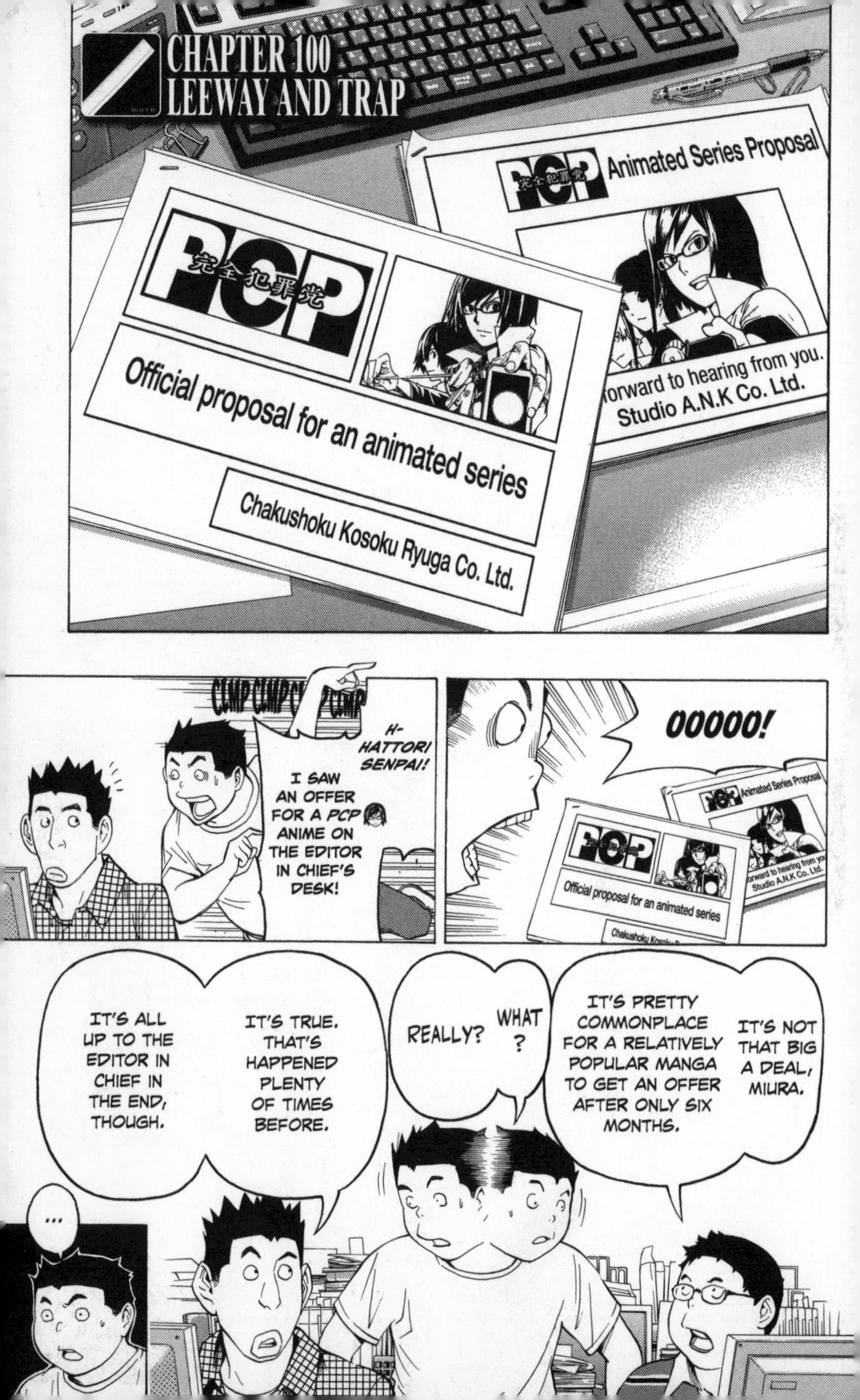
CHAPTER 100
LEEWAY AND TRAP
PCP 完全犯罪党 Animated Series Proposal
orward to hearing from you.
Studio A.N.K Co. Ltd.
PCP 完全犯罪党
Official proposal for an animated series
Chakushoku Kosoku Ryuga Co. Ltd.
OOOOO!
H-HATTORI SENPAI!
I SAW AN OFFER FOR A PCP ANIME ON THE EDITOR IN CHIEF'S DESK!
IT'S NOT THAT BIG A DEAL, MIURA.
IT'S PRETTY COMMONPLACE FOR A RELATIVELY POPULAR MANGA TO GET AN OFFER AFTER ONLY SIX MONTHS.
WHAT?
REALLY?
IT'S TRUE. THAT'S HAPPENED PLENTY OF TIMES BEFORE.
IT'S ALL UP TO THE EDITOR IN CHIEF IN THE END, THOUGH.
...

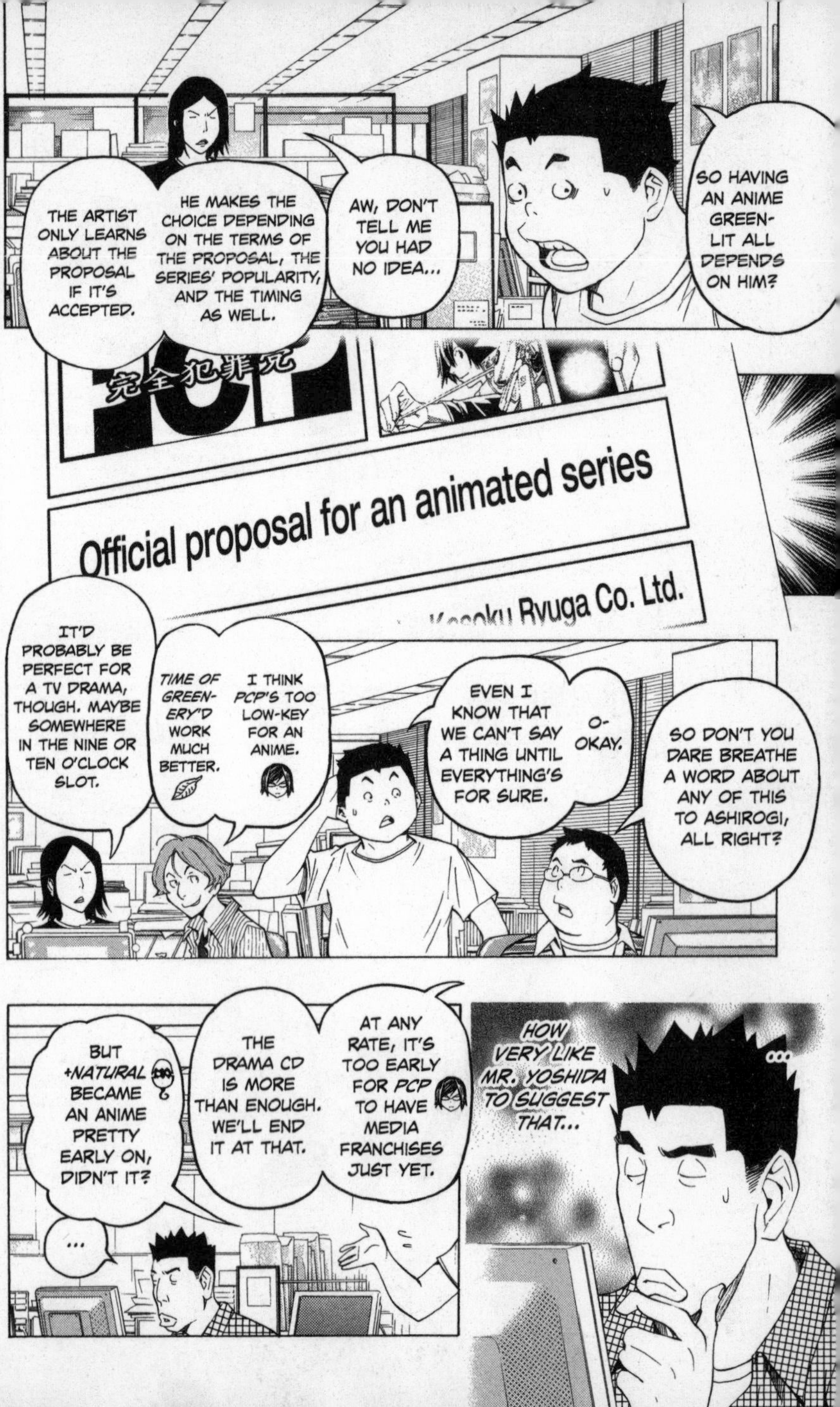
SO HAVING AN ANIME GREEN-LIT ALL DEPENDS ON HIM?
AW, DON'T TELL ME YOU HAD NO IDEA...
HE MAKES THE CHOICE DEPENDING ON THE TERMS OF THE PROPOSAL, THE SERIES' POPULARITY, AND THE TIMING AS WELL.
THE ARTIST ONLY LEARNS ABOUT THE PROPOSAL IF IT'S ACCEPTED.
Official proposal for an animated series
Ryuga Co. Ltd.
SO DON'T YOU DARE BREATHE A WORD ABOUT ANY OF THIS TO ASHIROGI, ALL RIGHT?
EVEN I KNOW THAT WE CAN'T SAY A THING UNTIL EVERYTHING'S FOR SURE.
O-OKAY.
I THINK *PCP*'S TOO LOW-KEY FOR AN ANIME.
TIME OF GREENERY'D WORK MUCH BETTER.
IT'D PROBABLY BE PERFECT FOR A TV DRAMA, THOUGH. MAYBE SOMEWHERE IN THE NINE OR TEN O'CLOCK SLOT.
...
HOW VERY LIKE MR. YOSHIDA TO SUGGEST THAT...
AT ANY RATE, IT'S TOO EARLY FOR *PCP* TO HAVE MEDIA FRANCHISES JUST YET.
THE DRAMA CD IS MORE THAN ENOUGH. WE'LL END IT AT THAT.
BUT *+NATURAL* BECAME AN ANIME PRETTY EARLY ON, DIDN'T IT?
...

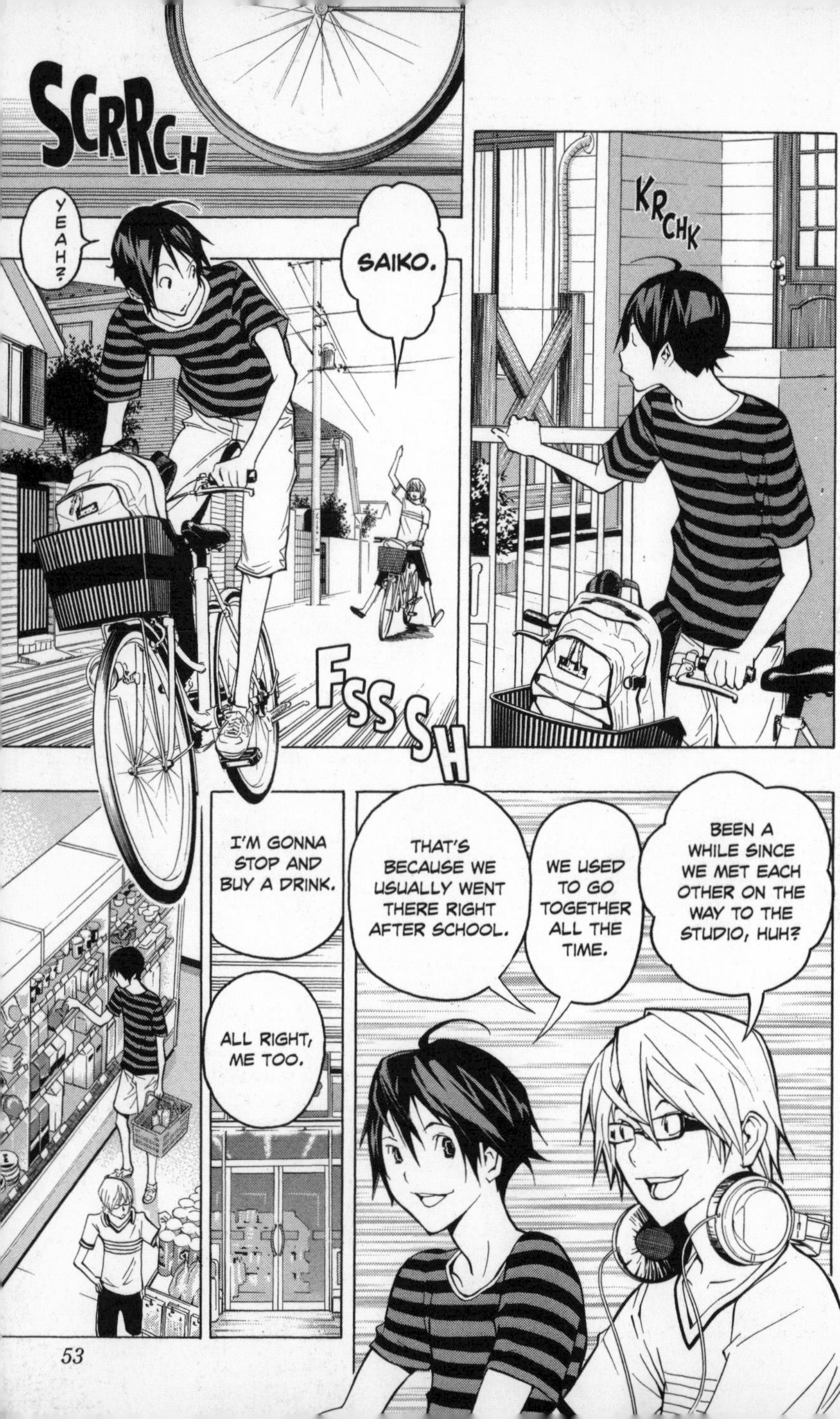
KRCHK
SCRRCH
SAIKO.
YEAH?
FSSSH
BEEN A WHILE SINCE WE MET EACH OTHER ON THE WAY TO THE STUDIO, HUH?
WE USED TO GO TOGETHER ALL THE TIME.
THAT'S BECAUSE WE USUALLY WENT THERE RIGHT AFTER SCHOOL.
I'M GONNA STOP AND BUY A DRINK.
ALL RIGHT, ME TOO.

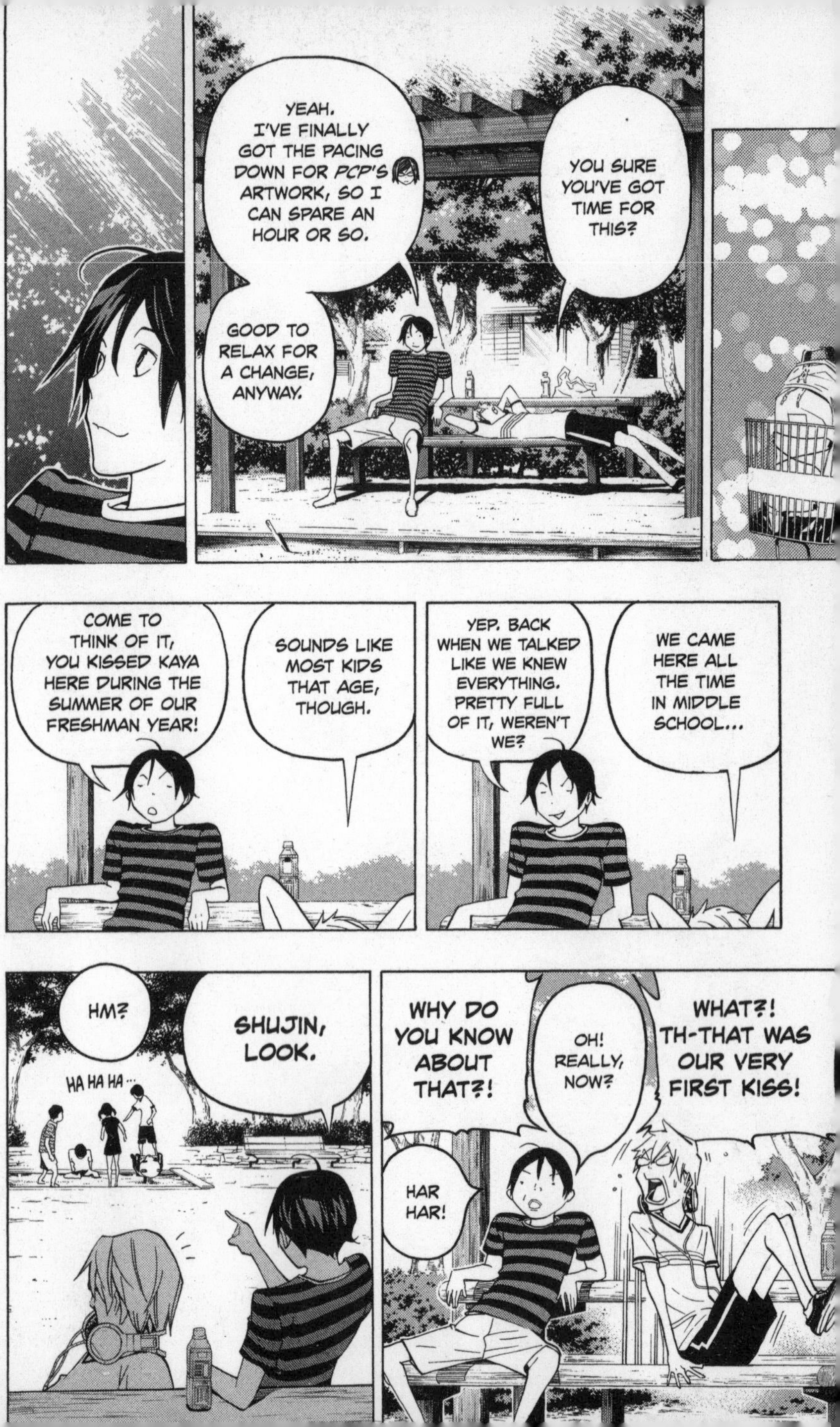
YOU SURE YOU'VE GOT TIME FOR THIS?
YEAH. I'VE FINALLY GOT THE PACING DOWN FOR PCP'S ARTWORK, SO I CAN SPARE AN HOUR OR SO.
GOOD TO RELAX FOR A CHANGE, ANYWAY.
WE CAME HERE ALL THE TIME IN MIDDLE SCHOOL...
YEP. BACK WHEN WE TALKED LIKE WE KNEW EVERYTHING. PRETTY FULL OF IT, WEREN'T WE?
SOUNDS LIKE MOST KIDS THAT AGE, THOUGH.
COME TO THINK OF IT, YOU KISSED KAYA HERE DURING THE SUMMER OF OUR FRESHMAN YEAR!
WHAT?! TH-THAT WAS OUR VERY FIRST KISS!
OH! REALLY, NOW?
WHY DO YOU KNOW ABOUT THAT?!
HAR HAR!
SHUJIN, LOOK.
HM?
HA HA HA...

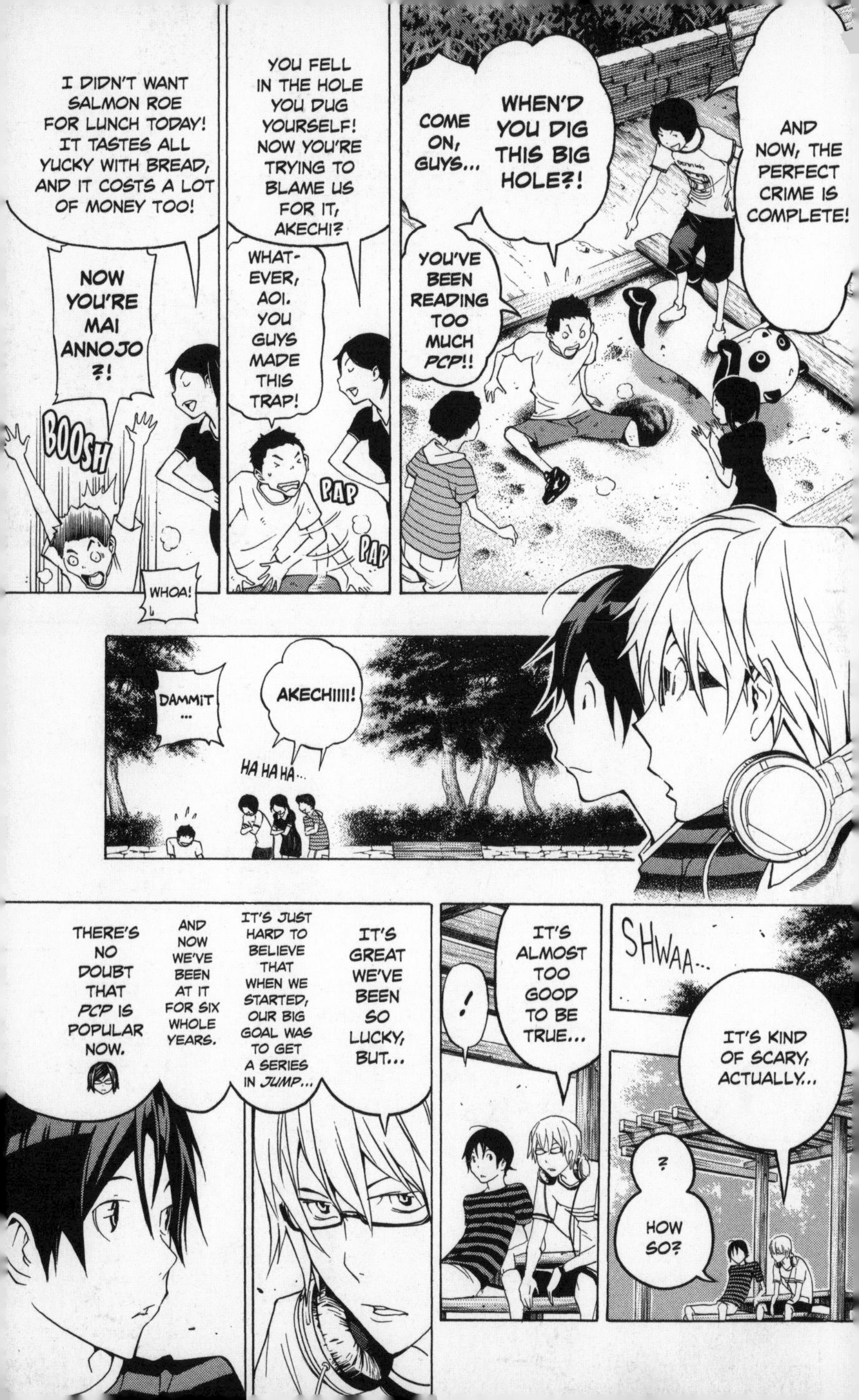
AND NOW, THE PERFECT CRIME IS COMPLETE!
WHEN'D YOU DIG THIS BIG HOLE?!
COME ON, GUYS...
YOU'VE BEEN READING TOO MUCH *PCP*!!
YOU FELL IN THE HOLE YOU DUG YOURSELF! NOW YOU'RE TRYING TO BLAME US FOR IT, AKECHI?
WHATEVER, AOI. YOU GUYS MADE THIS TRAP!
PAP
PAP
I DIDN'T WANT SALMON ROE FOR LUNCH TODAY! IT TASTES ALL YUCKY WITH BREAD, AND IT COSTS A LOT OF MONEY TOO!
NOW YOU'RE MAI ANNOJO?!
BOOSH
WHOA!
AKECHIIII!
DAMMIT...
HA HA HA...
SHWAA...
IT'S KIND OF SCARY, ACTUALLY...
?
HOW SO?
IT'S ALMOST TOO GOOD TO BE TRUE...
!
IT'S GREAT WE'VE BEEN SO LUCKY, BUT...
IT'S JUST HARD TO BELIEVE THAT WHEN WE STARTED, OUR BIG GOAL WAS TO GET A SERIES IN *JUMP*...
AND NOW WE'VE BEEN AT IT FOR SIX WHOLE YEARS.
THERE'S NO DOUBT THAT *PCP* IS POPULAR NOW.

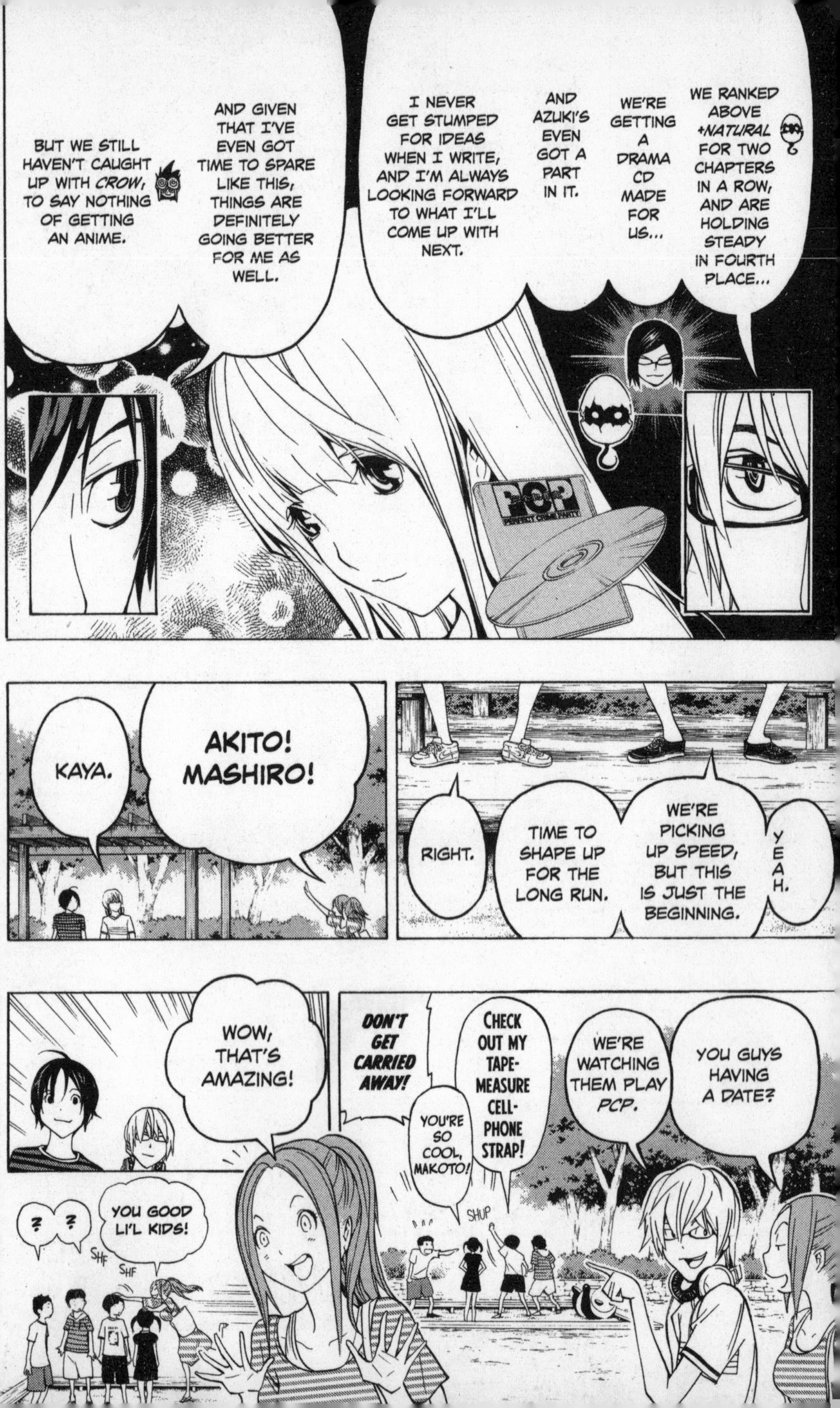
WE RANKED ABOVE +NATURAL FOR TWO CHAPTERS IN A ROW, AND ARE HOLDING STEADY IN FOURTH PLACE...
WE'RE GETTING A DRAMA CD MADE FOR US...
AND AZUKI'S EVEN GOT A PART IN IT.
I NEVER GET STUMPED FOR IDEAS WHEN I WRITE, AND I'M ALWAYS LOOKING FORWARD TO WHAT I'LL COME UP WITH NEXT.
AND GIVEN THAT I'VE EVEN GOT TIME TO SPARE LIKE THIS, THINGS ARE DEFINITELY GOING BETTER FOR ME AS WELL.
BUT WE STILL HAVEN'T CAUGHT UP WITH CROW, TO SAY NOTHING OF GETTING AN ANIME.
PCP
PERFECT CRIME PARTY
YEAH.
WE'RE PICKING UP SPEED, BUT THIS IS JUST THE BEGINNING.
TIME TO SHAPE UP FOR THE LONG RUN.
RIGHT.
AKITO! MASHIRO!
KAYA.
YOU GUYS HAVING A DATE?
WE'RE WATCHING THEM PLAY PCP.
CHECK OUT MY TAPE-MEASURE CELL-PHONE STRAP!
DON'T GET CARRIED AWAY!
YOU'RE SO COOL, MAKOTO!
SHUP
WOW, THAT'S AMAZING!
YOU GOOD LI'L KIDS!
? ?
SHF
SHF

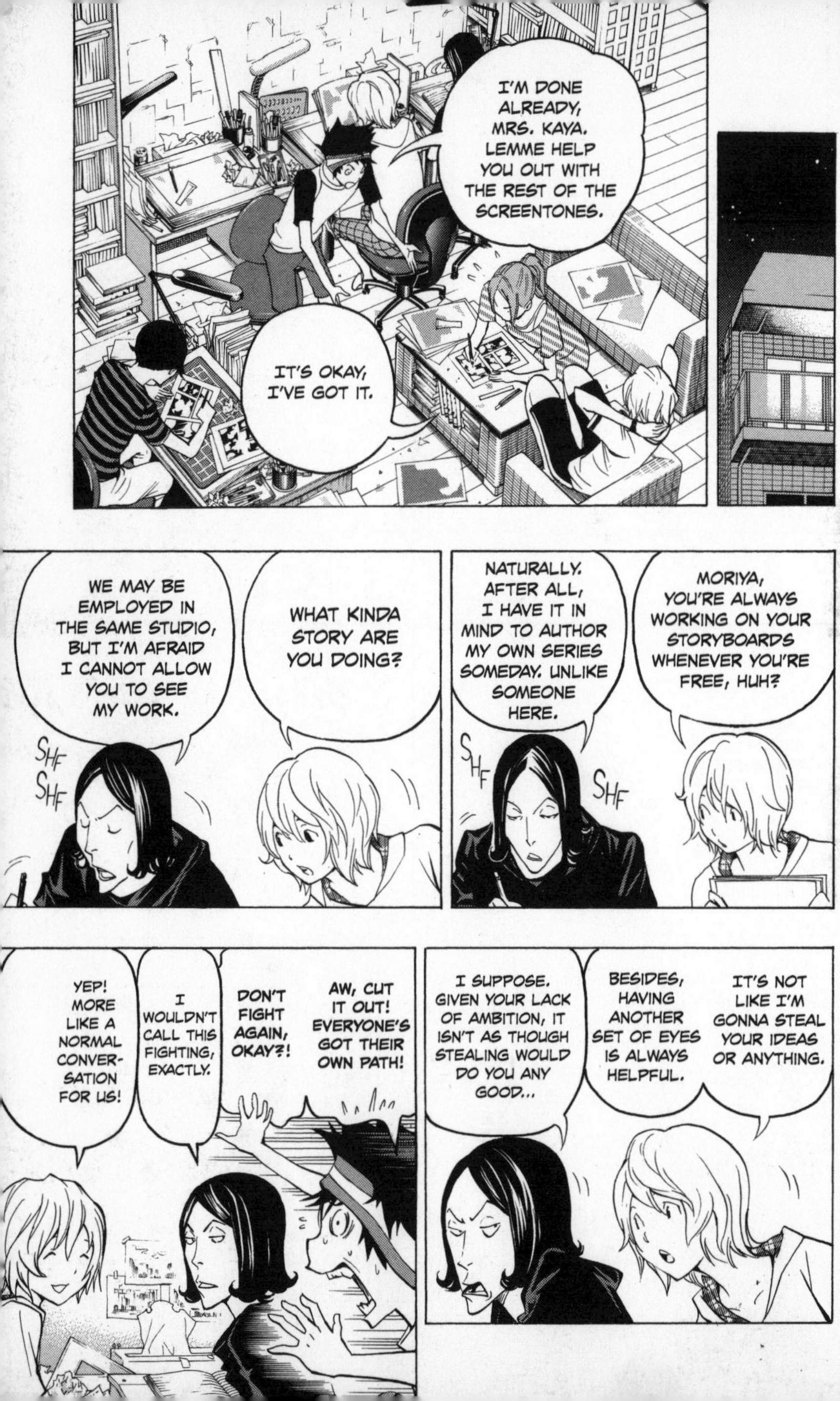
I'M DONE ALREADY, MRS. KAYA. LEMME HELP YOU OUT WITH THE REST OF THE SCREENTONES.
IT'S OKAY, I'VE GOT IT.
MORIYA, YOU'RE ALWAYS WORKING ON YOUR STORYBOARDS WHENEVER YOU'RE FREE, HUH?
NATURALLY. AFTER ALL, I HAVE IT IN MIND TO AUTHOR MY OWN SERIES SOMEDAY. UNLIKE SOMEONE HERE.
SHF
SHF
WHAT KINDA STORY ARE YOU DOING?
WE MAY BE EMPLOYED IN THE SAME STUDIO, BUT I'M AFRAID I CANNOT ALLOW YOU TO SEE MY WORK.
SHF
SHF
IT'S NOT LIKE I'M GONNA STEAL YOUR IDEAS OR ANYTHING.
BESIDES, HAVING ANOTHER SET OF EYES IS ALWAYS HELPFUL.
I SUPPOSE. GIVEN YOUR LACK OF AMBITION, IT ISN'T AS THOUGH STEALING WOULD DO YOU ANY GOOD...
AW, CUT IT OUT! EVERYONE'S GOT THEIR OWN PATH!
DON'T FIGHT AGAIN, OKAY?!
I WOULDN'T CALL THIS FIGHTING, EXACTLY.
YEP! MORE LIKE A NORMAL CONVERSATION FOR US!

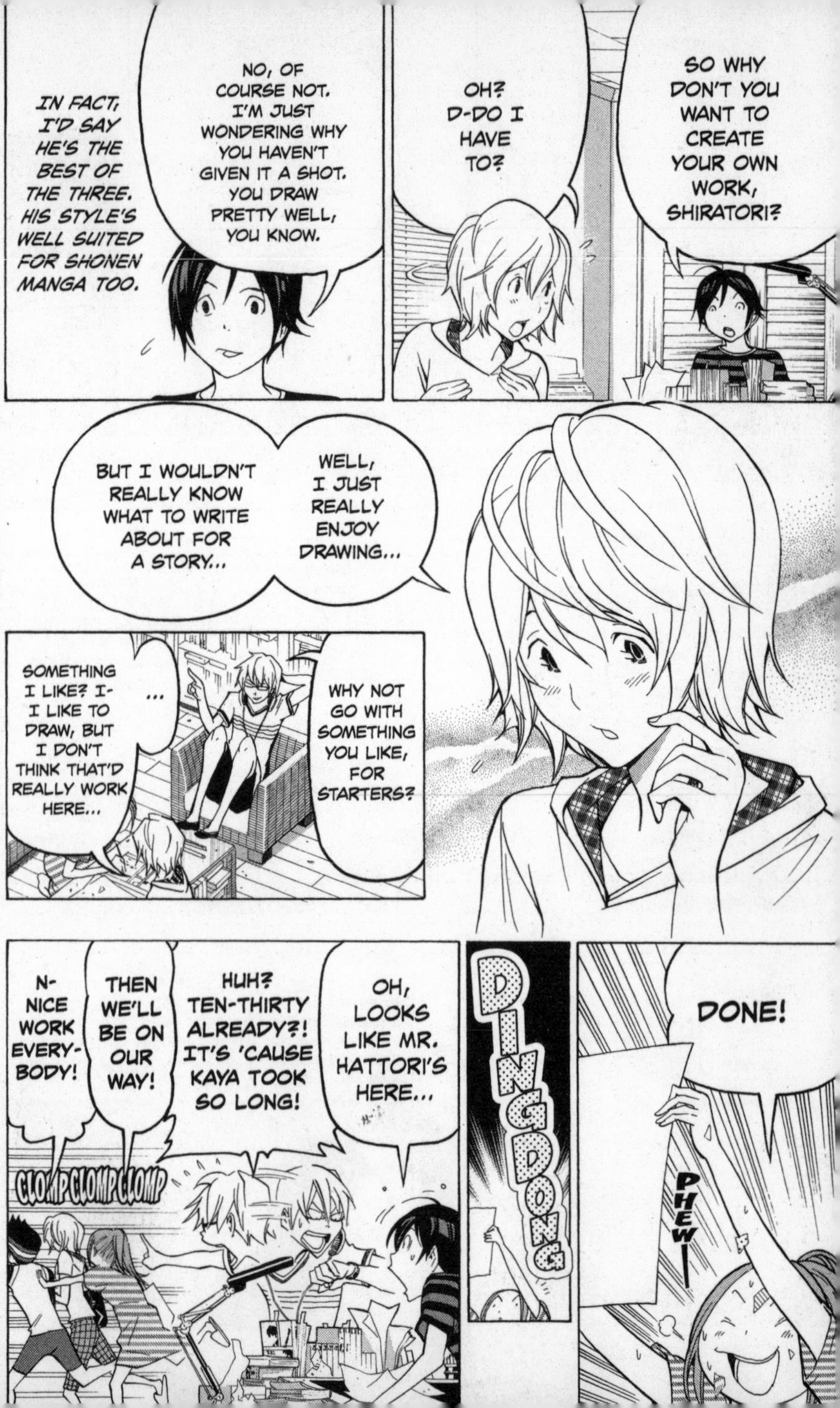
SO WHY DON'T YOU WANT TO CREATE YOUR OWN WORK, SHIRATORI?
OH? D-DO I HAVE TO?
NO, OF COURSE NOT. I'M JUST WONDERING WHY YOU HAVEN'T GIVEN IT A SHOT. YOU DRAW PRETTY WELL, YOU KNOW.
IN FACT, I'D SAY HE'S THE BEST OF THE THREE. HIS STYLE'S WELL SUITED FOR SHONEN MANGA TOO.
WELL, I JUST REALLY ENJOY DRAWING...
BUT I WOULDN'T REALLY KNOW WHAT TO WRITE ABOUT FOR A STORY...
WHY NOT GO WITH SOMETHING YOU LIKE, FOR STARTERS?
...
SOMETHING I LIKE? I-I LIKE TO DRAW, BUT I DON'T THINK THAT'D REALLY WORK HERE...
DONE!
PHEW!
DINGDONG
OH, LOOKS LIKE MR. HATTORI'S HERE...
HUH? TEN-THIRTY ALREADY?! IT'S 'CAUSE KAYA TOOK SO LONG!
THEN WE'LL BE ON OUR WAY!
N-NICE WORK EVERYBODY!
CLOMP CLOMP CLOMP

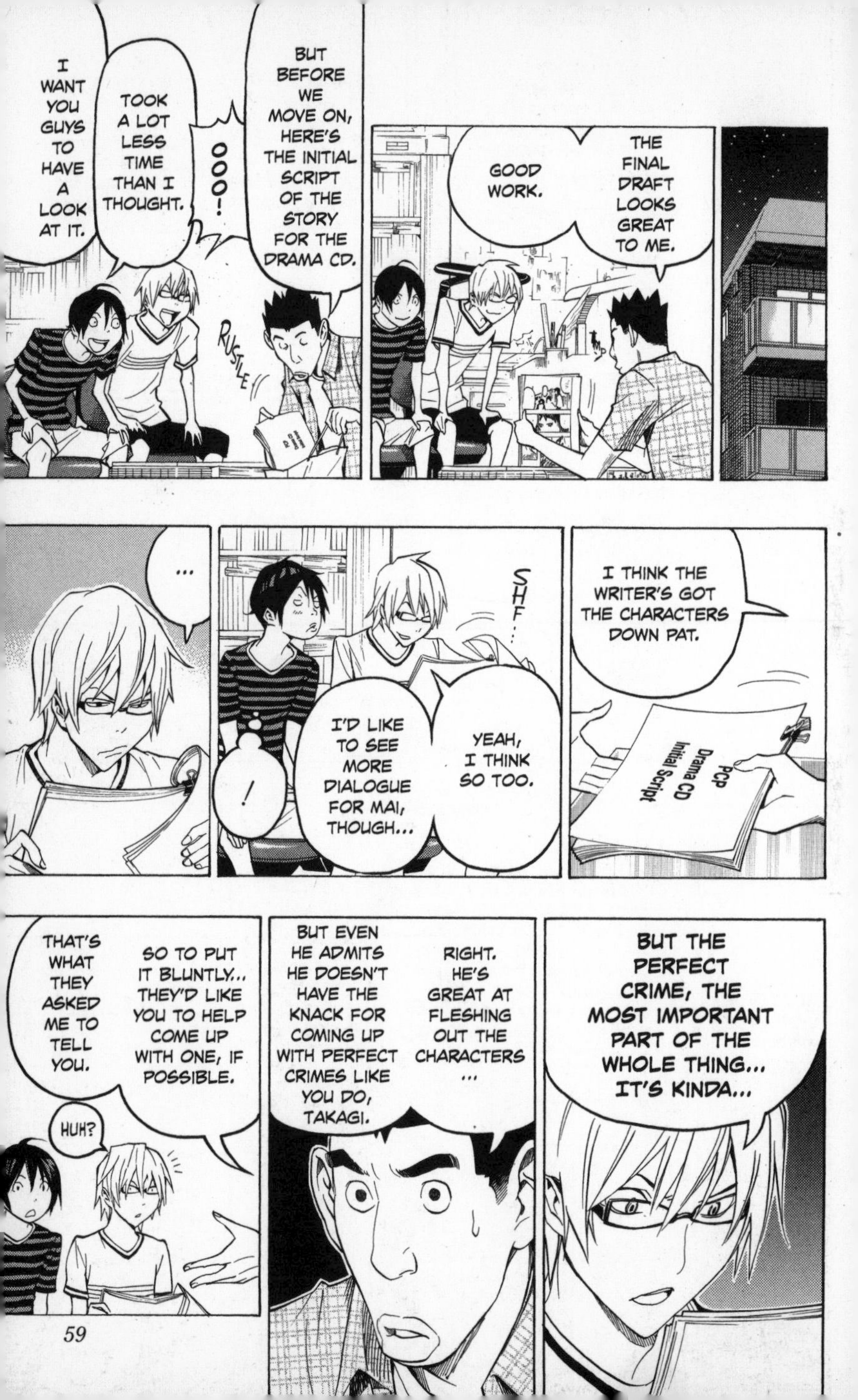
THE FINAL DRAFT LOOKS GREAT TO ME.
GOOD WORK.
BUT BEFORE WE MOVE ON, HERE'S THE INITIAL SCRIPT OF THE STORY FOR THE DRAMA CD.
RUSTLE
OOO!
TOOK A LOT LESS TIME THAN I THOUGHT.
I WANT YOU GUYS TO HAVE A LOOK AT IT.
I THINK THE WRITER'S GOT THE CHARACTERS DOWN PAT.
PCP Drama CD Initial Script
SHF...
YEAH, I THINK SO TOO.
I'D LIKE TO SEE MORE DIALOGUE FOR MAI, THOUGH...
!
...
BUT THE PERFECT CRIME, THE MOST IMPORTANT PART OF THE WHOLE THING... IT'S KINDA...
RIGHT. HE'S GREAT AT FLESHING OUT THE CHARACTERS ...
BUT EVEN HE ADMITS HE DOESN'T HAVE THE KNACK FOR COMING UP WITH PERFECT CRIMES LIKE YOU DO, TAKAGI.
SO TO PUT IT BLUNTLY... THEY'D LIKE YOU TO HELP COME UP WITH ONE, IF POSSIBLE.
THAT'S WHAT THEY ASKED ME TO TELL YOU.
HUH?

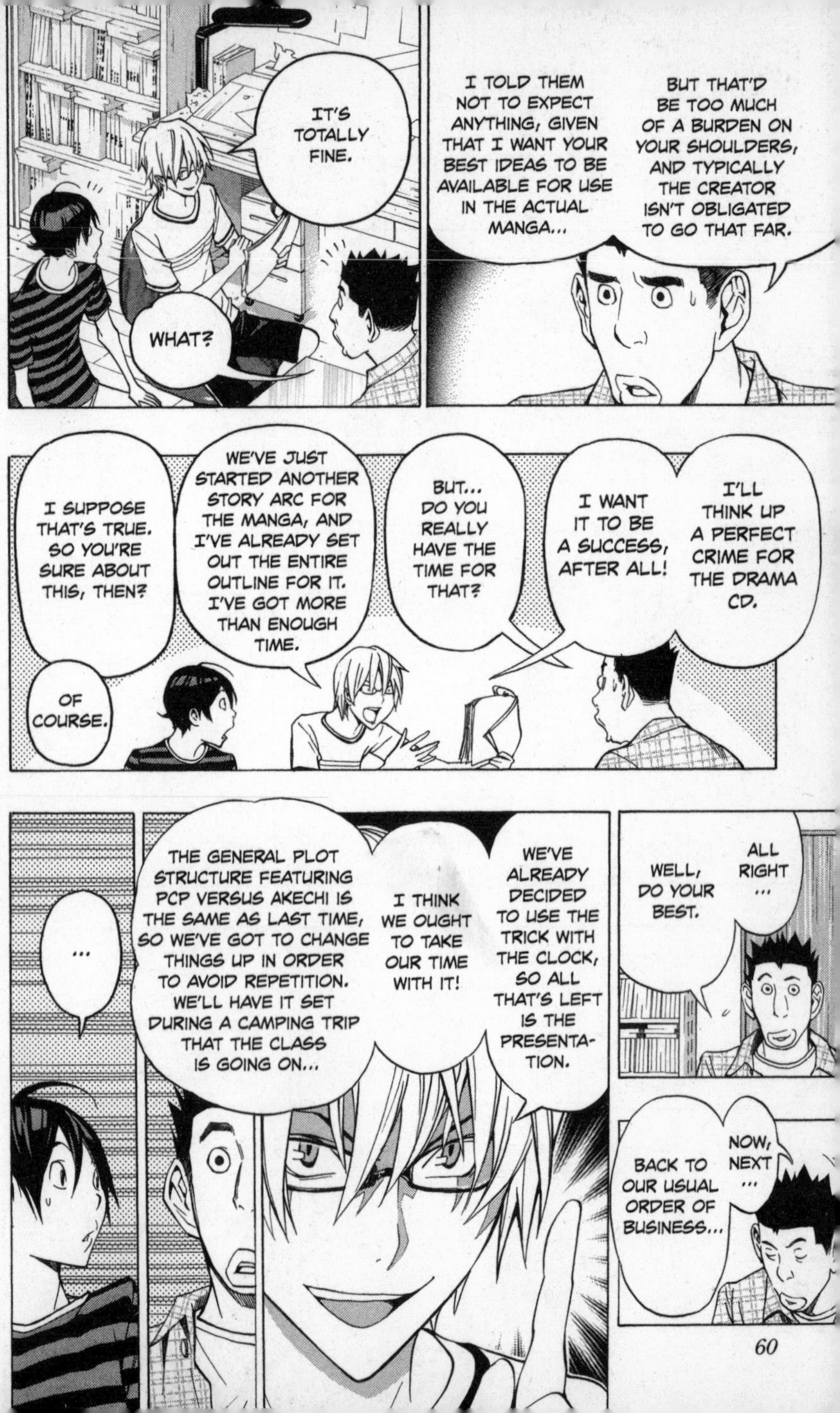
BUT THAT'D BE TOO MUCH OF A BURDEN ON YOUR SHOULDERS, AND TYPICALLY THE CREATOR ISN'T OBLIGATED TO GO THAT FAR.
I TOLD THEM NOT TO EXPECT ANYTHING, GIVEN THAT I WANT YOUR BEST IDEAS TO BE AVAILABLE FOR USE IN THE ACTUAL MANGA...
IT'S TOTALLY FINE.
WHAT?
I'LL THINK UP A PERFECT CRIME FOR THE DRAMA CD.
I WANT IT TO BE A SUCCESS, AFTER ALL!
BUT... DO YOU REALLY HAVE THE TIME FOR THAT?
WE'VE JUST STARTED ANOTHER STORY ARC FOR THE MANGA, AND I'VE ALREADY SET OUT THE ENTIRE OUTLINE FOR IT. I'VE GOT MORE THAN ENOUGH TIME.
I SUPPOSE THAT'S TRUE. SO YOU'RE SURE ABOUT THIS, THEN?
OF COURSE.
ALL RIGHT...
WELL, DO YOUR BEST.
NOW, NEXT...
BACK TO OUR USUAL ORDER OF BUSINESS...
WE'VE ALREADY DECIDED TO USE THE TRICK WITH THE CLOCK, SO ALL THAT'S LEFT IS THE PRESENTATION.
I THINK WE OUGHT TO TAKE OUR TIME WITH IT!
THE GENERAL PLOT STRUCTURE FEATURING PCP VERSUS AKECHI IS THE SAME AS LAST TIME, SO WE'VE GOT TO CHANGE THINGS UP IN ORDER TO AVOID REPETITION. WE'LL HAVE IT SET DURING A CAMPING TRIP THAT THE CLASS IS GOING ON...
...

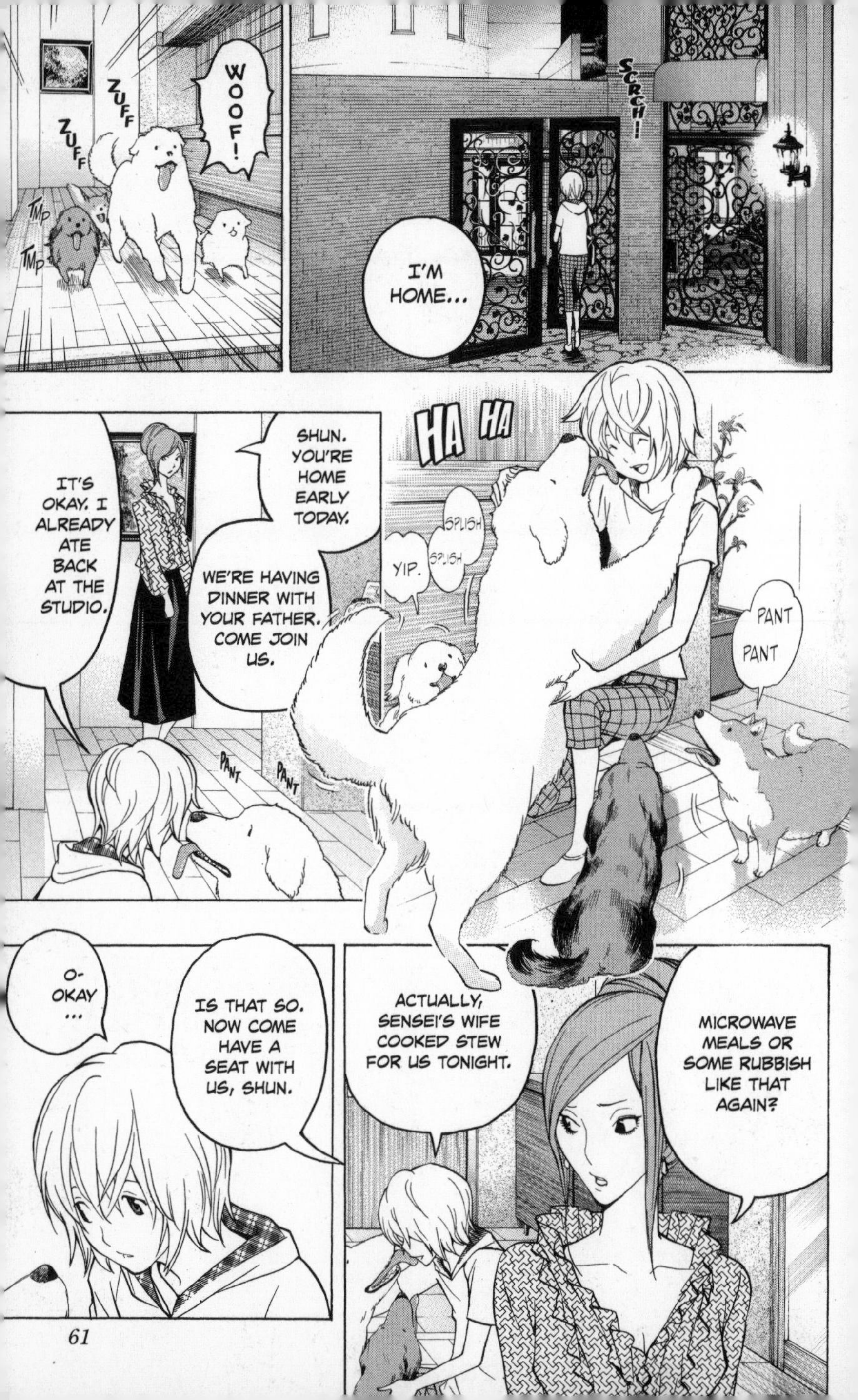
SCRCH!
I'M HOME...
WOOF!
ZUFF ZUFF
ZUFF
TMP
TMP
HA HA
SPLISH
SPLISH
YIP.
PANT
PANT
SHUN. YOU'RE HOME EARLY TODAY.
WE'RE HAVING DINNER WITH YOUR FATHER. COME JOIN US.
IT'S OKAY. I ALREADY ATE BACK AT THE STUDIO.
PANT
PANT
MICROWAVE MEALS OR SOME RUBBISH LIKE THAT AGAIN?
ACTUALLY, SENSEI'S WIFE COOKED STEW FOR US TONIGHT.
IS THAT SO. NOW COME HAVE A SEAT WITH US, SHUN.
O-OKAY...

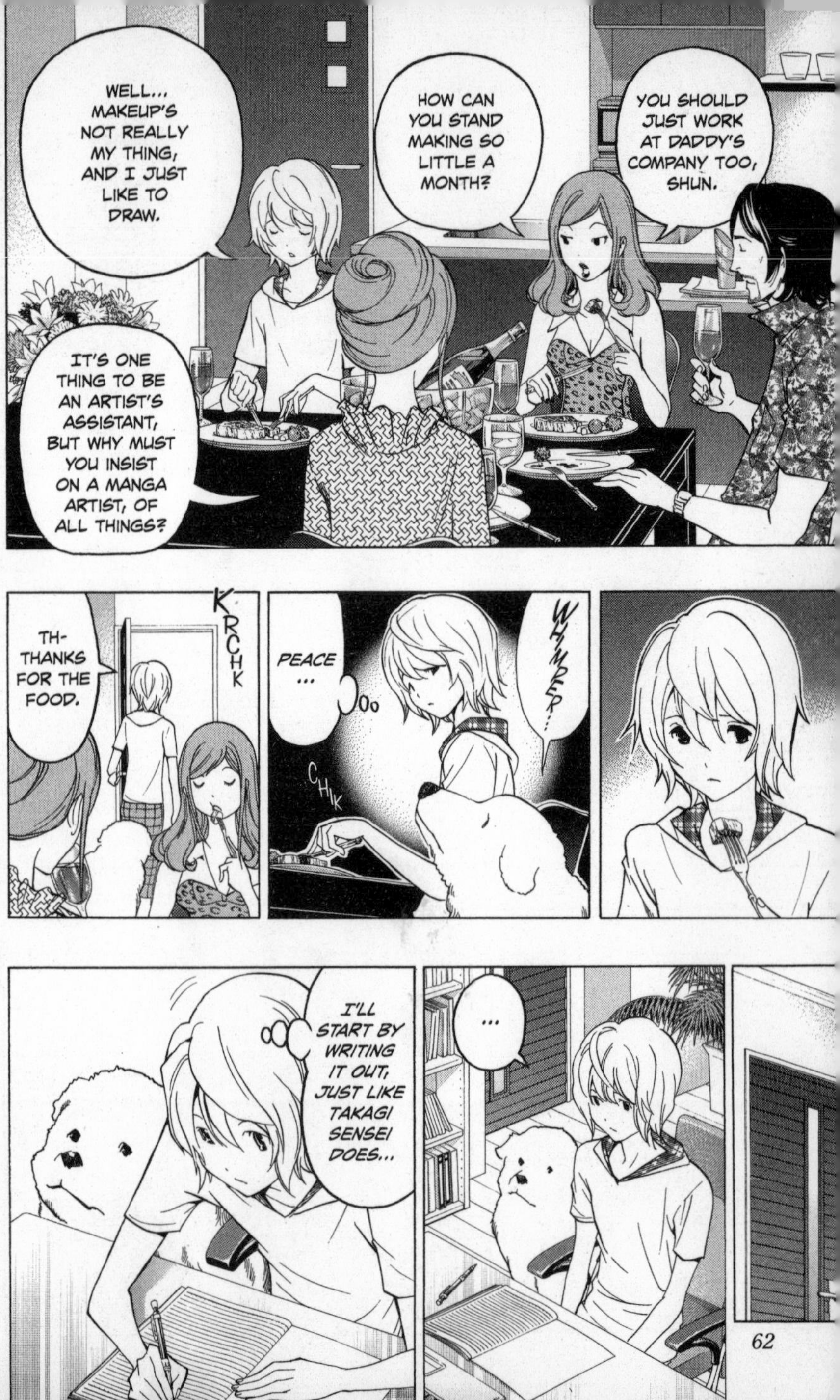
YOU SHOULD JUST WORK AT DADDY'S COMPANY TOO, SHUN.
HOW CAN YOU STAND MAKING SO LITTLE A MONTH?
WELL... MAKEUP'S NOT REALLY MY THING, AND I JUST LIKE TO DRAW.
IT'S ONE THING TO BE AN ARTIST'S ASSISTANT, BUT WHY MUST YOU INSIST ON A MANGA ARTIST, OF ALL THINGS?
WHIMPER...
PEACE...
CHIK
KRCHK
TH-THANKS FOR THE FOOD.
...
I'LL START BY WRITING IT OUT, JUST LIKE TAKAGI SENSEI DOES...

READ THIS WAY

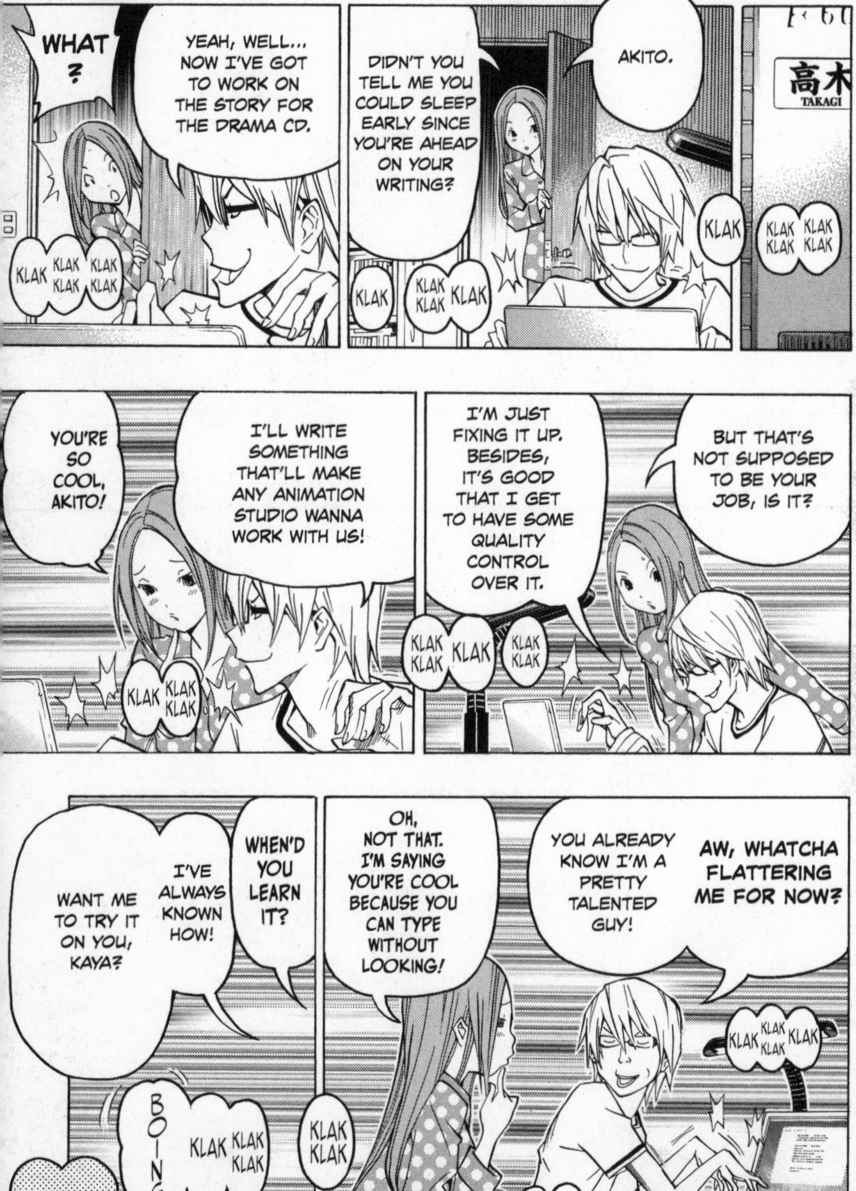

高木
TAKAGI
KLAK KLAK
KLAK KLAK
KLAK
AKITO.
DIDN'T YOU TELL ME YOU COULD SLEEP EARLY SINCE YOU'RE AHEAD ON YOUR WRITING?
KLAK
KLAK KLAK
KLAK
YEAH, WELL... NOW I'VE GOT TO WORK ON THE STORY FOR THE DRAMA CD.
WHAT?
KLAK KLAK
KLAK KLAK
KLAK
BUT THAT'S NOT SUPPOSED TO BE YOUR JOB, IS IT?
I'M JUST FIXING IT UP. BESIDES, IT'S GOOD THAT I GET TO HAVE SOME QUALITY CONTROL OVER IT.
KLAK KLAK
KLAK
KLAK KLAK
I'LL WRITE SOMETHING THAT'LL MAKE ANY ANIMATION STUDIO WANNA WORK WITH US!
YOU'RE SO COOL, AKITO!
KLAK KLAK
KLAK
AW, WHATCHA FLATTERING ME FOR NOW?
YOU ALREADY KNOW I'M A PRETTY TALENTED GUY!
OH, NOT THAT. I'M SAYING YOU'RE COOL BECAUSE YOU CAN TYPE WITHOUT LOOKING!
KLAK
KLAK KLAK
KLAK
KLAK KLAK
KLAK
KLAK KLAK
KLAK
WHEN'D YOU LEARN IT?
I'VE ALWAYS KNOWN HOW!
WANT ME TO TRY IT ON YOU, KAYA?
BOING
KLAK KLAK
KLAK
EEP!

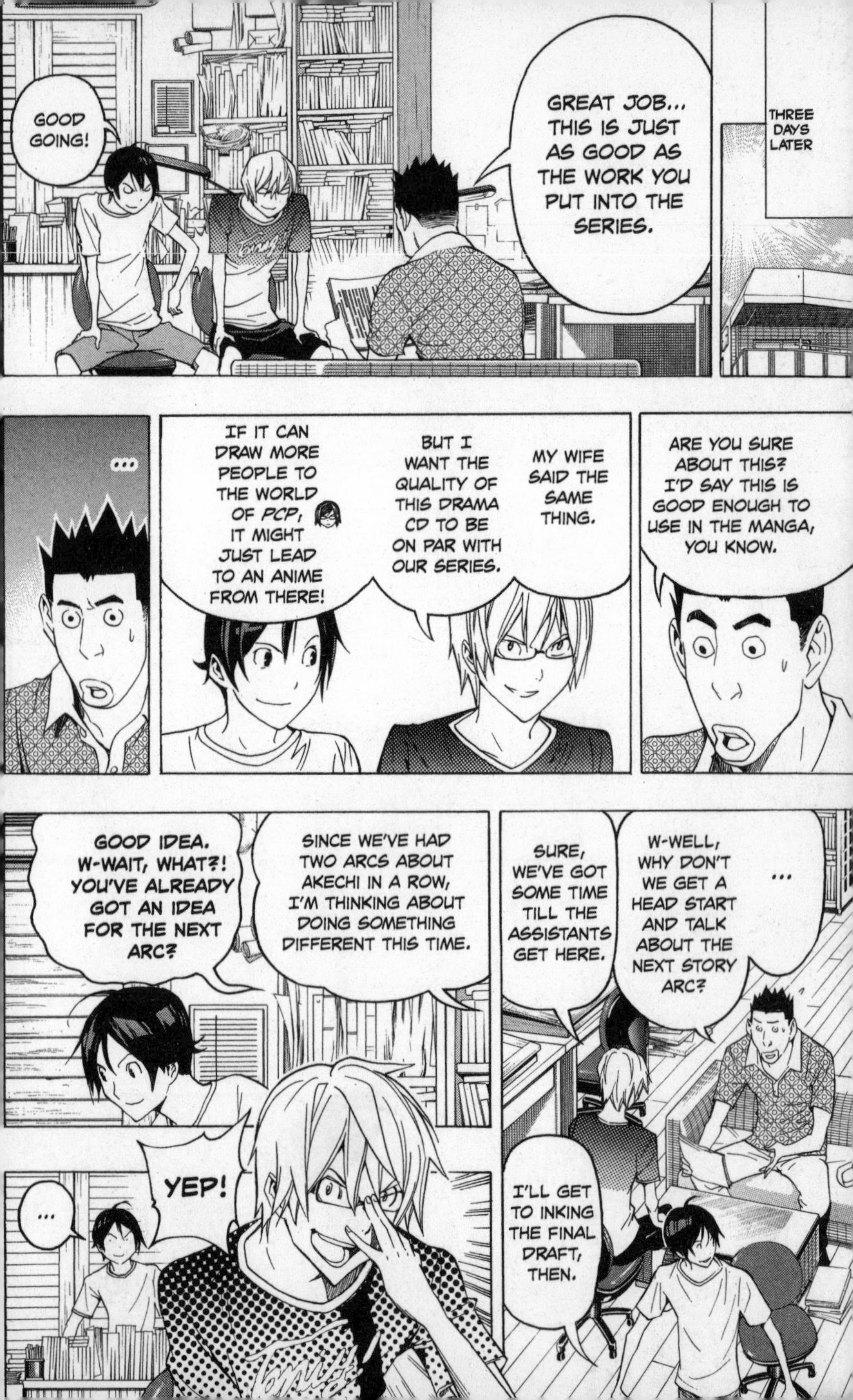
THREE DAYS LATER
GREAT JOB... THIS IS JUST AS GOOD AS THE WORK YOU PUT INTO THE SERIES.
GOOD GOING!
ARE YOU SURE ABOUT THIS? I'D SAY THIS IS GOOD ENOUGH TO USE IN THE MANGA, YOU KNOW.
MY WIFE SAID THE SAME THING.
BUT I WANT THE QUALITY OF THIS DRAMA CD TO BE ON PAR WITH OUR SERIES.
IF IT CAN DRAW MORE PEOPLE TO THE WORLD OF *PCP*, IT MIGHT JUST LEAD TO AN ANIME FROM THERE!
...
...
W-WELL, WHY DON'T WE GET A HEAD START AND TALK ABOUT THE NEXT STORY ARC?
SURE, WE'VE GOT SOME TIME TILL THE ASSISTANTS GET HERE.
I'LL GET TO INKING THE FINAL DRAFT, THEN.
SINCE WE'VE HAD TWO ARCS ABOUT AKECHI IN A ROW, I'M THINKING ABOUT DOING SOMETHING DIFFERENT THIS TIME.
GOOD IDEA. W-WAIT, WHAT?! YOU'VE ALREADY GOT AN IDEA FOR THE NEXT ARC?
YEP!
...

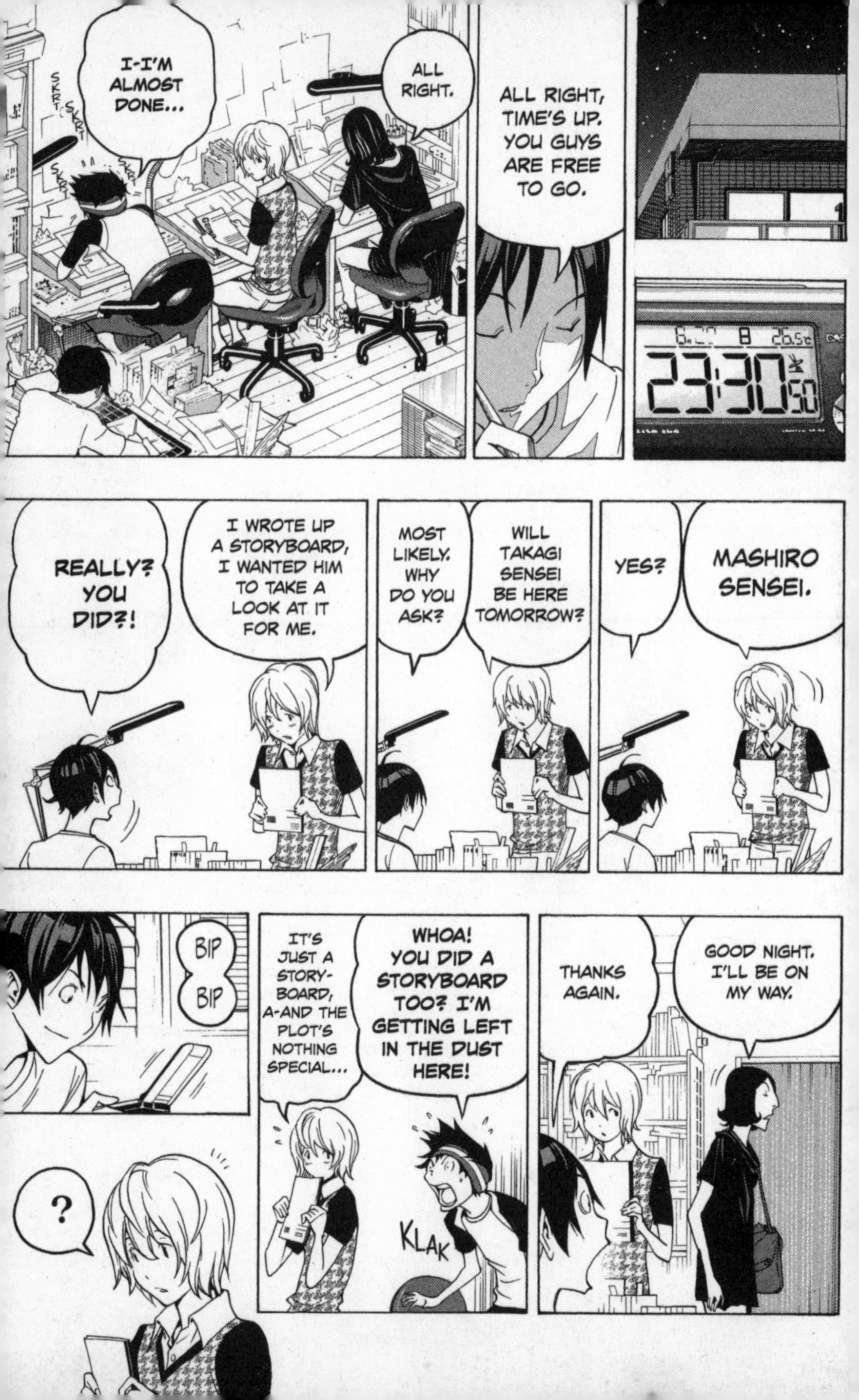
23:30
ALL RIGHT, TIME'S UP. YOU GUYS ARE FREE TO GO.
ALL RIGHT.
I-I'M ALMOST DONE...
SKRT SKRT SKRT SKRT
MASHIRO SENSEI.
YES?
WILL TAKAGI SENSEI BE HERE TOMORROW?
MOST LIKELY. WHY DO YOU ASK?
I WROTE UP A STORYBOARD, I WANTED HIM TO TAKE A LOOK AT IT FOR ME.
REALLY? YOU DID?!
GOOD NIGHT. I'LL BE ON MY WAY.
THANKS AGAIN.
WHOA! YOU DID A STORYBOARD TOO? I'M GETTING LEFT IN THE DUST HERE!
IT'S JUST A STORY-BOARD, A-AND THE PLOT'S NOTHING SPECIAL...
KLAK
BIP
BIP
?

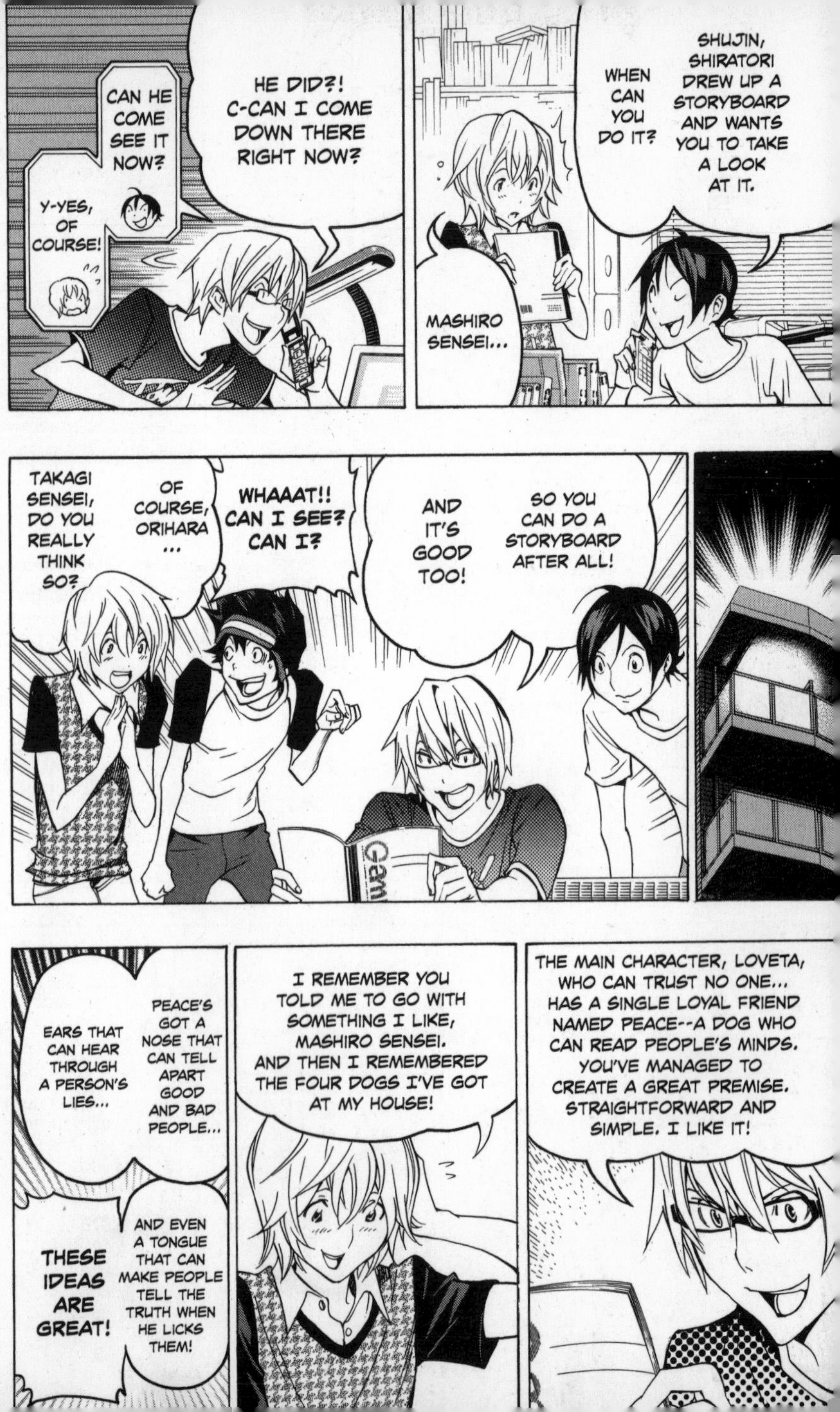
SHUJIN, SHIRATORI DREW UP A STORYBOARD AND WANTS YOU TO TAKE A LOOK AT IT.
WHEN CAN YOU DO IT?
MASHIRO SENSEI...
HE DID?! C-CAN I COME DOWN THERE RIGHT NOW?
CAN HE COME SEE IT NOW?
Y-YES, OF COURSE!
SO YOU CAN DO A STORYBOARD AFTER ALL!
AND IT'S GOOD TOO!
WHAAAT!! CAN I SEE? CAN I?
OF COURSE, ORIHARA...
TAKAGI SENSEI, DO YOU REALLY THINK SO?
THE MAIN CHARACTER, LOVETA, WHO CAN TRUST NO ONE... HAS A SINGLE LOYAL FRIEND NAMED PEACE--A DOG WHO CAN READ PEOPLE'S MINDS. YOU'VE MANAGED TO CREATE A GREAT PREMISE. STRAIGHTFORWARD AND SIMPLE. I LIKE IT!
I REMEMBER YOU TOLD ME TO GO WITH SOMETHING I LIKE, MASHIRO SENSEI. AND THEN I REMEMBERED THE FOUR DOGS I'VE GOT AT MY HOUSE!
PEACE'S GOT A NOSE THAT CAN TELL APART GOOD AND BAD PEOPLE...
EARS THAT CAN HEAR THROUGH A PERSON'S LIES...
AND EVEN A TONGUE THAT CAN MAKE PEOPLE TELL THE TRUTH WHEN HE LICKS THEM!
THESE IDEAS ARE GREAT!

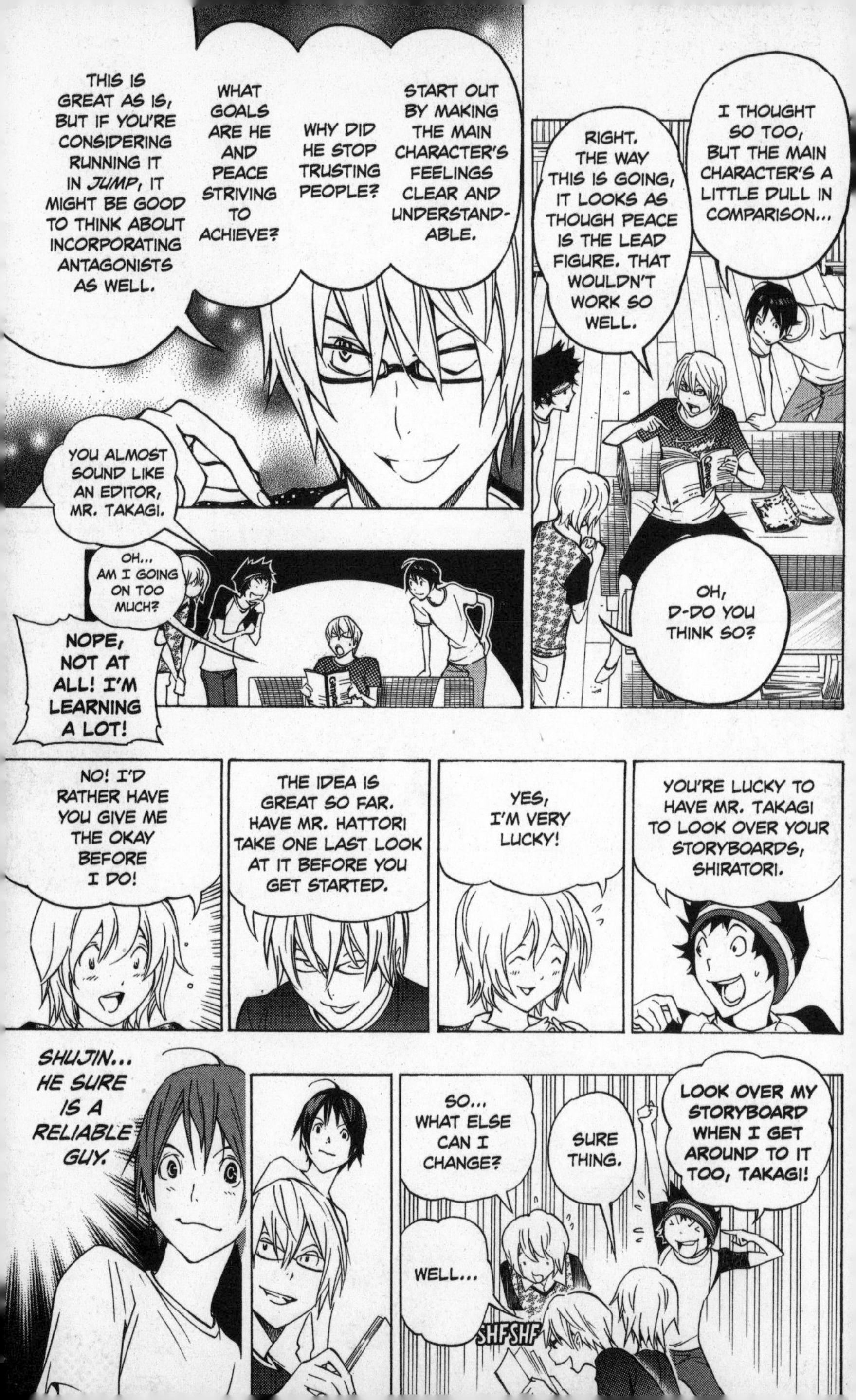
I THOUGHT SO TOO, BUT THE MAIN CHARACTER'S A LITTLE DULL IN COMPARISON...
RIGHT. THE WAY THIS IS GOING, IT LOOKS AS THOUGH PEACE IS THE LEAD FIGURE. THAT WOULDN'T WORK SO WELL.
OH, D-DO YOU THINK SO?
START OUT BY MAKING THE MAIN CHARACTER'S FEELINGS CLEAR AND UNDERSTAND-ABLE.
WHY DID HE STOP TRUSTING PEOPLE?
WHAT GOALS ARE HE AND PEACE STRIVING TO ACHIEVE?
THIS IS GREAT AS IS, BUT IF YOU'RE CONSIDERING RUNNING IT IN *JUMP*, IT MIGHT BE GOOD TO THINK ABOUT INCORPORATING ANTAGONISTS AS WELL.
YOU ALMOST SOUND LIKE AN EDITOR, MR. TAKAGI.
OH... AM I GOING ON TOO MUCH?
NOPE, NOT AT ALL! I'M LEARNING A LOT!
YOU'RE LUCKY TO HAVE MR. TAKAGI TO LOOK OVER YOUR STORYBOARDS, SHIRATORI.
YES, I'M VERY LUCKY!
THE IDEA IS GREAT SO FAR. HAVE MR. HATTORI TAKE ONE LAST LOOK AT IT BEFORE YOU GET STARTED.
NO! I'D RATHER HAVE YOU GIVE ME THE OKAY BEFORE I DO!
LOOK OVER MY STORYBOARD WHEN I GET AROUND TO IT TOO, TAKAGI!
SURE THING.
SO... WHAT ELSE CAN I CHANGE?
WELL...
SHF SHF
SHUJIN... HE SURE IS A RELIABLE GUY.

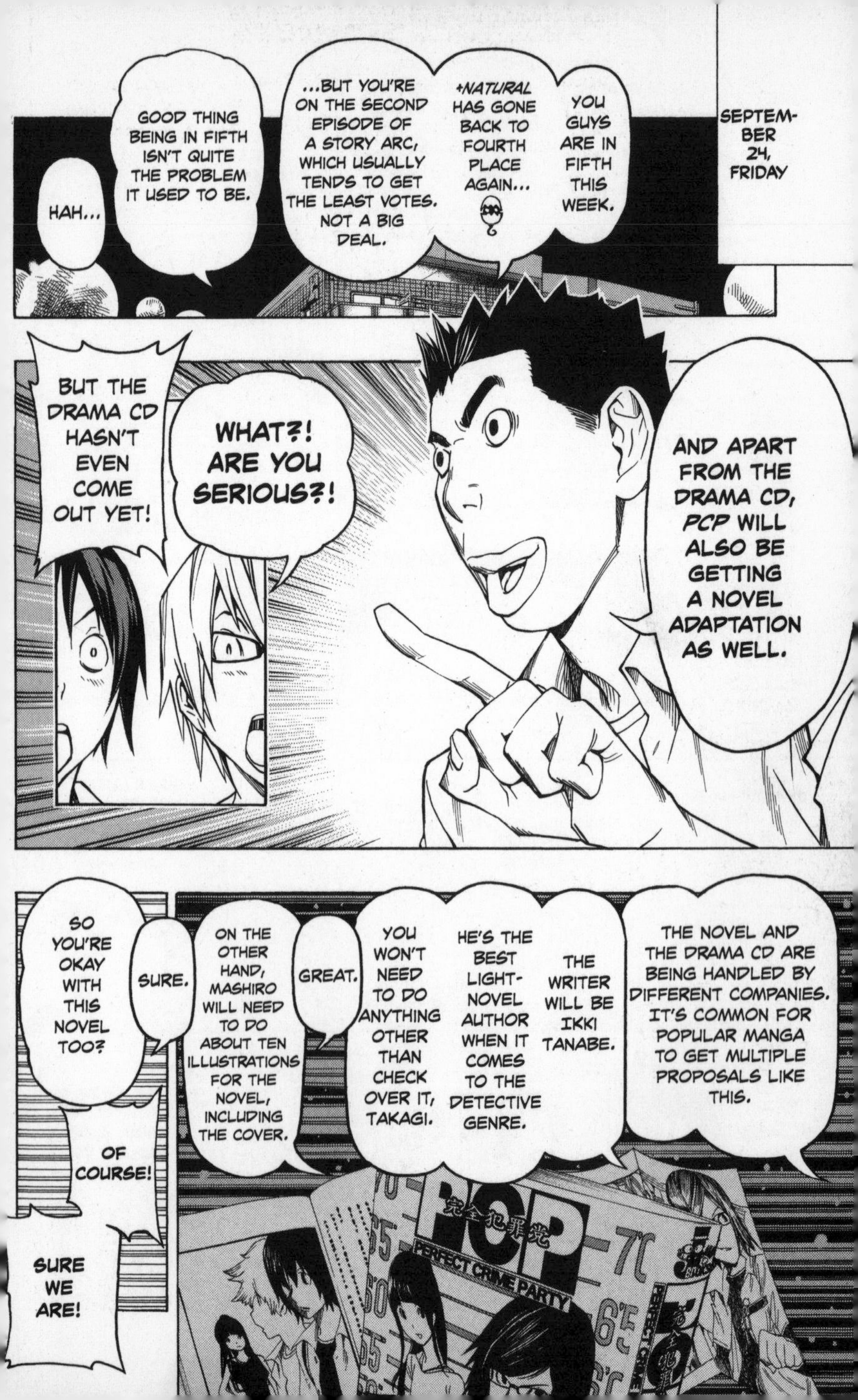
SEPTEMBER 24, FRIDAY
YOU GUYS ARE IN FIFTH THIS WEEK.
+NATURAL HAS GONE BACK TO FOURTH PLACE AGAIN...
...BUT YOU'RE ON THE SECOND EPISODE OF A STORY ARC, WHICH USUALLY TENDS TO GET THE LEAST VOTES. NOT A BIG DEAL.
GOOD THING BEING IN FIFTH ISN'T QUITE THE PROBLEM IT USED TO BE.
HAH...
AND APART FROM THE DRAMA CD, *PCP* WILL ALSO BE GETTING A NOVEL ADAPTATION AS WELL.
WHAT?! ARE YOU SERIOUS?!
BUT THE DRAMA CD HASN'T EVEN COME OUT YET!
THE NOVEL AND THE DRAMA CD ARE BEING HANDLED BY DIFFERENT COMPANIES. IT'S COMMON FOR POPULAR MANGA TO GET MULTIPLE PROPOSALS LIKE THIS.
THE WRITER WILL BE IKKI TANABE.
HE'S THE BEST LIGHT-NOVEL AUTHOR WHEN IT COMES TO THE DETECTIVE GENRE.
YOU WON'T NEED TO DO ANYTHING OTHER THAN CHECK OVER IT, TAKAGI.
GREAT.
ON THE OTHER HAND, MASHIRO WILL NEED TO DO ABOUT TEN ILLUSTRATIONS FOR THE NOVEL, INCLUDING THE COVER.
SURE.
SO YOU'RE OKAY WITH THIS NOVEL TOO?
OF COURSE!
SURE WE ARE!
PCP
完全犯罪党
PERFECT CRIME PARTY

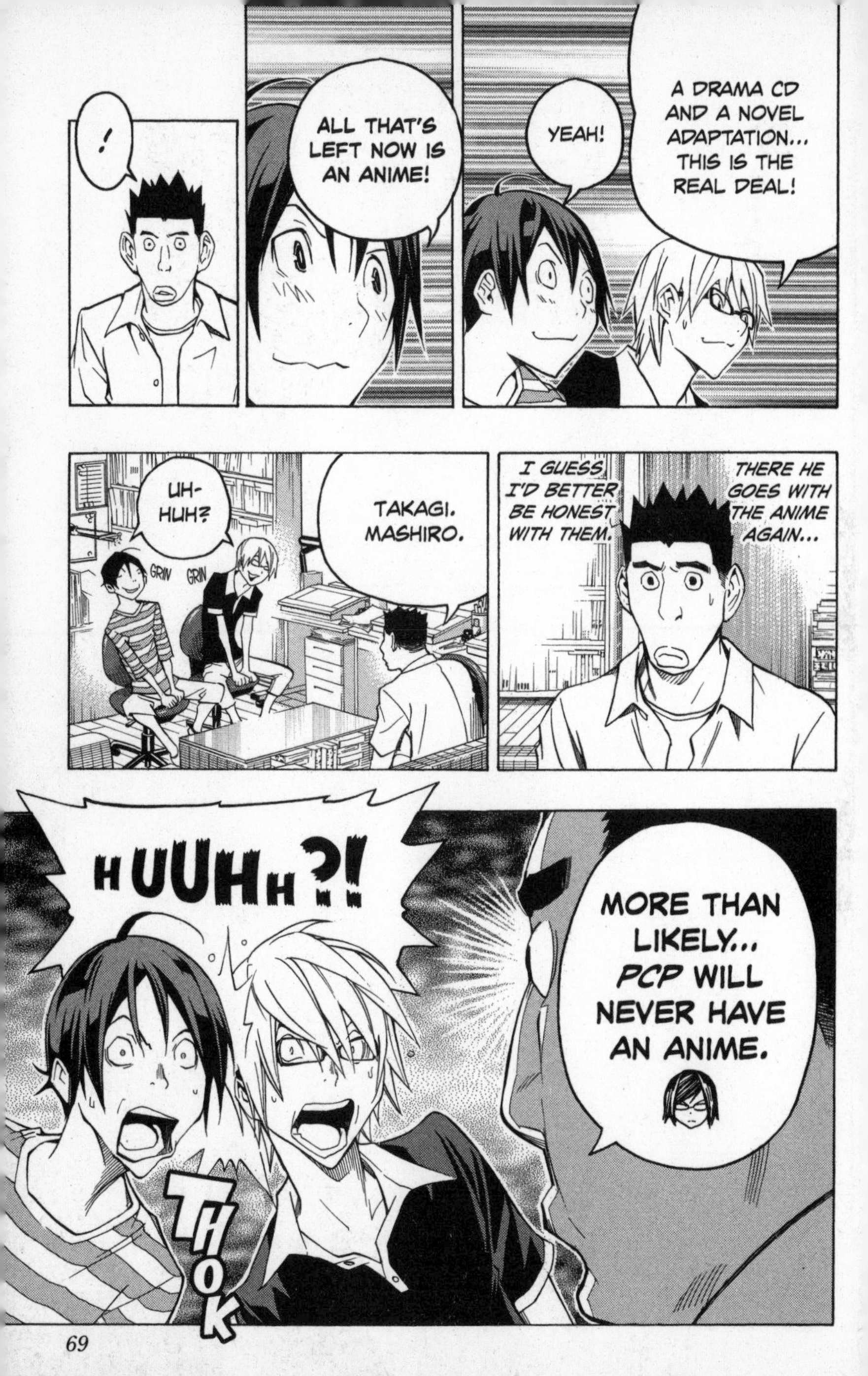
A DRAMA CD AND A NOVEL ADAPTATION... THIS IS THE REAL DEAL!
YEAH!
ALL THAT'S LEFT NOW IS AN ANIME!
!
THERE HE GOES WITH THE ANIME AGAIN...
I GUESS I'D BETTER BE HONEST WITH THEM.
TAKAGI. MASHIRO.
UH-HUH?
GRIN
GRIN
MORE THAN LIKELY... PCP WILL NEVER HAVE AN ANIME.
HUUHH?!
THOK

OHBA'S STORYBOARD

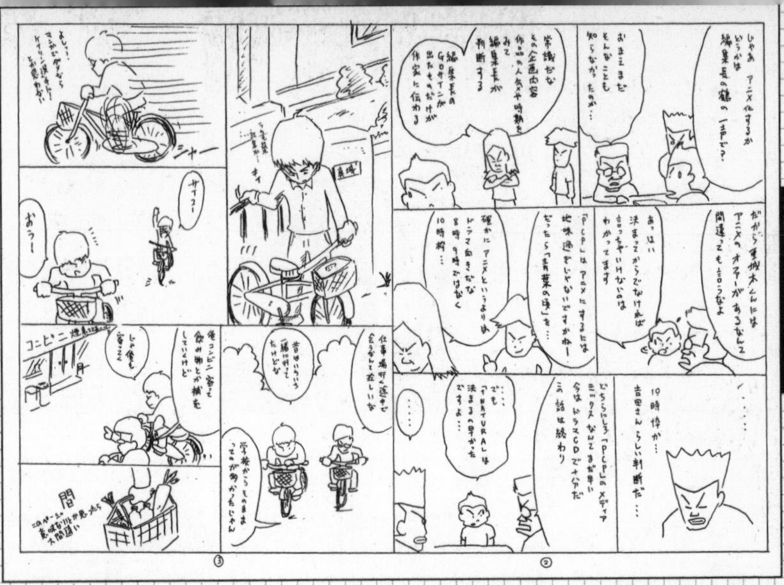
じゃあ アニメ化するかどうかは 編集長の鶴の一声で?
おまえまで そんなことも 知らなかったのか…
常識だな その企画内容 作品の人気や時期をみて 編集長が判断する
編集長のGOサインが出たものだけが 作家に伝わる
だから真城くんには アニメのオファーがあるなんて 間違っても言うなよ
あっはい 決まってからでなければ 言っちゃいけないのは わかってます
「PCP」はアニメにするには 地味過ぎじゃないですかねー だったら「青葉の頃」を…
確かにアニメというよりは ドラマ向きだな 8時9時台ではなく 10時枠…
……
10時枠か… 吉田さんらしい判断だ…
どちらにしろ「PCP」のメディアミックスなんてまだ早い 今はドラマCDで十分だ この話は終わり
でも「+NATURAL」は 決まるの早かったですよね…
……
サイコー
おう
仕事場行く途中で 会うなんて 珍しいな
昔はいっしょに 一緒に行ってたけどな
学校からそのまま ってのが多かったじゃん
俺コンビニ寄って 飲み物とか補充していくけど
じゃ俺も 寄ってく
コンビニ
間

OBATA'S STORYBOARD

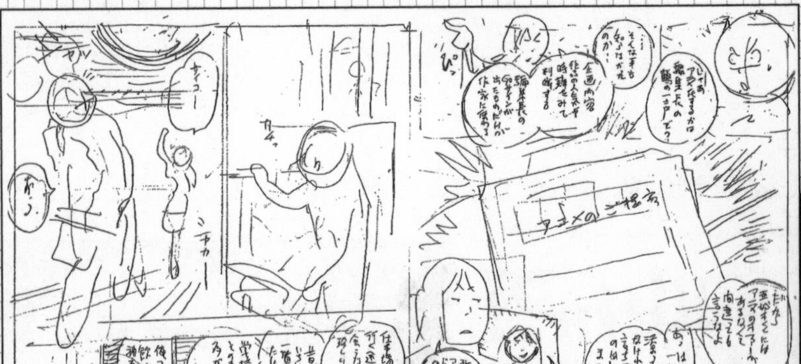

COMPLETE!

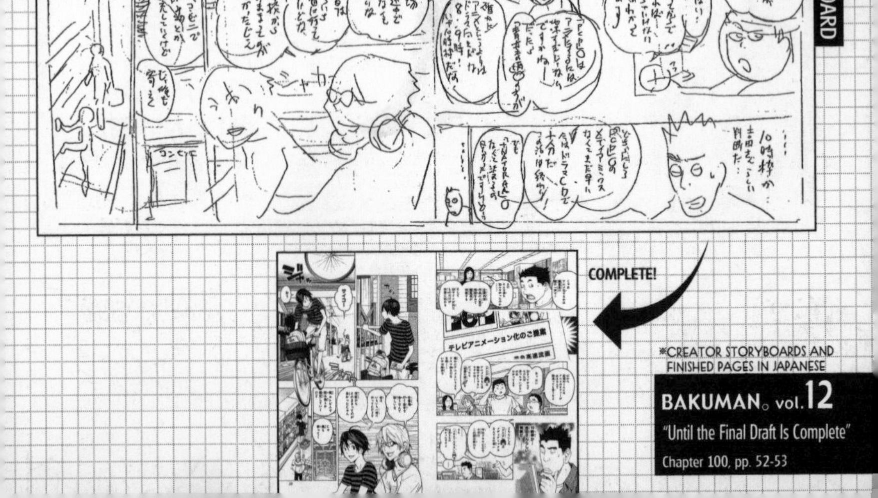

※CREATOR STORYBOARDS AND FINISHED PAGES IN JAPANESE

BAKUMAN。 vol.12

"Until the Final Draft Is Complete"

Chapter 100, pp. 52-53

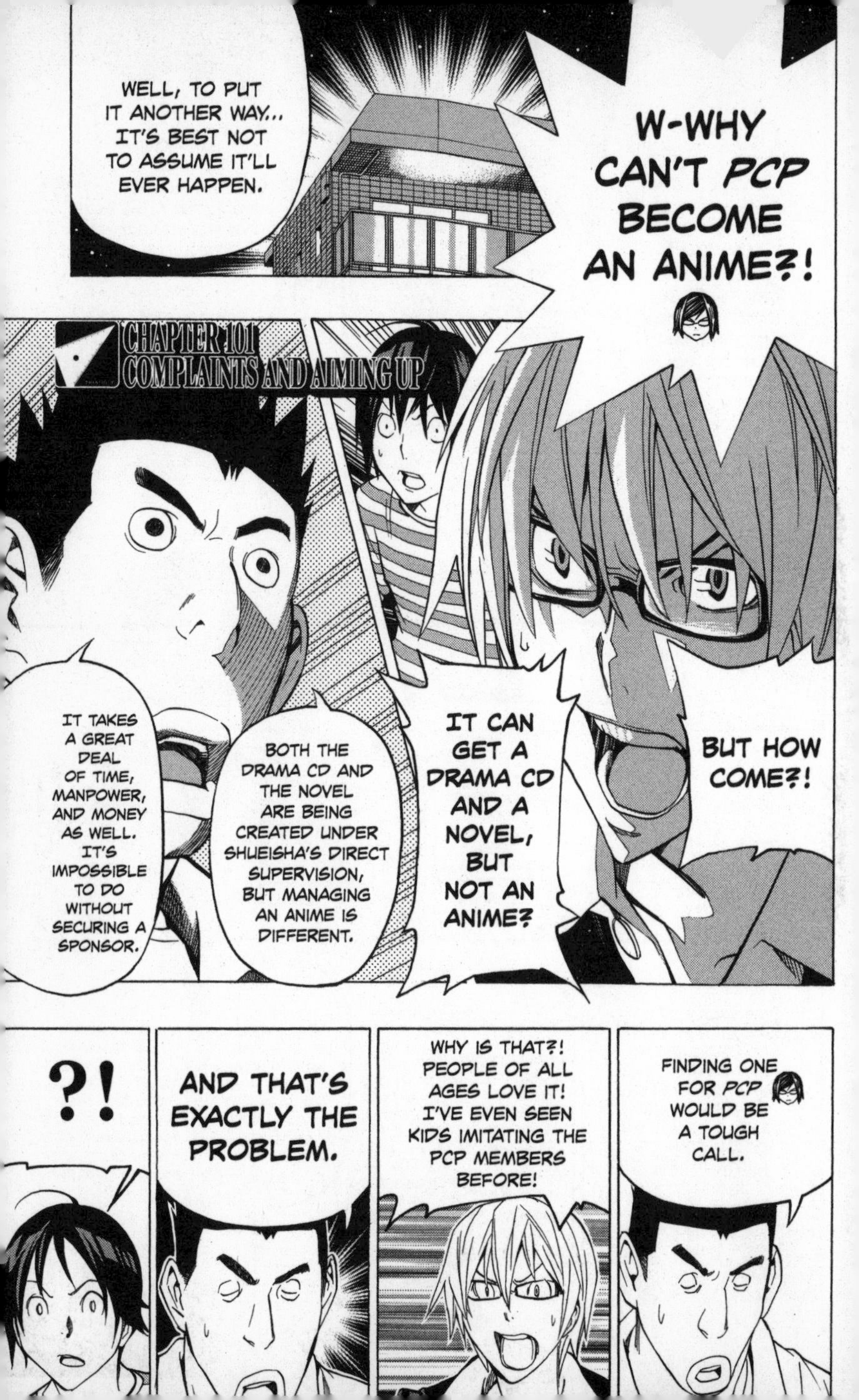
WELL, TO PUT IT ANOTHER WAY... IT'S BEST NOT TO ASSUME IT'LL EVER HAPPEN.
W-WHY CAN'T *PCP* BECOME AN ANIME?!
CHAPTER 101 COMPLAINTS AND AIMING UP
BUT HOW COME?!
IT CAN GET A DRAMA CD AND A NOVEL, BUT NOT AN ANIME?
BOTH THE DRAMA CD AND THE NOVEL ARE BEING CREATED UNDER SHUEISHA'S DIRECT SUPERVISION, BUT MANAGING AN ANIME IS DIFFERENT.
IT TAKES A GREAT DEAL OF TIME, MANPOWER, AND MONEY AS WELL. IT'S IMPOSSIBLE TO DO WITHOUT SECURING A SPONSOR.
FINDING ONE FOR *PCP* WOULD BE A TOUGH CALL.
WHY IS THAT?! PEOPLE OF ALL AGES LOVE IT! I'VE EVEN SEEN KIDS IMITATING THE PCP MEMBERS BEFORE!
AND THAT'S EXACTLY THE PROBLEM.
?!

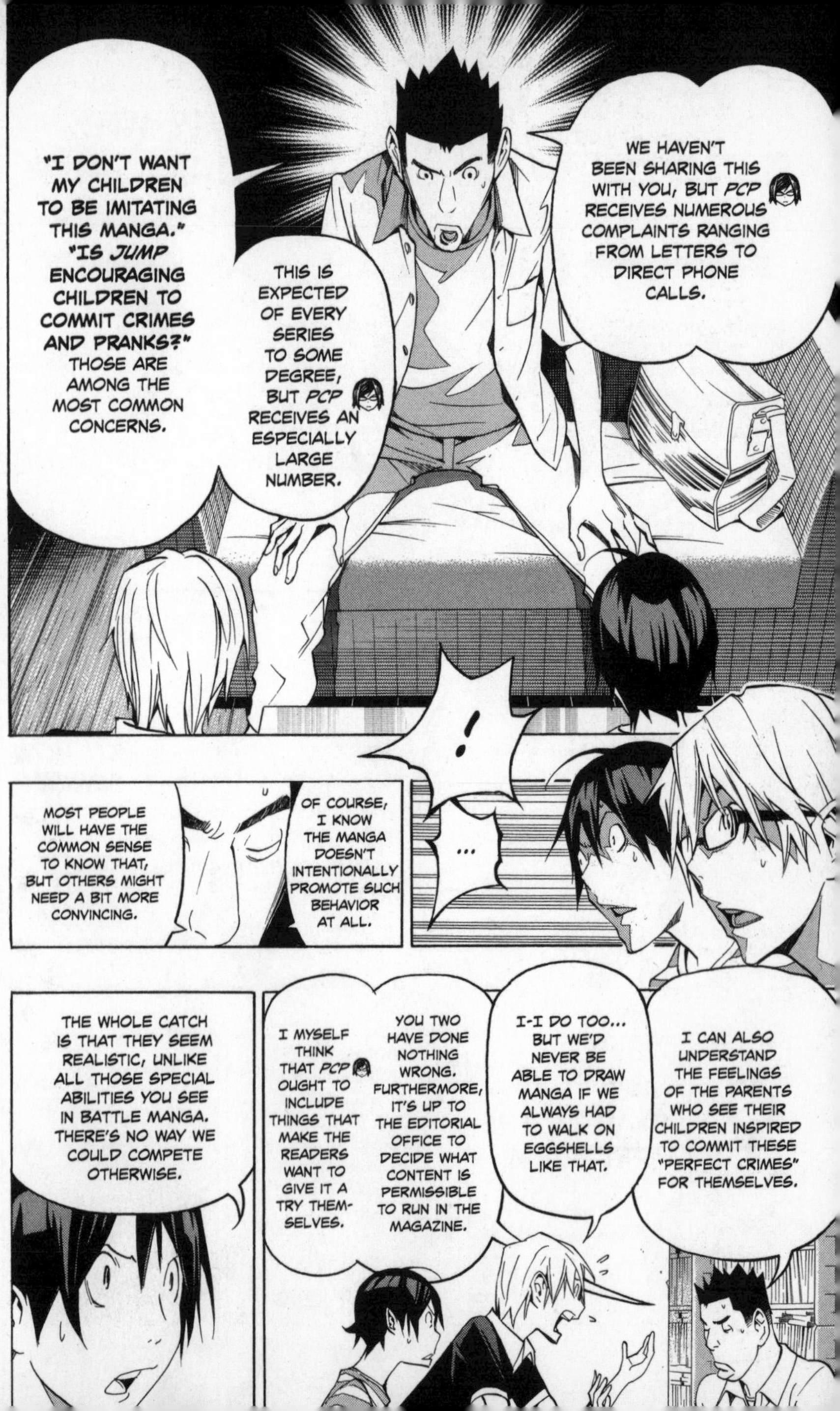
WE HAVEN'T BEEN SHARING THIS WITH YOU, BUT *PCP* RECEIVES NUMEROUS COMPLAINTS RANGING FROM LETTERS TO DIRECT PHONE CALLS.
THIS IS EXPECTED OF EVERY SERIES TO SOME DEGREE, BUT *PCP* RECEIVES AN ESPECIALLY LARGE NUMBER.
"I DON'T WANT MY CHILDREN TO BE IMITATING THIS MANGA." "IS *JUMP* ENCOURAGING CHILDREN TO COMMIT CRIMES AND PRANKS?" THOSE ARE AMONG THE MOST COMMON CONCERNS.
!
...
OF COURSE, I KNOW THE MANGA DOESN'T INTENTIONALLY PROMOTE SUCH BEHAVIOR AT ALL.
MOST PEOPLE WILL HAVE THE COMMON SENSE TO KNOW THAT, BUT OTHERS MIGHT NEED A BIT MORE CONVINCING.
I CAN ALSO UNDERSTAND THE FEELINGS OF THE PARENTS WHO SEE THEIR CHILDREN INSPIRED TO COMMIT THESE "PERFECT CRIMES" FOR THEMSELVES.
I-I DO TOO... BUT WE'D NEVER BE ABLE TO DRAW MANGA IF WE ALWAYS HAD TO WALK ON EGGSHELLS LIKE THAT.
YOU TWO HAVE DONE NOTHING WRONG. FURTHERMORE, IT'S UP TO THE EDITORIAL OFFICE TO DECIDE WHAT CONTENT IS PERMISSIBLE TO RUN IN THE MAGAZINE.
I MYSELF THINK THAT *PCP* OUGHT TO INCLUDE THINGS THAT MAKE THE READERS WANT TO GIVE IT A TRY THEMSELVES.
THE WHOLE CATCH IS THAT THEY SEEM REALISTIC, UNLIKE ALL THOSE SPECIAL ABILITIES YOU SEE IN BATTLE MANGA. THERE'S NO WAY WE COULD COMPETE OTHERWISE.

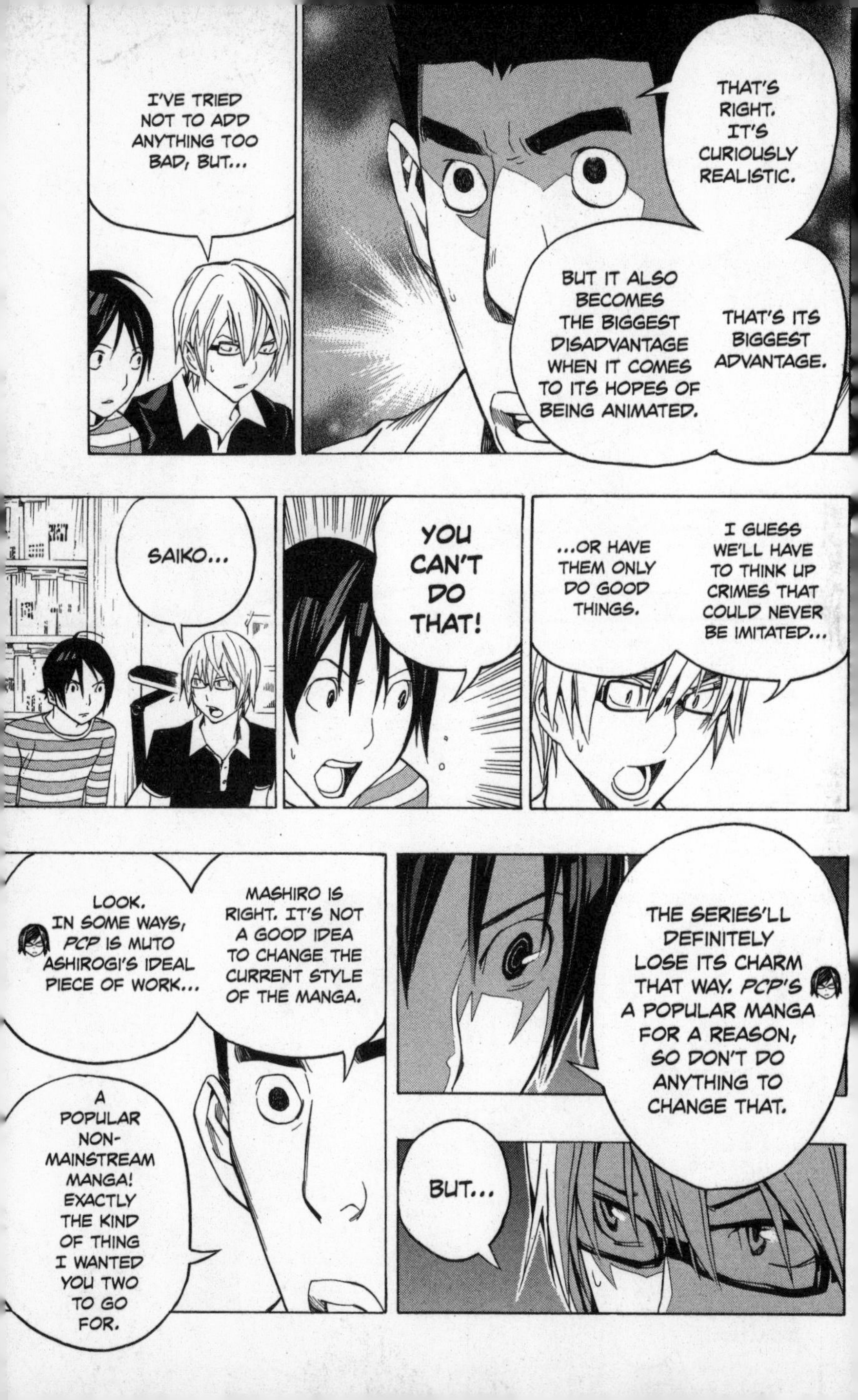
THAT'S RIGHT. IT'S CURIOUSLY REALISTIC.
THAT'S ITS BIGGEST ADVANTAGE.
BUT IT ALSO BECOMES THE BIGGEST DISADVANTAGE WHEN IT COMES TO ITS HOPES OF BEING ANIMATED.
I'VE TRIED NOT TO ADD ANYTHING TOO BAD, BUT...
I GUESS WE'LL HAVE TO THINK UP CRIMES THAT COULD NEVER BE IMITATED...
...OR HAVE THEM ONLY DO GOOD THINGS.
YOU CAN'T DO THAT!
SAIKO...
THE SERIES'LL DEFINITELY LOSE ITS CHARM THAT WAY. *PCP*'S A POPULAR MANGA FOR A REASON, SO DON'T DO ANYTHING TO CHANGE THAT.
BUT...
MASHIRO IS RIGHT. IT'S NOT A GOOD IDEA TO CHANGE THE CURRENT STYLE OF THE MANGA.
LOOK. IN SOME WAYS, *PCP* IS MUTO ASHIROGI'S IDEAL PIECE OF WORK...
A POPULAR NON-MAINSTREAM MANGA! EXACTLY THE KIND OF THING I WANTED YOU TWO TO GO FOR.

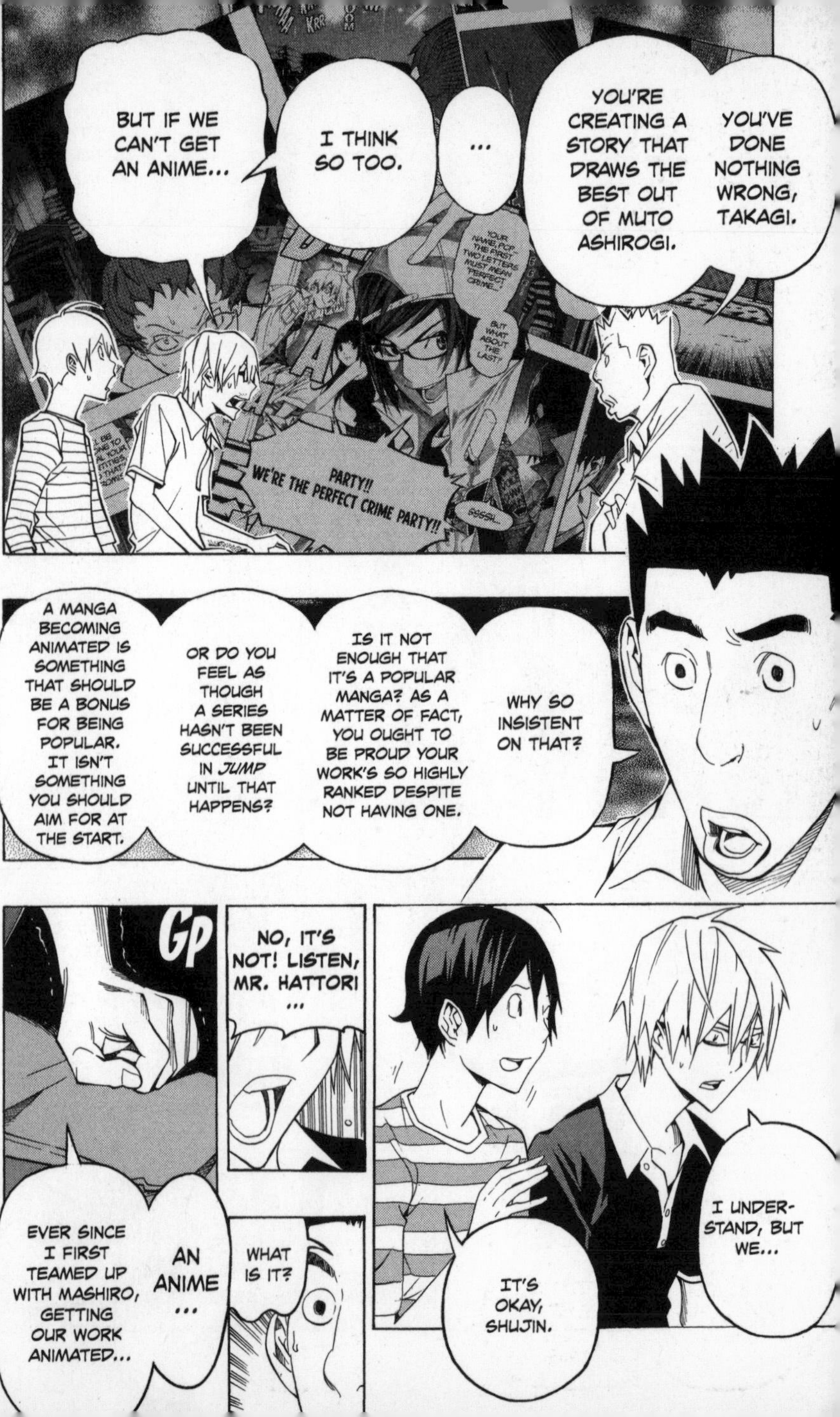
YOU'VE DONE NOTHING WRONG, TAKAGI.
YOU'RE CREATING A STORY THAT DRAWS THE BEST OUT OF MUTO ASHIROGI.
...
I THINK SO TOO.
BUT IF WE CAN'T GET AN ANIME...
YOUR NAME, PCP. THE FIRST TWO LETTERS MUST MEAN "PERFECT CRIME"...
BUT WHAT ABOUT THE LAST?
PARTY!! WE'RE THE PERFECT CRIME PARTY!!
WHY SO INSISTENT ON THAT?
IS IT NOT ENOUGH THAT IT'S A POPULAR MANGA? AS A MATTER OF FACT, YOU OUGHT TO BE PROUD YOUR WORK'S SO HIGHLY RANKED DESPITE NOT HAVING ONE.
OR DO YOU FEEL AS THOUGH A SERIES HASN'T BEEN SUCCESSFUL IN *JUMP* UNTIL THAT HAPPENS?
A MANGA BECOMING ANIMATED IS SOMETHING THAT SHOULD BE A BONUS FOR BEING POPULAR. IT ISN'T SOMETHING YOU SHOULD AIM FOR AT THE START.
I UNDER-STAND, BUT WE...
IT'S OKAY, SHUJIN.
NO, IT'S NOT! LISTEN, MR. HATTORI...
GP
WHAT IS IT?
AN ANIME...
EVER SINCE I FIRST TEAMED UP WITH MASHIRO, GETTING OUR WORK ANIMATED...

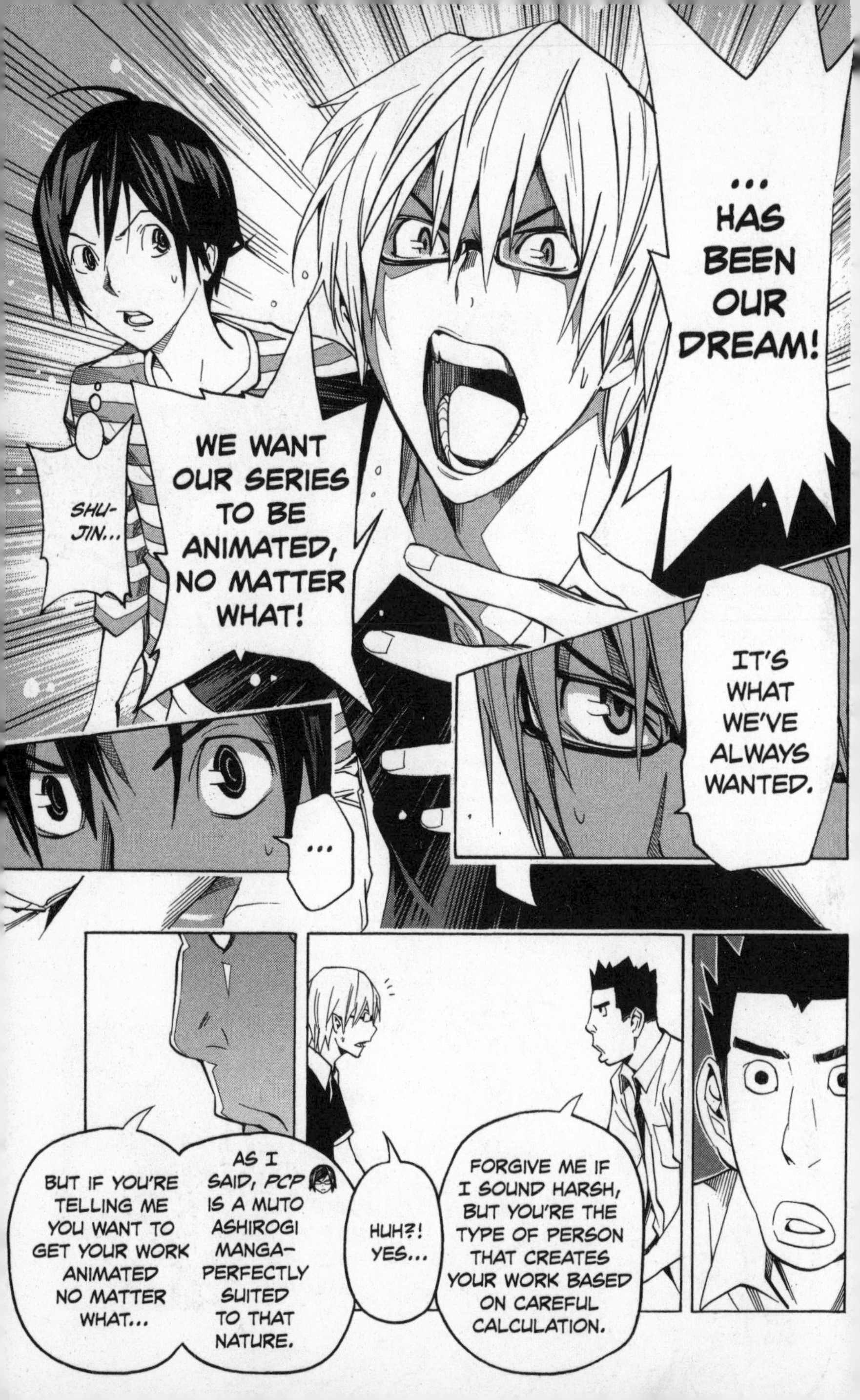
...HAS BEEN OUR DREAM!
WE WANT OUR SERIES TO BE ANIMATED, NO MATTER WHAT!
SHU-JIN...
IT'S WHAT WE'VE ALWAYS WANTED.
...
FORGIVE ME IF I SOUND HARSH, BUT YOU'RE THE TYPE OF PERSON THAT CREATES YOUR WORK BASED ON CAREFUL CALCULATION.
HUH?! YES...
AS I SAID, *PCP* IS A MUTO ASHIROGI MANGA—PERFECTLY SUITED TO THAT NATURE.
BUT IF YOU'RE TELLING ME YOU WANT TO GET YOUR WORK ANIMATED NO MATTER WHAT...

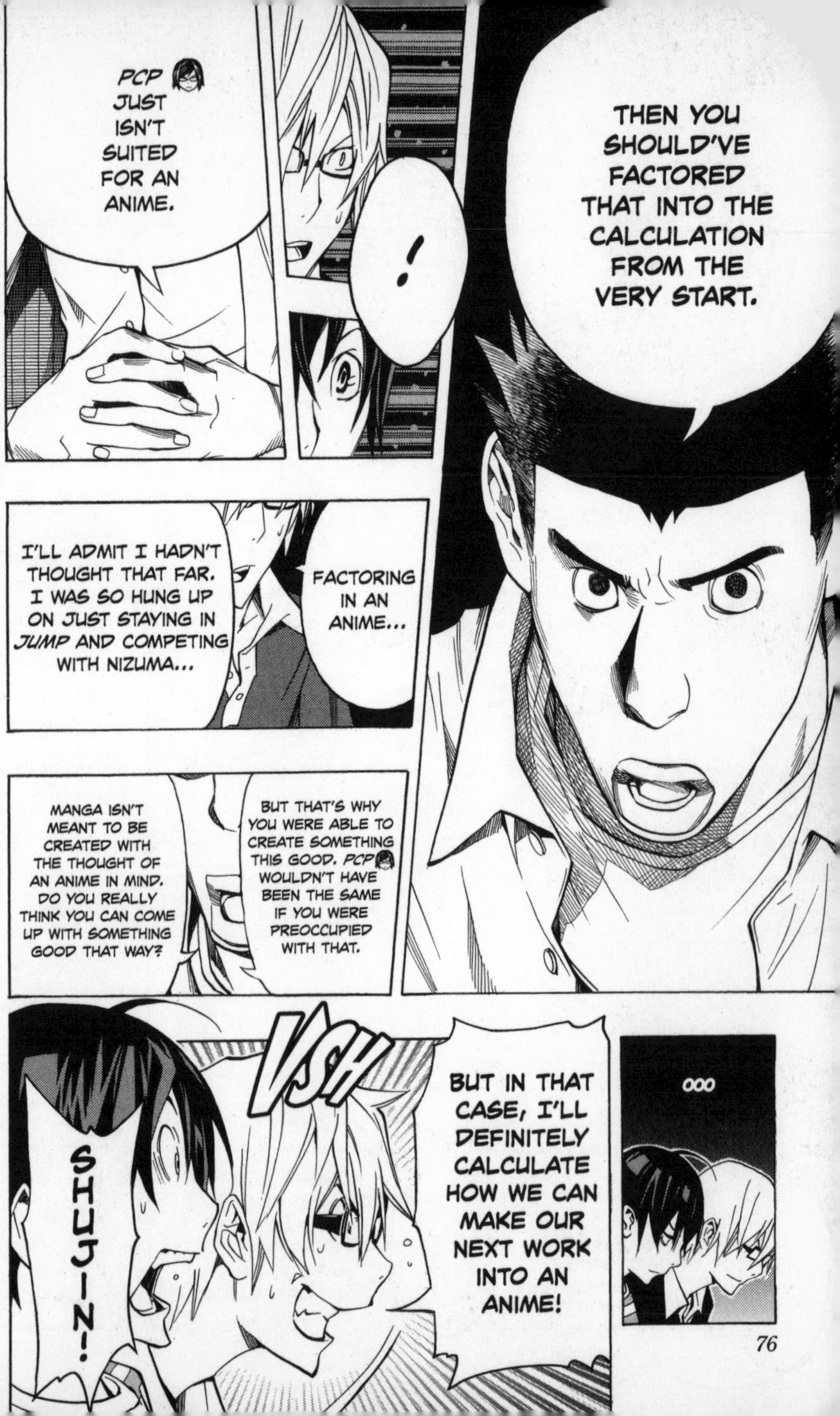
THEN YOU SHOULD'VE FACTORED THAT INTO THE CALCULATION FROM THE VERY START.
!
PCP JUST ISN'T SUITED FOR AN ANIME.
FACTORING IN AN ANIME...
I'LL ADMIT I HADN'T THOUGHT THAT FAR. I WAS SO HUNG UP ON JUST STAYING IN *JUMP* AND COMPETING WITH NIZUMA...
BUT THAT'S WHY YOU WERE ABLE TO CREATE SOMETHING THIS GOOD. PCP WOULDN'T HAVE BEEN THE SAME IF YOU WERE PREOCCUPIED WITH THAT.
MANGA ISN'T MEANT TO BE CREATED WITH THE THOUGHT OF AN ANIME IN MIND. DO YOU REALLY THINK YOU CAN COME UP WITH SOMETHING GOOD THAT WAY?
ooo
BUT IN THAT CASE, I'LL DEFINITELY CALCULATE HOW WE CAN MAKE OUR NEXT WORK INTO AN ANIME!
VSH
SHUJIN!

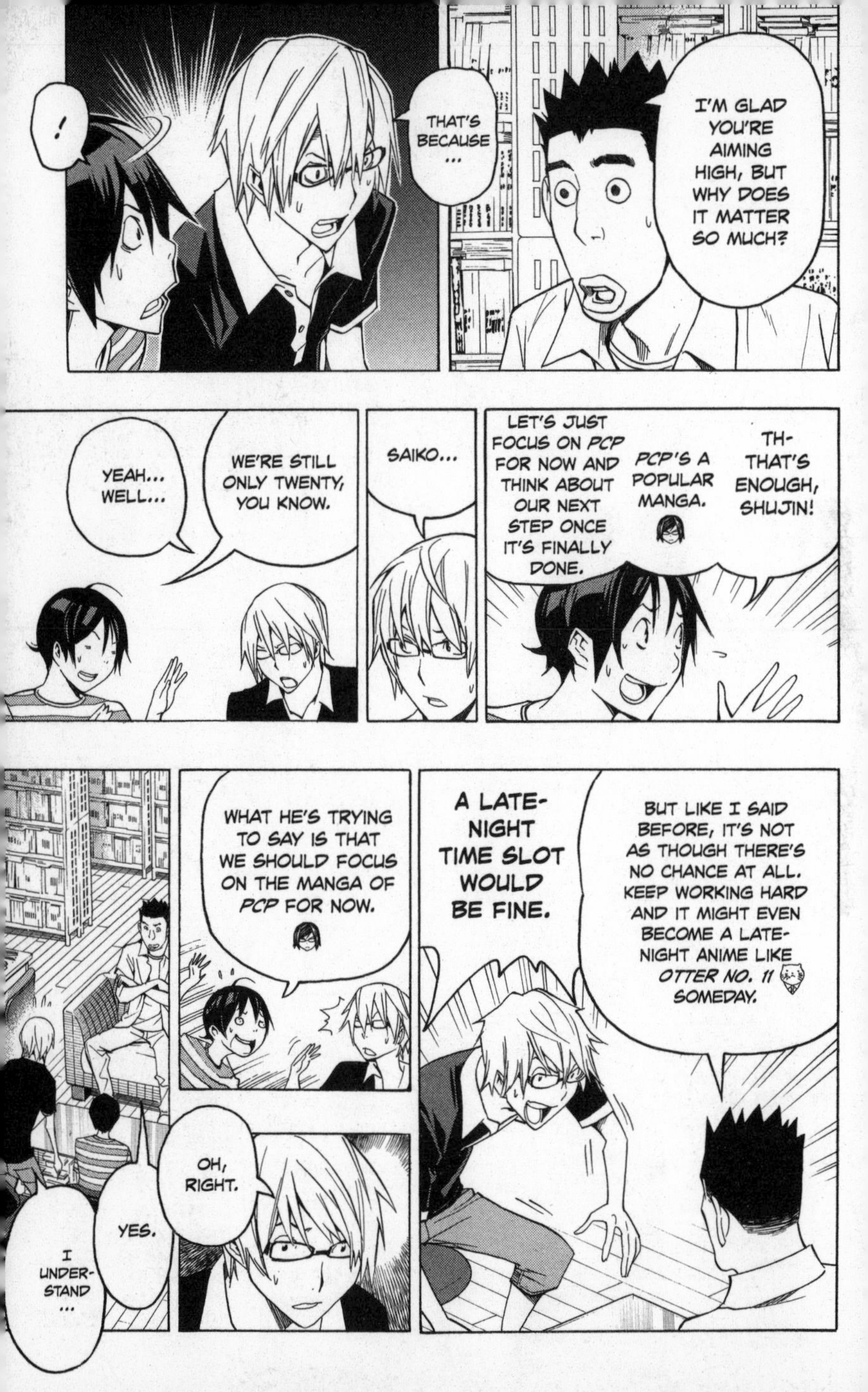
I'M GLAD YOU'RE AIMING HIGH, BUT WHY DOES IT MATTER SO MUCH?
THAT'S BECAUSE ...
!
TH- THAT'S ENOUGH, SHUJIN!
PCP'S A POPULAR MANGA.
LET'S JUST FOCUS ON PCP FOR NOW AND THINK ABOUT OUR NEXT STEP ONCE IT'S FINALLY DONE.
SAIKO...
WE'RE STILL ONLY TWENTY, YOU KNOW.
YEAH... WELL...
BUT LIKE I SAID BEFORE, IT'S NOT AS THOUGH THERE'S NO CHANCE AT ALL. KEEP WORKING HARD AND IT MIGHT EVEN BECOME A LATE-NIGHT ANIME LIKE OTTER NO. 11 SOMEDAY.
A LATE-NIGHT TIME SLOT WOULD BE FINE.
WHAT HE'S TRYING TO SAY IS THAT WE SHOULD FOCUS ON THE MANGA OF PCP FOR NOW.
OH, RIGHT.
YES.
I UNDERSTAND ...

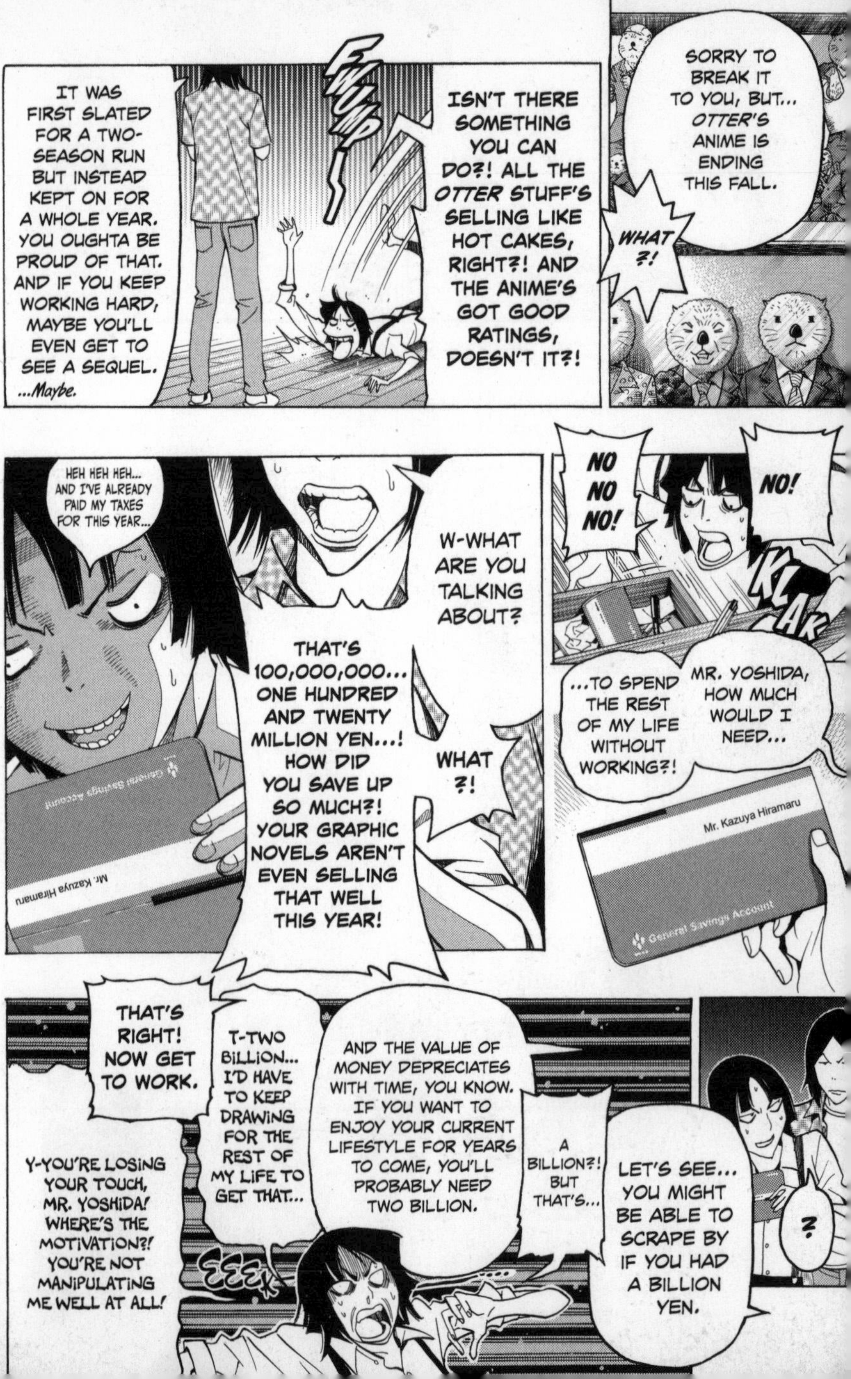
SORRY TO BREAK IT TO YOU, BUT... OTTER'S ANIME IS ENDING THIS FALL.
WHAT?!
FWUMP
ISN'T THERE SOMETHING YOU CAN DO?! ALL THE OTTER STUFF'S SELLING LIKE HOT CAKES, RIGHT?! AND THE ANIME'S GOT GOOD RATINGS, DOESN'T IT?!
IT WAS FIRST SLATED FOR A TWO-SEASON RUN BUT INSTEAD KEPT ON FOR A WHOLE YEAR. YOU OUGHTA BE PROUD OF THAT. AND IF YOU KEEP WORKING HARD, MAYBE YOU'LL EVEN GET TO SEE A SEQUEL. ...Maybe.
NO!
NO NO NO!
KLAK
MR. YOSHIDA, HOW MUCH WOULD I NEED...
...TO SPEND THE REST OF MY LIFE WITHOUT WORKING?!
Mr. Kazuya Hiramaru
General Savings Account
W-WHAT ARE YOU TALKING ABOUT?
HEH HEH HEH... AND I'VE ALREADY PAID MY TAXES FOR THIS YEAR...
WHAT?!
THAT'S 100,000,000... ONE HUNDRED AND TWENTY MILLION YEN...! HOW DID YOU SAVE UP SO MUCH?! YOUR GRAPHIC NOVELS AREN'T EVEN SELLING THAT WELL THIS YEAR!
General Savings Account
Mr. Kazuya Hiramaru
?
LET'S SEE... YOU MIGHT BE ABLE TO SCRAPE BY IF YOU HAD A BILLION YEN.
A BILLION?! BUT THAT'S...
AND THE VALUE OF MONEY DEPRECIATES WITH TIME, YOU KNOW. IF YOU WANT TO ENJOY YOUR CURRENT LIFESTYLE FOR YEARS TO COME, YOU'LL PROBABLY NEED TWO BILLION.
T-TWO BILLION... I'D HAVE TO KEEP DRAWING FOR THE REST OF MY LIFE TO GET THAT...
THAT'S RIGHT! NOW GET TO WORK.
Y-YOU'RE LOSING YOUR TOUCH, MR. YOSHIDA! WHERE'S THE MOTIVATION?! YOU'RE NOT MANIPULATING ME WELL AT ALL!
EEEK

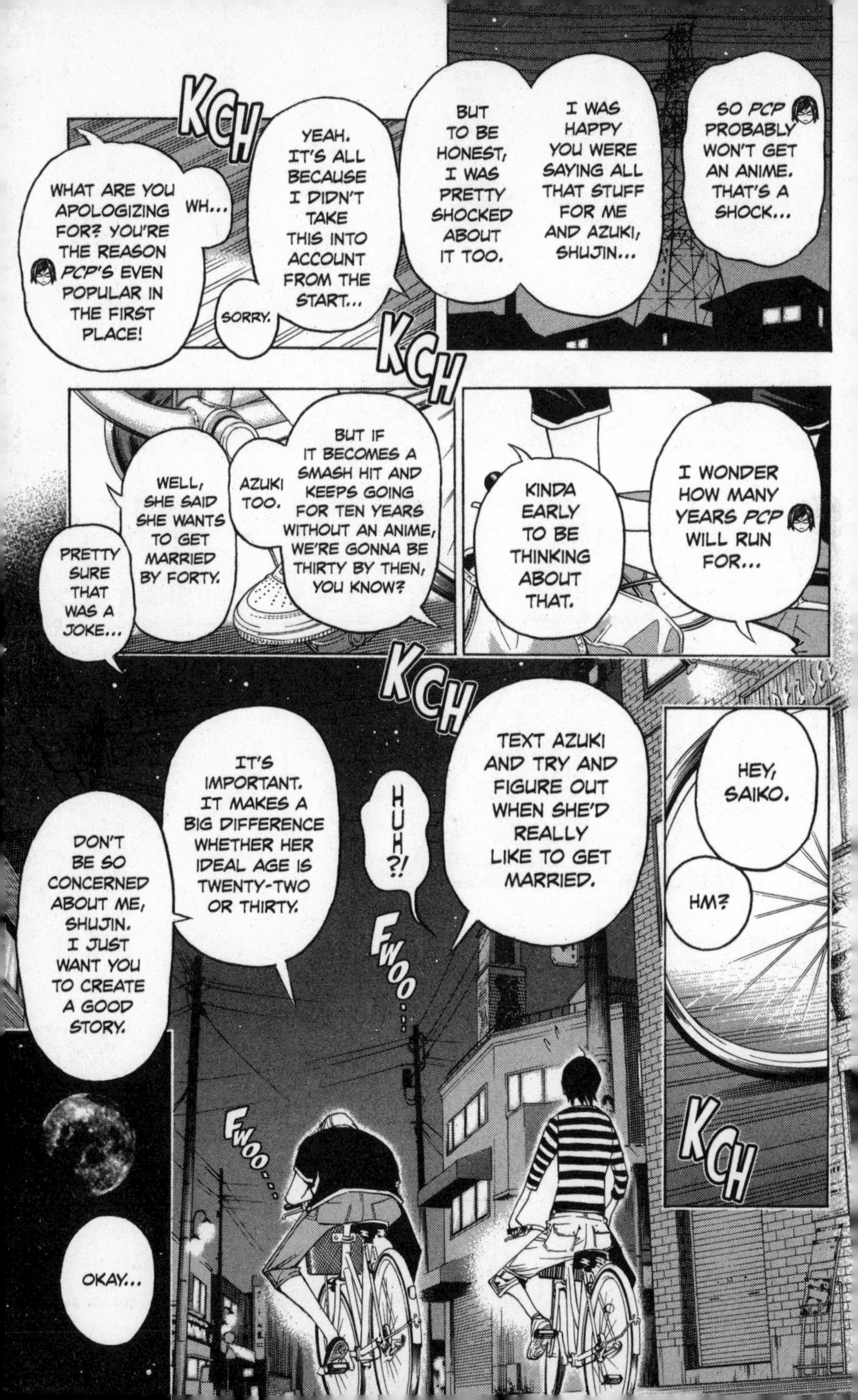
SO PCP PROBABLY WON'T GET AN ANIME. THAT'S A SHOCK...
I WAS HAPPY YOU WERE SAYING ALL THAT STUFF FOR ME AND AZUKI, SHUJIN...
BUT TO BE HONEST, I WAS PRETTY SHOCKED ABOUT IT TOO.
KCH
YEAH. IT'S ALL BECAUSE I DIDN'T TAKE THIS INTO ACCOUNT FROM THE START...
SORRY.
KCH
WH...
WHAT ARE YOU APOLOGIZING FOR? YOU'RE THE REASON PCP'S EVEN POPULAR IN THE FIRST PLACE!
I WONDER HOW MANY YEARS PCP WILL RUN FOR...
KINDA EARLY TO BE THINKING ABOUT THAT.
BUT IF IT BECOMES A SMASH HIT AND KEEPS GOING FOR TEN YEARS WITHOUT AN ANIME, WE'RE GONNA BE THIRTY BY THEN, YOU KNOW?
AZUKI TOO.
WELL, SHE SAID SHE WANTS TO GET MARRIED BY FORTY.
PRETTY SURE THAT WAS A JOKE...
KCH
HEY, SAIKO.
HM?
KCH
TEXT AZUKI AND TRY AND FIGURE OUT WHEN SHE'D REALLY LIKE TO GET MARRIED.
HUH?!
IT'S IMPORTANT. IT MAKES A BIG DIFFERENCE WHETHER HER IDEAL AGE IS TWENTY-TWO OR THIRTY.
FWOO...
DON'T BE SO CONCERNED ABOUT ME, SHUJIN. I JUST WANT YOU TO CREATE A GOOD STORY.
FWOO...
OKAY...

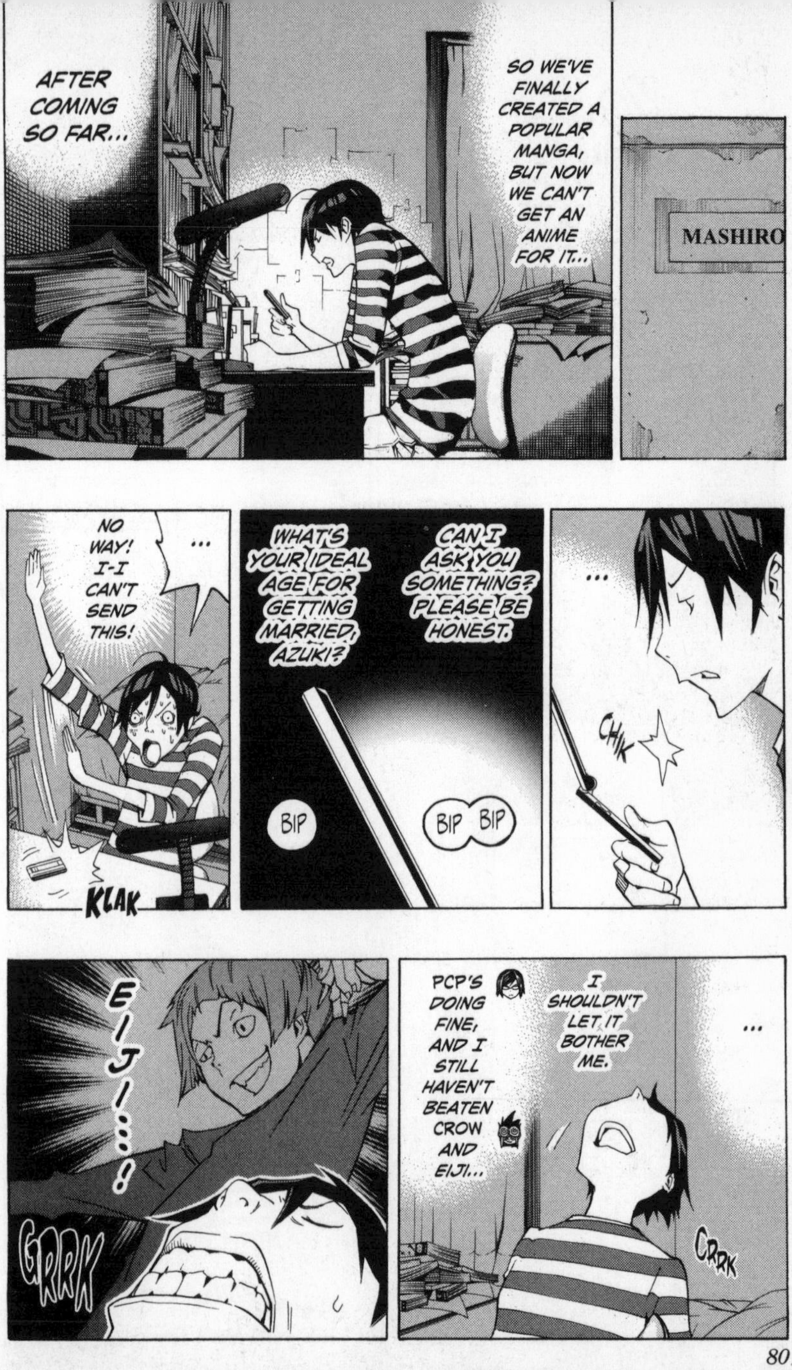

MASHIRO
SO WE'VE FINALLY CREATED A POPULAR MANGA, BUT NOW WE CAN'T GET AN ANIME FOR IT...
AFTER COMING SO FAR...
...
CHIK
CAN I ASK YOU SOMETHING? PLEASE BE HONEST.
WHAT'S YOUR IDEAL AGE FOR GETTING MARRIED, AZUKI?
BIP BIP
BIP
...
NO WAY! I-I CAN'T SEND THIS!
KLAK
...
I SHOULDN'T LET IT BOTHER ME.
PCP'S DOING FINE, AND I STILL HAVEN'T BEATEN CROW AND EIJI...
CRRK
EIJI...!
GRRK

READ THIS WAY

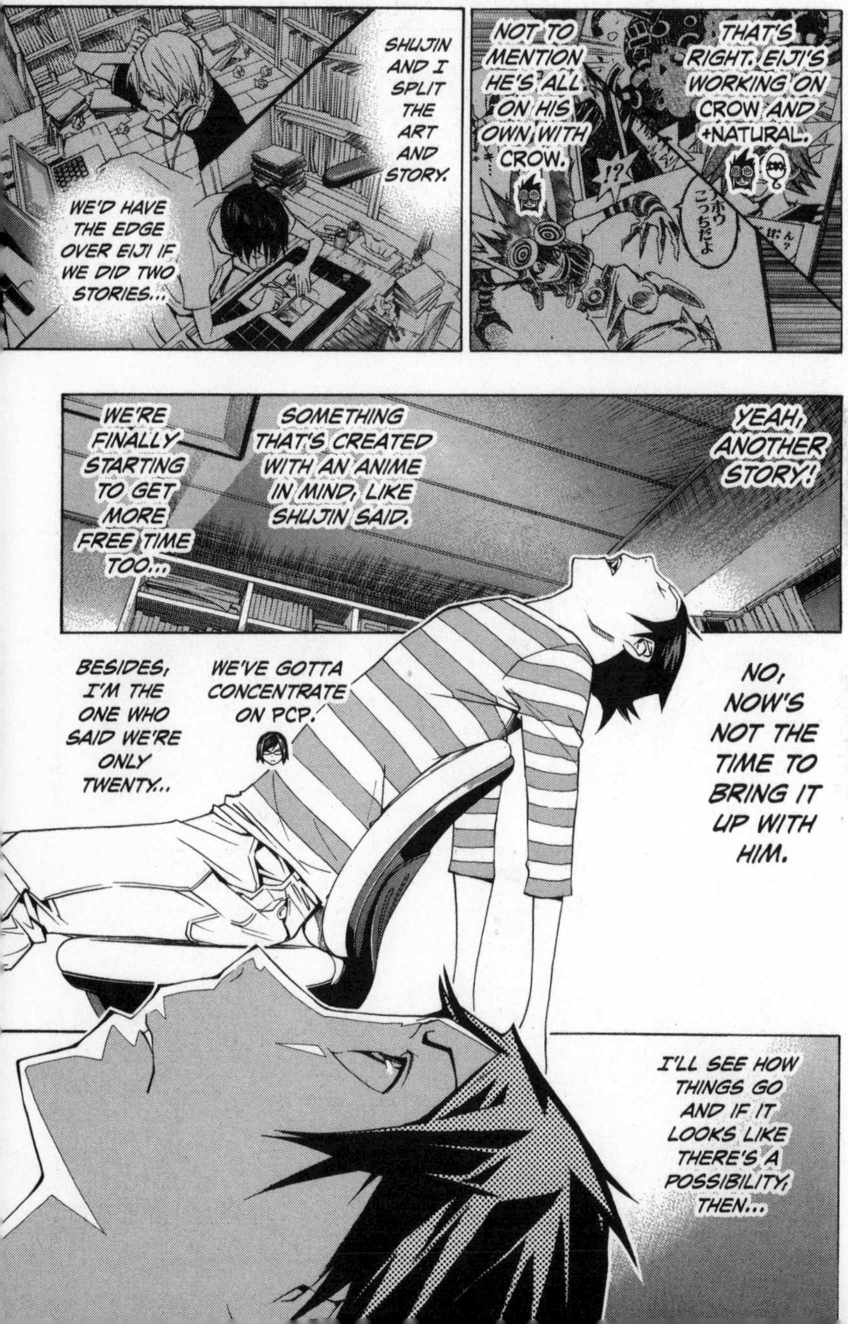
THAT'S RIGHT. EIJI'S WORKING ON CROW AND +NATURAL.
NOT TO MENTION HE'S ALL ON HIS OWN WITH CROW.
!?
SHUJIN AND I SPLIT THE ART AND STORY.
WE'D HAVE THE EDGE OVER EIJI IF WE DID TWO STORIES...
YEAH, ANOTHER STORY!
SOMETHING THAT'S CREATED WITH AN ANIME IN MIND, LIKE SHUJIN SAID.
WE'RE FINALLY STARTING TO GET MORE FREE TIME TOO...
NO, NOW'S NOT THE TIME TO BRING IT UP WITH HIM.
WE'VE GOTTA CONCENTRATE ON PCP.
BESIDES, I'M THE ONE WHO SAID WE'RE ONLY TWENTY...
I'LL SEE HOW THINGS GO AND IF IT LOOKS LIKE THERE'S A POSSIBILITY, THEN...

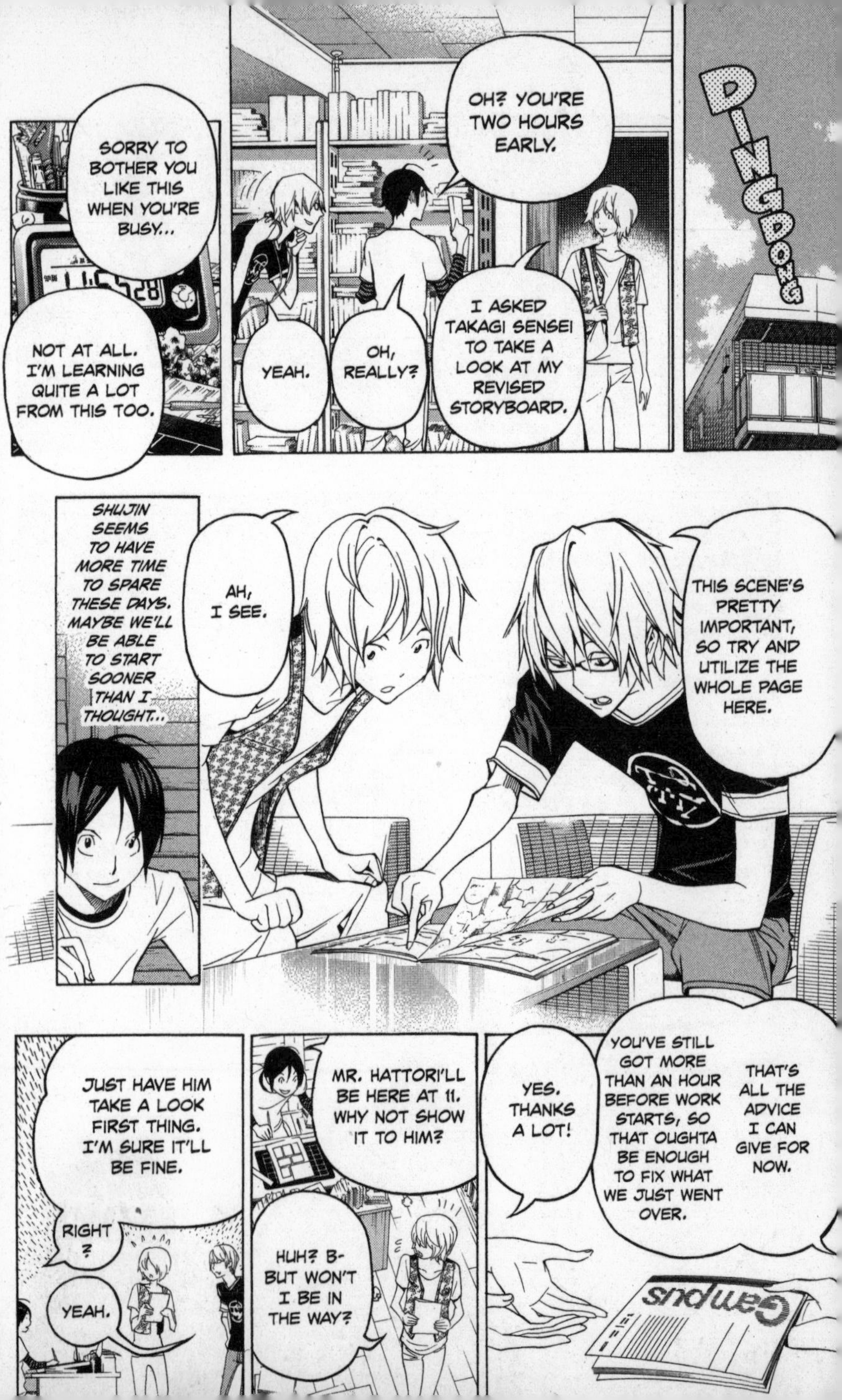
DINGDONG
OH? YOU'RE TWO HOURS EARLY.
I ASKED TAKAGI SENSEI TO TAKE A LOOK AT MY REVISED STORYBOARD.
OH, REALLY?
YEAH.
SORRY TO BOTHER YOU LIKE THIS WHEN YOU'RE BUSY...
NOT AT ALL. I'M LEARNING QUITE A LOT FROM THIS TOO.
THIS SCENE'S PRETTY IMPORTANT, SO TRY AND UTILIZE THE WHOLE PAGE HERE.
AH, I SEE.
SHUJIN SEEMS TO HAVE MORE TIME TO SPARE THESE DAYS. MAYBE WE'LL BE ABLE TO START SOONER THAN I THOUGHT...
THAT'S ALL THE ADVICE I CAN GIVE FOR NOW.
YOU'VE STILL GOT MORE THAN AN HOUR BEFORE WORK STARTS, SO THAT OUGHTA BE ENOUGH TO FIX WHAT WE JUST WENT OVER.
YES. THANKS A LOT!
Gampus
MR. HATTORI'LL BE HERE AT 11. WHY NOT SHOW IT TO HIM?
HUH? B-BUT WON'T I BE IN THE WAY?
JUST HAVE HIM TAKE A LOOK FIRST THING. I'M SURE IT'LL BE FINE.
RIGHT?
YEAH.

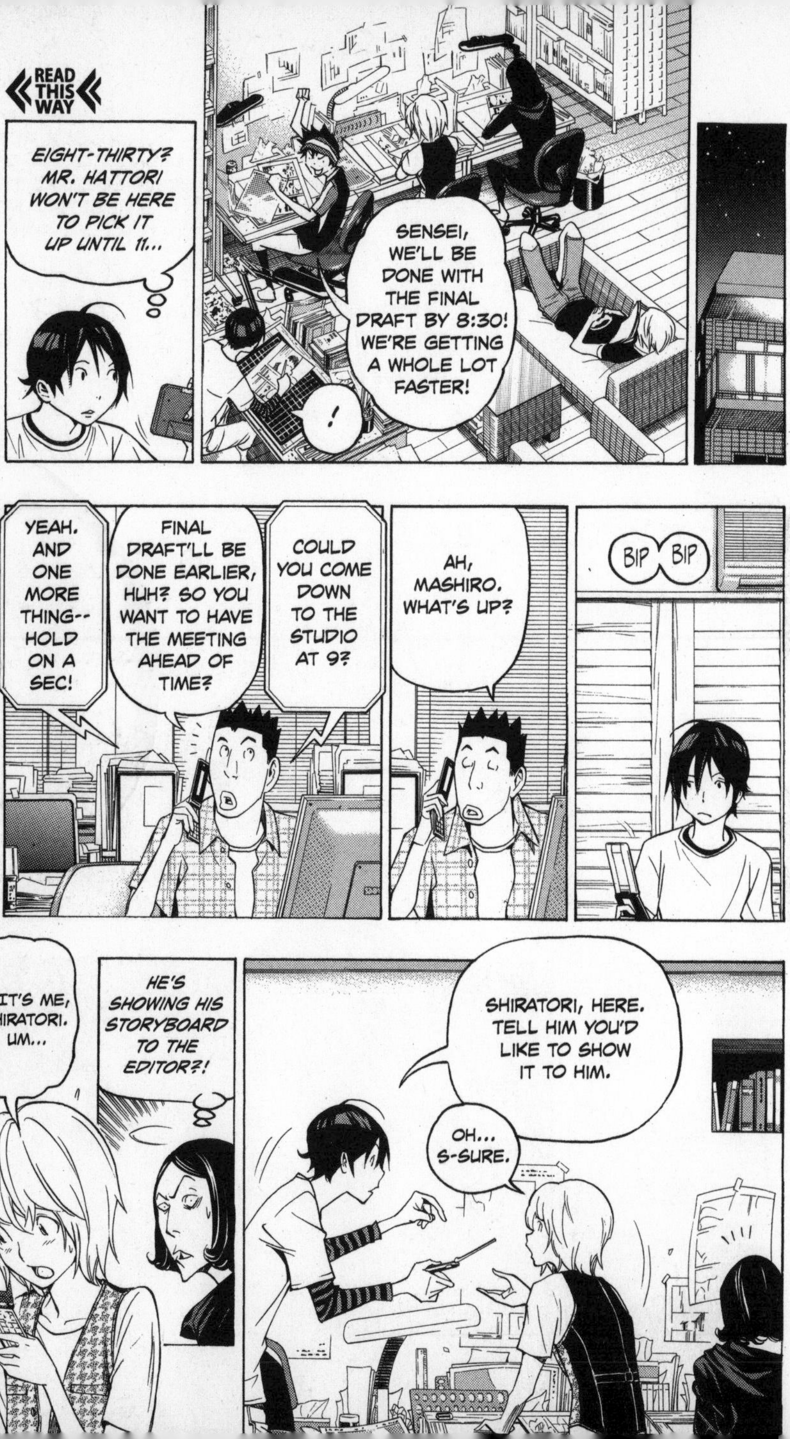
READ THIS WAY
SENSEI, WE'LL BE DONE WITH THE FINAL DRAFT BY 8:30! WE'RE GETTING A WHOLE LOT FASTER!
!
EIGHT-THIRTY? MR. HATTORI WON'T BE HERE TO PICK IT UP UNTIL 11...
BIP BIP
AH, MASHIRO. WHAT'S UP?
COULD YOU COME DOWN TO THE STUDIO AT 9?
FINAL DRAFT'LL BE DONE EARLIER, HUH? SO YOU WANT TO HAVE THE MEETING AHEAD OF TIME?
YEAH. AND ONE MORE THING--HOLD ON A SEC!
SHIRATORI, HERE. TELL HIM YOU'D LIKE TO SHOW IT TO HIM.
OH... S-SURE.
HE'S SHOWING HIS STORYBOARD TO THE EDITOR?!
I-IT'S ME, SHIRATORI. UM...

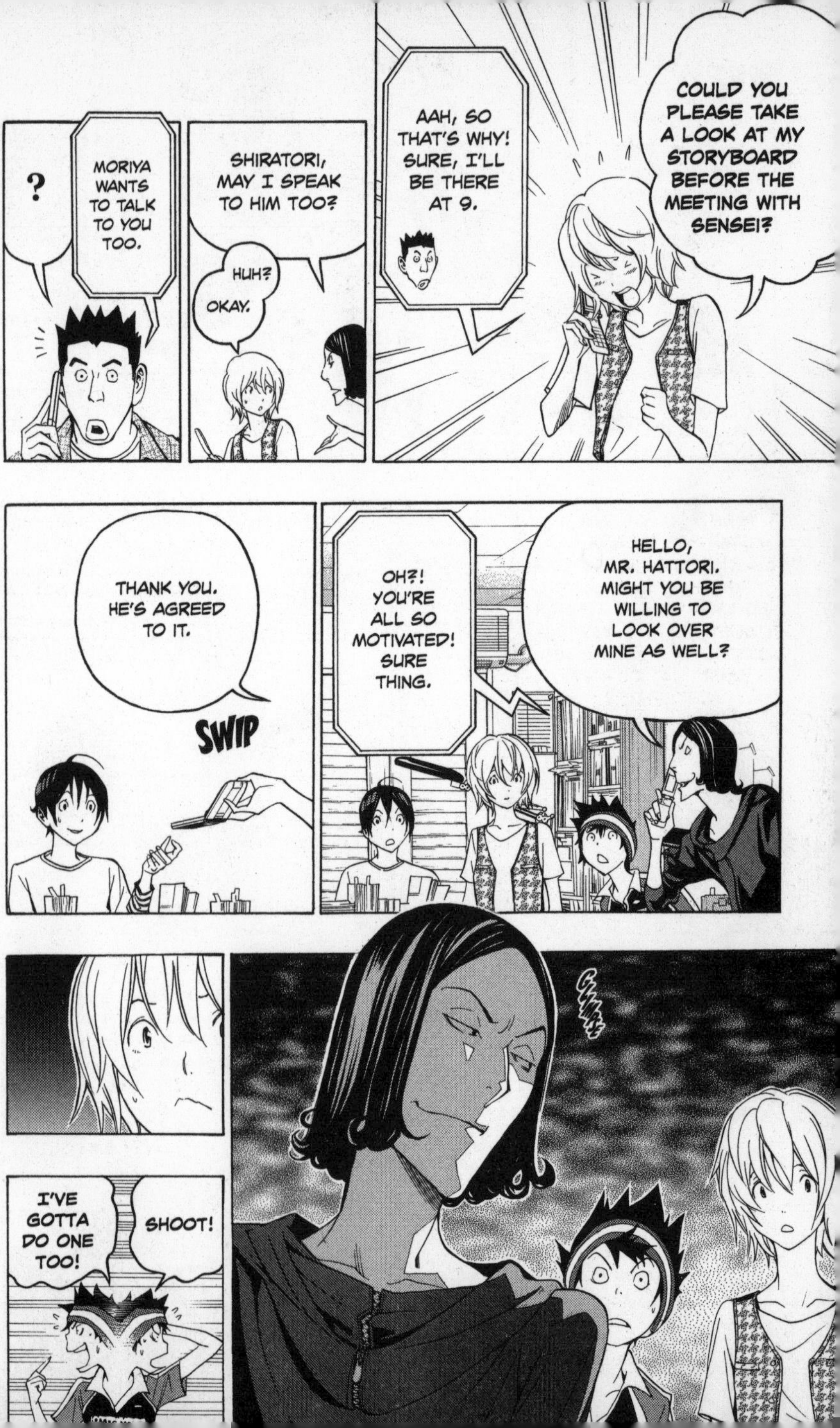
COULD YOU PLEASE TAKE A LOOK AT MY STORYBOARD BEFORE THE MEETING WITH SENSEI?
AAH, SO THAT'S WHY! SURE, I'LL BE THERE AT 9.
SHIRATORI, MAY I SPEAK TO HIM TOO?
HUH?
OKAY.
MORIYA WANTS TO TALK TO YOU TOO.
?
HELLO, MR. HATTORI. MIGHT YOU BE WILLING TO LOOK OVER MINE AS WELL?
OH?! YOU'RE ALL SO MOTIVATED! SURE THING.
THANK YOU. HE'S AGREED TO IT.
SWIP
SHOOT!
I'VE GOTTA DO ONE TOO!

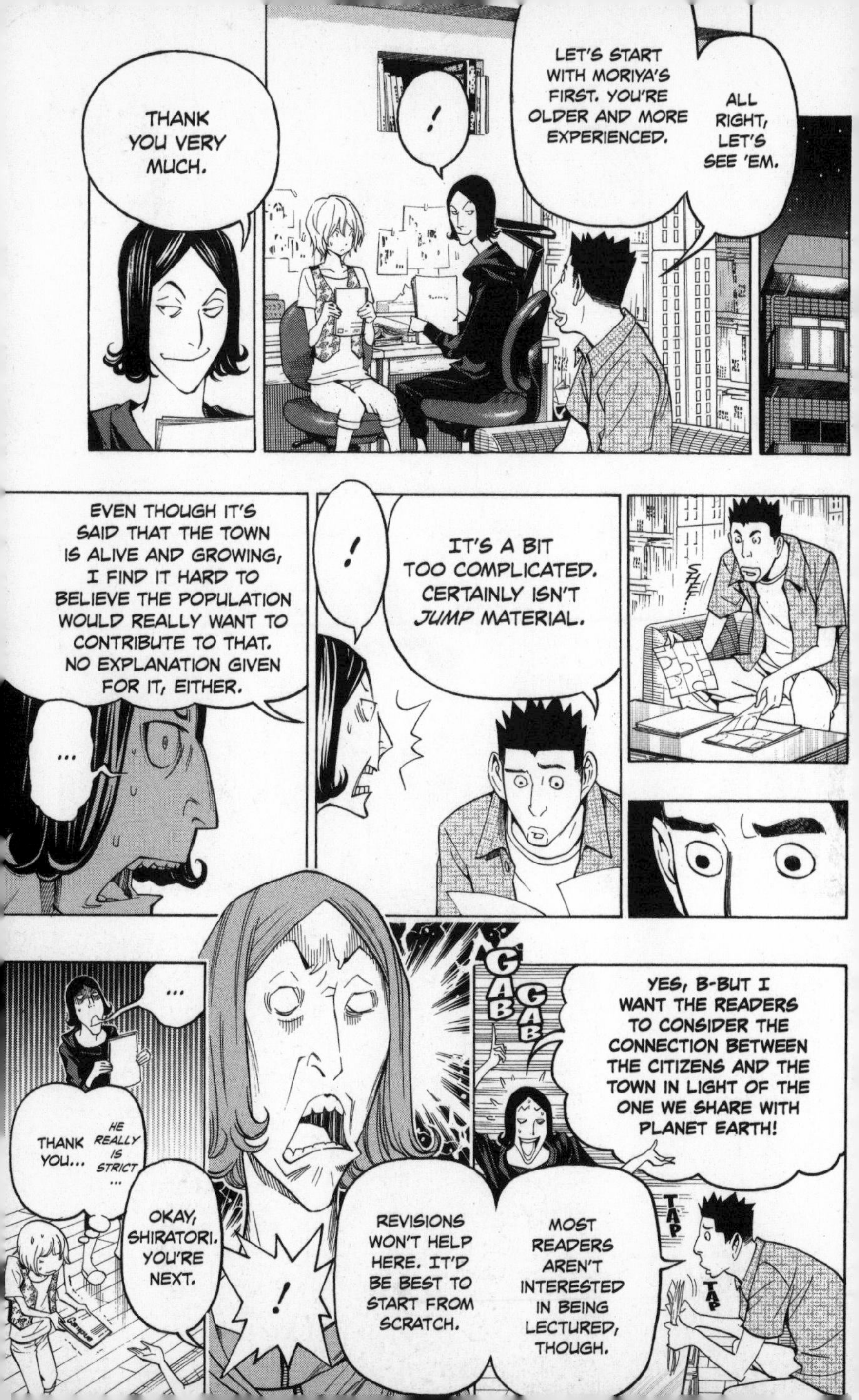
ALL RIGHT, LET'S SEE 'EM.
LET'S START WITH MORIYA'S FIRST. YOU'RE OLDER AND MORE EXPERIENCED.
!
THANK YOU VERY MUCH.
IT'S A BIT TOO COMPLICATED. CERTAINLY ISN'T *JUMP* MATERIAL.
!
EVEN THOUGH IT'S SAID THAT THE TOWN IS ALIVE AND GROWING, I FIND IT HARD TO BELIEVE THE POPULATION WOULD REALLY WANT TO CONTRIBUTE TO THAT. NO EXPLANATION GIVEN FOR IT, EITHER.
...
YES, B-BUT I WANT THE READERS TO CONSIDER THE CONNECTION BETWEEN THE CITIZENS AND THE TOWN IN LIGHT OF THE ONE WE SHARE WITH PLANET EARTH!
GAB GAB
TAP TAP
MOST READERS AREN'T INTERESTED IN BEING LECTURED, THOUGH.
REVISIONS WON'T HELP HERE. IT'D BE BEST TO START FROM SCRATCH.
!
...
THANK YOU...
HE REALLY IS STRICT...
OKAY, SHIRATORI. YOU'RE NEXT.

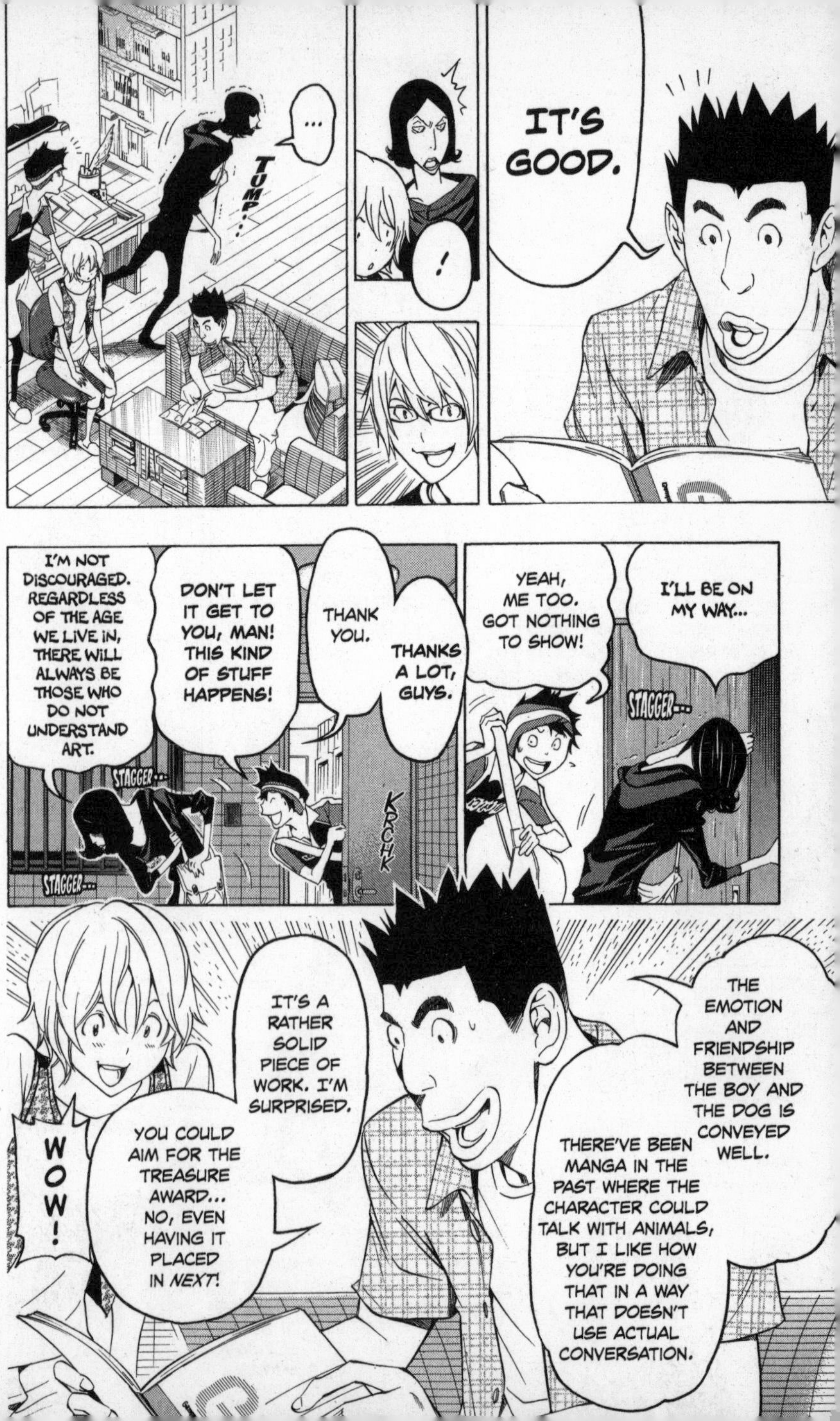
IT'S GOOD.
!
...
TUMP...
I'LL BE ON MY WAY...
YEAH, ME TOO. GOT NOTHING TO SHOW!
STAGGER...
THANKS A LOT, GUYS.
THANK YOU.
DON'T LET IT GET TO YOU, MAN! THIS KIND OF STUFF HAPPENS!
I'M NOT DISCOURAGED. REGARDLESS OF THE AGE WE LIVE IN, THERE WILL ALWAYS BE THOSE WHO DO NOT UNDERSTAND ART.
KRCHK
STAGGER...
STAGGER...
THE EMOTION AND FRIENDSHIP BETWEEN THE BOY AND THE DOG IS CONVEYED WELL.
THERE'VE BEEN MANGA IN THE PAST WHERE THE CHARACTER COULD TALK WITH ANIMALS, BUT I LIKE HOW YOU'RE DOING THAT IN A WAY THAT DOESN'T USE ACTUAL CONVERSATION.
IT'S A RATHER SOLID PIECE OF WORK. I'M SURPRISED.
YOU COULD AIM FOR THE TREASURE AWARD... NO, EVEN HAVING IT PLACED IN *NEXT*!
WOW!

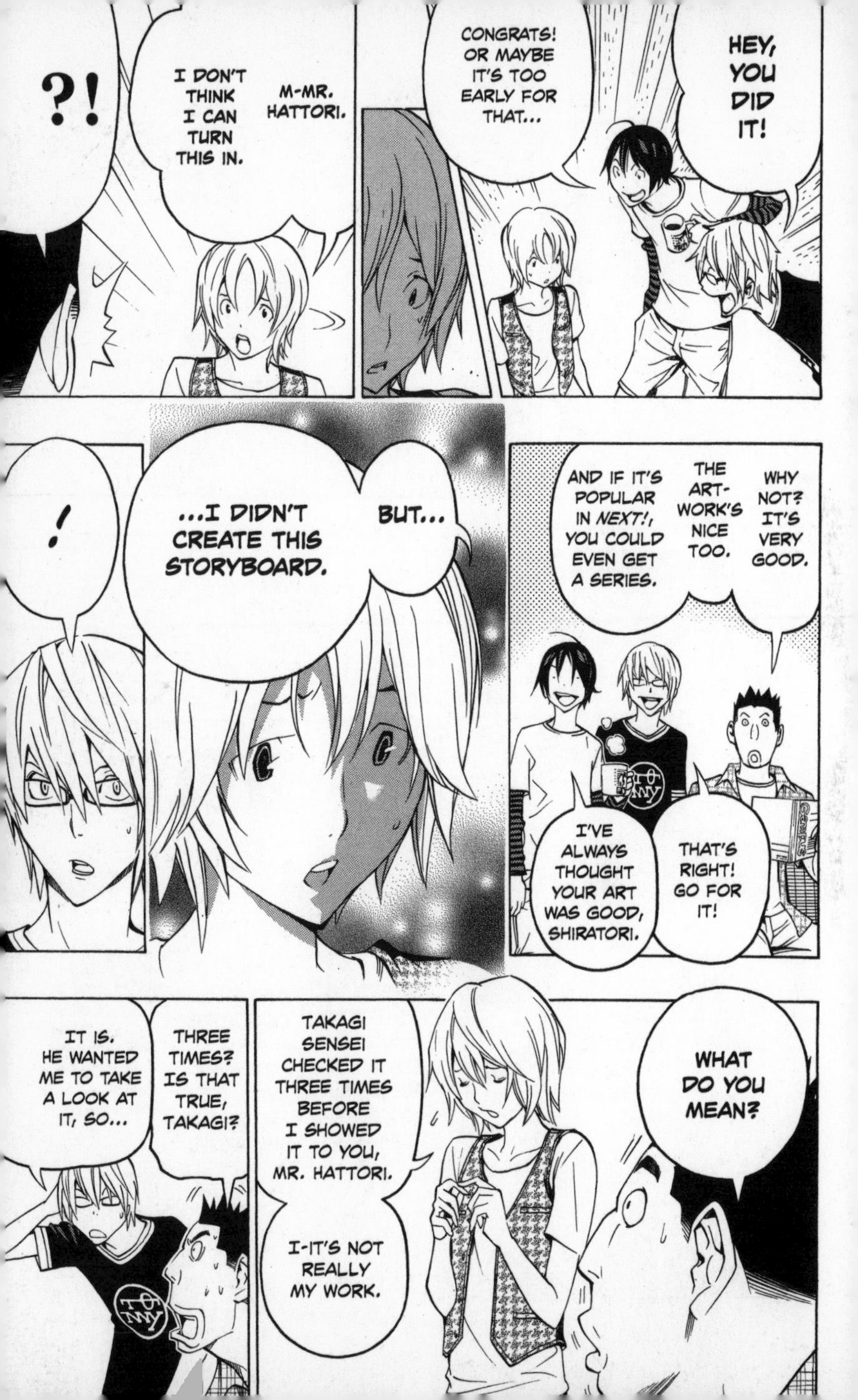
HEY, YOU DID IT!
CONGRATS! OR MAYBE IT'S TOO EARLY FOR THAT...
M-MR. HATTORI.
I DON'T THINK I CAN TURN THIS IN.
?!
WHY NOT? IT'S VERY GOOD.
THE ART-WORK'S NICE TOO.
AND IF IT'S POPULAR IN *NEXT!*, YOU COULD EVEN GET A SERIES.
THAT'S RIGHT! GO FOR IT!
I'VE ALWAYS THOUGHT YOUR ART WAS GOOD, SHIRATORI.
BUT...
...I DIDN'T CREATE THIS STORYBOARD.
!
WHAT DO YOU MEAN?
TAKAGI SENSEI CHECKED IT THREE TIMES BEFORE I SHOWED IT TO YOU, MR. HATTORI.
I-IT'S NOT REALLY MY WORK.
THREE TIMES? IS THAT TRUE, TAKAGI?
IT IS. HE WANTED ME TO TAKE A LOOK AT IT, SO...

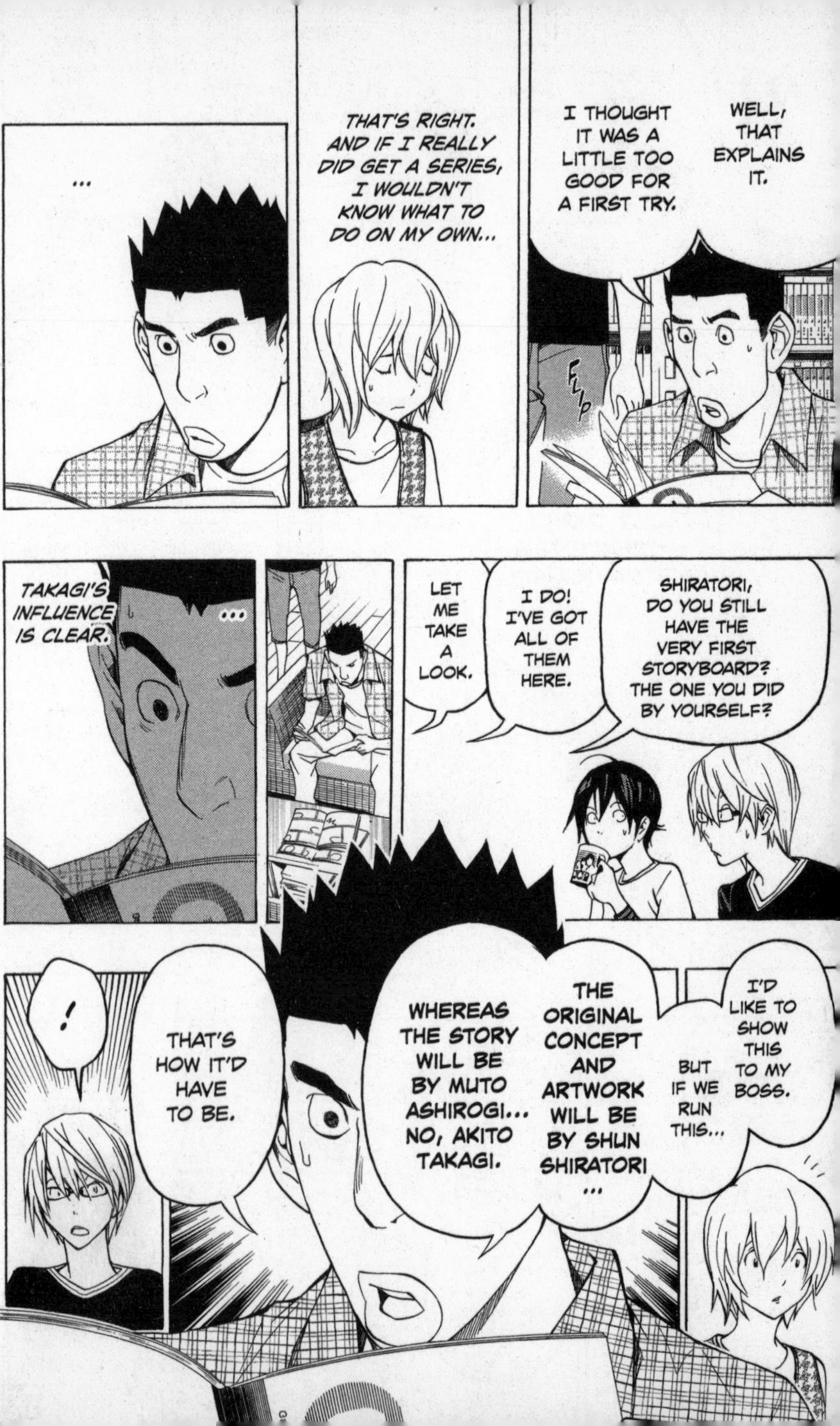
WELL, THAT EXPLAINS IT.
I THOUGHT IT WAS A LITTLE TOO GOOD FOR A FIRST TRY.
FLIP
THAT'S RIGHT. AND IF I REALLY DID GET A SERIES, I WOULDN'T KNOW WHAT TO DO ON MY OWN...
...
SHIRATORI, DO YOU STILL HAVE THE VERY FIRST STORYBOARD? THE ONE YOU DID BY YOURSELF?
I DO! I'VE GOT ALL OF THEM HERE.
LET ME TAKE A LOOK.
...
TAKAGI'S INFLUENCE IS CLEAR.
I'D LIKE TO SHOW THIS TO MY BOSS.
BUT IF WE RUN THIS...
THE ORIGINAL CONCEPT AND ARTWORK WILL BE BY SHUN SHIRATORI...
WHEREAS THE STORY WILL BE BY MUTO ASHIROGI... NO, AKITO TAKAGI.
THAT'S HOW IT'D HAVE TO BE.
!

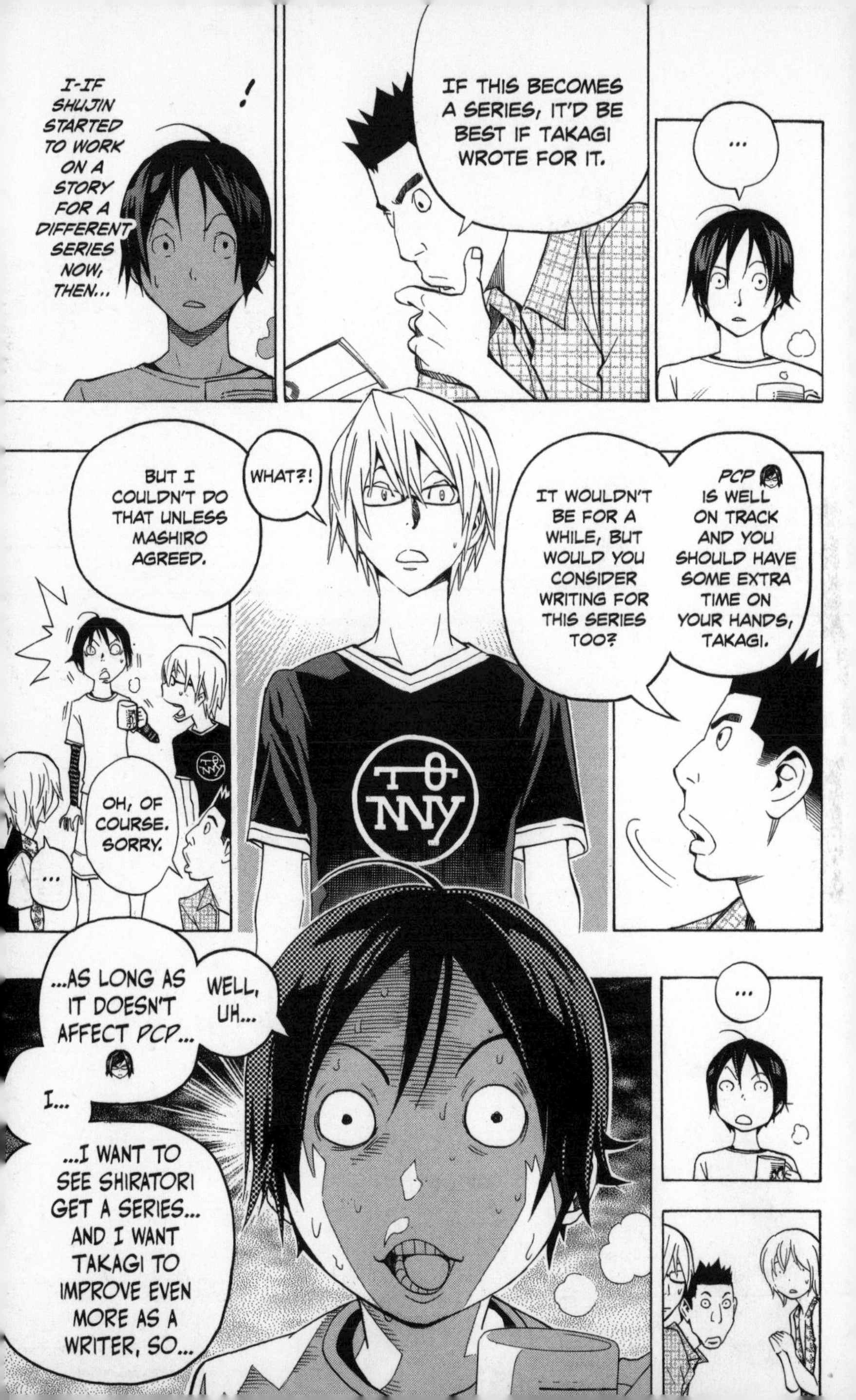
...
IF THIS BECOMES A SERIES, IT'D BE BEST IF TAKAGI WROTE FOR IT.
!
I-IF SHUJIN STARTED TO WORK ON A STORY FOR A DIFFERENT SERIES NOW, THEN...
PCP IS WELL ON TRACK AND YOU SHOULD HAVE SOME EXTRA TIME ON YOUR HANDS, TAKAGI.
IT WOULDN'T BE FOR A WHILE, BUT WOULD YOU CONSIDER WRITING FOR THIS SERIES TOO?
WHAT?!
BUT I COULDN'T DO THAT UNLESS MASHIRO AGREED.
OH, OF COURSE. SORRY.
...
...
WELL, UH...
...AS LONG AS IT DOESN'T AFFECT PCP...
I...
...I WANT TO SEE SHIRATORI GET A SERIES... AND I WANT TAKAGI TO IMPROVE EVEN MORE AS A WRITER, SO...

OHBA'S STORYBOARD

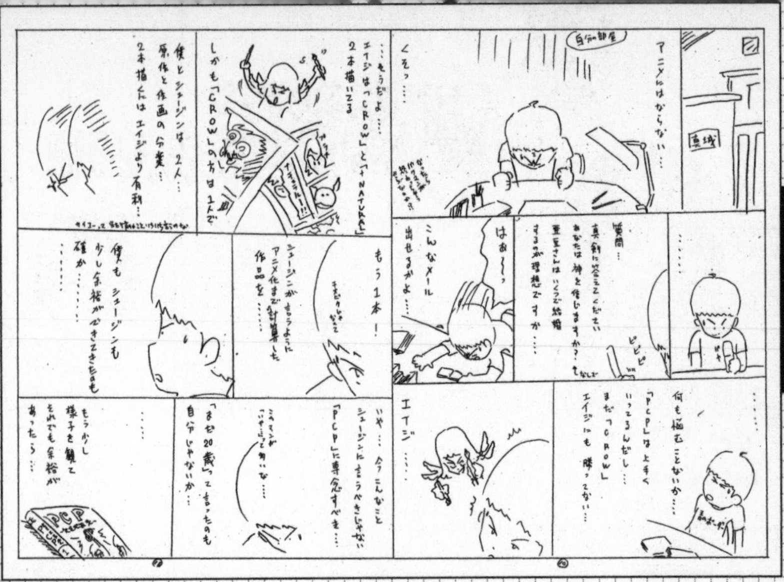
自分部屋
アニメにはならない…
真城
くそっ…
……
ピピピ
質問… 真剣に答えてください
あなたは神を信じますか？
亜豆さんはいくつで結婚するのが理想ですか…
はぁ～っ
こんなメール出せるかよ…
……
何も悩むことないか…
「PCP」は上手くいってるんだし…
まだ「CROW」エイジにも勝ってない…
エイジ……
…もうだよ… エイジは「CROW」と「+NATURAL」2本描いてる
しかも「CROW」の方は1人で
僕とシュージンは2人… 原作と作画の分業… 2本描くんはエイジより有利…
もう1本！
シュージンがもうように アニメ化まで計算した作品を……
僕もシュージンも少し余裕ができてきたのも
確か……
いや…今こんなことシュージンに言うべきじゃない
「PCP」に専念すべき…
「まだ20歳」って言ったのも自分じゃないか…
……
もう少し様子を観て
それでも余裕があったら…

OBATA'S STORYBOARD

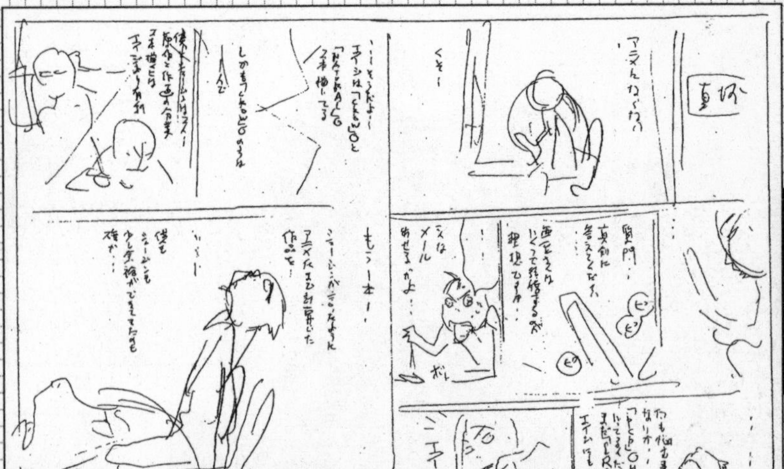

COMPLETE!

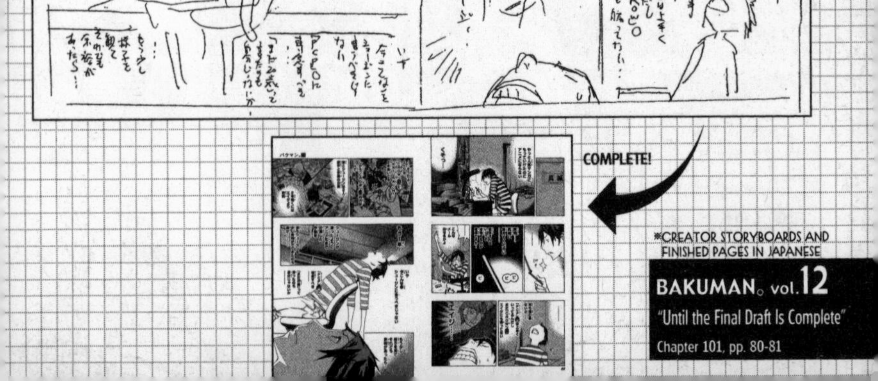

※CREATOR STORYBOARDS AND FINISHED PAGES IN JAPANESE

BAKUMAN。 vol.12

"Until the Final Draft Is Complete"

Chapter 101, pp. 80-81

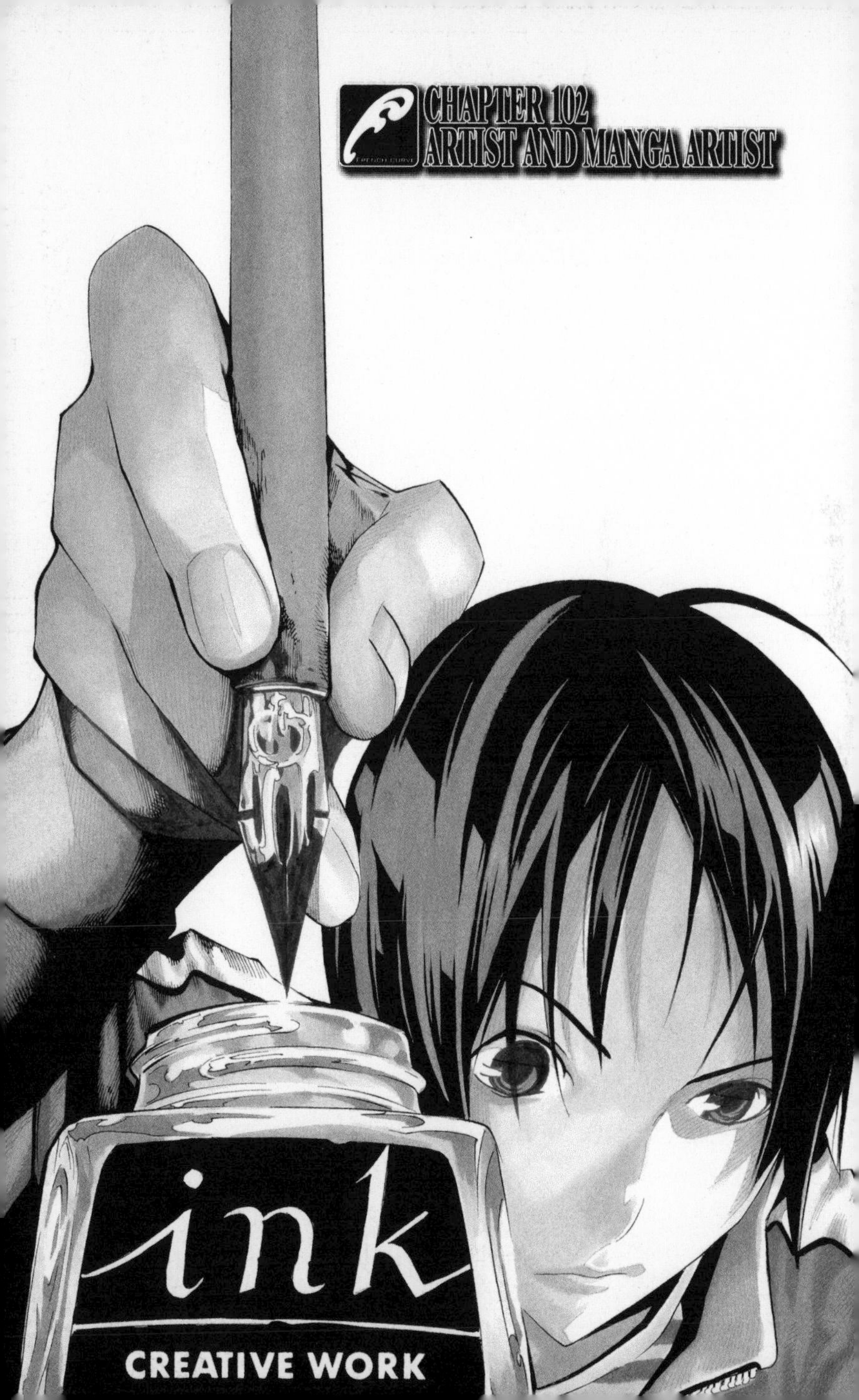
CHAPTER 102
ARTIST AND MANGA ARTIST
ink
CREATIVE WORK

BAKUMAN。

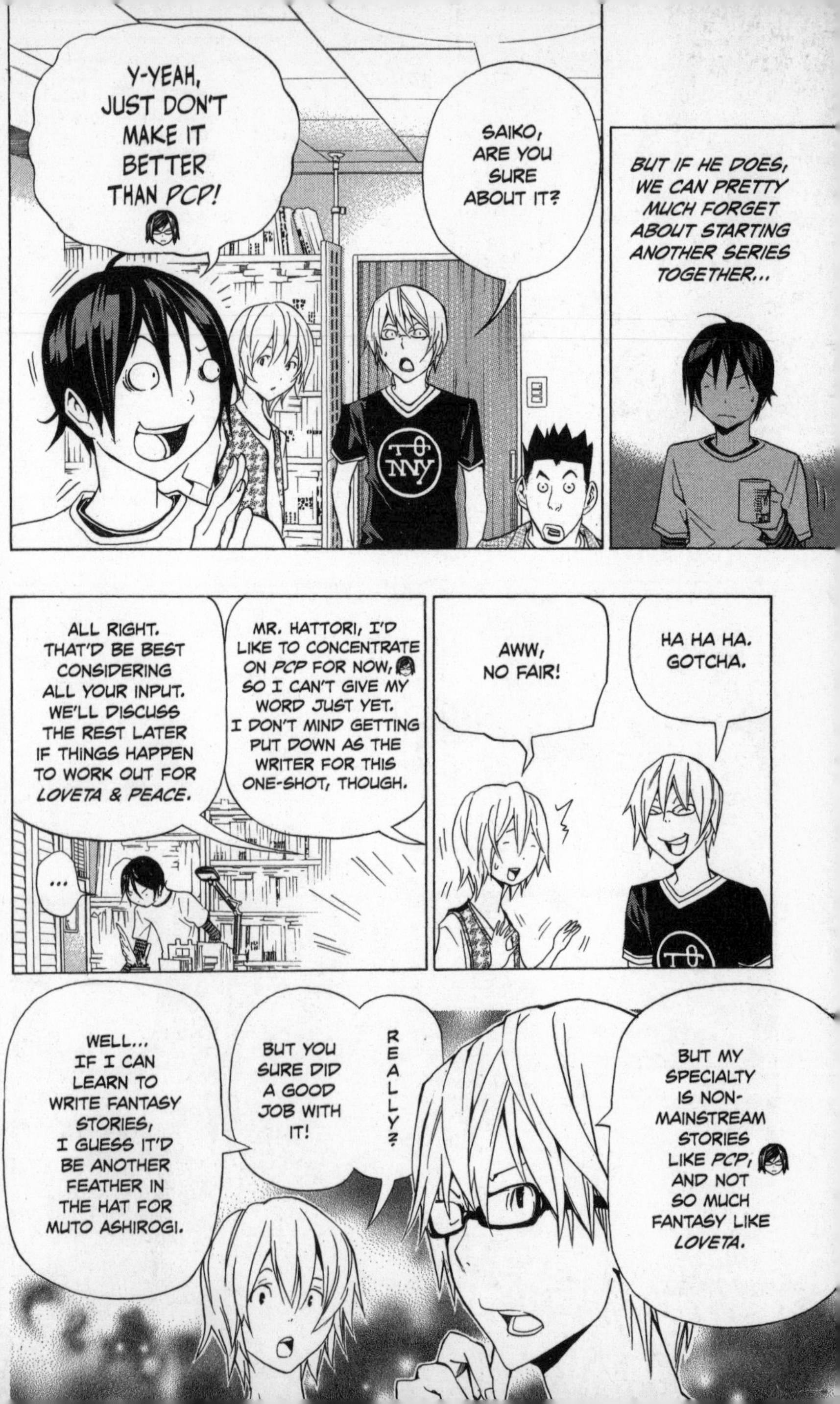
BUT IF HE DOES, WE CAN PRETTY MUCH FORGET ABOUT STARTING ANOTHER SERIES TOGETHER...
SAIKO, ARE YOU SURE ABOUT IT?
Y-YEAH, JUST DON'T MAKE IT BETTER THAN PCP!
HA HA HA. GOTCHA.
AWW, NO FAIR!
MR. HATTORI, I'D LIKE TO CONCENTRATE ON PCP FOR NOW, SO I CAN'T GIVE MY WORD JUST YET. I DON'T MIND GETTING PUT DOWN AS THE WRITER FOR THIS ONE-SHOT, THOUGH.
ALL RIGHT. THAT'D BE BEST CONSIDERING ALL YOUR INPUT. WE'LL DISCUSS THE REST LATER IF THINGS HAPPEN TO WORK OUT FOR LOVETA & PEACE.
...
BUT MY SPECIALTY IS NON-MAINSTREAM STORIES LIKE PCP, AND NOT SO MUCH FANTASY LIKE LOVETA.
REALLY?
BUT YOU SURE DID A GOOD JOB WITH IT!
WELL... IF I CAN LEARN TO WRITE FANTASY STORIES, I GUESS IT'D BE ANOTHER FEATHER IN THE HAT FOR MUTO ASHIROGI.

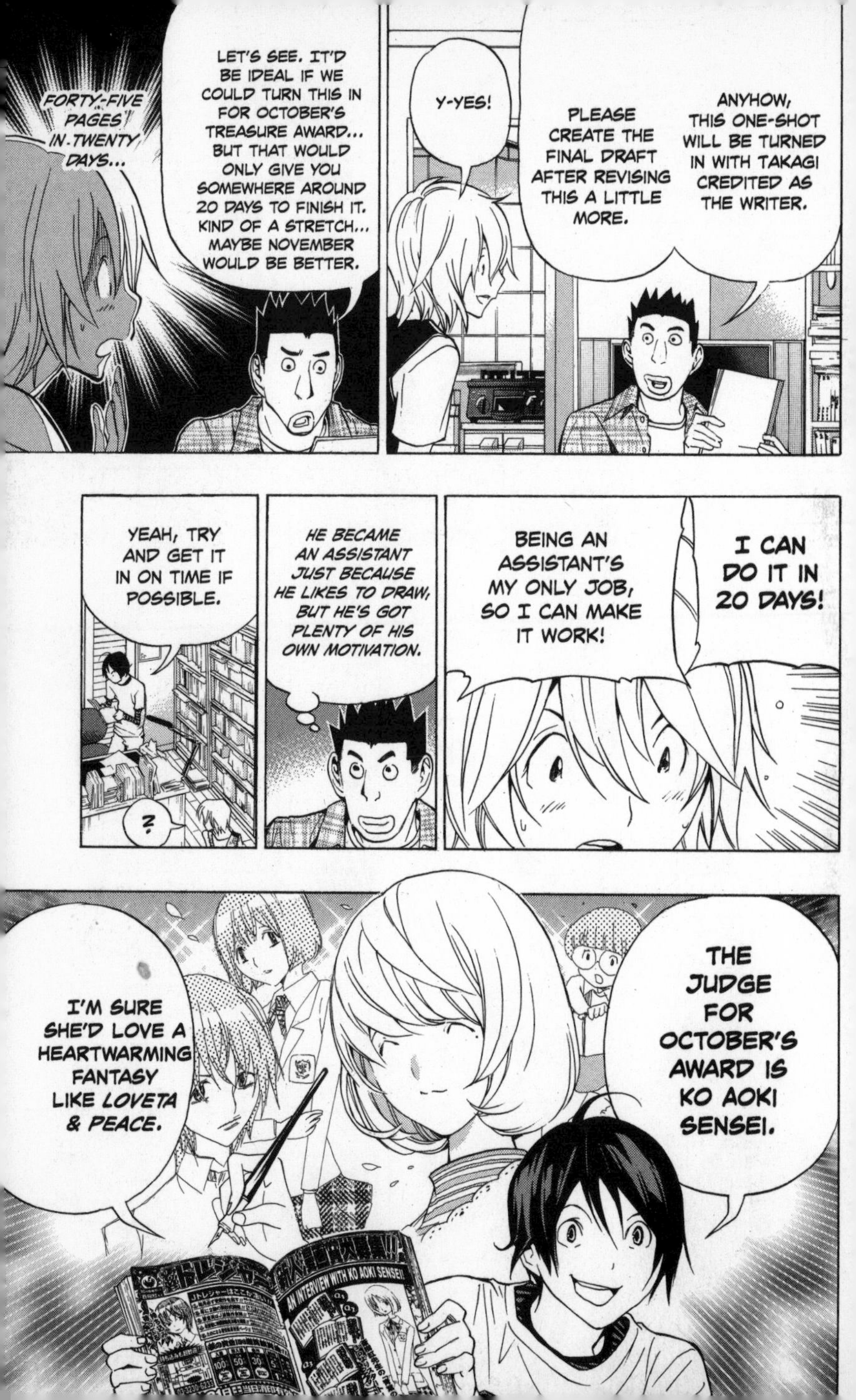
ANYHOW, THIS ONE-SHOT WILL BE TURNED IN WITH TAKAGI CREDITED AS THE WRITER.
PLEASE CREATE THE FINAL DRAFT AFTER REVISING THIS A LITTLE MORE.
Y-YES!
LET'S SEE. IT'D BE IDEAL IF WE COULD TURN THIS IN FOR OCTOBER'S TREASURE AWARD... BUT THAT WOULD ONLY GIVE YOU SOMEWHERE AROUND 20 DAYS TO FINISH IT. KIND OF A STRETCH... MAYBE NOVEMBER WOULD BE BETTER.
FORTY-FIVE PAGES IN TWENTY DAYS...
I CAN DO IT IN 20 DAYS!
BEING AN ASSISTANT'S MY ONLY JOB, SO I CAN MAKE IT WORK!
HE BECAME AN ASSISTANT JUST BECAUSE HE LIKES TO DRAW, BUT HE'S GOT PLENTY OF HIS OWN MOTIVATION.
YEAH, TRY AND GET IT IN ON TIME IF POSSIBLE.
?
THE JUDGE FOR OCTOBER'S AWARD IS KO AOKI SENSEI.
I'M SURE SHE'D LOVE A HEARTWARMING FANTASY LIKE LOVETA & PEACE.
AN INTERVIEW WITH KO AOKI SENSEI!

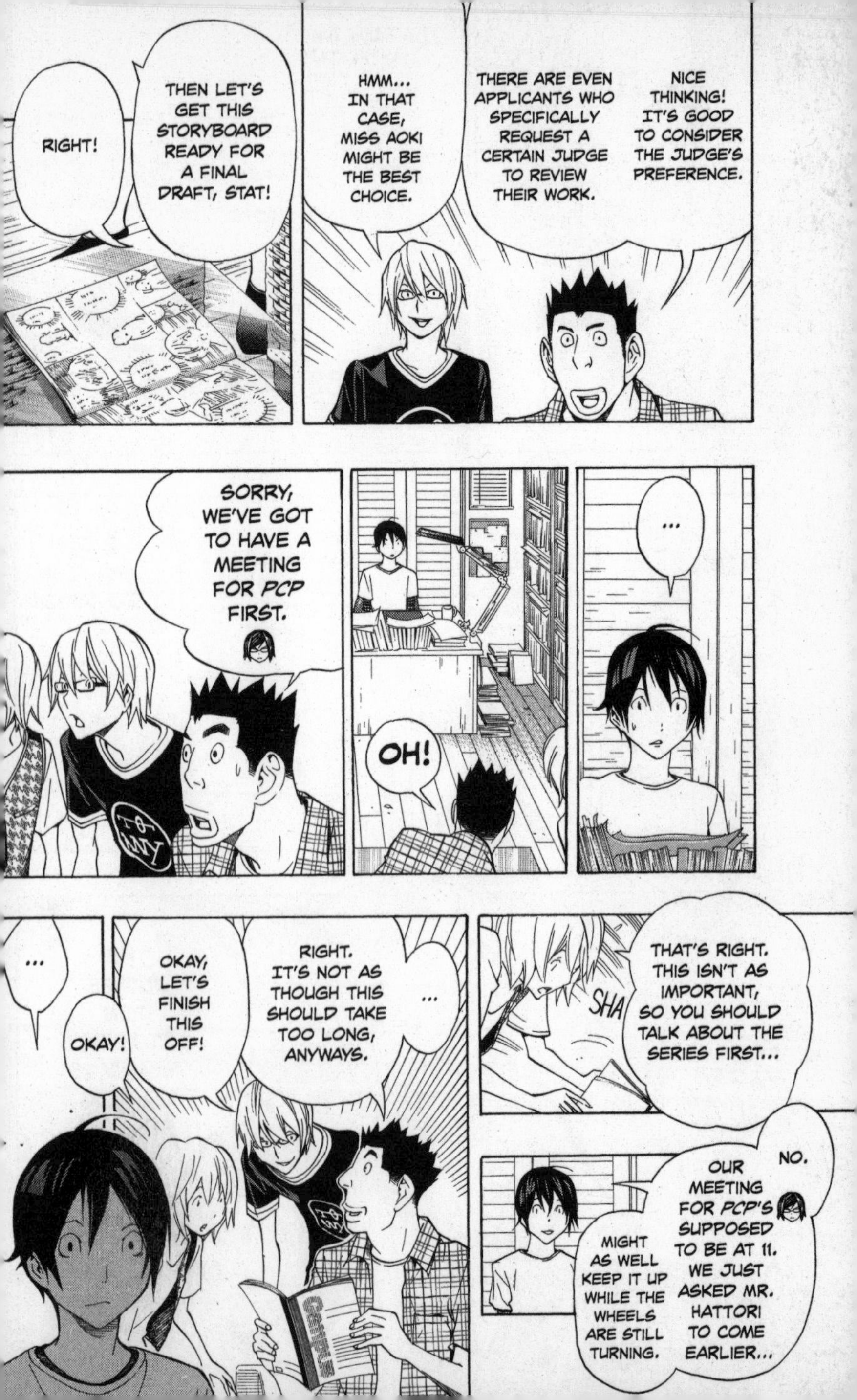
NICE THINKING! IT'S GOOD TO CONSIDER THE JUDGE'S PREFERENCE.
THERE ARE EVEN APPLICANTS WHO SPECIFICALLY REQUEST A CERTAIN JUDGE TO REVIEW THEIR WORK.
HMM... IN THAT CASE, MISS AOKI MIGHT BE THE BEST CHOICE.
THEN LET'S GET THIS STORYBOARD READY FOR A FINAL DRAFT, STAT!
RIGHT!
...
OH!
SORRY, WE'VE GOT TO HAVE A MEETING FOR *PCP* FIRST.
SHA
THAT'S RIGHT. THIS ISN'T AS IMPORTANT, SO YOU SHOULD TALK ABOUT THE SERIES FIRST...
NO.
OUR MEETING FOR *PCP*'S SUPPOSED TO BE AT 11. WE JUST ASKED MR. HATTORI TO COME EARLIER...
MIGHT AS WELL KEEP IT UP WHILE THE WHEELS ARE STILL TURNING.
...
RIGHT. IT'S NOT AS THOUGH THIS SHOULD TAKE TOO LONG, ANYWAYS.
OKAY, LET'S FINISH THIS OFF!
OKAY!
...

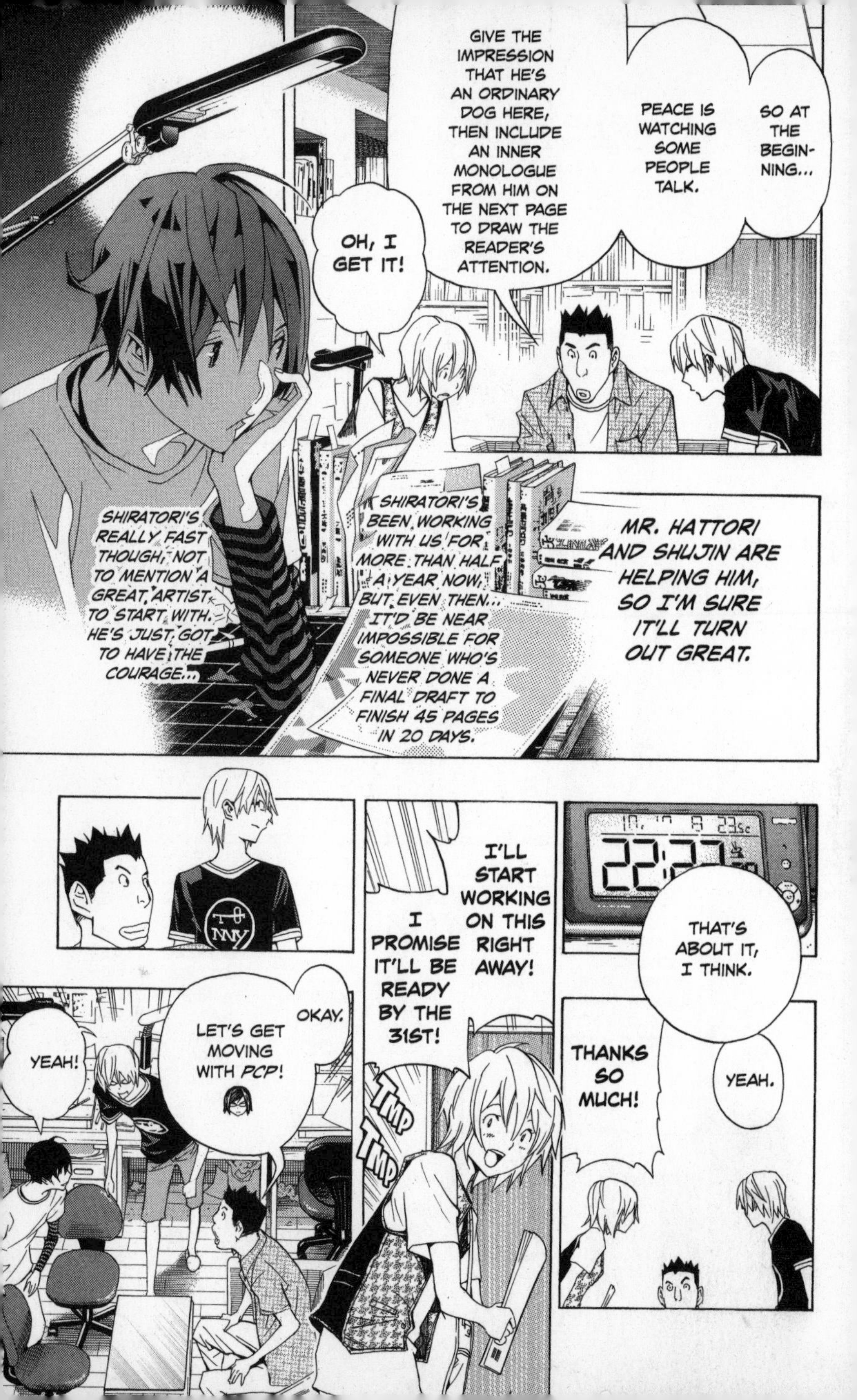
SO AT THE BEGINNING...
PEACE IS WATCHING SOME PEOPLE TALK.
GIVE THE IMPRESSION THAT HE'S AN ORDINARY DOG HERE, THEN INCLUDE AN INNER MONOLOGUE FROM HIM ON THE NEXT PAGE TO DRAW THE READER'S ATTENTION.
OH, I GET IT!
MR. HATTORI AND SHUJIN ARE HELPING HIM, SO I'M SURE IT'LL TURN OUT GREAT.
SHIRATORI'S BEEN WORKING WITH US FOR MORE THAN HALF A YEAR NOW, BUT EVEN THEN... IT'D BE NEAR IMPOSSIBLE FOR SOMEONE WHO'S NEVER DONE A FINAL DRAFT TO FINISH 45 PAGES IN 20 DAYS.
SHIRATORI'S REALLY FAST THOUGH, NOT TO MENTION A GREAT ARTIST TO START WITH. HE'S JUST GOT TO HAVE THE COURAGE...
THAT'S ABOUT IT, I THINK.
YEAH.
THANKS SO MUCH!
I'LL START WORKING ON THIS RIGHT AWAY!
I PROMISE IT'LL BE READY BY THE 31ST!
TMP
TMP
OKAY.
LET'S GET MOVING WITH PCP!
YEAH!

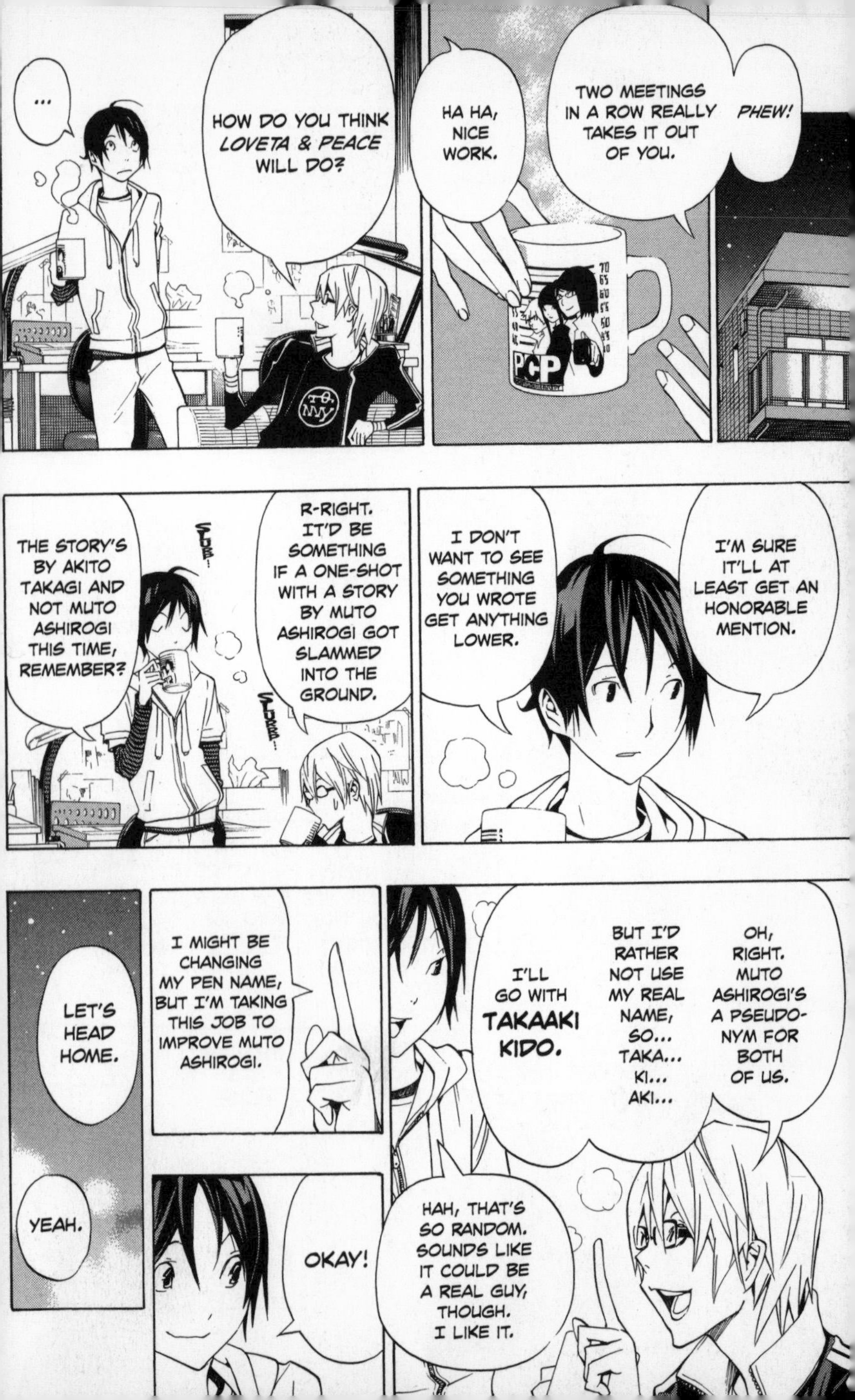
PHEW!
TWO MEETINGS IN A ROW REALLY TAKES IT OUT OF YOU.
HA HA, NICE WORK.
HOW DO YOU THINK *LOVETA & PEACE* WILL DO?
...
I'M SURE IT'LL AT LEAST GET AN HONORABLE MENTION.
I DON'T WANT TO SEE SOMETHING YOU WROTE GET ANYTHING LOWER.
R-RIGHT. IT'D BE SOMETHING IF A ONE-SHOT WITH A STORY BY MUTO ASHIROGI GOT SLAMMED INTO THE GROUND.
THE STORY'S BY AKITO TAKAGI AND NOT MUTO ASHIROGI THIS TIME, REMEMBER?
OH, RIGHT. MUTO ASHIROGI'S A PSEUDONYM FOR BOTH OF US.
BUT I'D RATHER NOT USE MY REAL NAME, SO... TAKA... KI... AKI...
I'LL GO WITH **TAKAAKI KIDO.**
HAH, THAT'S SO RANDOM. SOUNDS LIKE IT COULD BE A REAL GUY, THOUGH. I LIKE IT.
I MIGHT BE CHANGING MY PEN NAME, BUT I'M TAKING THIS JOB TO IMPROVE MUTO ASHIROGI.
OKAY!
LET'S HEAD HOME.
YEAH.

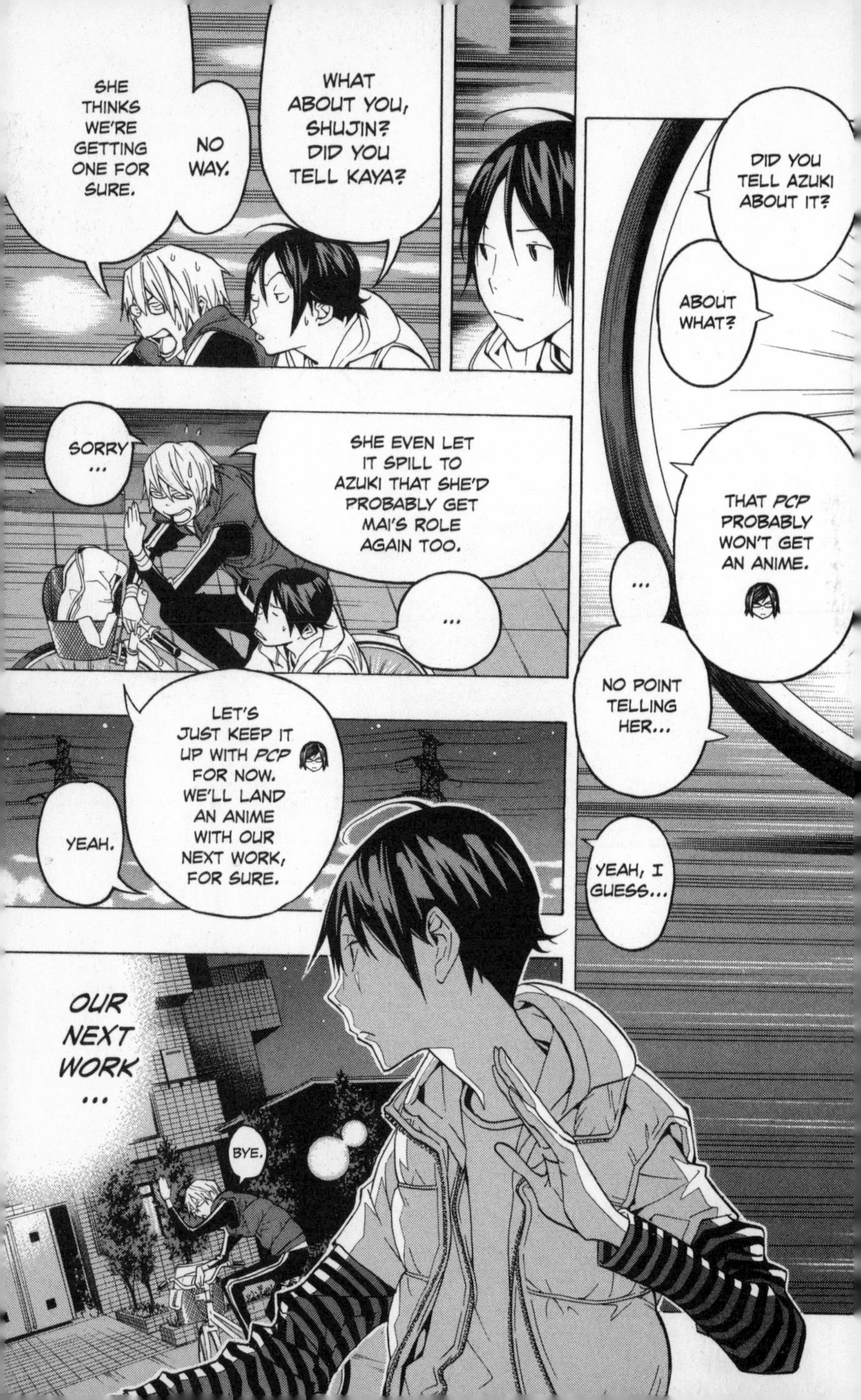
DID YOU TELL AZUKI ABOUT IT?
ABOUT WHAT?
THAT *PCP* PROBABLY WON'T GET AN ANIME.
...
NO POINT TELLING HER...
YEAH, I GUESS...
WHAT ABOUT YOU, SHUJIN? DID YOU TELL KAYA?
NO WAY.
SHE THINKS WE'RE GETTING ONE FOR SURE.
SHE EVEN LET IT SPILL TO AZUKI THAT SHE'D PROBABLY GET MAI'S ROLE AGAIN TOO.
SORRY...
...
LET'S JUST KEEP IT UP WITH *PCP* FOR NOW. WE'LL LAND AN ANIME WITH OUR NEXT WORK, FOR SURE.
YEAH.
OUR NEXT WORK...
BYE.

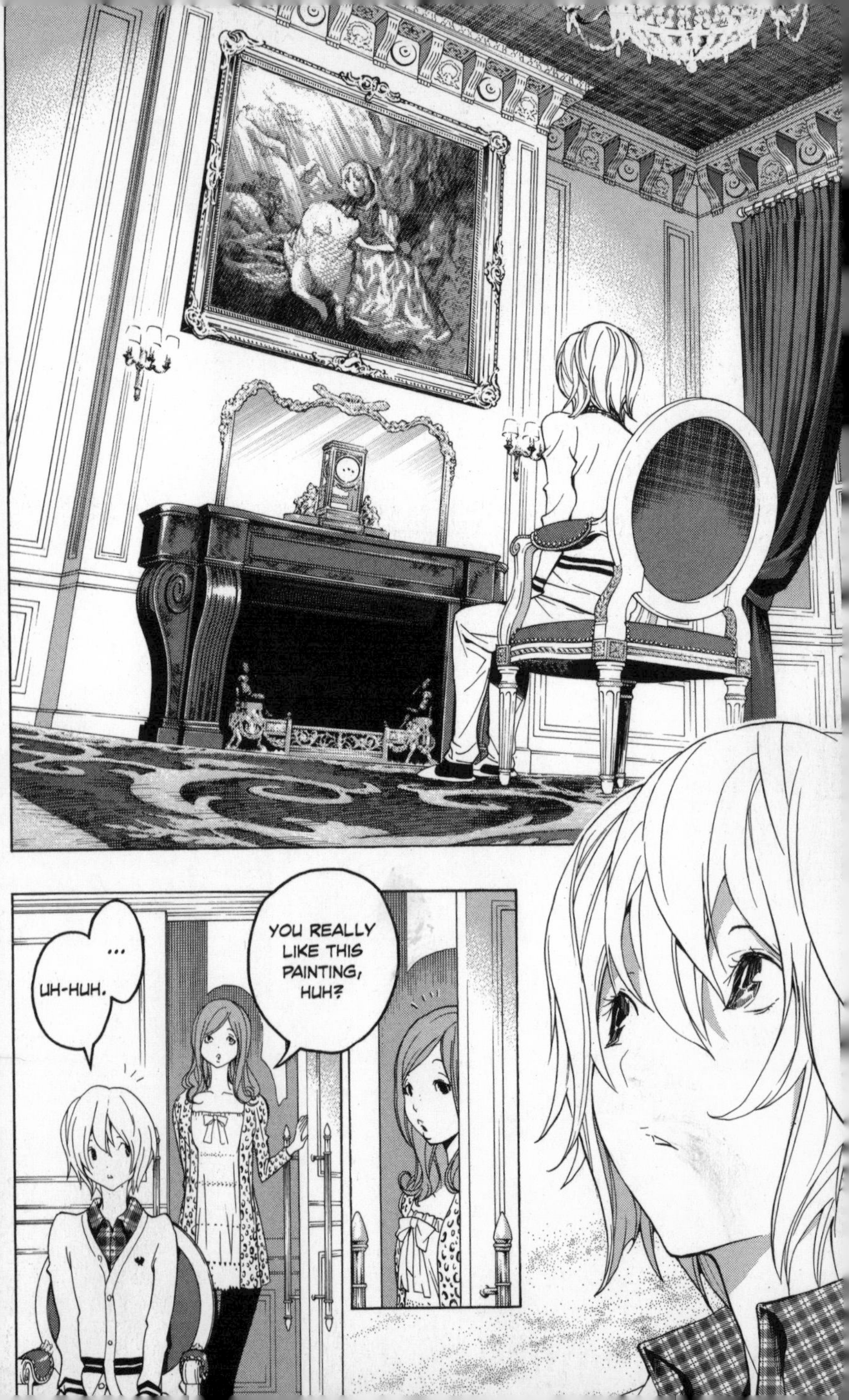
YOU REALLY LIKE THIS PAINTING, HUH?
... UH-HUH.

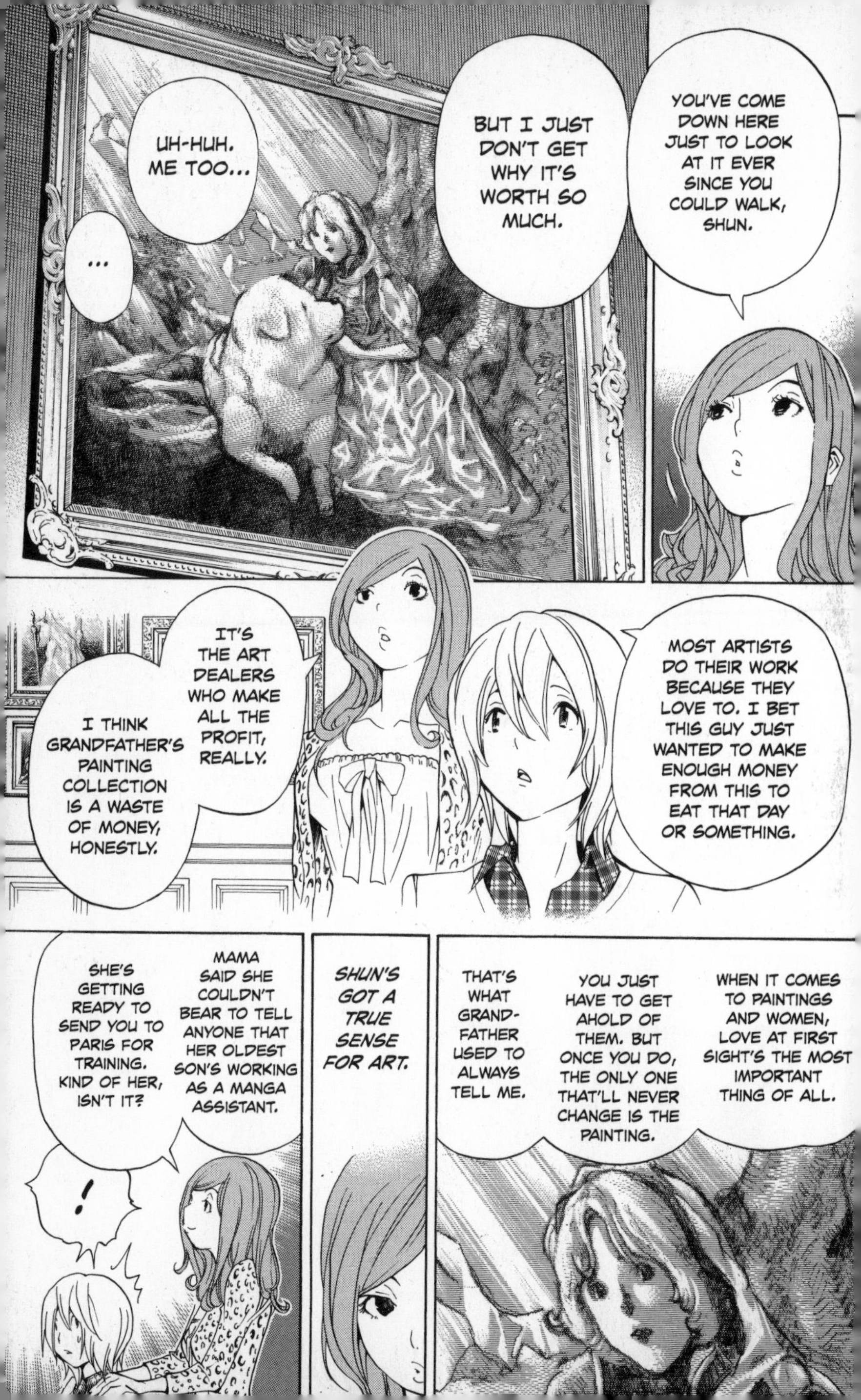
YOU'VE COME DOWN HERE JUST TO LOOK AT IT EVER SINCE YOU COULD WALK, SHUN.
BUT I JUST DON'T GET WHY IT'S WORTH SO MUCH.
UH-HUH. ME TOO...
...
MOST ARTISTS DO THEIR WORK BECAUSE THEY LOVE TO. I BET THIS GUY JUST WANTED TO MAKE ENOUGH MONEY FROM THIS TO EAT THAT DAY OR SOMETHING.
IT'S THE ART DEALERS WHO MAKE ALL THE PROFIT, REALLY.
I THINK GRANDFATHER'S PAINTING COLLECTION IS A WASTE OF MONEY, HONESTLY.
WHEN IT COMES TO PAINTINGS AND WOMEN, LOVE AT FIRST SIGHT'S THE MOST IMPORTANT THING OF ALL.
YOU JUST HAVE TO GET AHOLD OF THEM. BUT ONCE YOU DO, THE ONLY ONE THAT'LL NEVER CHANGE IS THE PAINTING.
THAT'S WHAT GRAND-FATHER USED TO ALWAYS TELL ME.
SHUN'S GOT A TRUE SENSE FOR ART.
MAMA SAID SHE COULDN'T BEAR TO TELL ANYONE THAT HER OLDEST SON'S WORKING AS A MANGA ASSISTANT.
SHE'S GETTING READY TO SEND YOU TO PARIS FOR TRAINING. KIND OF HER, ISN'T IT?
!

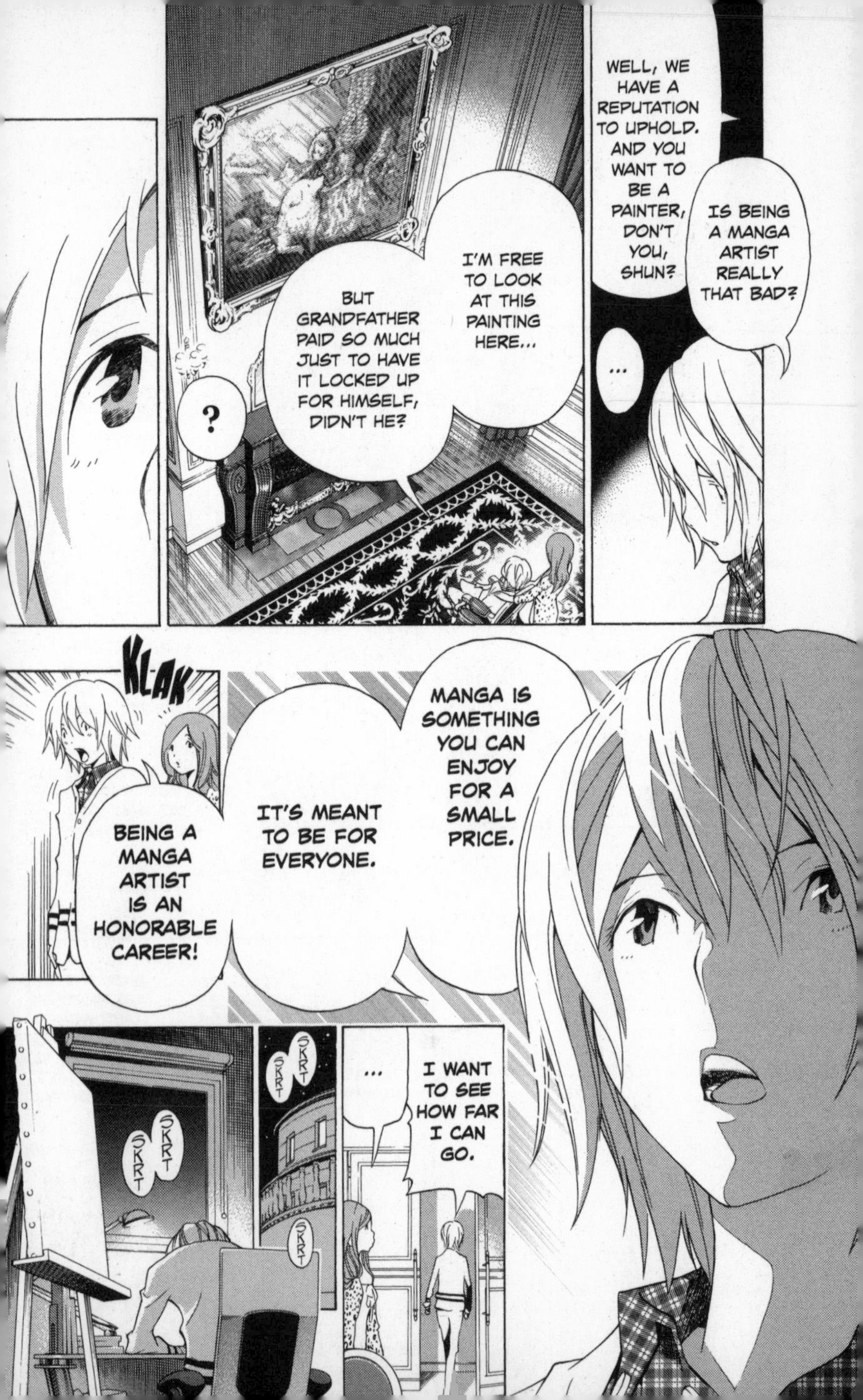
WELL, WE HAVE A REPUTATION TO UPHOLD. AND YOU WANT TO BE A PAINTER, DON'T YOU, SHUN?
IS BEING A MANGA ARTIST REALLY THAT BAD?
...
I'M FREE TO LOOK AT THIS PAINTING HERE...
BUT GRANDFATHER PAID SO MUCH JUST TO HAVE IT LOCKED UP FOR HIMSELF, DIDN'T HE?
?
MANGA IS SOMETHING YOU CAN ENJOY FOR A SMALL PRICE.
IT'S MEANT TO BE FOR EVERYONE.
BEING A MANGA ARTIST IS AN HONORABLE CAREER!
KLAK
I WANT TO SEE HOW FAR I CAN GO.
...
SKRT SKRT
SKRT
SKRT SKRT

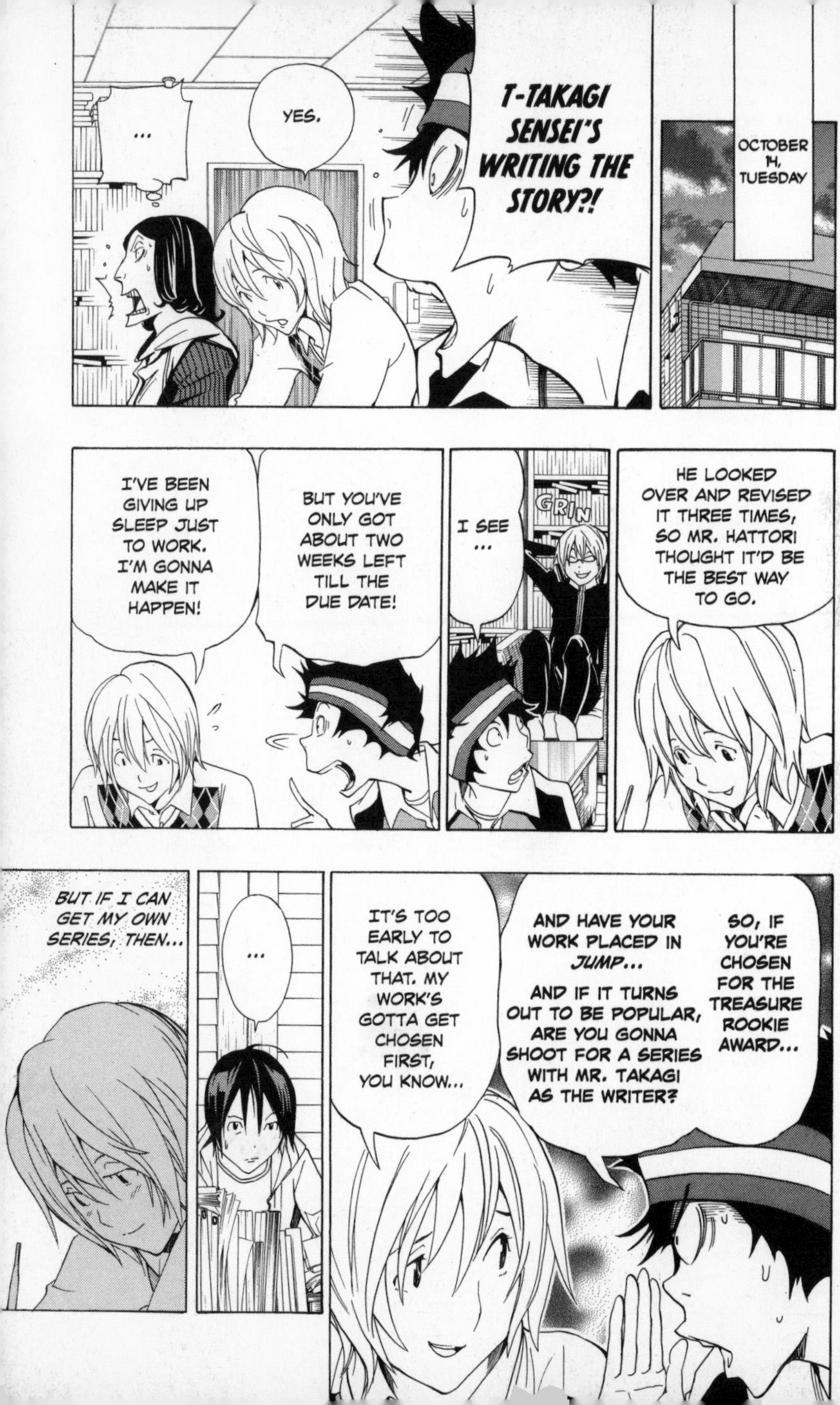
OCTOBER 14, TUESDAY
T-TAKAGI SENSEI'S WRITING THE STORY?!
YES.
...
HE LOOKED OVER AND REVISED IT THREE TIMES, SO MR. HATTORI THOUGHT IT'D BE THE BEST WAY TO GO.
GRIN
I SEE ...
BUT YOU'VE ONLY GOT ABOUT TWO WEEKS LEFT TILL THE DUE DATE!
I'VE BEEN GIVING UP SLEEP JUST TO WORK. I'M GONNA MAKE IT HAPPEN!
SO, IF YOU'RE CHOSEN FOR THE TREASURE ROOKIE AWARD...
AND HAVE YOUR WORK PLACED IN *JUMP*...
AND IF IT TURNS OUT TO BE POPULAR, ARE YOU GONNA SHOOT FOR A SERIES WITH MR. TAKAGI AS THE WRITER?
IT'S TOO EARLY TO TALK ABOUT THAT. MY WORK'S GOTTA GET CHOSEN FIRST, YOU KNOW...
...
BUT IF I CAN GET MY OWN SERIES, THEN...

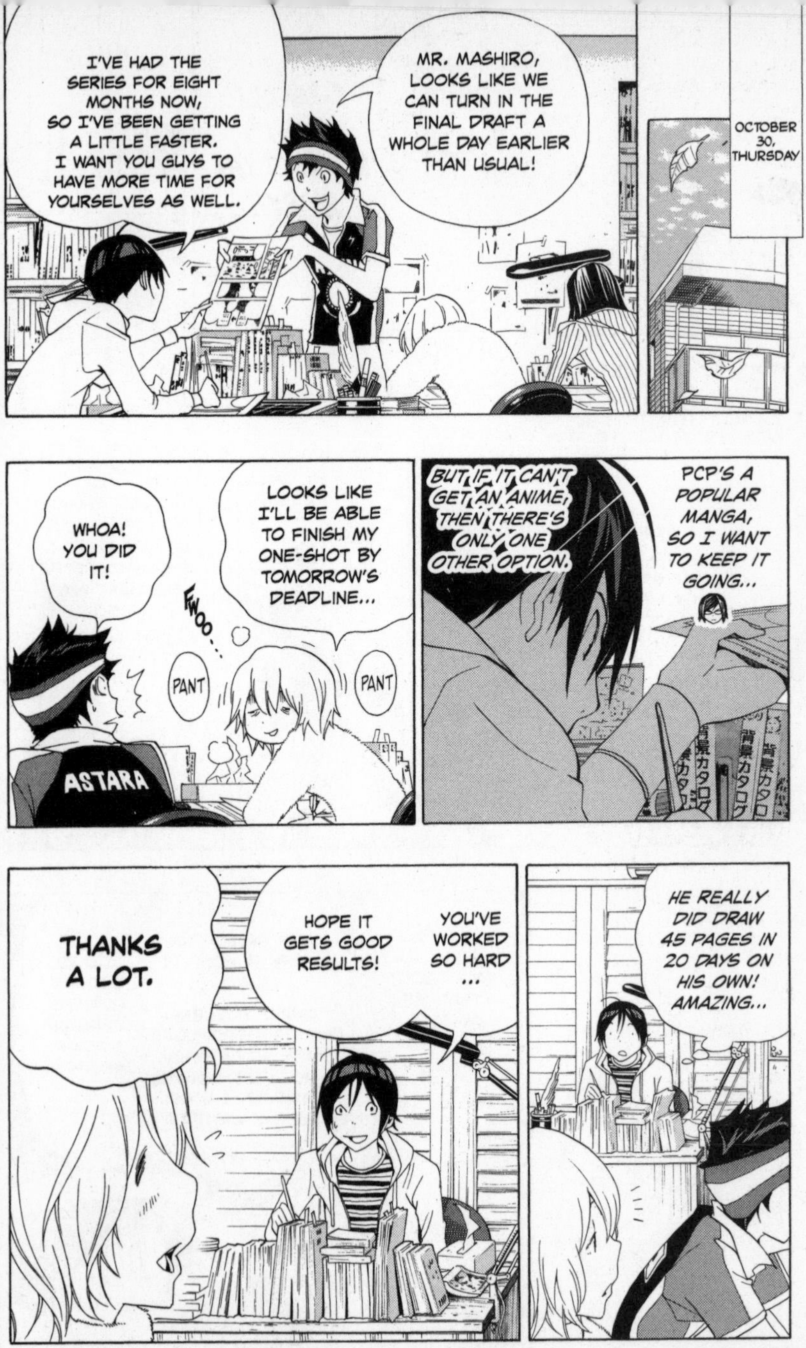
OCTOBER 30, THURSDAY
MR. MASHIRO, LOOKS LIKE WE CAN TURN IN THE FINAL DRAFT A WHOLE DAY EARLIER THAN USUAL!
I'VE HAD THE SERIES FOR EIGHT MONTHS NOW, SO I'VE BEEN GETTING A LITTLE FASTER. I WANT YOU GUYS TO HAVE MORE TIME FOR YOURSELVES AS WELL.
PCP'S A POPULAR MANGA, SO I WANT TO KEEP IT GOING...
BUT IF IT CAN'T GET AN ANIME, THEN THERE'S ONLY ONE OTHER OPTION.
LOOKS LIKE I'LL BE ABLE TO FINISH MY ONE-SHOT BY TOMORROW'S DEADLINE...
FWOO...
PANT
PANT
WHOA! YOU DID IT!
ASTARA
HE REALLY DID DRAW 45 PAGES IN 20 DAYS ON HIS OWN! AMAZING...
YOU'VE WORKED SO HARD...
HOPE IT GETS GOOD RESULTS!
THANKS A LOT.

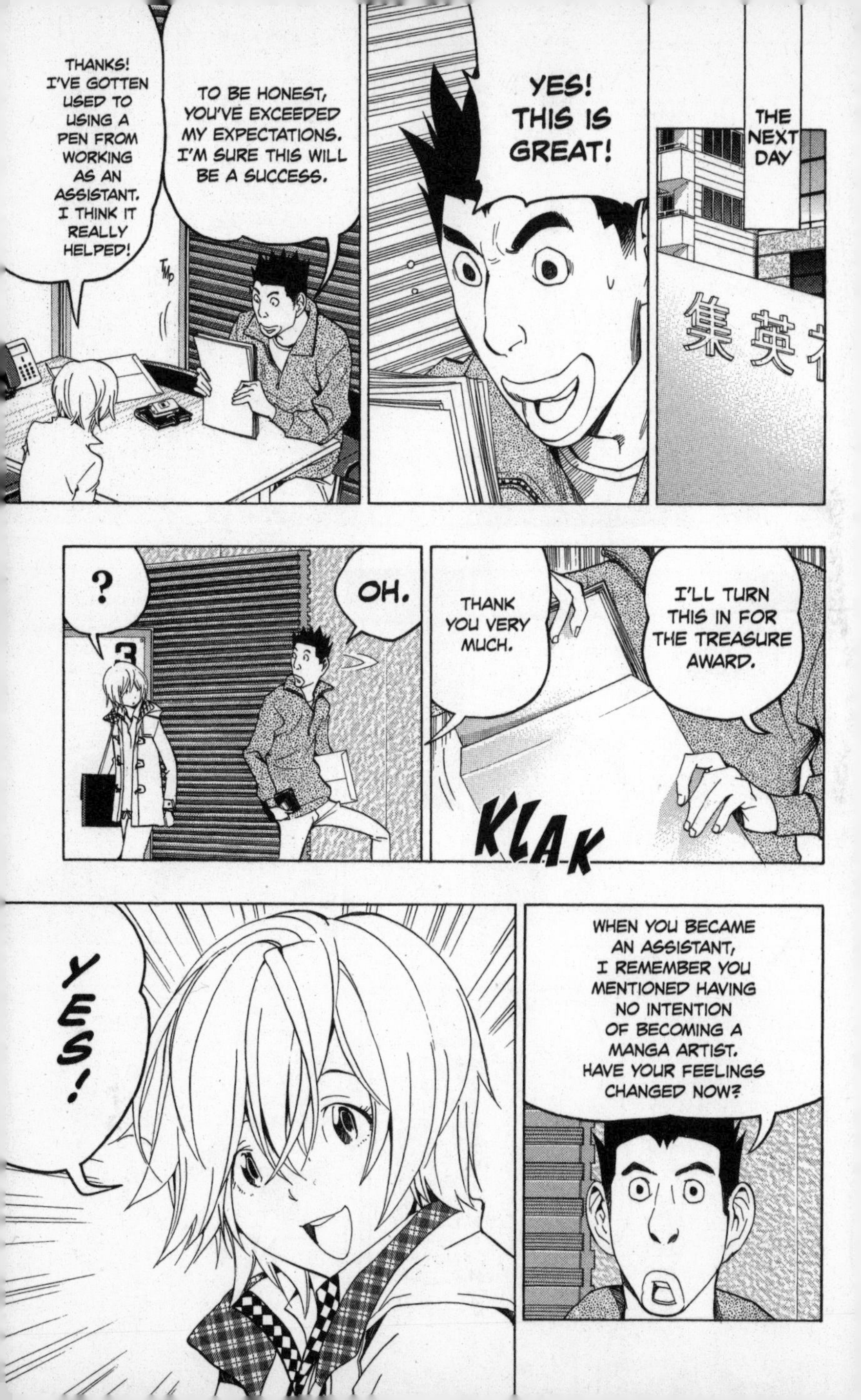
THE NEXT DAY
YES! THIS IS GREAT!
TO BE HONEST, YOU'VE EXCEEDED MY EXPECTATIONS. I'M SURE THIS WILL BE A SUCCESS.
THANKS! I'VE GOTTEN USED TO USING A PEN FROM WORKING AS AN ASSISTANT. I THINK IT REALLY HELPED!
TMP
I'LL TURN THIS IN FOR THE TREASURE AWARD.
THANK YOU VERY MUCH.
KLAK
OH.
?
WHEN YOU BECAME AN ASSISTANT, I REMEMBER YOU MENTIONED HAVING NO INTENTION OF BECOMING A MANGA ARTIST. HAVE YOUR FEELINGS CHANGED NOW?
YES!

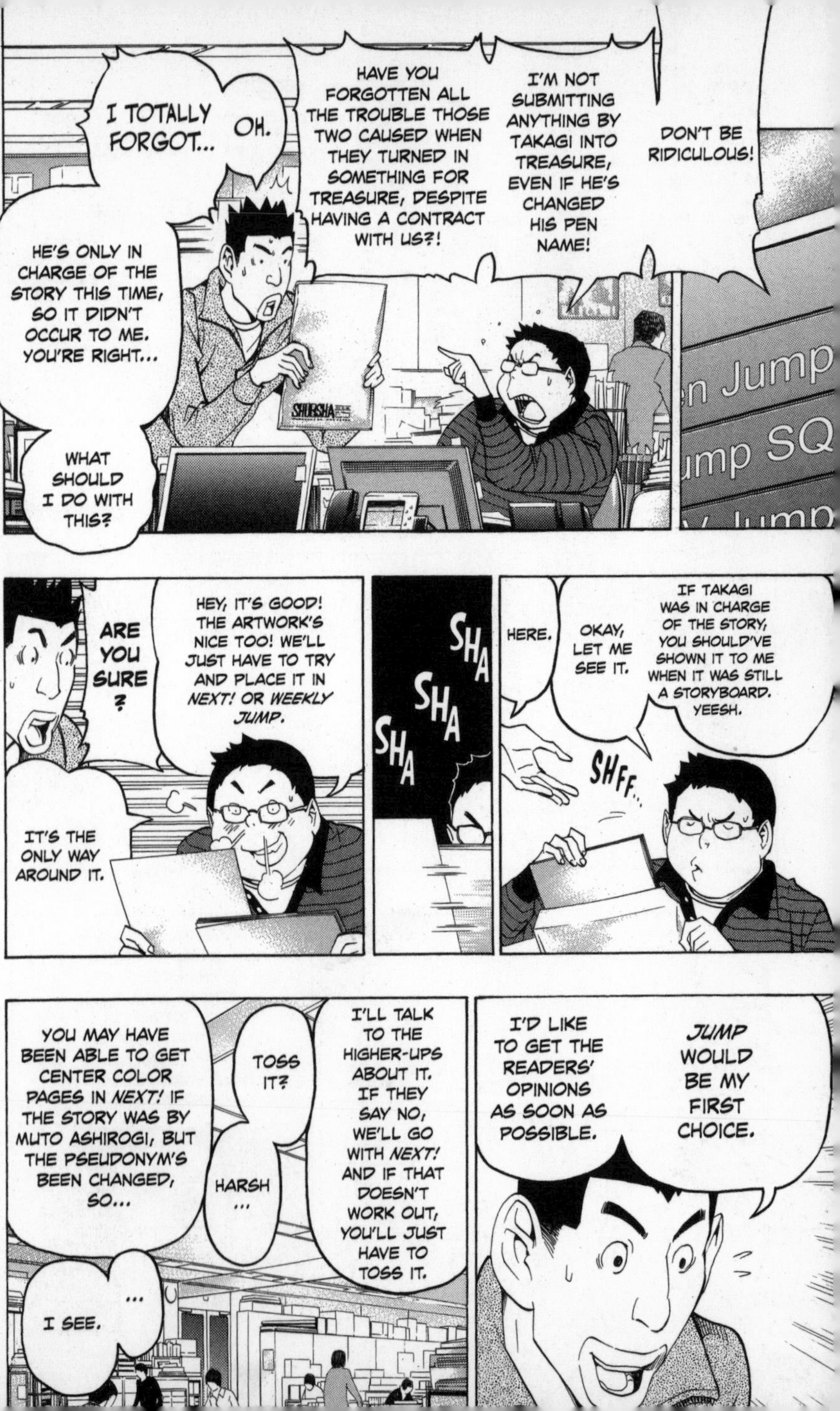
DON'T BE RIDICULOUS!
I'M NOT SUBMITTING ANYTHING BY TAKAGI INTO TREASURE, EVEN IF HE'S CHANGED HIS PEN NAME!
HAVE YOU FORGOTTEN ALL THE TROUBLE THOSE TWO CAUSED WHEN THEY TURNED IN SOMETHING FOR TREASURE, DESPITE HAVING A CONTRACT WITH US?!
OH.
I TOTALLY FORGOT...
HE'S ONLY IN CHARGE OF THE STORY THIS TIME, SO IT DIDN'T OCCUR TO ME. YOU'RE RIGHT...
WHAT SHOULD I DO WITH THIS?
IF TAKAGI WAS IN CHARGE OF THE STORY, YOU SHOULD'VE SHOWN IT TO ME WHEN IT WAS STILL A STORYBOARD. YEESH.
OKAY, LET ME SEE IT.
HERE.
SHFF...
SHA
SHA
SHA
HEY, IT'S GOOD! THE ARTWORK'S NICE TOO! WE'LL JUST HAVE TO TRY AND PLACE IT IN *NEXT!* OR *WEEKLY JUMP*.
ARE YOU SURE?
IT'S THE ONLY WAY AROUND IT.
JUMP WOULD BE MY FIRST CHOICE.
I'D LIKE TO GET THE READERS' OPINIONS AS SOON AS POSSIBLE.
I'LL TALK TO THE HIGHER-UPS ABOUT IT. IF THEY SAY NO, WE'LL GO WITH *NEXT!* AND IF THAT DOESN'T WORK OUT, YOU'LL JUST HAVE TO TOSS IT.
TOSS IT?
YOU MAY HAVE BEEN ABLE TO GET CENTER COLOR PAGES IN *NEXT!* IF THE STORY WAS BY MUTO ASHIROGI, BUT THE PSEUDONYM'S BEEN CHANGED, SO...
HARSH...
... I SEE.

READ THIS WAY

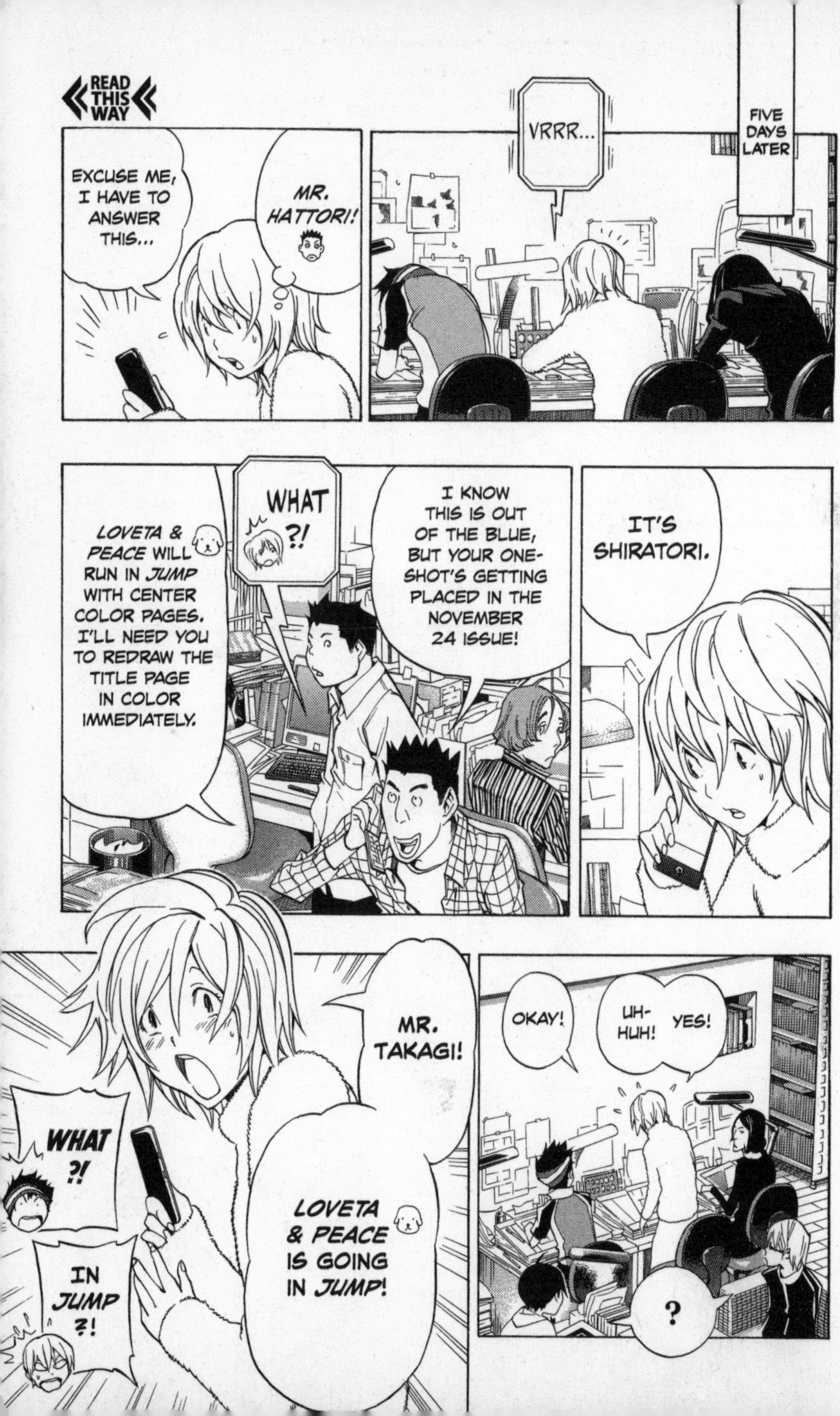
FIVE DAYS LATER
VRRR...
MR. HATTORI!
EXCUSE ME, I HAVE TO ANSWER THIS...
IT'S SHIRATORI.
I KNOW THIS IS OUT OF THE BLUE, BUT YOUR ONE-SHOT'S GETTING PLACED IN THE NOVEMBER 24 ISSUE!
WHAT ?!
LOVETA & PEACE WILL RUN IN *JUMP* WITH CENTER COLOR PAGES. I'LL NEED YOU TO REDRAW THE TITLE PAGE IN COLOR IMMEDIATELY.
YES!
UH-HUH!
OKAY!
?
MR. TAKAGI!
LOVETA & PEACE IS GOING IN *JUMP*!
WHAT ?!
IN *JUMP* ?!

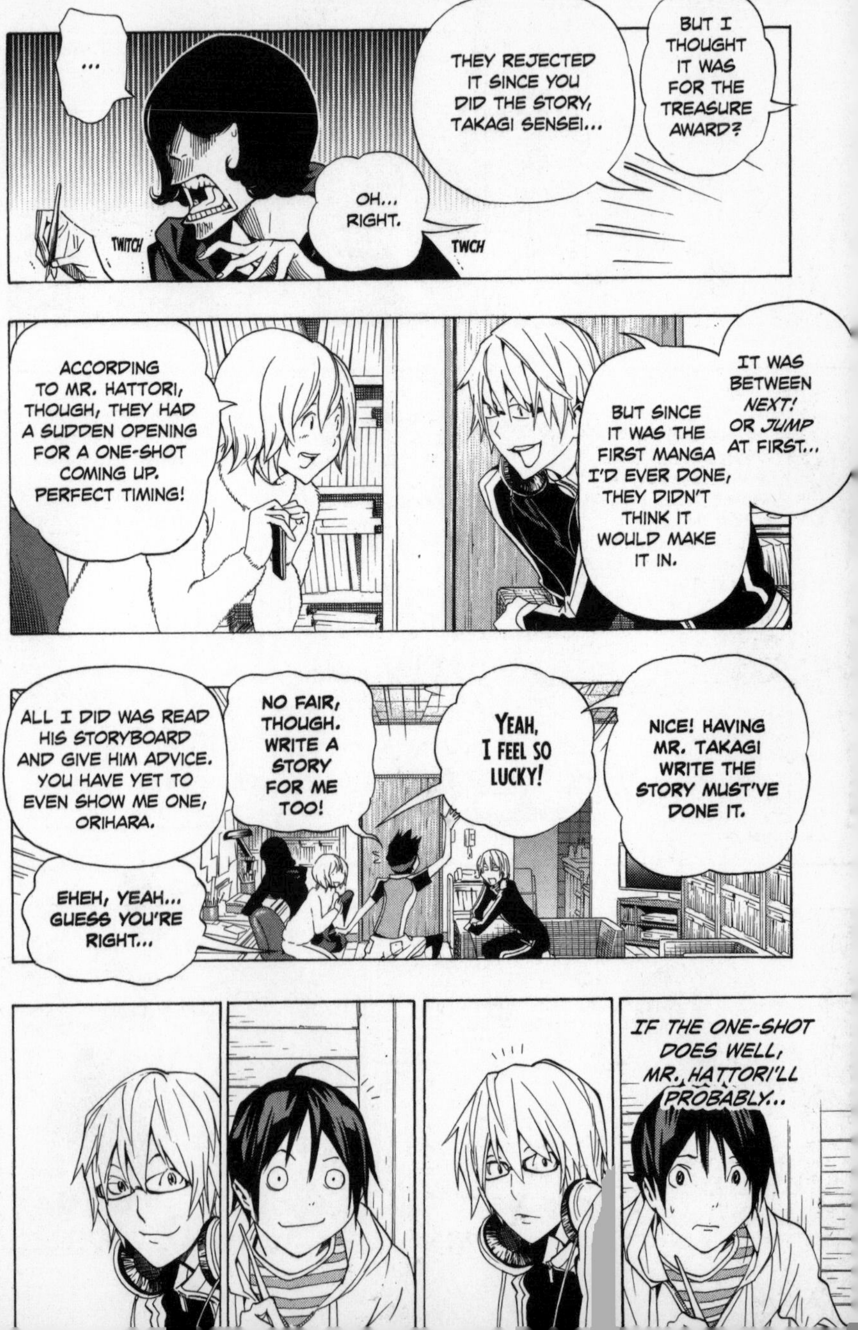
BUT I THOUGHT IT WAS FOR THE TREASURE AWARD?
THEY REJECTED IT SINCE YOU DID THE STORY, TAKAGI SENSEI...
OH... RIGHT.
TWCH
...
TWITCH
IT WAS BETWEEN *NEXT!* OR *JUMP* AT FIRST...
BUT SINCE IT WAS THE FIRST MANGA I'D EVER DONE, THEY DIDN'T THINK IT WOULD MAKE IT IN.
ACCORDING TO MR. HATTORI, THOUGH, THEY HAD A SUDDEN OPENING FOR A ONE-SHOT COMING UP. PERFECT TIMING!
NICE! HAVING MR. TAKAGI WRITE THE STORY MUST'VE DONE IT.
YEAH, I FEEL SO LUCKY!
NO FAIR, THOUGH. WRITE A STORY FOR ME TOO!
ALL I DID WAS READ HIS STORYBOARD AND GIVE HIM ADVICE. YOU HAVE YET TO EVEN SHOW ME ONE, ORIHARA.
EHEH, YEAH... GUESS YOU'RE RIGHT...
IF THE ONE-SHOT DOES WELL, MR. HATTORI'LL PROBABLY...

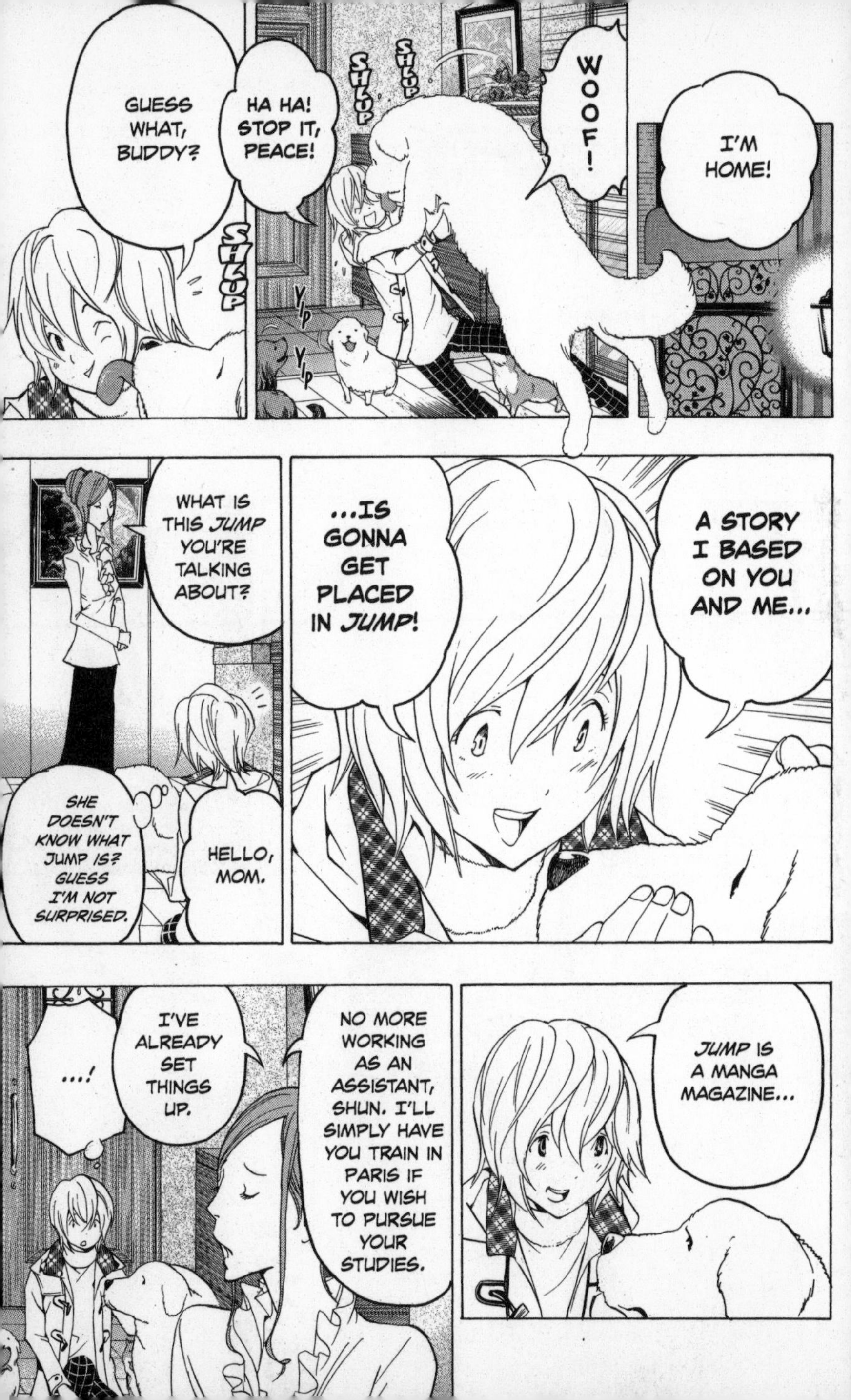

I'M HOME!
WOOF!
SHLUP
SHLUP
HA HA! STOP IT, PEACE!
SHLUP
YIP
YIP
GUESS WHAT, BUDDY?
A STORY I BASED ON YOU AND ME...
...IS GONNA GET PLACED IN *JUMP*!
WHAT IS THIS *JUMP* YOU'RE TALKING ABOUT?
HELLO, MOM.
SHE DOESN'T KNOW WHAT JUMP IS? GUESS I'M NOT SURPRISED.
JUMP IS A MANGA MAGAZINE...
NO MORE WORKING AS AN ASSISTANT, SHUN. I'LL SIMPLY HAVE YOU TRAIN IN PARIS IF YOU WISH TO PURSUE YOUR STUDIES.
I'VE ALREADY SET THINGS UP.
...!

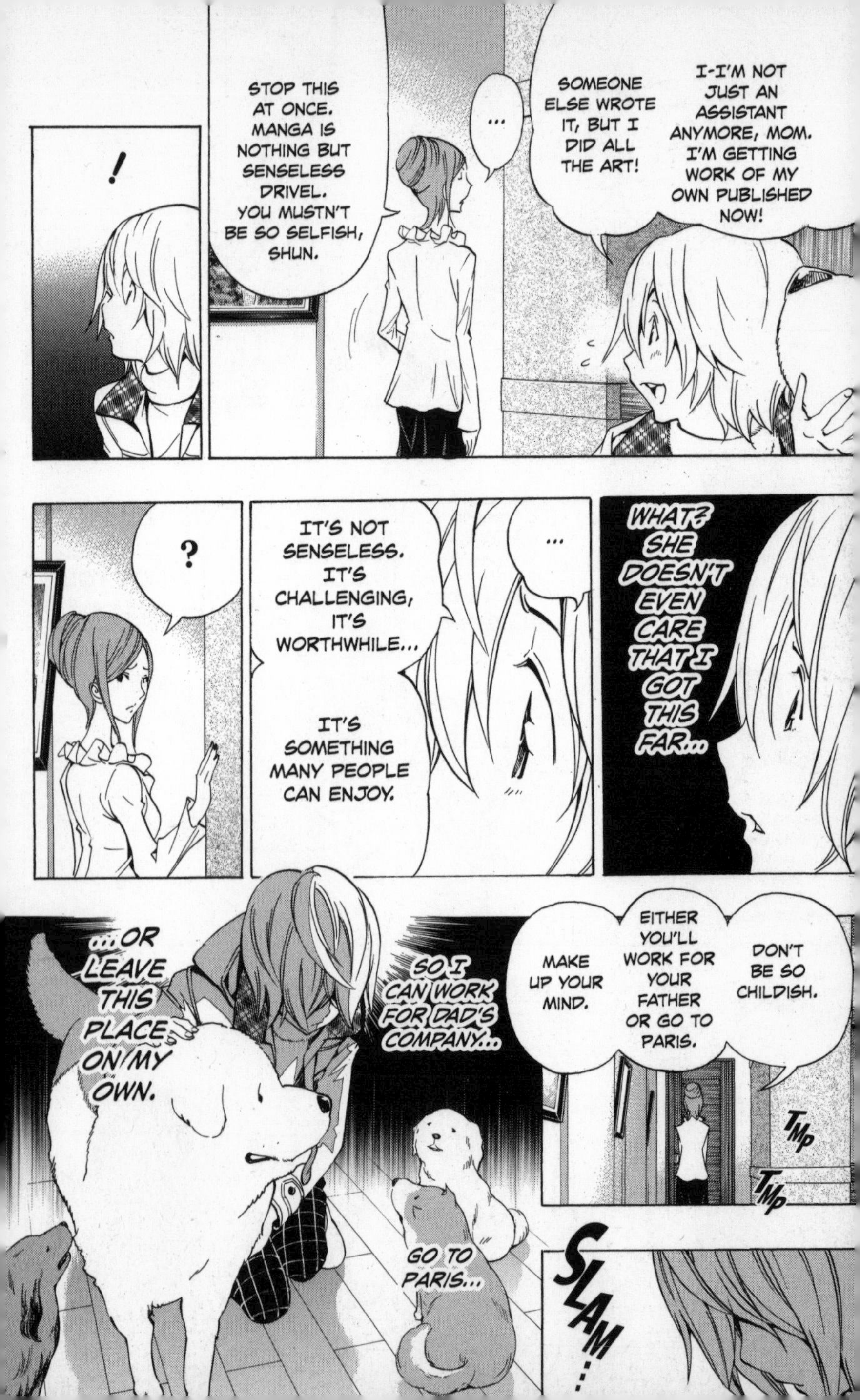
I-I'M NOT JUST AN ASSISTANT ANYMORE, MOM. I'M GETTING WORK OF MY OWN PUBLISHED NOW!
SOMEONE ELSE WROTE IT, BUT I DID ALL THE ART!
...
STOP THIS AT ONCE. MANGA IS NOTHING BUT SENSELESS DRIVEL. YOU MUSTN'T BE SO SELFISH, SHUN.
!
WHAT? SHE DOESN'T EVEN CARE THAT I GOT THIS FAR...
...
IT'S NOT SENSELESS. IT'S CHALLENGING, IT'S WORTHWHILE...
IT'S SOMETHING MANY PEOPLE CAN ENJOY.
?
DON'T BE SO CHILDISH.
EITHER YOU'LL WORK FOR YOUR FATHER OR GO TO PARIS.
MAKE UP YOUR MIND.
TMP
TMP
SLAM...
SO I CAN WORK FOR DAD'S COMPANY...
...OR LEAVE THIS PLACE ON MY OWN.
GO TO PARIS...

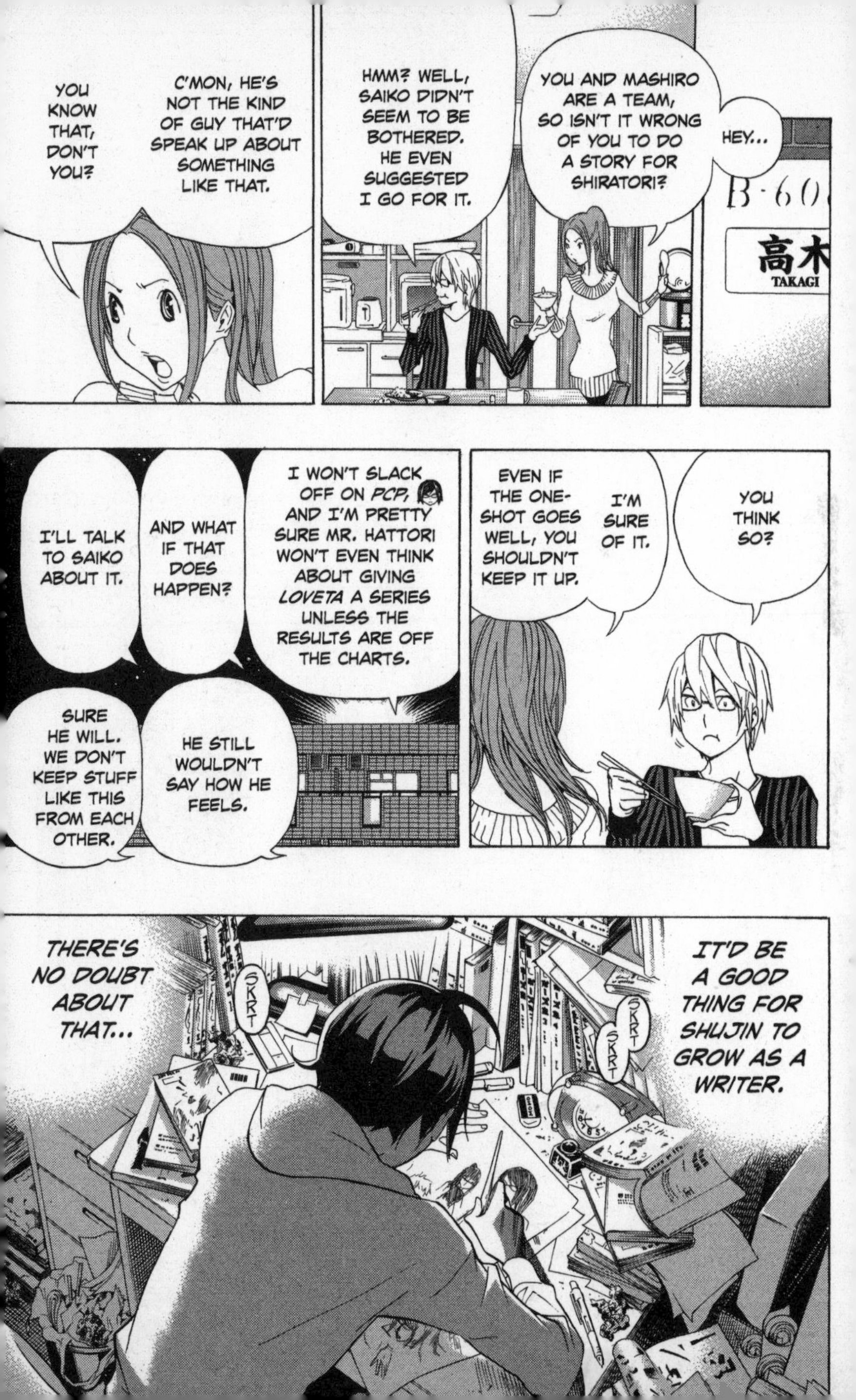
B-60
高木
TAKAGI
HEY...
YOU AND MASHIRO ARE A TEAM, SO ISN'T IT WRONG OF YOU TO DO A STORY FOR SHIRATORI?
HMM? WELL, SAIKO DIDN'T SEEM TO BE BOTHERED. HE EVEN SUGGESTED I GO FOR IT.
C'MON, HE'S NOT THE KIND OF GUY THAT'D SPEAK UP ABOUT SOMETHING LIKE THAT.
YOU KNOW THAT, DON'T YOU?
YOU THINK SO?
I'M SURE OF IT.
EVEN IF THE ONE-SHOT GOES WELL, YOU SHOULDN'T KEEP IT UP.
I WON'T SLACK OFF ON *PCP*, AND I'M PRETTY SURE MR. HATTORI WON'T EVEN THINK ABOUT GIVING *LOVETA* A SERIES UNLESS THE RESULTS ARE OFF THE CHARTS.
AND WHAT IF THAT DOES HAPPEN?
I'LL TALK TO SAIKO ABOUT IT.
HE STILL WOULDN'T SAY HOW HE FEELS.
SURE HE WILL. WE DON'T KEEP STUFF LIKE THIS FROM EACH OTHER.
IT'D BE A GOOD THING FOR SHUJIN TO GROW AS A WRITER.
SKRT
SKRT
SKRT
THERE'S NO DOUBT ABOUT THAT...

OHBA'S STORYBOARD

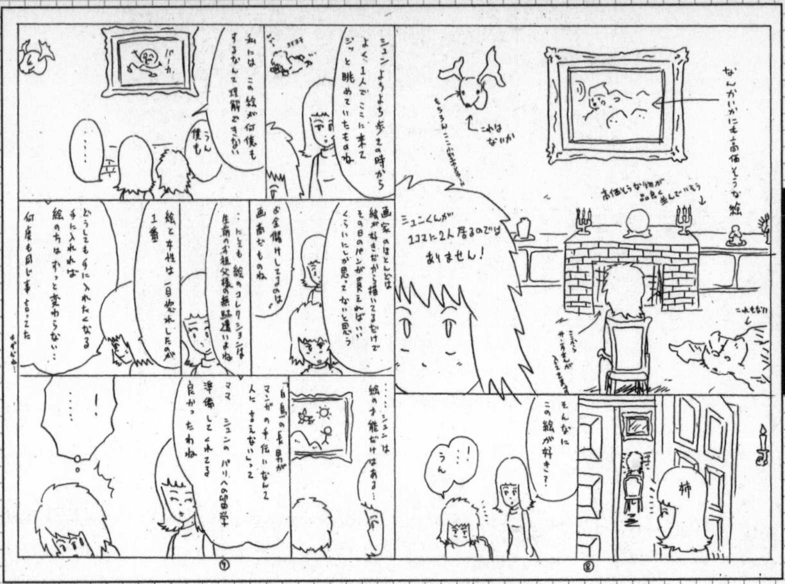
なんかいかにも高価そうな絵
これはないか
高価そうな物が品良く並んでいそう
シュンくんが1コマに2人居るのではありません!
これもないか
そんなにこの絵が好き?
…!
うん
姉
シュンよちよち歩きの時からよく1人でここに来てジッと眺めていたものね
私にはこの絵が何億もするなんて理解できない
うん僕も
……
画家のほとんどは絵が好きだから描いてるだけでその日のパンが買えればいいくらいにしか思ってないと思う
お金儲けしてるのは画商だものね
…にしても絵のコレクションは生前のお祖父様の無駄遣いよね
絵と女性は一目惚れしたのが1番
どうしても手に入れたくなる
手に入れれば絵の方はずっと変わらない…
何度も同じ事言ってた
…シュンは絵の才能だけはある…
「白鳥の長男がマンガの手伝いなんて人に言えない」って
ママシュンのパリへの留学準備してくれてる
良かったわね
!
……

OBATA'S STORYBOARD

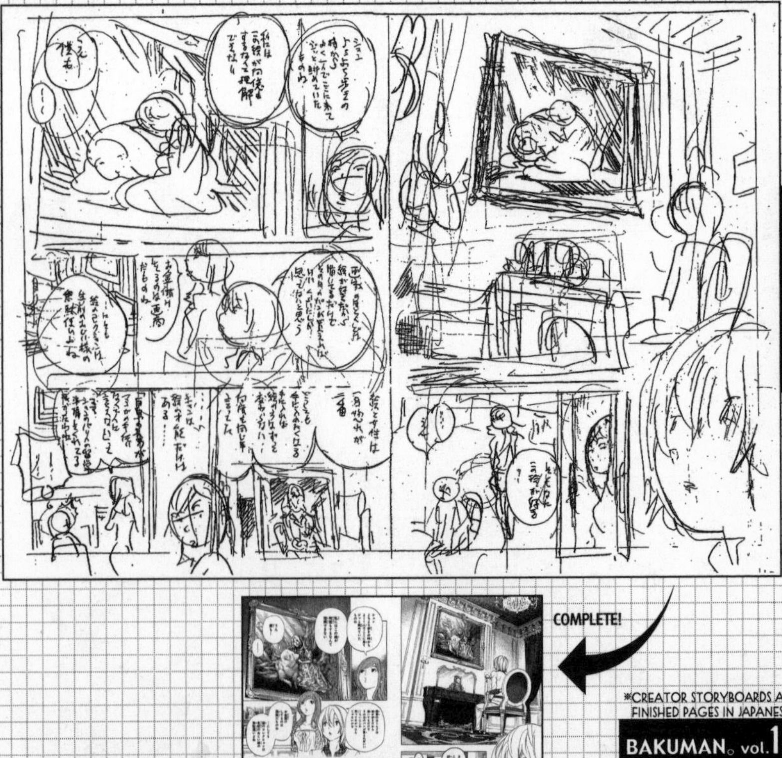

COMPLETE!

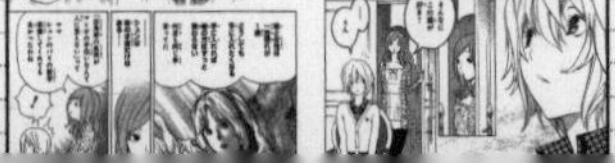

※CREATOR STORYBOARDS AND FINISHED PAGES IN JAPANESE

BAKUMAN。vol.12

"Until the Final Draft Is Complete"

Chapter 102, pp. 100-101

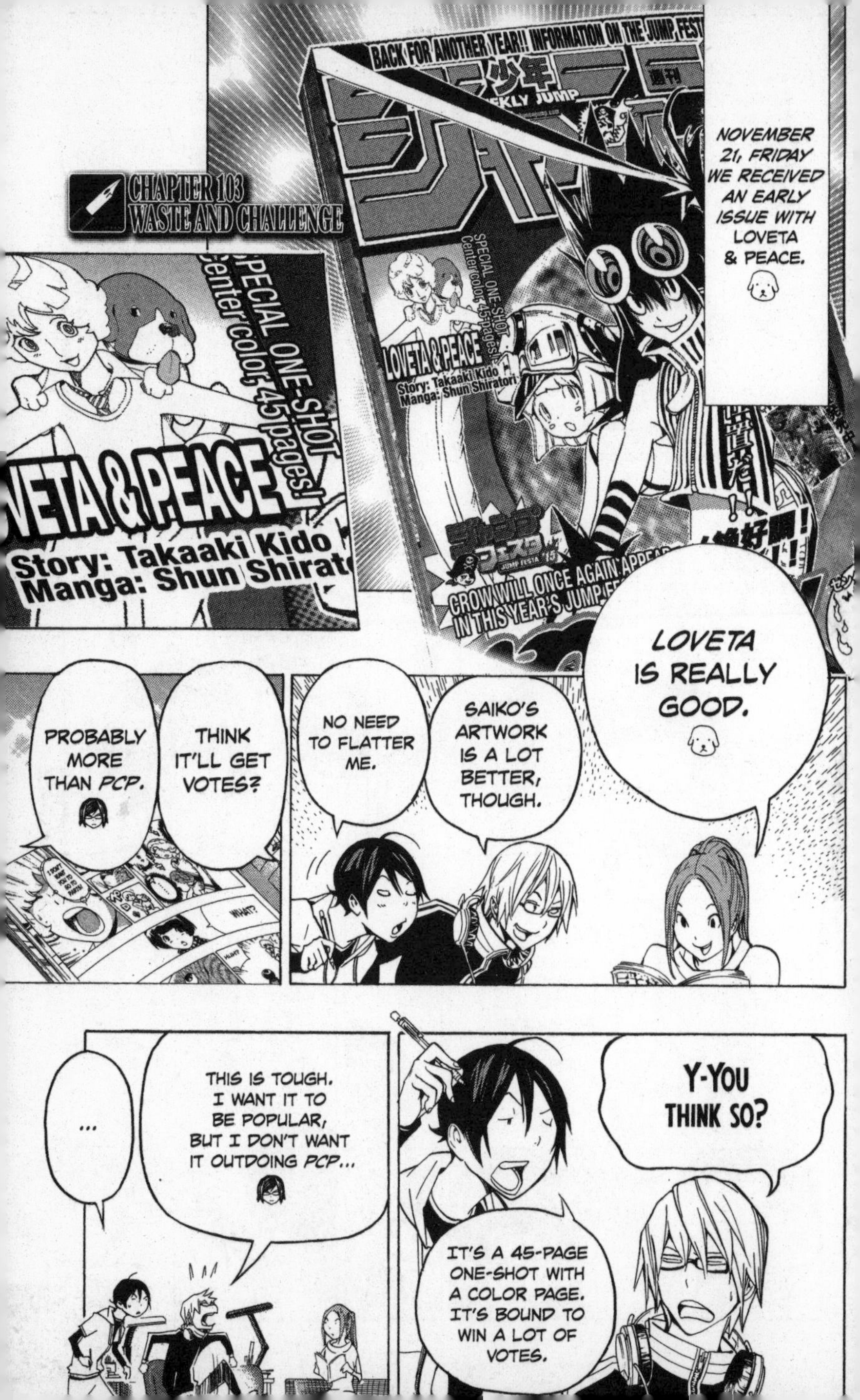
NOVEMBER 21, FRIDAY WE RECEIVED AN EARLY ISSUE WITH LOVETA & PEACE.
BACK FOR ANOTHER YEAR!! INFORMATION ON THE JUMP FEST
SPECIAL ONE-SHOT Center color, 45 pages!
LOVETA & PEACE
Story: Takaaki Kido
Manga: Shun Shiratori
CHAPTER 103 WASTE AND CHALLENGE
LOVETA IS REALLY GOOD.
SAIKO'S ARTWORK IS A LOT BETTER, THOUGH.
NO NEED TO FLATTER ME.
THINK IT'LL GET VOTES?
PROBABLY MORE THAN PCP.
Y-YOU THINK SO?
IT'S A 45-PAGE ONE-SHOT WITH A COLOR PAGE. IT'S BOUND TO WIN A LOT OF VOTES.
THIS IS TOUGH. I WANT IT TO BE POPULAR, BUT I DON'T WANT IT OUTDOING PCP...
...

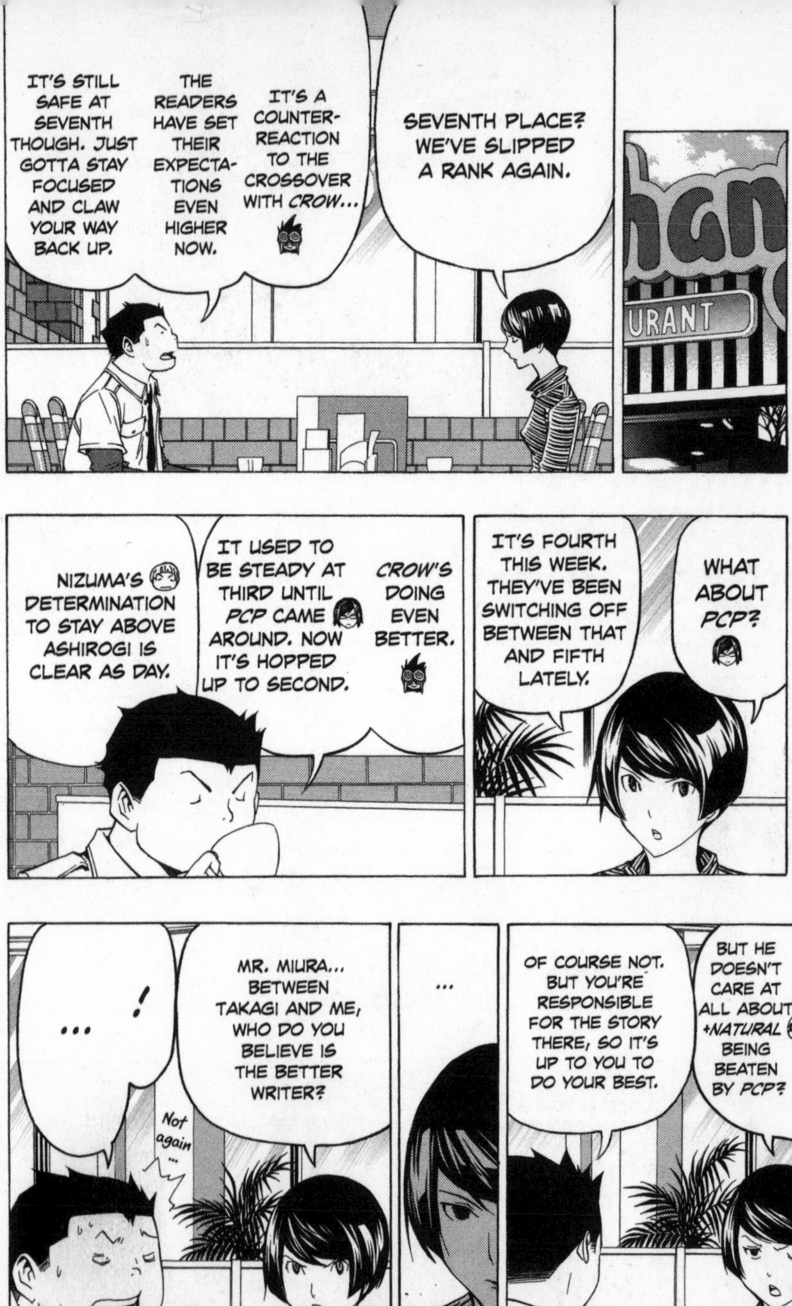
SEVENTH PLACE? WE'VE SLIPPED A RANK AGAIN.
IT'S A COUNTER-REACTION TO THE CROSSOVER WITH *CROW*...
THE READERS HAVE SET THEIR EXPECTATIONS EVEN HIGHER NOW.
IT'S STILL SAFE AT SEVENTH THOUGH. JUST GOTTA STAY FOCUSED AND CLAW YOUR WAY BACK UP.
WHAT ABOUT *PCP*?
IT'S FOURTH THIS WEEK. THEY'VE BEEN SWITCHING OFF BETWEEN THAT AND FIFTH LATELY.
CROW'S DOING EVEN BETTER.
IT USED TO BE STEADY AT THIRD UNTIL *PCP* CAME AROUND. NOW IT'S HOPPED UP TO SECOND.
NIZUMA'S DETERMINATION TO STAY ABOVE ASHIROGI IS CLEAR AS DAY.
BUT HE DOESN'T CARE AT ALL ABOUT *+NATURAL* BEING BEATEN BY *PCP*?
OF COURSE NOT. BUT YOU'RE RESPONSIBLE FOR THE STORY THERE, SO IT'S UP TO YOU TO DO YOUR BEST.
...
MR. MIURA... BETWEEN TAKAGI AND ME, WHO DO YOU BELIEVE IS THE BETTER WRITER?
...!
Not again...

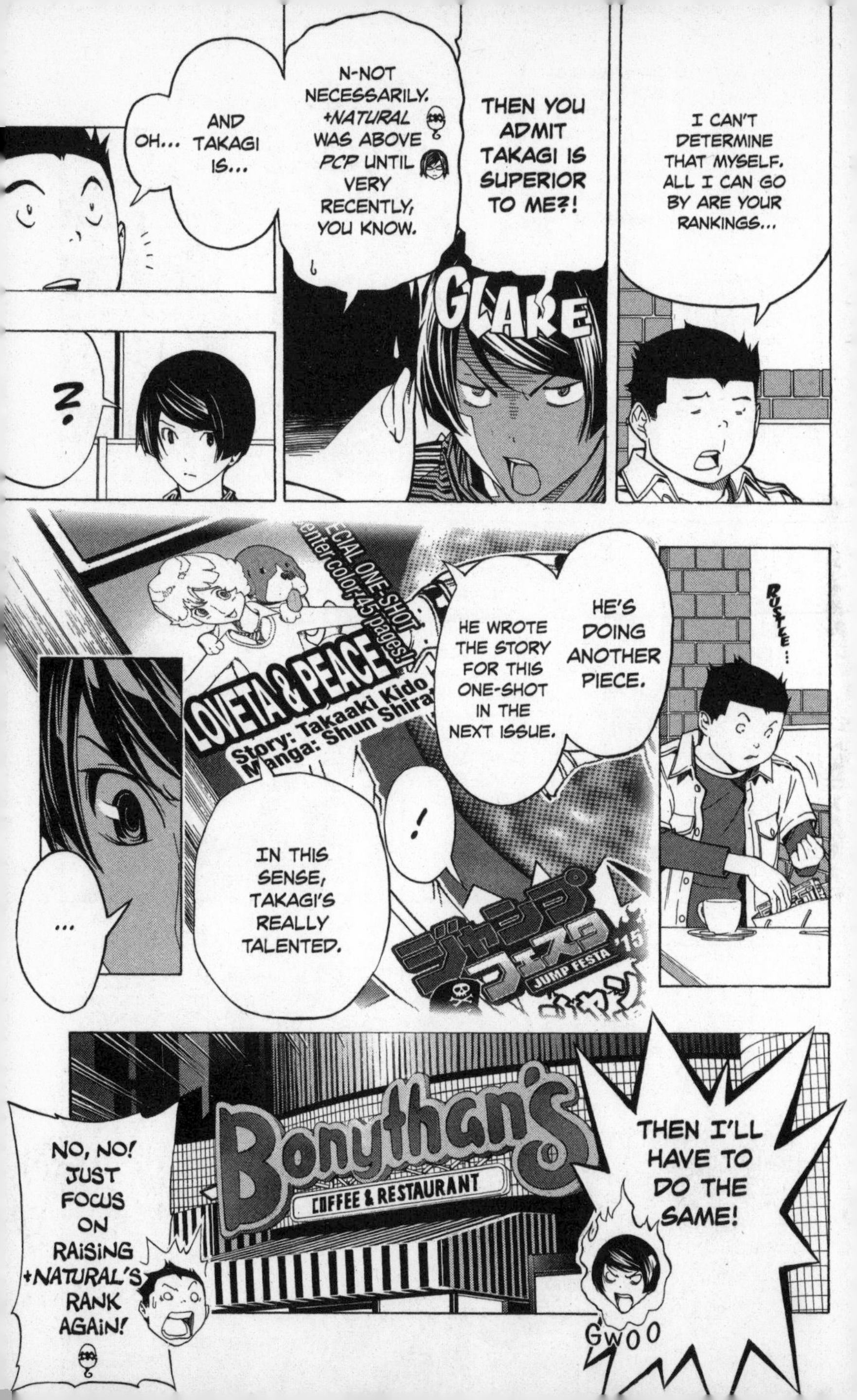
I CAN'T DETERMINE THAT MYSELF. ALL I CAN GO BY ARE YOUR RANKINGS...
THEN YOU ADMIT TAKAGI IS SUPERIOR TO ME?!
N-NOT NECESSARILY. +NATURAL WAS ABOVE PCP UNTIL VERY RECENTLY, YOU KNOW.
GLARE
AND TAKAGI IS...
OH...
?
RUSTLE...
HE'S DOING ANOTHER PIECE.
HE WROTE THE STORY FOR THIS ONE-SHOT IN THE NEXT ISSUE.
!
SPECIAL ONE-SHOT
center color 45 pages!
LOVETA & PEACE
Story: Takaaki Kido
Manga: Shun Shira
IN THIS SENSE, TAKAGI'S REALLY TALENTED.
ジャンプフェスタ
JUMP FESTA '15
...
THEN I'LL HAVE TO DO THE SAME!
GWOO
Bonythan's
COFFEE & RESTAURANT
NO, NO! JUST FOCUS ON RAISING +NATURAL'S RANK AGAIN!

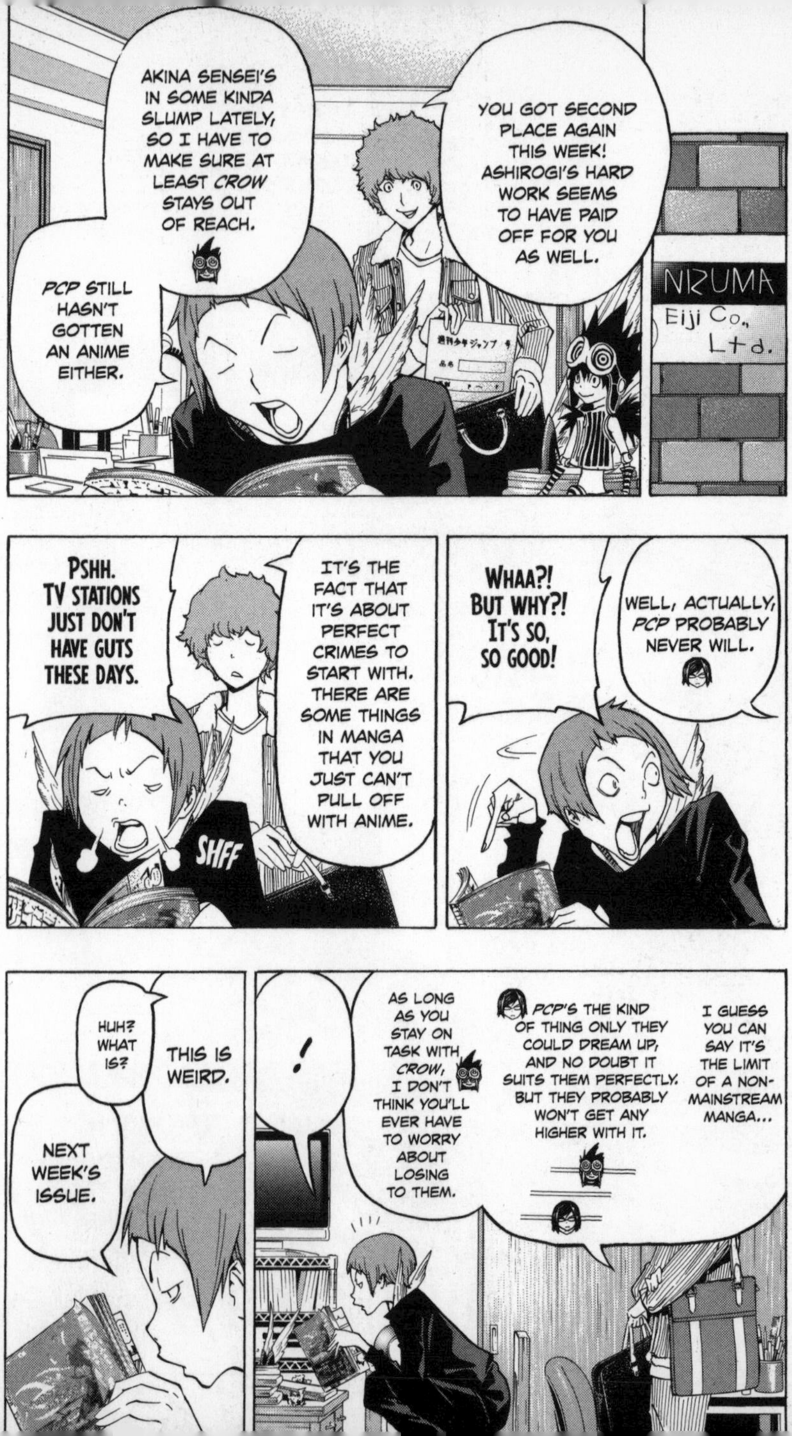
YOU GOT SECOND PLACE AGAIN THIS WEEK! ASHIROGI'S HARD WORK SEEMS TO HAVE PAID OFF FOR YOU AS WELL.
AKINA SENSEI'S IN SOME KINDA SLUMP LATELY, SO I HAVE TO MAKE SURE AT LEAST *CROW* STAYS OUT OF REACH.
NIZUMA Eiji Co., Ltd.
PCP STILL HASN'T GOTTEN AN ANIME EITHER.
WELL, ACTUALLY, *PCP* PROBABLY NEVER WILL.
WHAA?! BUT WHY?! IT'S SO, SO GOOD!
IT'S THE FACT THAT IT'S ABOUT PERFECT CRIMES TO START WITH. THERE ARE SOME THINGS IN MANGA THAT YOU JUST CAN'T PULL OFF WITH ANIME.
PSHH. TV STATIONS JUST DON'T HAVE GUTS THESE DAYS.
SHFF
I GUESS YOU CAN SAY IT'S THE LIMIT OF A NON-MAINSTREAM MANGA...
PCP'S THE KIND OF THING ONLY THEY COULD DREAM UP, AND NO DOUBT IT SUITS THEM PERFECTLY. BUT THEY PROBABLY WON'T GET ANY HIGHER WITH IT.
AS LONG AS YOU STAY ON TASK WITH *CROW*, I DON'T THINK YOU'LL EVER HAVE TO WORRY ABOUT LOSING TO THEM.
!
THIS IS WEIRD.
HUH? WHAT IS?
NEXT WEEK'S ISSUE.

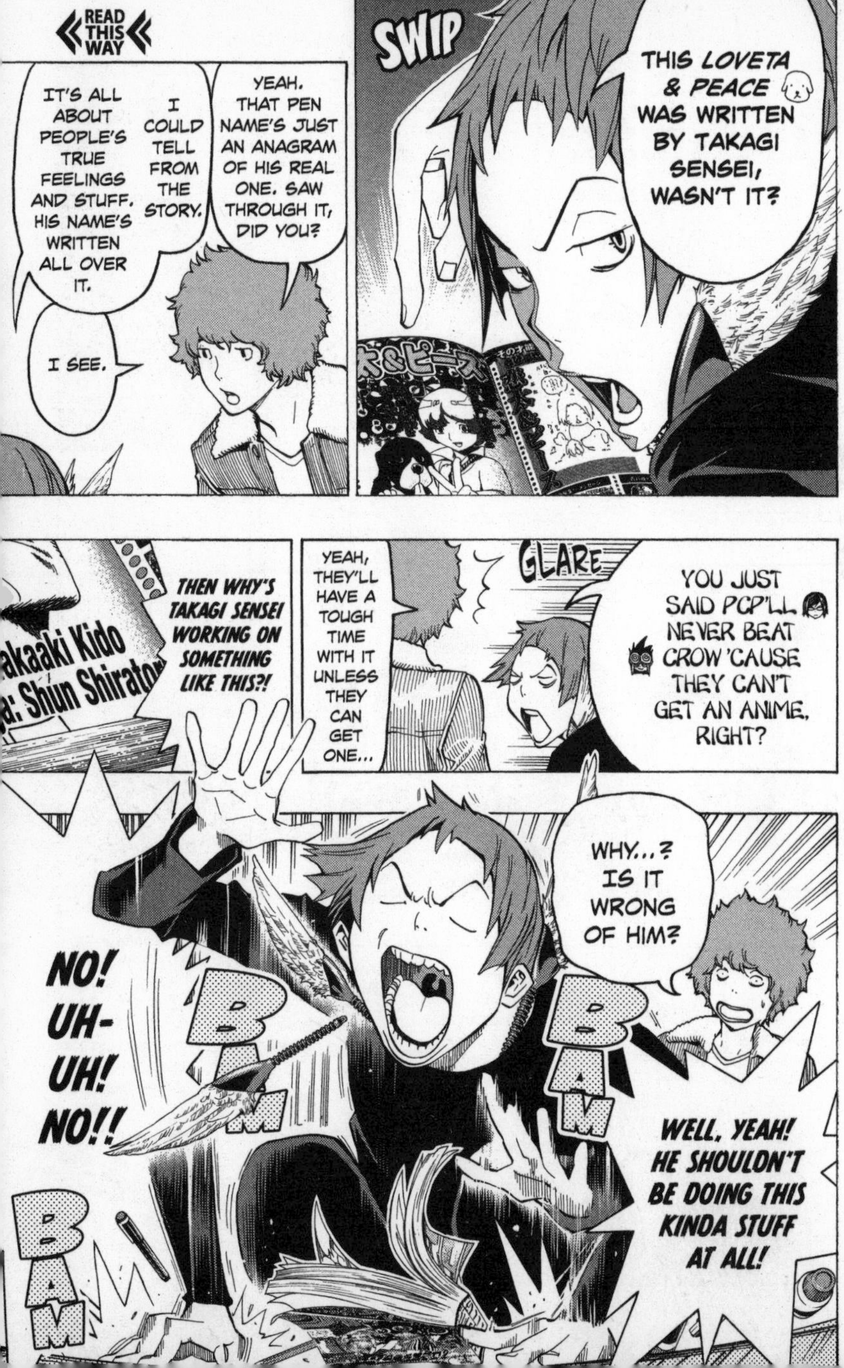
READ THIS WAY
SWIP
THIS LOVETA & PEACE WAS WRITTEN BY TAKAGI SENSEI, WASN'T IT?
YEAH. THAT PEN NAME'S JUST AN ANAGRAM OF HIS REAL ONE. SAW THROUGH IT, DID YOU?
I COULD TELL FROM THE STORY.
IT'S ALL ABOUT PEOPLE'S TRUE FEELINGS AND STUFF. HIS NAME'S WRITTEN ALL OVER IT.
I SEE.
GLARE
YOU JUST SAID PCP'LL NEVER BEAT CROW 'CAUSE THEY CAN'T GET AN ANIME, RIGHT?
YEAH, THEY'LL HAVE A TOUGH TIME WITH IT UNLESS THEY CAN GET ONE...
THEN WHY'S TAKAGI SENSEI WORKING ON SOMETHING LIKE THIS?!
akaaki Kido
a: Shun Shirato
WHY...? IS IT WRONG OF HIM?
BAM
WELL, YEAH! HE SHOULDN'T BE DOING THIS KINDA STUFF AT ALL!
BAM
NO! UH-UH! NO!!
BAM

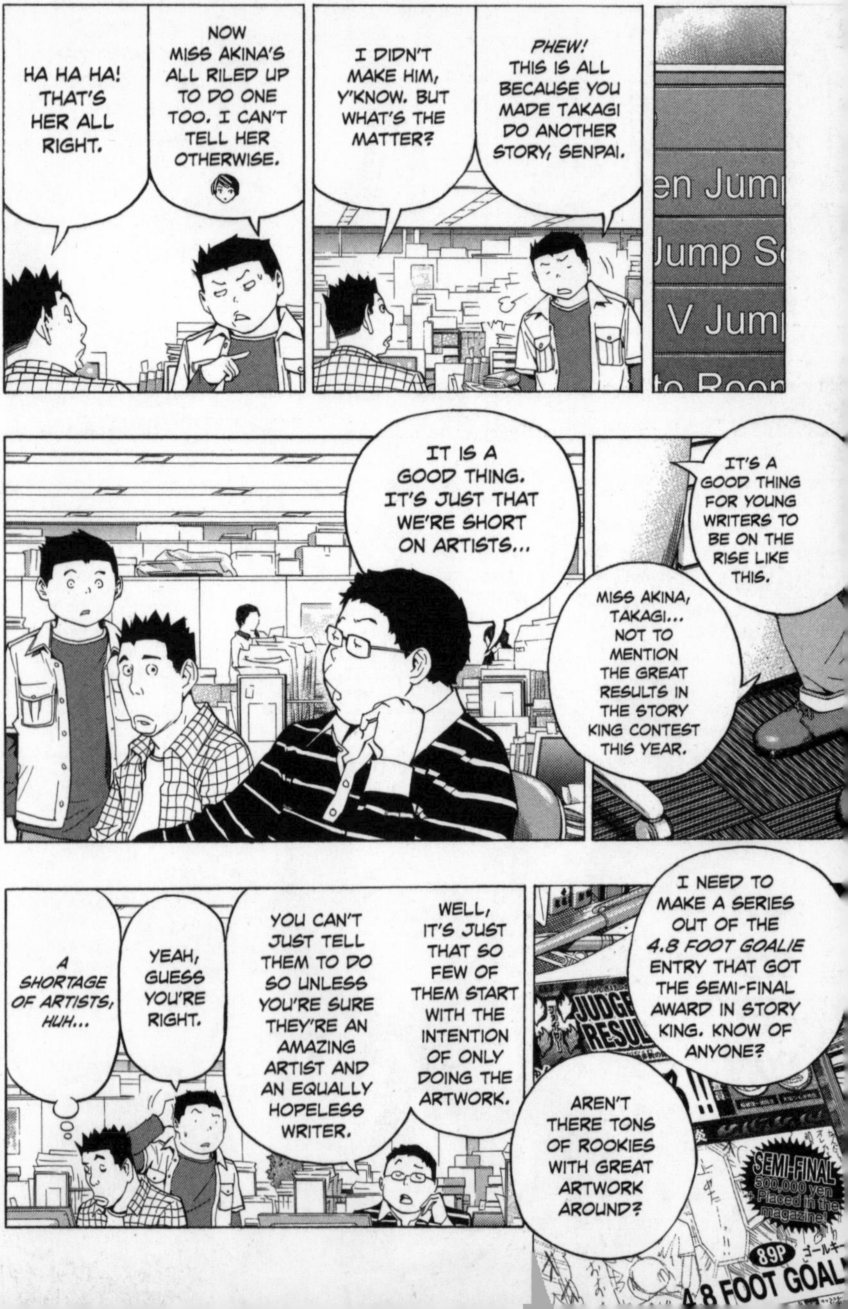

en Jump
Jump S
V Jump
PHEW! THIS IS ALL BECAUSE YOU MADE TAKAGI DO ANOTHER STORY, SENPAI.
I DIDN'T MAKE HIM, Y'KNOW. BUT WHAT'S THE MATTER?
NOW MISS AKINA'S ALL RILED UP TO DO ONE TOO. I CAN'T TELL HER OTHERWISE.
HA HA HA! THAT'S HER ALL RIGHT.
IT'S A GOOD THING FOR YOUNG WRITERS TO BE ON THE RISE LIKE THIS.
MISS AKINA, TAKAGI... NOT TO MENTION THE GREAT RESULTS IN THE STORY KING CONTEST THIS YEAR.
IT IS A GOOD THING. IT'S JUST THAT WE'RE SHORT ON ARTISTS...
I NEED TO MAKE A SERIES OUT OF THE 4.8 FOOT GOALIE ENTRY THAT GOT THE SEMI-FINAL AWARD IN STORY KING. KNOW OF ANYONE?
AREN'T THERE TONS OF ROOKIES WITH GREAT ARTWORK AROUND?
SEMI-FINAL
500,000 yen
Placed in the magazine!
89P
4.8 FOOT GOAL
WELL, IT'S JUST THAT SO FEW OF THEM START WITH THE INTENTION OF ONLY DOING THE ARTWORK.
YOU CAN'T JUST TELL THEM TO DO SO UNLESS YOU'RE SURE THEY'RE AN AMAZING ARTIST AND AN EQUALLY HOPELESS WRITER.
YEAH, GUESS YOU'RE RIGHT.
A SHORTAGE OF ARTISTS, HUH...

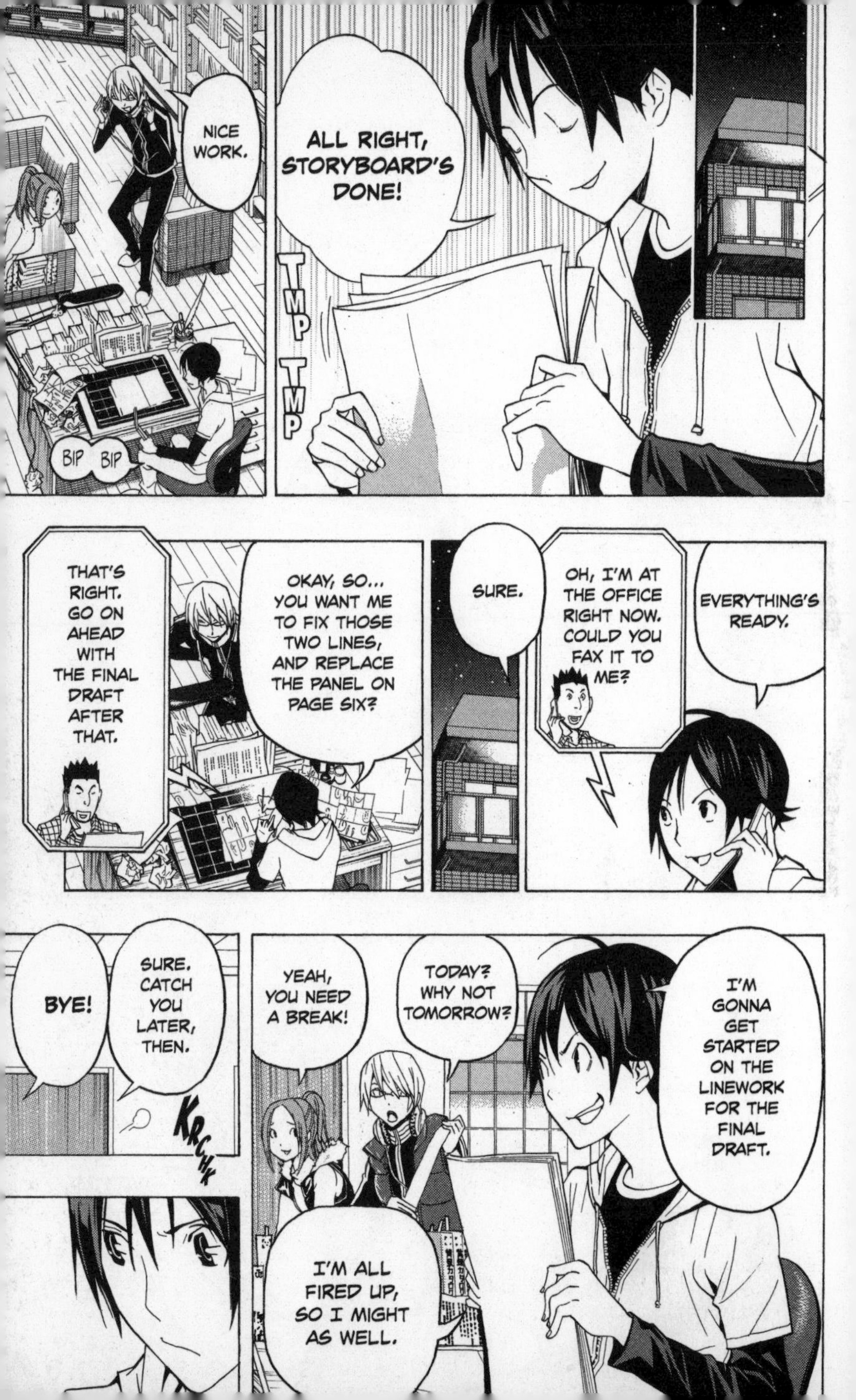
ALL RIGHT, STORYBOARD'S DONE!
TMP TMP
NICE WORK.
BIP BIP
EVERYTHING'S READY.
OH, I'M AT THE OFFICE RIGHT NOW. COULD YOU FAX IT TO ME?
SURE.
OKAY, SO... YOU WANT ME TO FIX THOSE TWO LINES, AND REPLACE THE PANEL ON PAGE SIX?
THAT'S RIGHT. GO ON AHEAD WITH THE FINAL DRAFT AFTER THAT.
I'M GONNA GET STARTED ON THE LINEWORK FOR THE FINAL DRAFT.
TODAY? WHY NOT TOMORROW?
YEAH, YOU NEED A BREAK!
I'M ALL FIRED UP, SO I MIGHT AS WELL.
SURE. CATCH YOU LATER, THEN.
BYE!
KRCHK

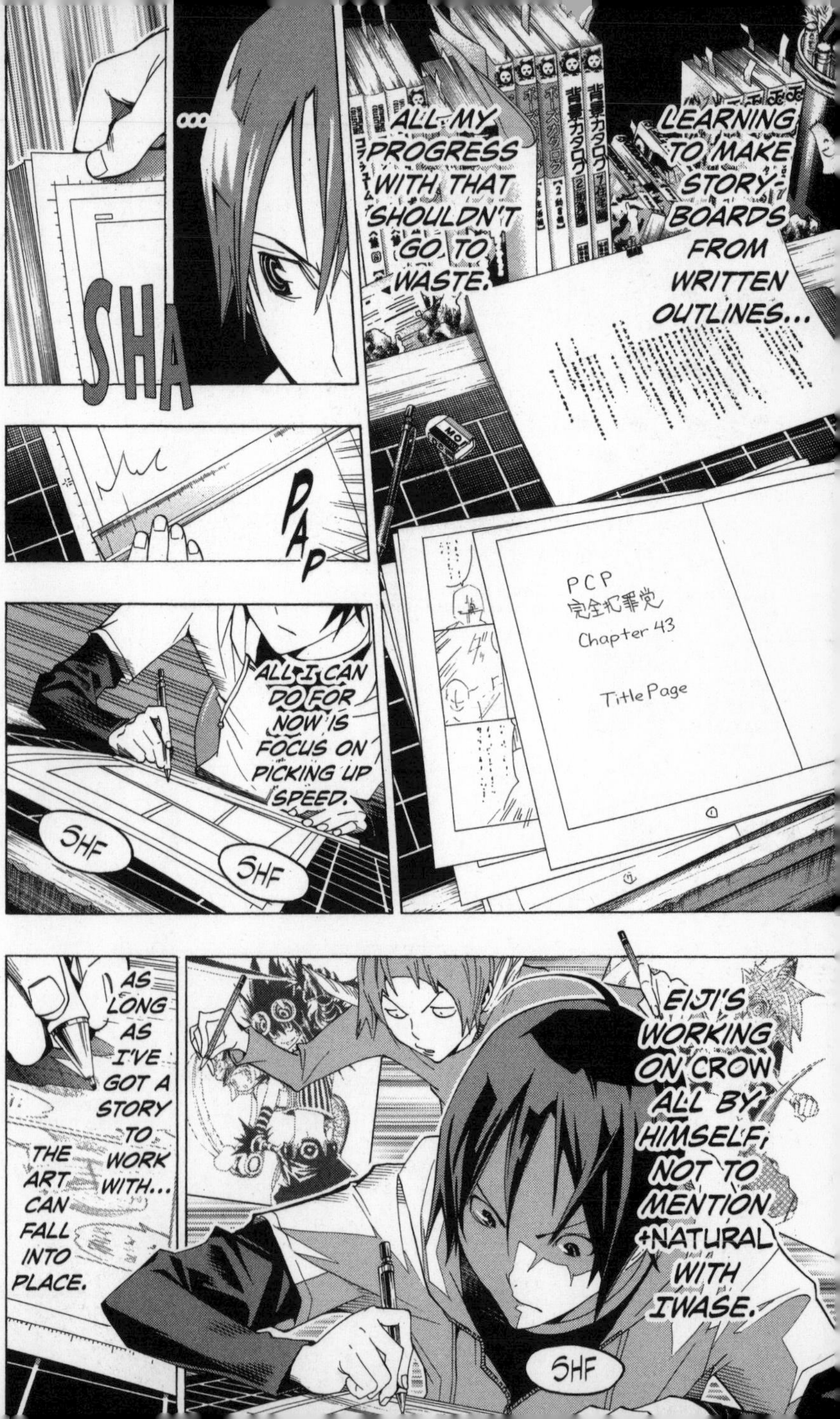
LEARNING TO MAKE STORYBOARDS FROM WRITTEN OUTLINES...
ALL MY PROGRESS WITH THAT SHOULDN'T GO TO WASTE.
...
SHA
PAP
PCP
完全犯罪党
Chapter 43
Title Page
ALL I CAN DO FOR NOW IS FOCUS ON PICKING UP SPEED.
SHF
SHF
EIJI'S WORKING ON CROW ALL BY HIMSELF, NOT TO MENTION +NATURAL WITH IWASE.
SHF
AS LONG AS I'VE GOT A STORY TO WORK WITH...
THE ART CAN FALL INTO PLACE.

READ THIS WAY

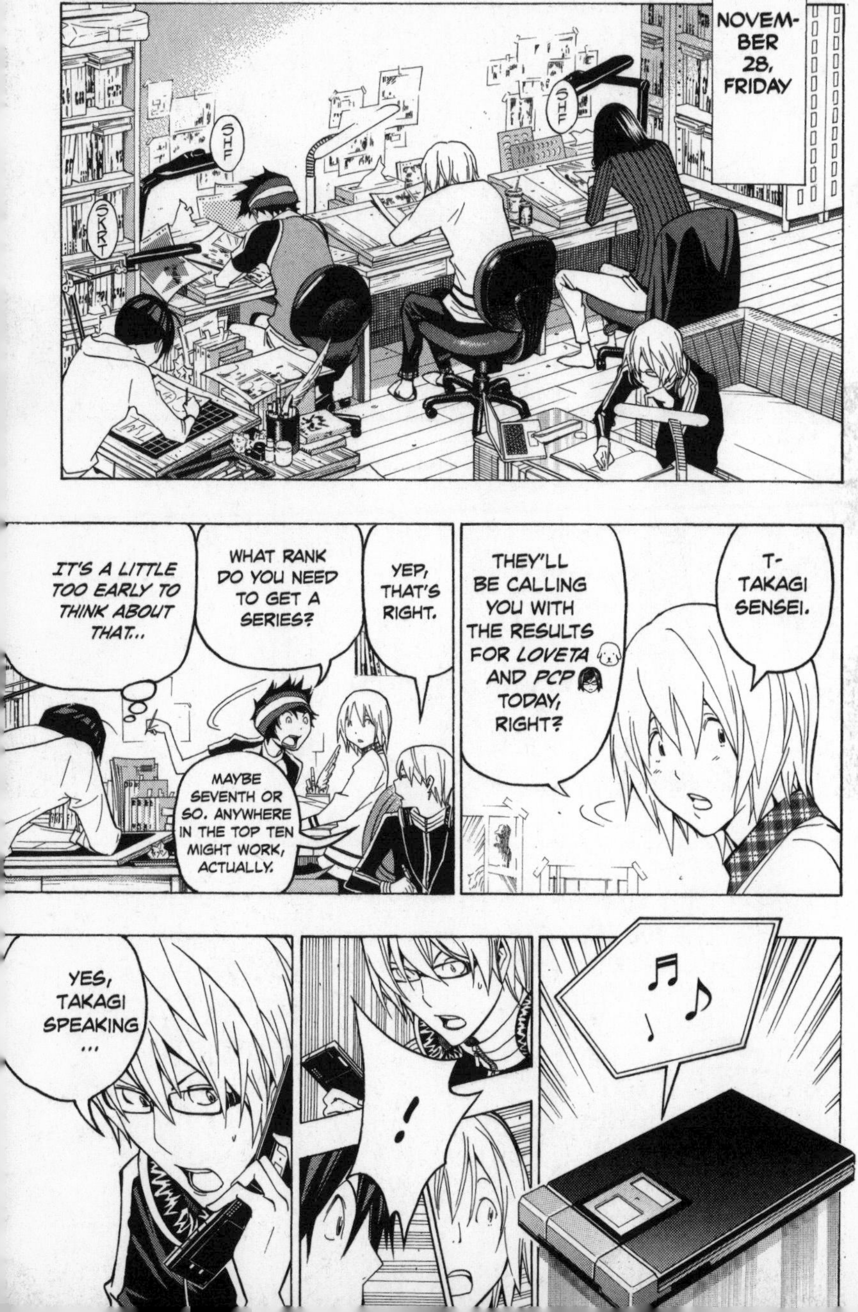
NOVEMBER 28, FRIDAY
SHF
SHF
SKRT
T-TAKAGI SENSEI.
THEY'LL BE CALLING YOU WITH THE RESULTS FOR *LOVETA* AND *PCP* TODAY, RIGHT?
YEP, THAT'S RIGHT.
WHAT RANK DO YOU NEED TO GET A SERIES?
IT'S A LITTLE TOO EARLY TO THINK ABOUT THAT...
MAYBE SEVENTH OR SO. ANYWHERE IN THE TOP TEN MIGHT WORK, ACTUALLY.
!
YES, TAKAGI SPEAKING ...

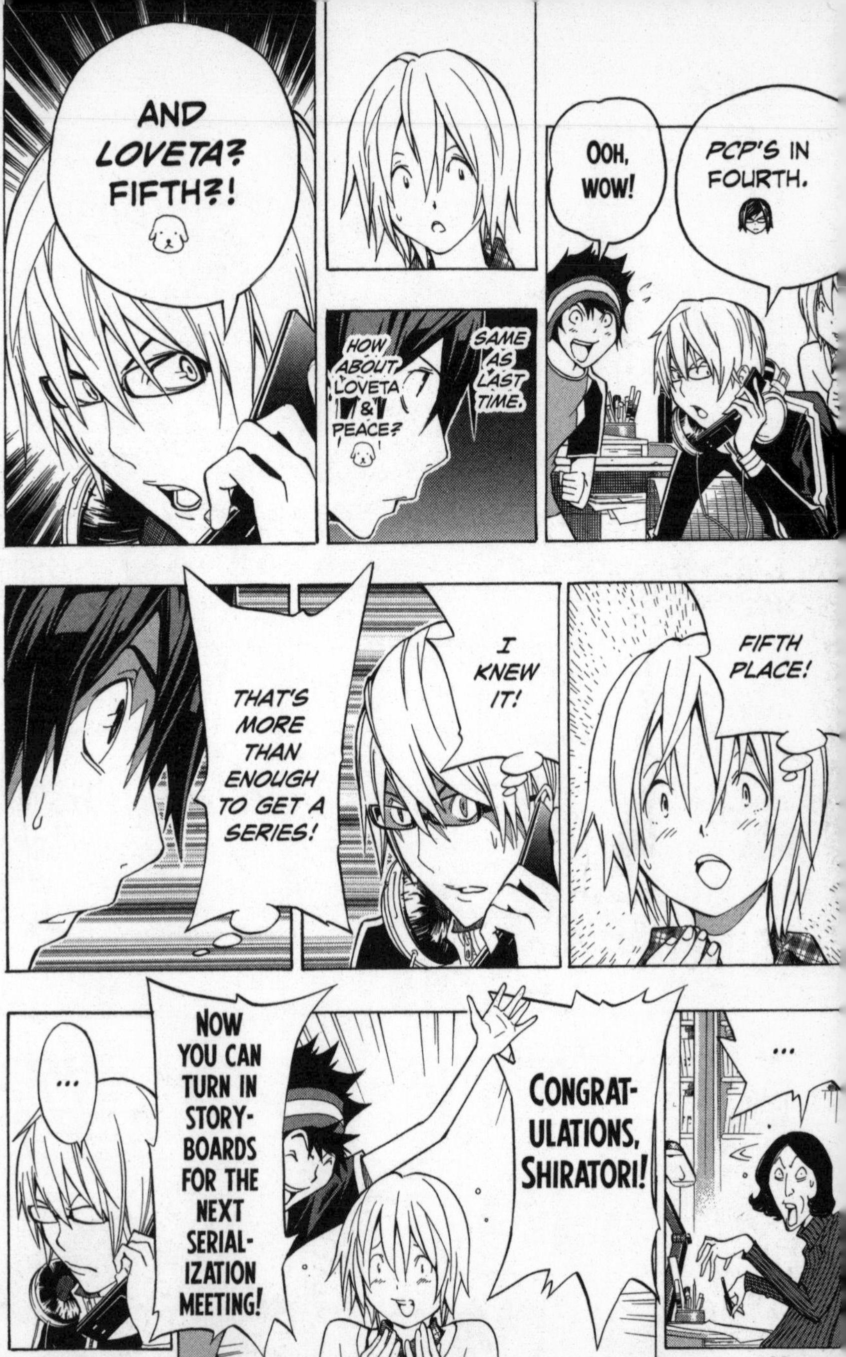
PCP'S IN FOURTH.
OOH, WOW!
HOW ABOUT LOVETA & PEACE?
SAME AS LAST TIME.
AND LOVETA? FIFTH?!
FIFTH PLACE!
I KNEW IT!
THAT'S MORE THAN ENOUGH TO GET A SERIES!
...
CONGRAT-ULATIONS, SHIRATORI!
NOW YOU CAN TURN IN STORY-BOARDS FOR THE NEXT SERIAL-IZATION MEETING!
...

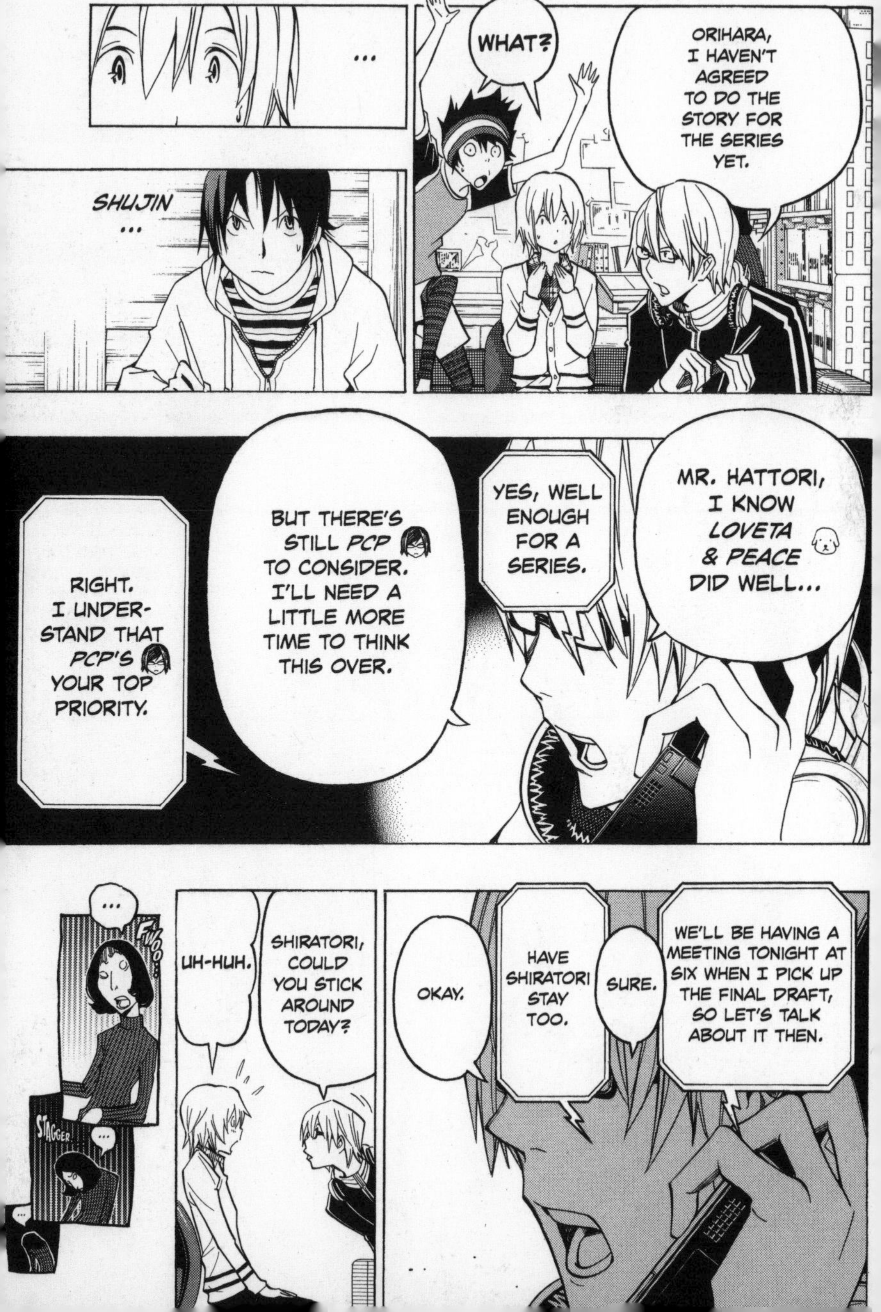
ORIHARA, I HAVEN'T AGREED TO DO THE STORY FOR THE SERIES YET.
WHAT?
...
SHUJIN ...
MR. HATTORI, I KNOW LOVETA & PEACE DID WELL...
YES, WELL ENOUGH FOR A SERIES.
BUT THERE'S STILL PCP TO CONSIDER. I'LL NEED A LITTLE MORE TIME TO THINK THIS OVER.
RIGHT. I UNDERSTAND THAT PCP'S YOUR TOP PRIORITY.
WE'LL BE HAVING A MEETING TONIGHT AT SIX WHEN I PICK UP THE FINAL DRAFT, SO LET'S TALK ABOUT IT THEN.
SURE.
HAVE SHIRATORI STAY TOO.
OKAY.
SHIRATORI, COULD YOU STICK AROUND TODAY?
UH-HUH.
...
FWOO
STAGGER
...
...

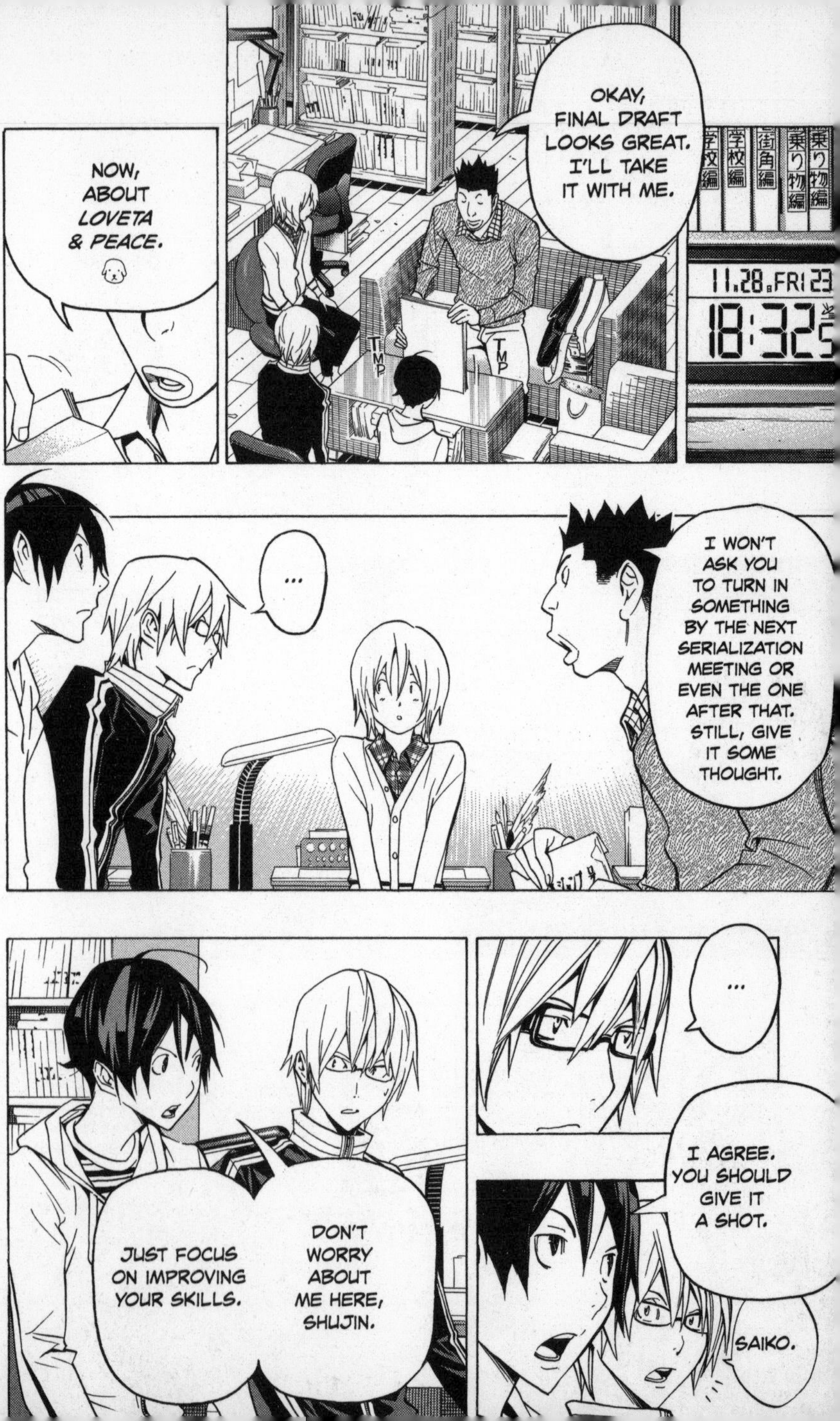
OKAY, FINAL DRAFT LOOKS GREAT. I'LL TAKE IT WITH ME.
TMP
TMP
NOW, ABOUT *LOVETA & PEACE.*
I WON'T ASK YOU TO TURN IN SOMETHING BY THE NEXT SERIALIZATION MEETING OR EVEN THE ONE AFTER THAT. STILL, GIVE IT SOME THOUGHT.
...
...
I AGREE. YOU SHOULD GIVE IT A SHOT.
SAIKO.
DON'T WORRY ABOUT ME HERE, SHUJIN.
JUST FOCUS ON IMPROVING YOUR SKILLS.

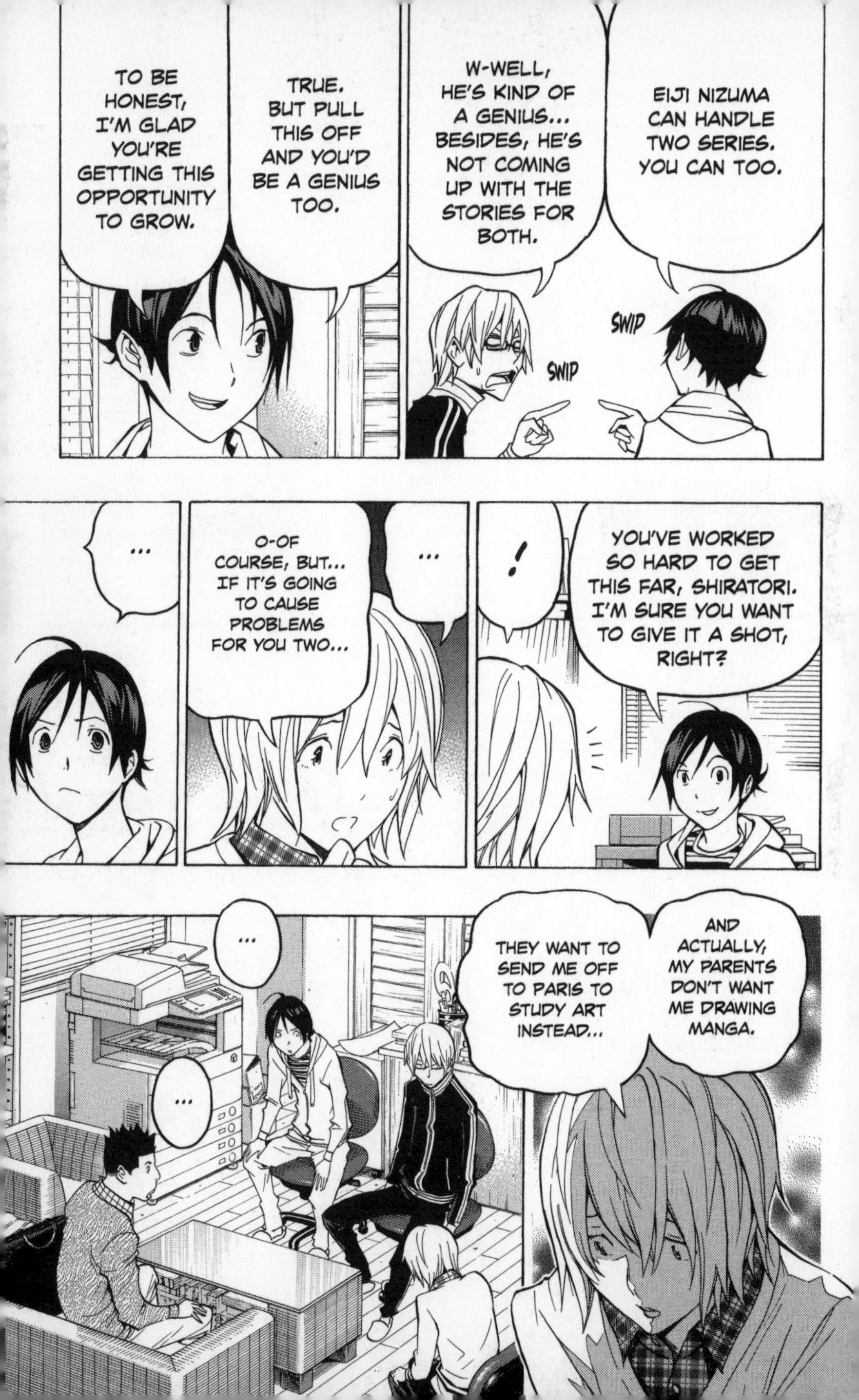
EIJI NIZUMA CAN HANDLE TWO SERIES. YOU CAN TOO.
W-WELL, HE'S KIND OF A GENIUS... BESIDES, HE'S NOT COMING UP WITH THE STORIES FOR BOTH.
SWIP
SWIP
TRUE. BUT PULL THIS OFF AND YOU'D BE A GENIUS TOO.
TO BE HONEST, I'M GLAD YOU'RE GETTING THIS OPPORTUNITY TO GROW.
YOU'VE WORKED SO HARD TO GET THIS FAR, SHIRATORI. I'M SURE YOU WANT TO GIVE IT A SHOT, RIGHT?
!
...
O-OF COURSE, BUT... IF IT'S GOING TO CAUSE PROBLEMS FOR YOU TWO...
...
AND ACTUALLY, MY PARENTS DON'T WANT ME DRAWING MANGA.
THEY WANT TO SEND ME OFF TO PARIS TO STUDY ART INSTEAD...
...
...

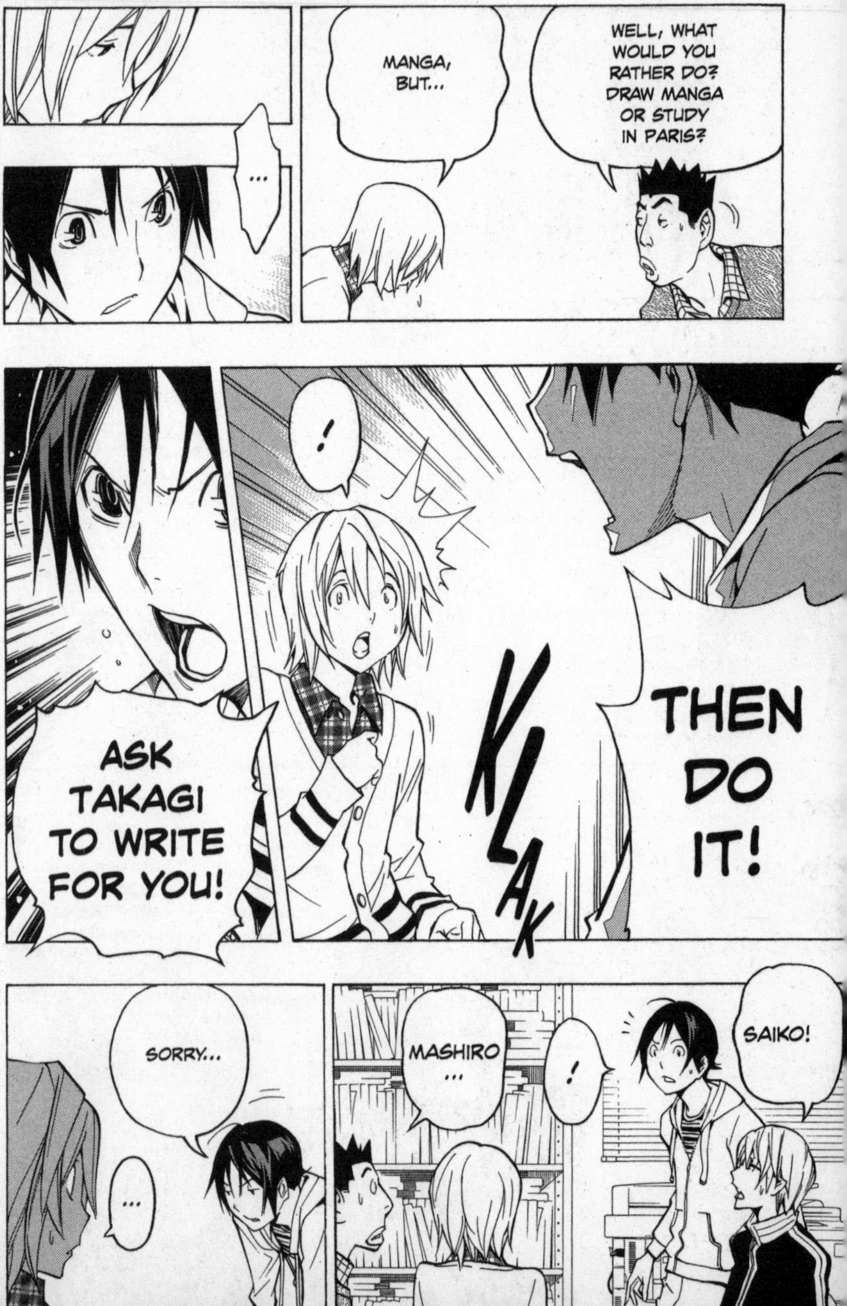
WELL, WHAT WOULD YOU RATHER DO? DRAW MANGA OR STUDY IN PARIS?
MANGA, BUT...
...
THEN DO IT!
KLAK
!
ASK TAKAGI TO WRITE FOR YOU!
SAIKO!
!
MASHIRO ...
SORRY...
...

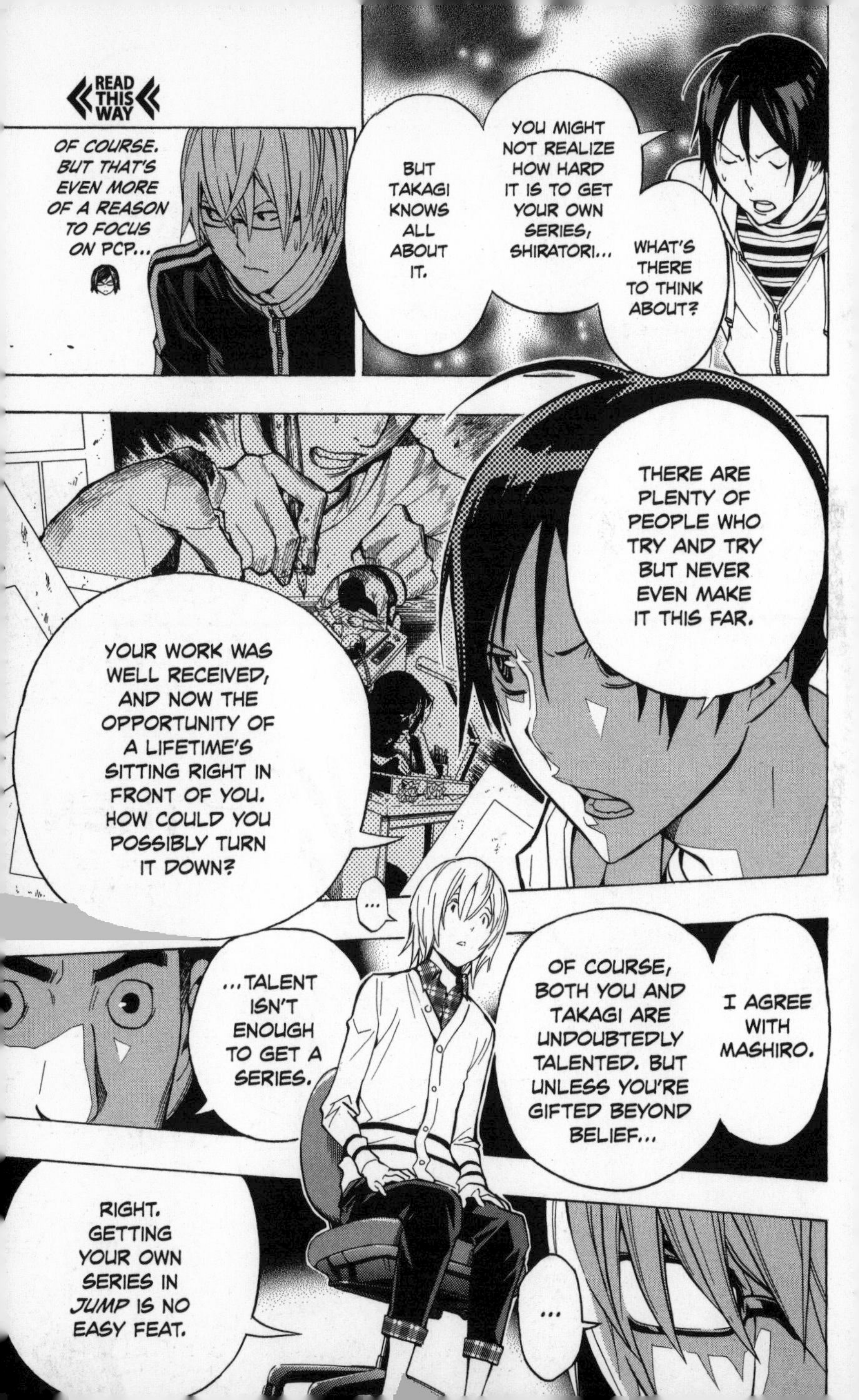
READ THIS WAY
WHAT'S THERE TO THINK ABOUT?
YOU MIGHT NOT REALIZE HOW HARD IT IS TO GET YOUR OWN SERIES, SHIRATORI...
BUT TAKAGI KNOWS ALL ABOUT IT.
OF COURSE. BUT THAT'S EVEN MORE OF A REASON TO FOCUS ON PCP...
THERE ARE PLENTY OF PEOPLE WHO TRY AND TRY BUT NEVER EVEN MAKE IT THIS FAR.
YOUR WORK WAS WELL RECEIVED, AND NOW THE OPPORTUNITY OF A LIFETIME'S SITTING RIGHT IN FRONT OF YOU. HOW COULD YOU POSSIBLY TURN IT DOWN?
...
I AGREE WITH MASHIRO.
OF COURSE, BOTH YOU AND TAKAGI ARE UNDOUBTEDLY TALENTED. BUT UNLESS YOU'RE GIFTED BEYOND BELIEF...
...TALENT ISN'T ENOUGH TO GET A SERIES.
...
RIGHT. GETTING YOUR OWN SERIES IN *JUMP* IS NO EASY FEAT.

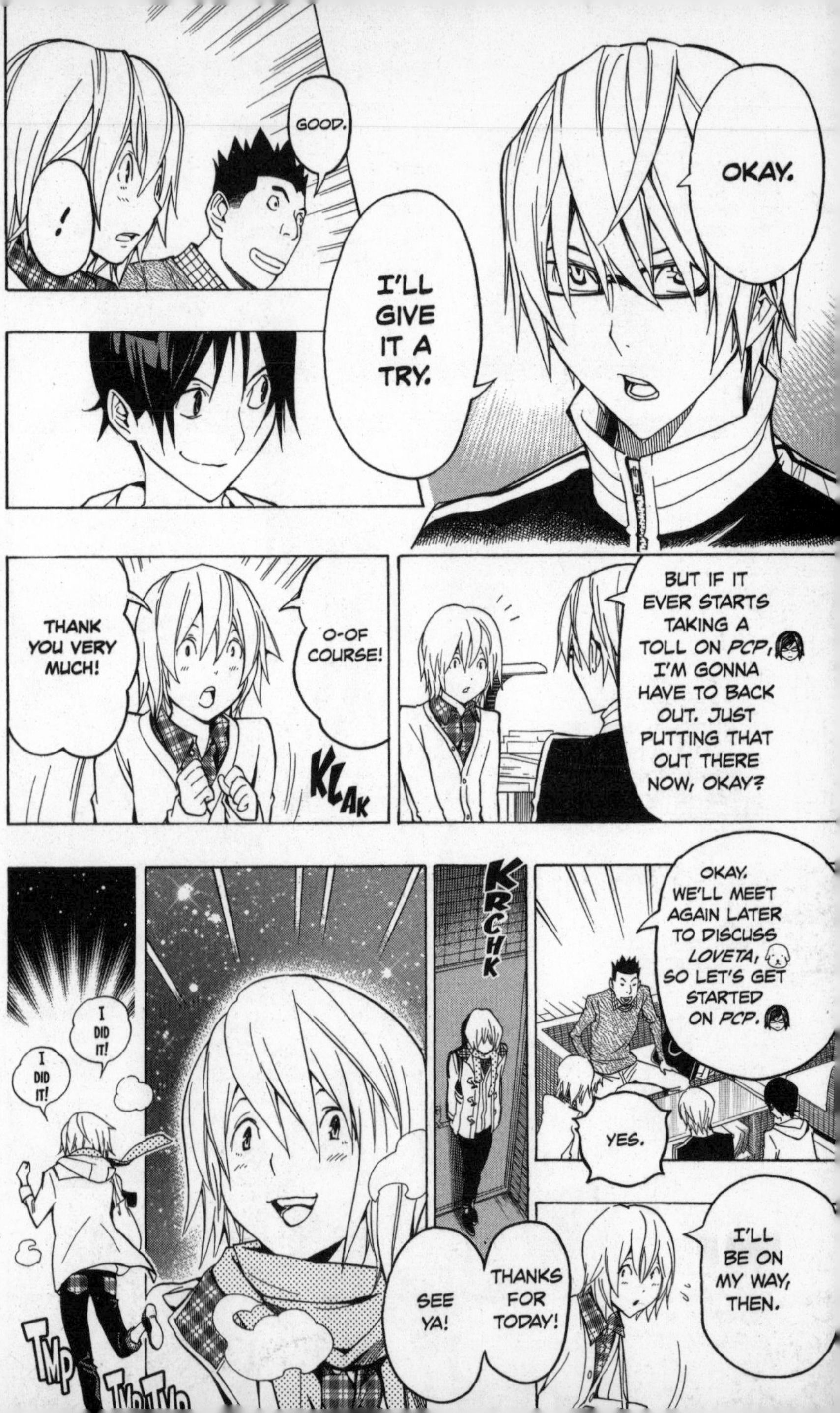
OKAY.
I'LL GIVE IT A TRY.
GOOD.
!
BUT IF IT EVER STARTS TAKING A TOLL ON *PCP*, I'M GONNA HAVE TO BACK OUT. JUST PUTTING THAT OUT THERE NOW, OKAY?
O-OF COURSE!
THANK YOU VERY MUCH!
KLAK
OKAY. WE'LL MEET AGAIN LATER TO DISCUSS *LOVETA*, SO LET'S GET STARTED ON *PCP*.
YES.
I'LL BE ON MY WAY, THEN.
KRCHK
THANKS FOR TODAY!
SEE YA!
I DID IT!
I DID IT!
TMP

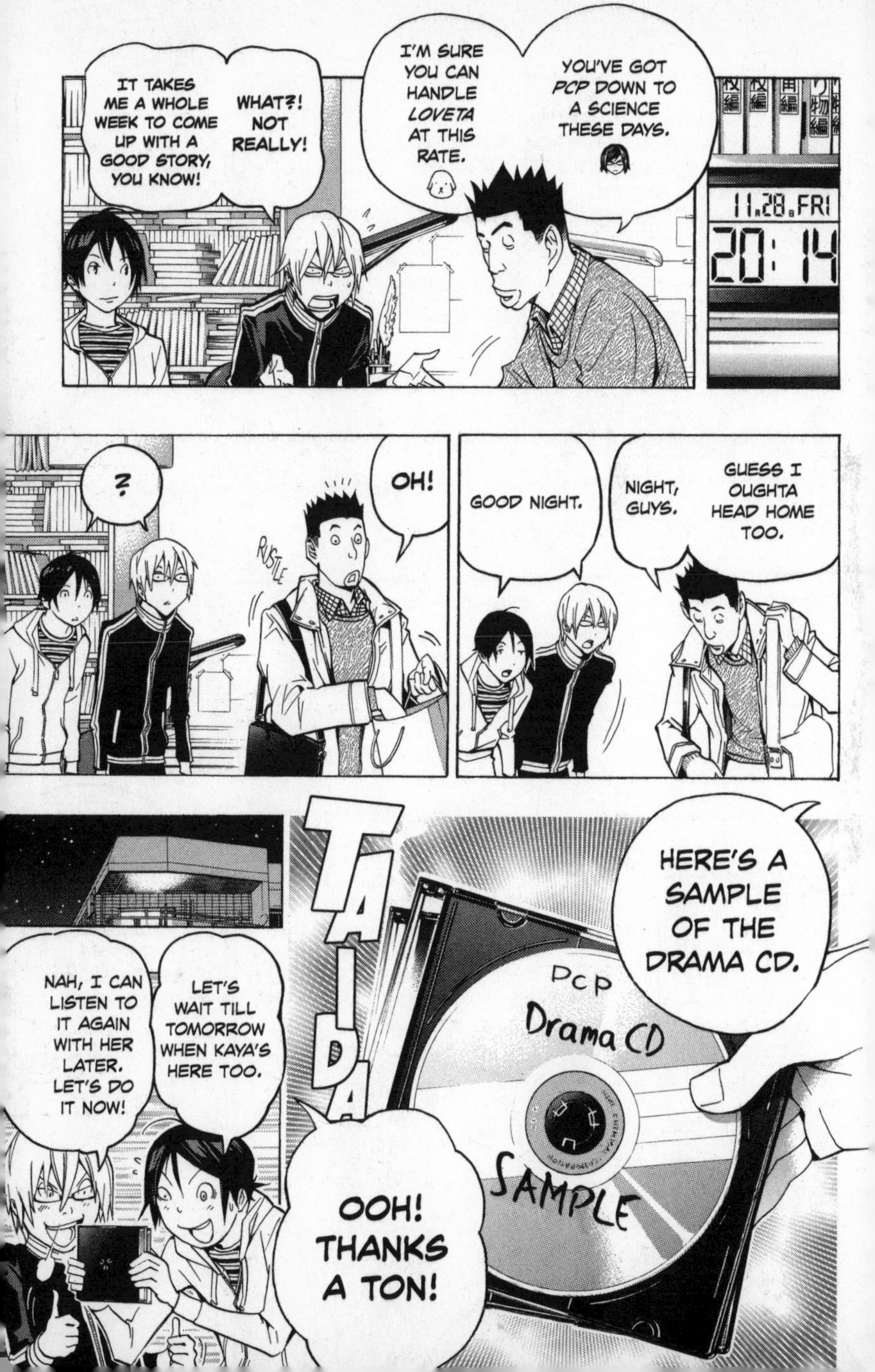
20:14
YOU'VE GOT PCP DOWN TO A SCIENCE THESE DAYS.
I'M SURE YOU CAN HANDLE LOVETA AT THIS RATE.
WHAT?! NOT REALLY!
IT TAKES ME A WHOLE WEEK TO COME UP WITH A GOOD STORY, YOU KNOW!
GUESS I OUGHTA HEAD HOME TOO.
NIGHT, GUYS.
GOOD NIGHT.
OH!
RUSTLE
?
HERE'S A SAMPLE OF THE DRAMA CD.
TA-DA
PCP Drama CD
SAMPLE
OOH! THANKS A TON!
LET'S WAIT TILL TOMORROW WHEN KAYA'S HERE TOO.
NAH, I CAN LISTEN TO IT AGAIN WITH HER LATER. LET'S DO IT NOW!

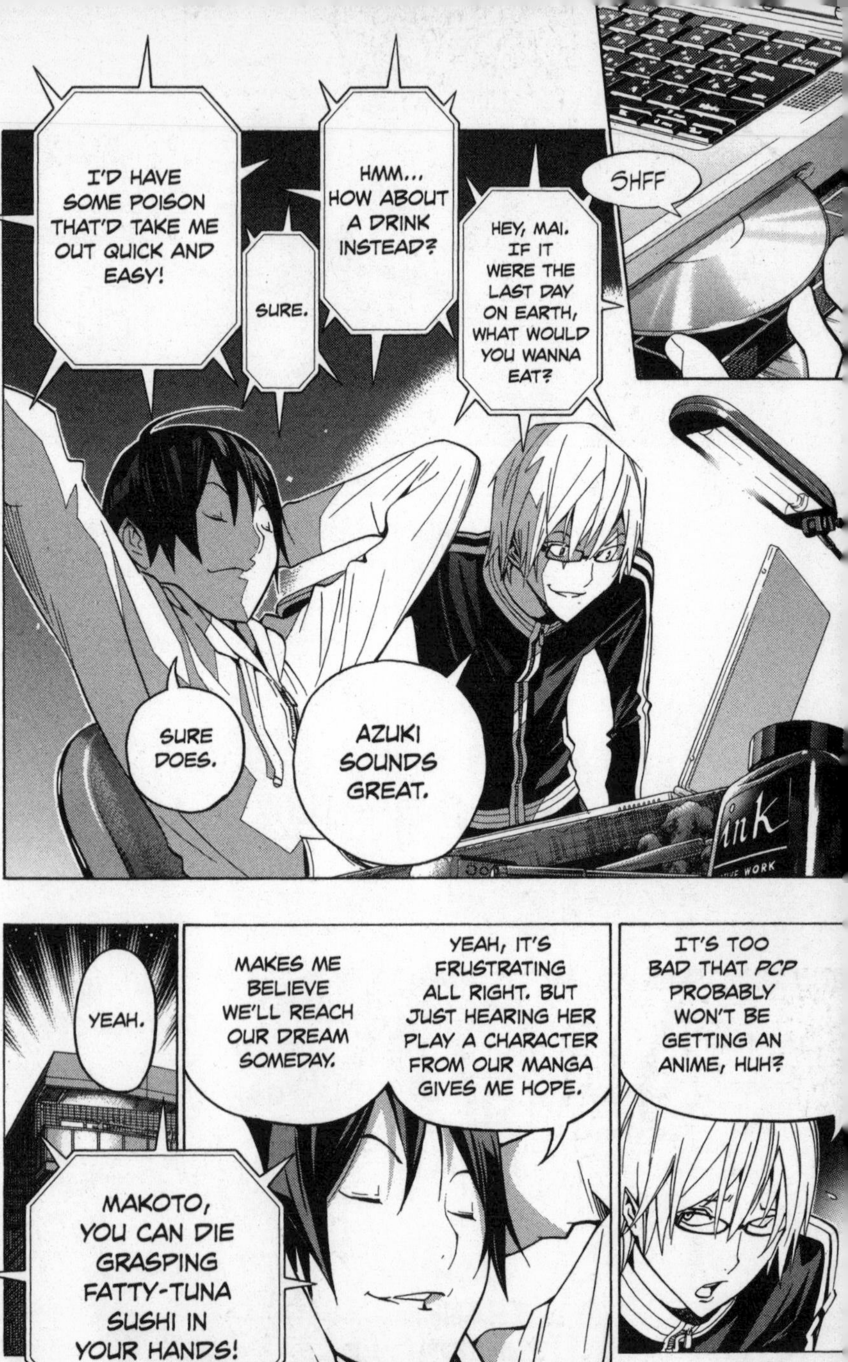
SHFF
HEY, MAI. IF IT WERE THE LAST DAY ON EARTH, WHAT WOULD YOU WANNA EAT?
HMM... HOW ABOUT A DRINK INSTEAD?
SURE.
I'D HAVE SOME POISON THAT'D TAKE ME OUT QUICK AND EASY!
ink
AZUKI SOUNDS GREAT.
SURE DOES.
IT'S TOO BAD THAT *PCP* PROBABLY WON'T BE GETTING AN ANIME, HUH?
YEAH, IT'S FRUSTRATING ALL RIGHT. BUT JUST HEARING HER PLAY A CHARACTER FROM OUR MANGA GIVES ME HOPE.
MAKES ME BELIEVE WE'LL REACH OUR DREAM SOMEDAY.
YEAH.
MAKOTO, YOU CAN DIE GRASPING FATTY-TUNA SUSHI IN YOUR HANDS!

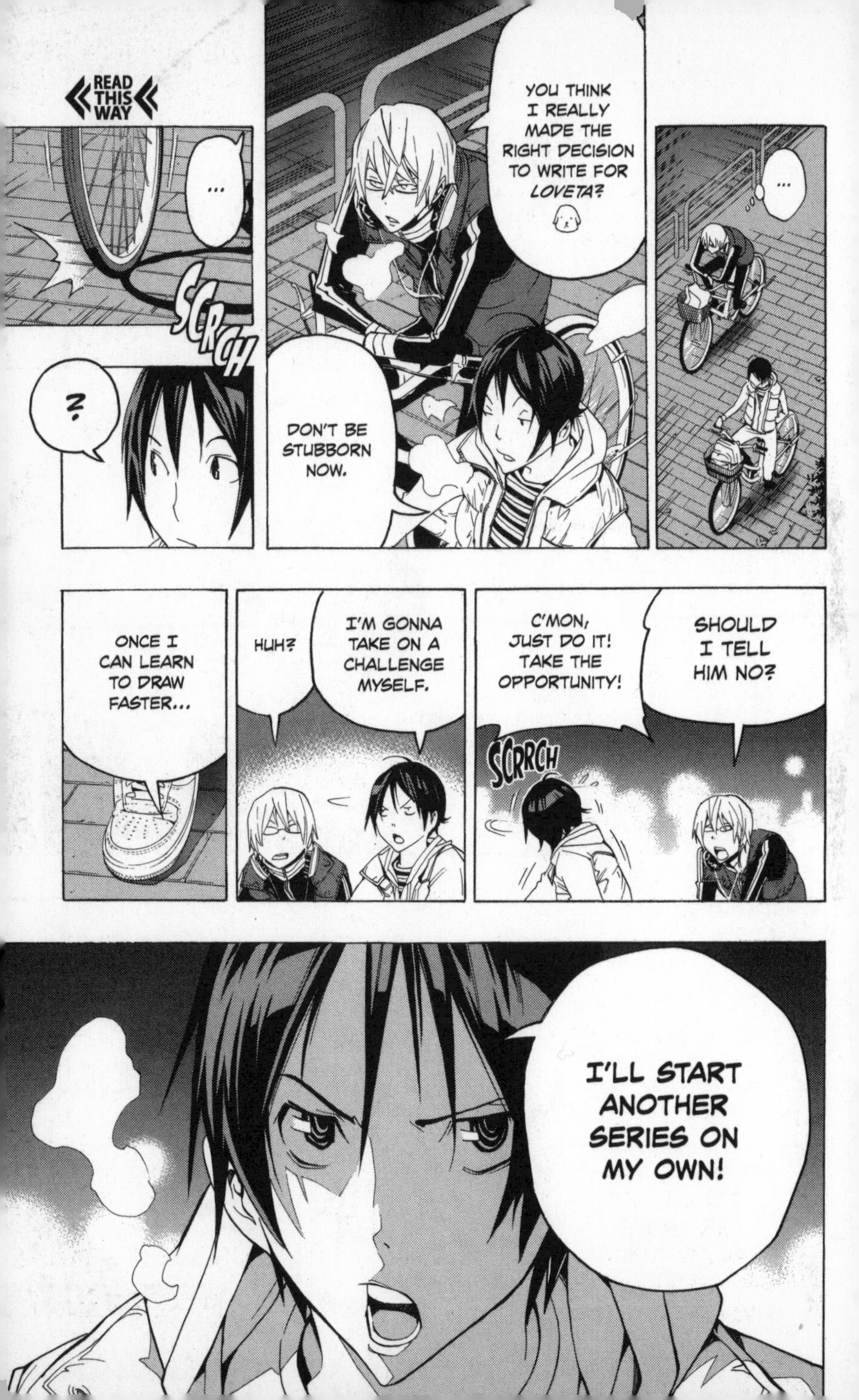
READ THIS WAY
...
YOU THINK I REALLY MADE THE RIGHT DECISION TO WRITE FOR *LOVETA*?
DON'T BE STUBBORN NOW.
...
SCRCH
?
SHOULD I TELL HIM NO?
C'MON, JUST DO IT! TAKE THE OPPORTUNITY!
SCRRCH
I'M GONNA TAKE ON A CHALLENGE MYSELF.
HUH?
ONCE I CAN LEARN TO DRAW FASTER...
I'LL START ANOTHER SERIES ON MY OWN!

OHBA'S STORYBOARD

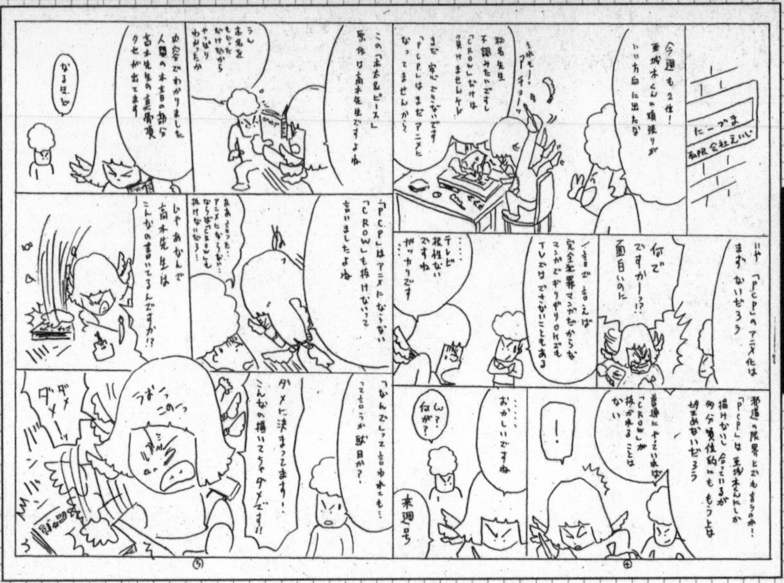

たーづま
有限会社えいじ
今週も2位! 亜城木くんの頑張りがいい方向に出たな
アチョーッ
秋名先生不調みたいですし「CROW」だけは負けませんしね
まだ安心できないです「PCP」はまだアニメになってませんから
いや「PCP」のアニメ化はまずないだろう
何でですかーっ!? 面白いのに
一言で言えば完全犯罪マンガだからな マンガでギリギリOKでもTVでは出来ないこともある
……テレビ規制ですね
ガッカリです
邪道の限界とかもあるのか…
「PCP」は亜城木くんにしか描けないし合っているが多分人気順位的にももう上はないだろう
普通にやっていれば「CROW」が抜かれることはない
!
……おかしいですね
ん? 何が?
来週号
この「ぷ太&ピース」原作は高木先生ですよね
うん 本名をもじっただけだからやっぱりわかったか
内容でわかりました 人間の本音の部分 高木先生の真骨頂 クセが出てます
なるほど
「PCP」はアニメにならない「CROW」も抜けないって言いましたよね
じゃあなんで高木先生はこんなの書いてるんですか!?
「なんでっ」て言われても… ってゆーか駄目か?
ダメに決まってます! こんなの描いてちゃダメです!!
うぬっ このっ
ダメ ダメーッ

OBATA'S STORYBOARD

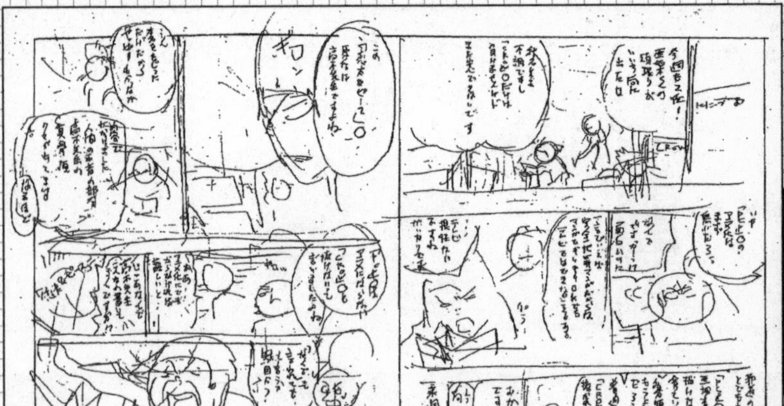

COMPLETE!

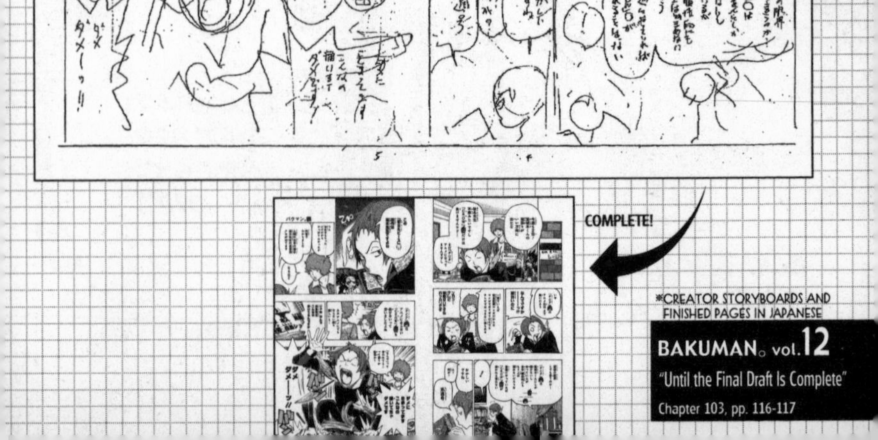

※CREATOR STORYBOARDS AND FINISHED PAGES IN JAPANESE

BAKUMAN。 vol.12

"Until the Final Draft Is Complete"

Chapter 103, pp. 116-117

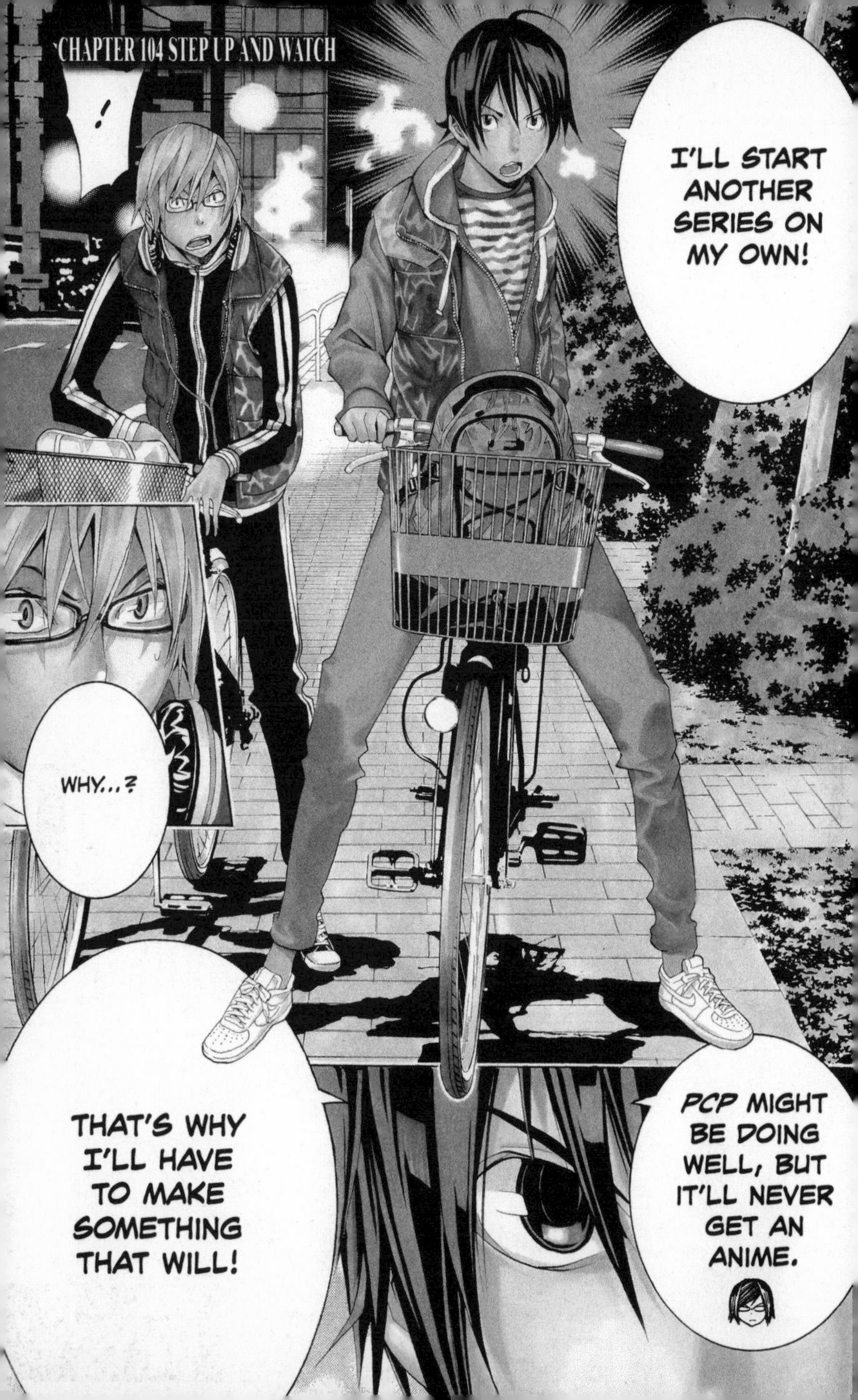
CHAPTER 104 STEP UP AND WATCH
I'LL START ANOTHER SERIES ON MY OWN!
!
WHY...?
PCP MIGHT BE DOING WELL, BUT IT'LL NEVER GET AN ANIME.
THAT'S WHY I'LL HAVE TO MAKE SOMETHING THAT WILL!

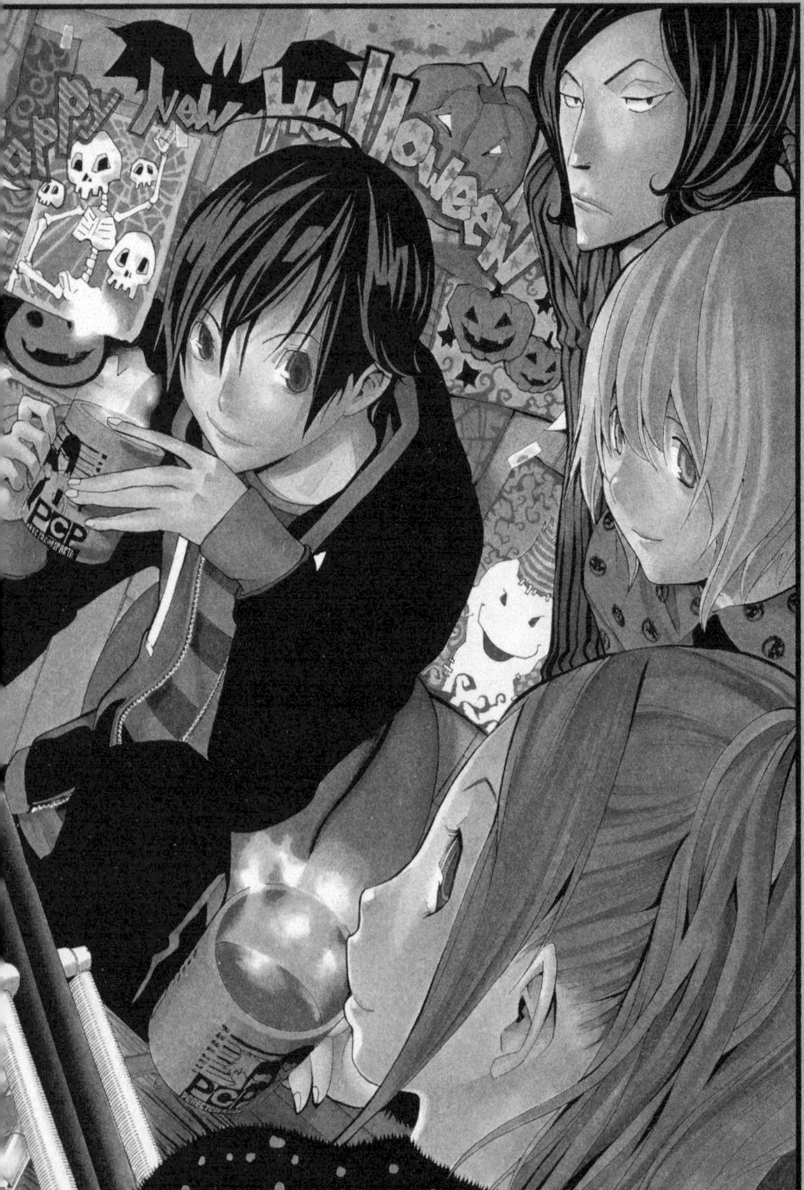
appy New Halloween
PCP
PCP

CHAPTER 104
STEP UP AND WATCH

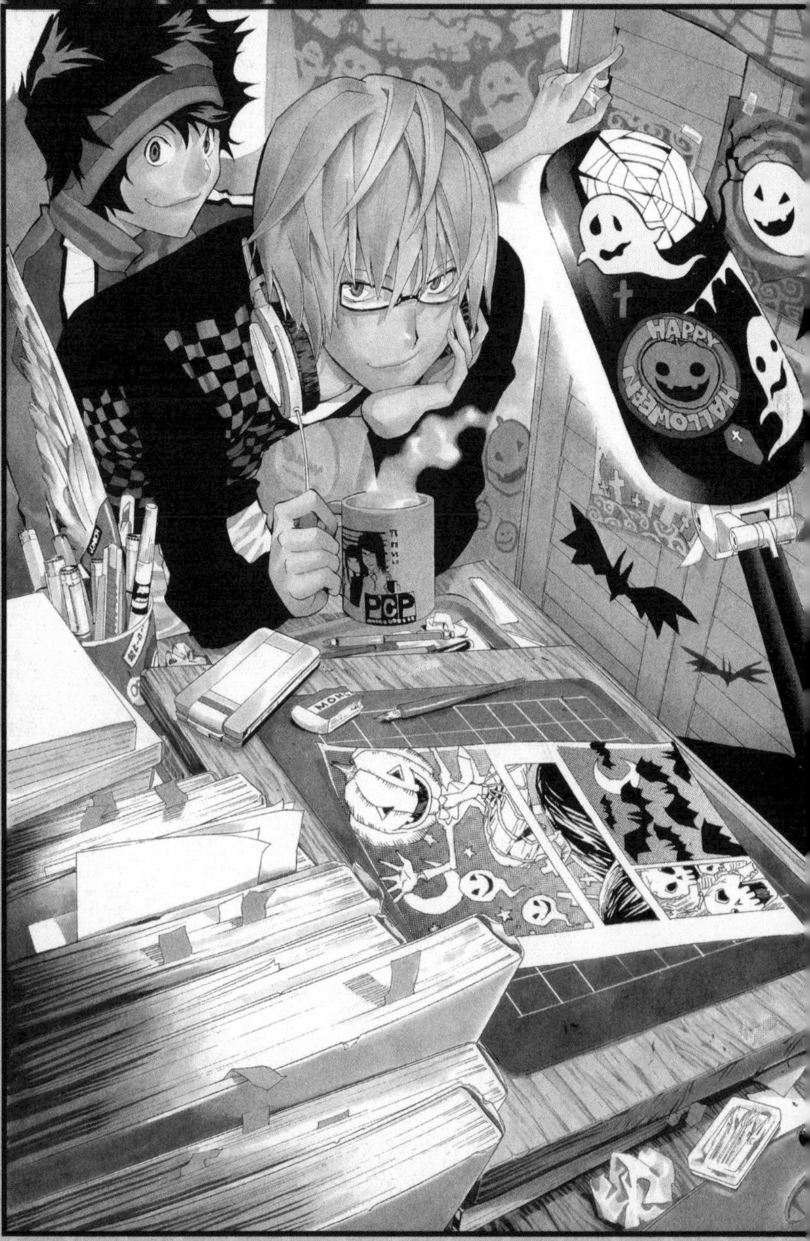
HAPPY HALLOWEEN
PCP

BAKUMAN。

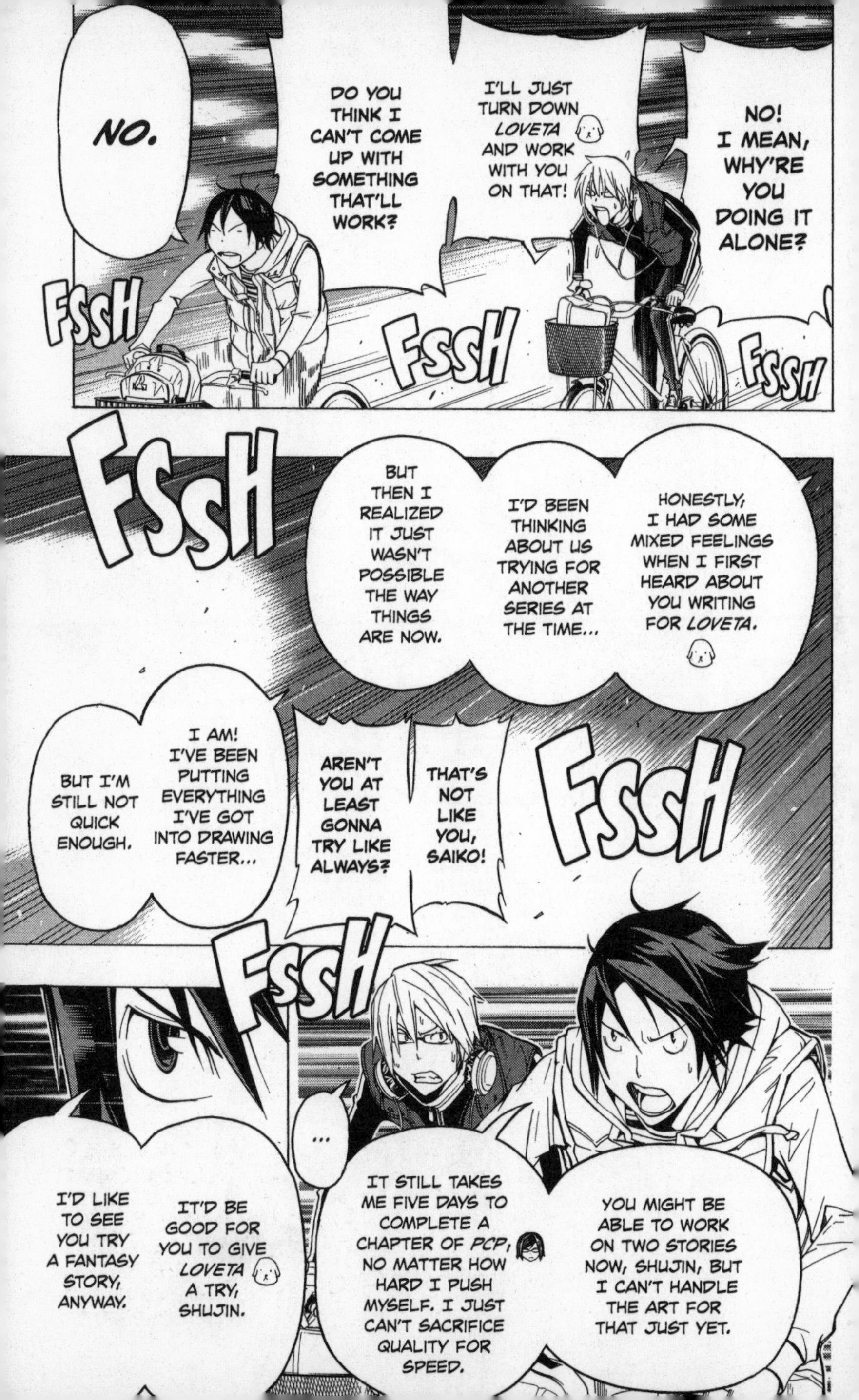

NO! I MEAN, WHY'RE YOU DOING IT ALONE?
I'LL JUST TURN DOWN *LOVETA* AND WORK WITH YOU ON THAT!
DO YOU THINK I CAN'T COME UP WITH SOMETHING THAT'LL WORK?
NO.
FSSH
FSSH
FSSH
FSSH
HONESTLY, I HAD SOME MIXED FEELINGS WHEN I FIRST HEARD ABOUT YOU WRITING FOR *LOVETA*.
I'D BEEN THINKING ABOUT US TRYING FOR ANOTHER SERIES AT THE TIME...
BUT THEN I REALIZED IT JUST WASN'T POSSIBLE THE WAY THINGS ARE NOW.
FSSH
THAT'S NOT LIKE YOU, SAIKO!
AREN'T YOU AT LEAST GONNA TRY LIKE ALWAYS?
I AM! I'VE BEEN PUTTING EVERYTHING I'VE GOT INTO DRAWING FASTER...
BUT I'M STILL NOT QUICK ENOUGH.
YOU MIGHT BE ABLE TO WORK ON TWO STORIES NOW, SHUJIN, BUT I CAN'T HANDLE THE ART FOR THAT JUST YET.
IT STILL TAKES ME FIVE DAYS TO COMPLETE A CHAPTER OF *PCP*, NO MATTER HOW HARD I PUSH MYSELF. I JUST CAN'T SACRIFICE QUALITY FOR SPEED.
...
FSSH
IT'D BE GOOD FOR YOU TO GIVE *LOVETA* A TRY, SHUJIN.
I'D LIKE TO SEE YOU TRY A FANTASY STORY, ANYWAY.

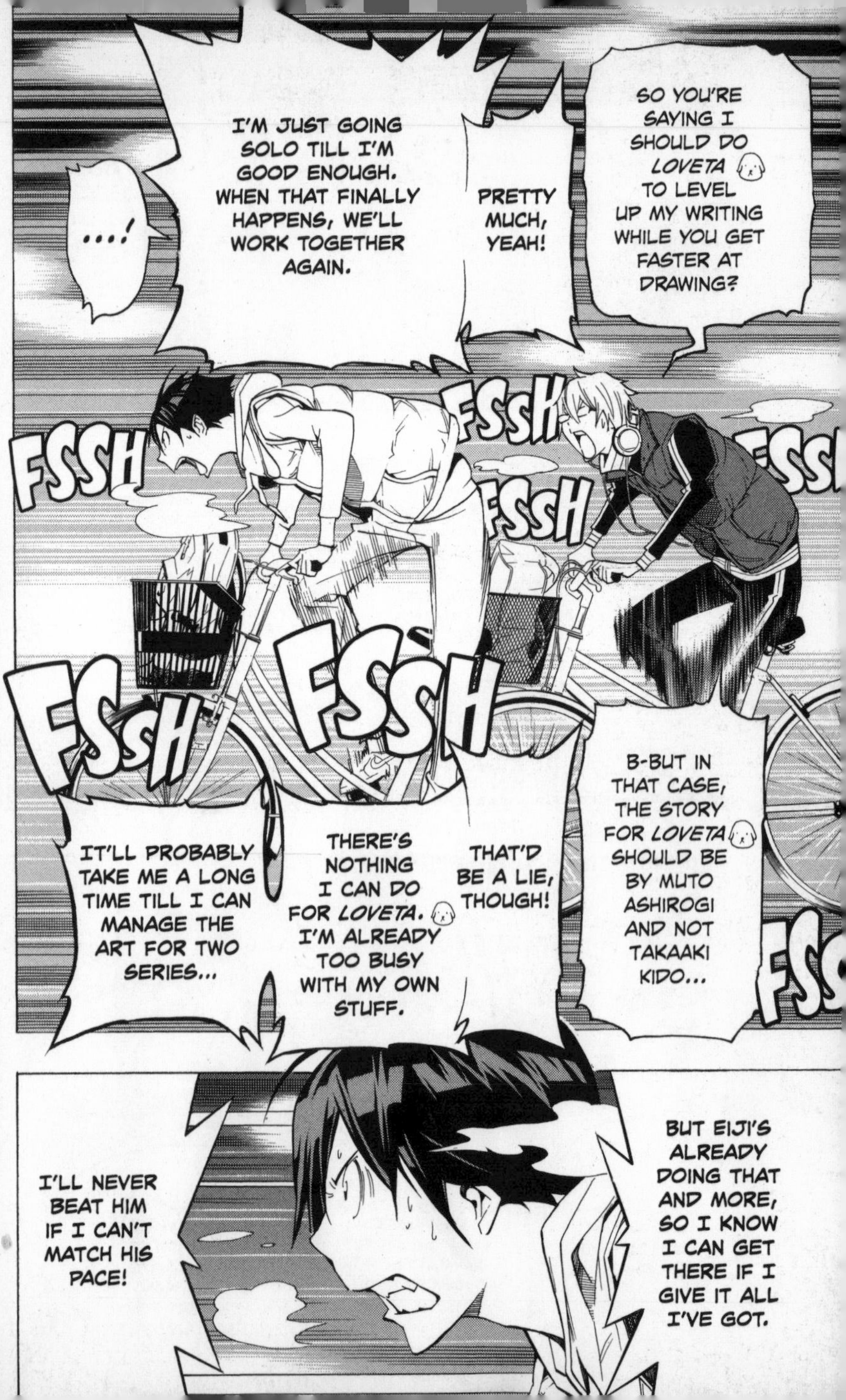
SO YOU'RE SAYING I SHOULD DO *LOVETA* TO LEVEL UP MY WRITING WHILE YOU GET FASTER AT DRAWING?
PRETTY MUCH, YEAH!
I'M JUST GOING SOLO TILL I'M GOOD ENOUGH. WHEN THAT FINALLY HAPPENS, WE'LL WORK TOGETHER AGAIN.
...!
FSSH
FSSH
FSSH
FSSH
FSSH
FSSH
B-BUT IN THAT CASE, THE STORY FOR *LOVETA* SHOULD BE BY MUTO ASHIROGI AND NOT TAKAAKI KIDO...
THAT'D BE A LIE, THOUGH!
THERE'S NOTHING I CAN DO FOR *LOVETA*. I'M ALREADY TOO BUSY WITH MY OWN STUFF.
IT'LL PROBABLY TAKE ME A LONG TIME TILL I CAN MANAGE THE ART FOR TWO SERIES...
BUT EIJI'S ALREADY DOING THAT AND MORE, SO I KNOW I CAN GET THERE IF I GIVE IT ALL I'VE GOT.
I'LL NEVER BEAT HIM IF I CAN'T MATCH HIS PACE!

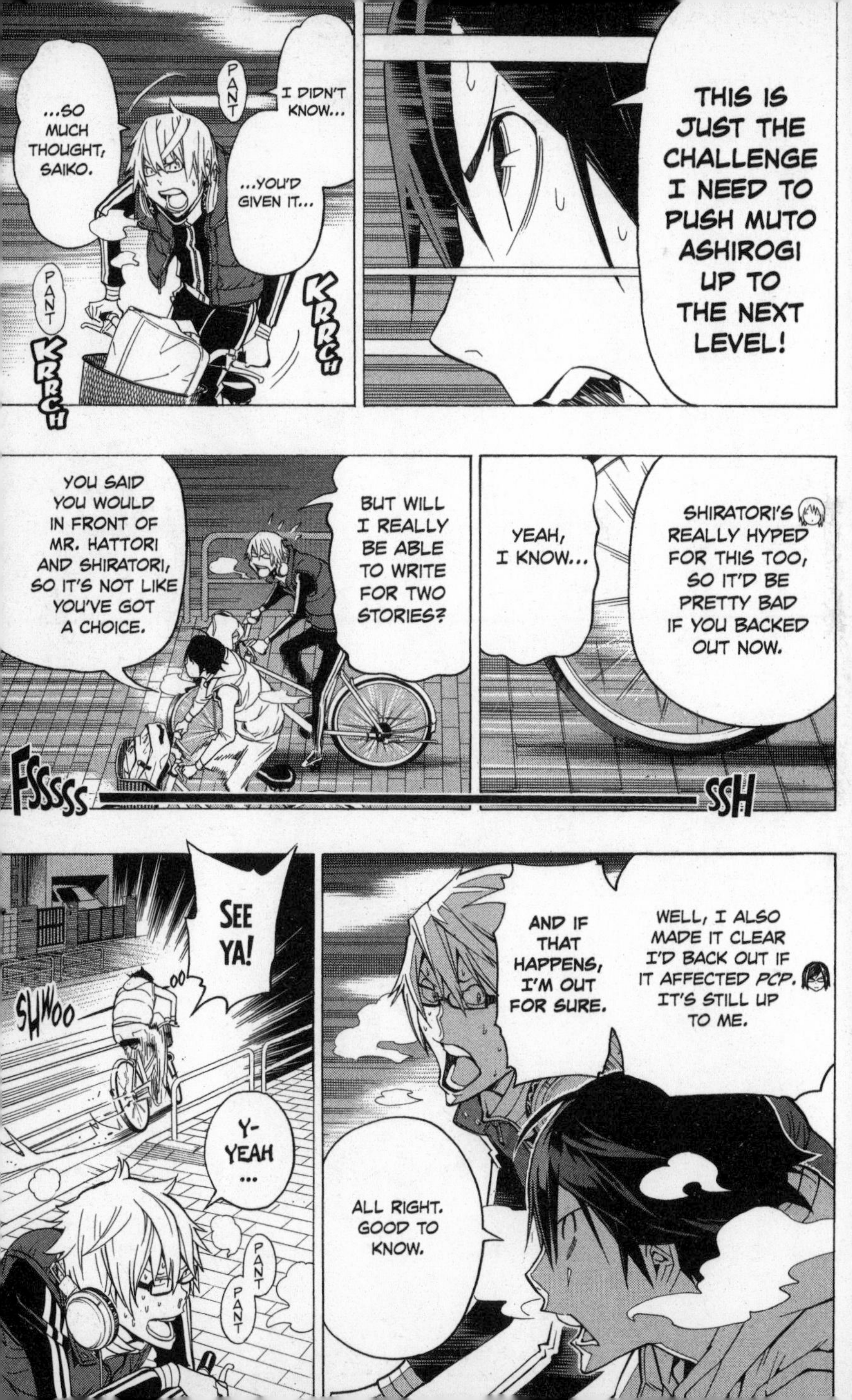
THIS IS JUST THE CHALLENGE I NEED TO PUSH MUTO ASHIROGI UP TO THE NEXT LEVEL!
I DIDN'T KNOW...
...YOU'D GIVEN IT...
PANT
...SO MUCH THOUGHT, SAIKO.
KRRCH
PANT
KRRCH
SHIRATORI'S REALLY HYPED FOR THIS TOO, SO IT'D BE PRETTY BAD IF YOU BACKED OUT NOW.
YEAH, I KNOW...
SSH
BUT WILL I REALLY BE ABLE TO WRITE FOR TWO STORIES?
YOU SAID YOU WOULD IN FRONT OF MR. HATTORI AND SHIRATORI, SO IT'S NOT LIKE YOU'VE GOT A CHOICE.
FSSSSS
WELL, I ALSO MADE IT CLEAR I'D BACK OUT IF IT AFFECTED *PCP*. IT'S STILL UP TO ME.
AND IF THAT HAPPENS, I'M OUT FOR SURE.
ALL RIGHT. GOOD TO KNOW.
SEE YA!
SHWOO
Y-YEAH...
PANT
PANT

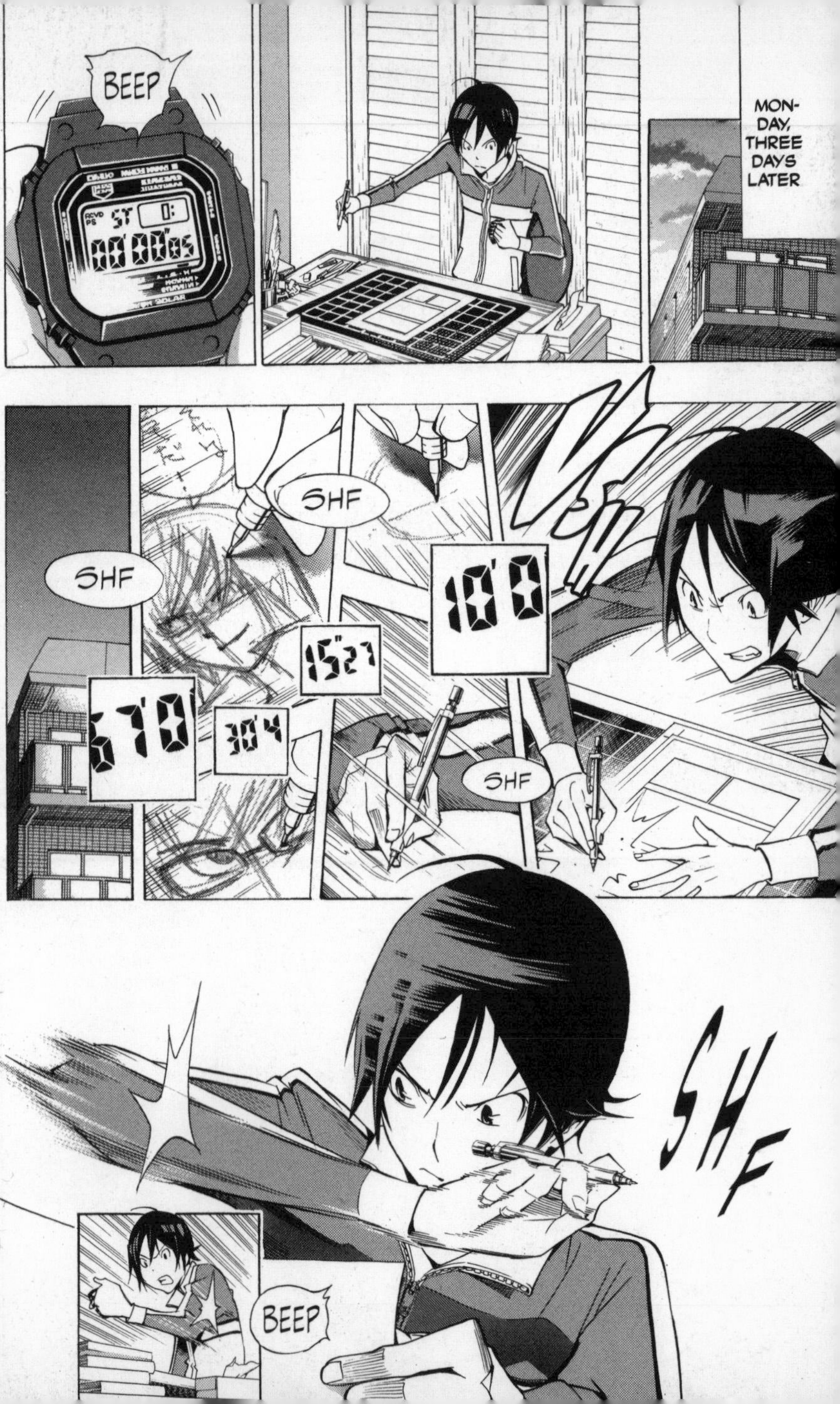
MON-DAY, THREE DAYS LATER
BEEP
SHF
SHF
SHF
SHF
BEEP

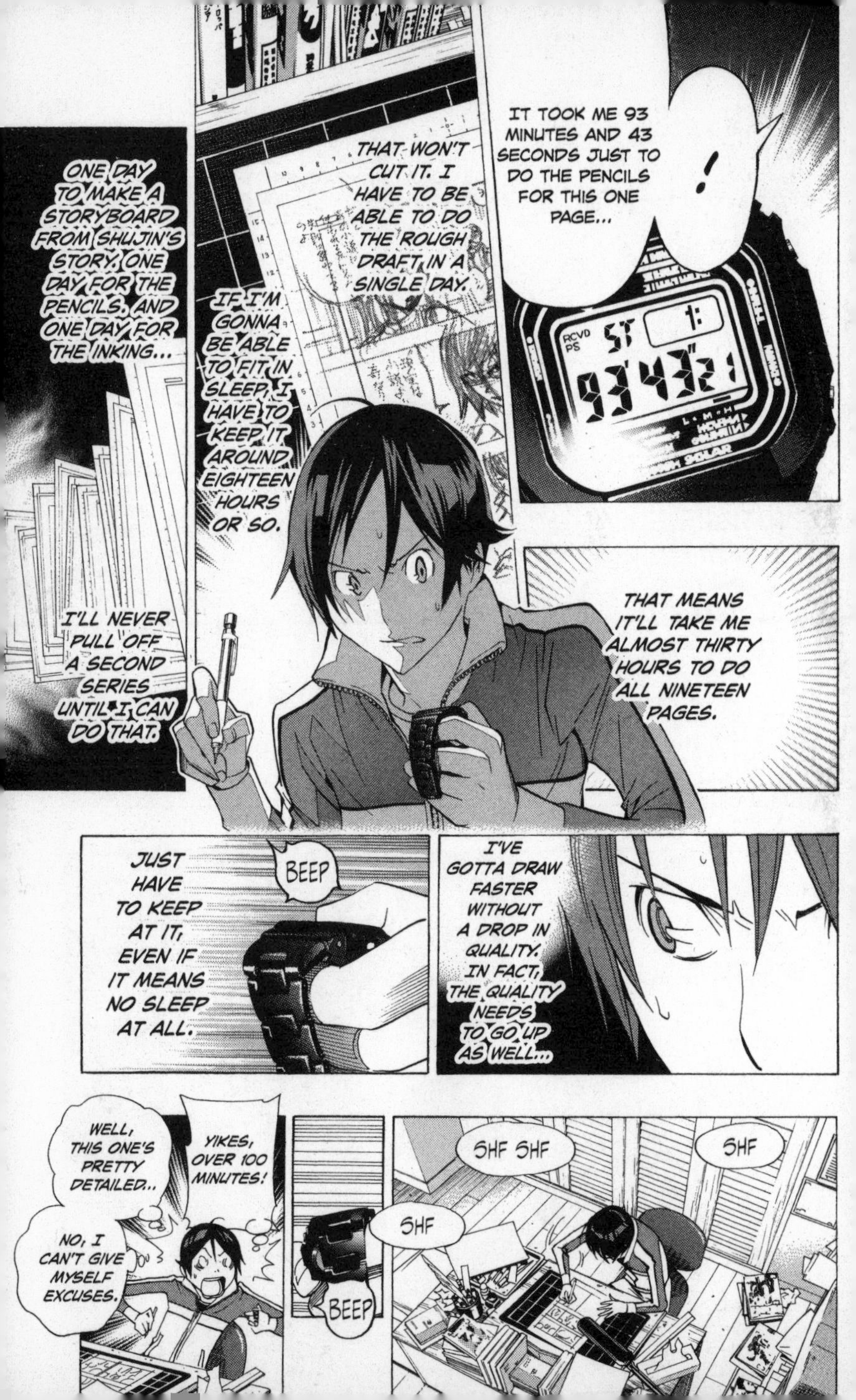
!
IT TOOK ME 93 MINUTES AND 43 SECONDS JUST TO DO THE PENCILS FOR THIS ONE PAGE...
THAT MEANS IT'LL TAKE ME ALMOST THIRTY HOURS TO DO ALL NINETEEN PAGES.
THAT WON'T CUT IT. I HAVE TO BE ABLE TO DO THE ROUGH DRAFT IN A SINGLE DAY.
IF I'M GONNA BE ABLE TO FIT IN SLEEP, I HAVE TO KEEP IT AROUND EIGHTEEN HOURS OR SO.
ONE DAY TO MAKE A STORYBOARD FROM SHUJIN'S STORY. ONE DAY FOR THE PENCILS. AND ONE DAY FOR THE INKING...
I'LL NEVER PULL OFF A SECOND SERIES UNTIL I CAN DO THAT.
I'VE GOTTA DRAW FASTER WITHOUT A DROP IN QUALITY. IN FACT, THE QUALITY NEEDS TO GO UP AS WELL...
BEEP
JUST HAVE TO KEEP AT IT, EVEN IF IT MEANS NO SLEEP AT ALL.
SHF
SHF SHF
SHF
BEEP
YIKES, OVER 100 MINUTES!
WELL, THIS ONE'S PRETTY DETAILED...
NO, I CAN'T GIVE MYSELF EXCUSES.

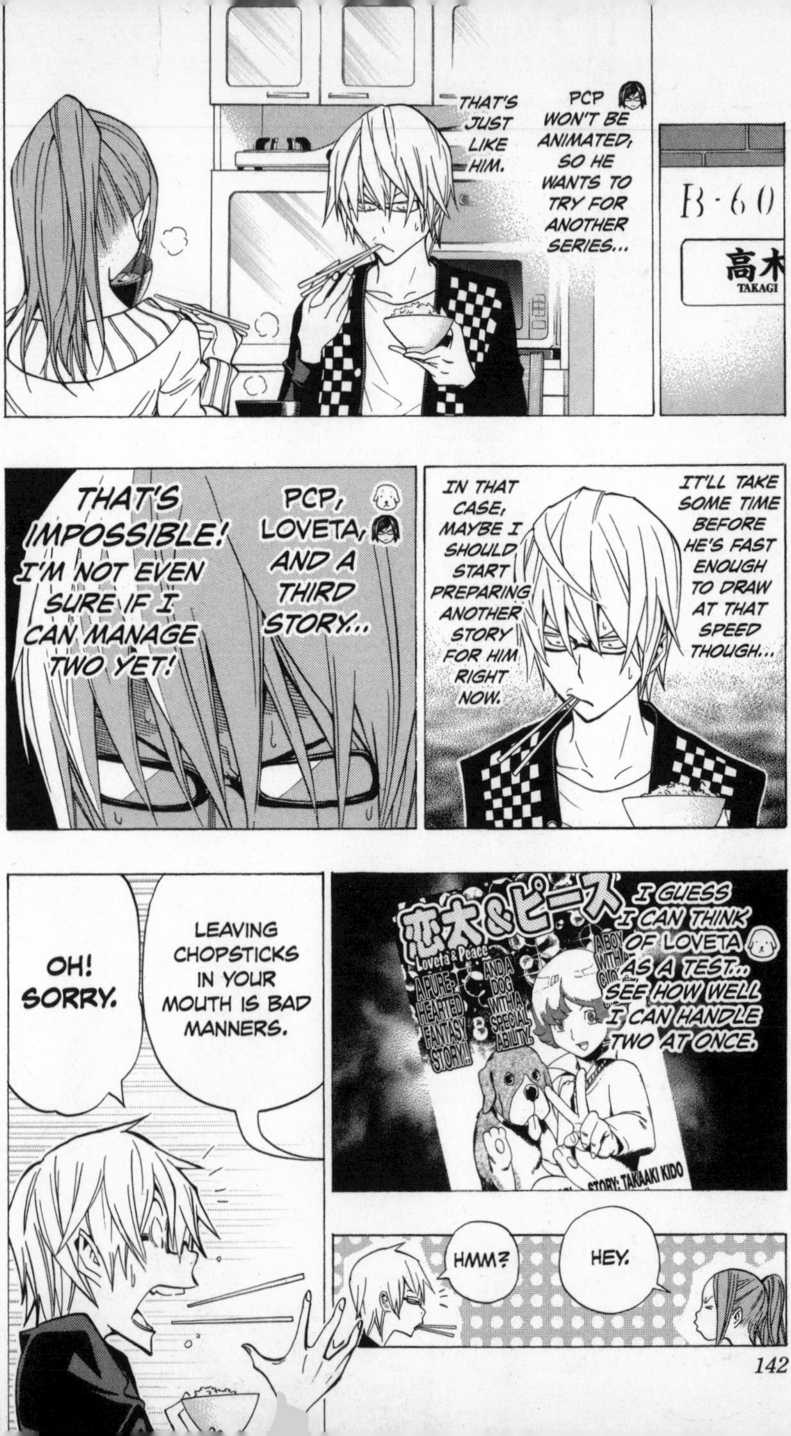
B-60
高木
TAKAGI
PCP WON'T BE ANIMATED, SO HE WANTS TO TRY FOR ANOTHER SERIES...
THAT'S JUST LIKE HIM.
IT'LL TAKE SOME TIME BEFORE HE'S FAST ENOUGH TO DRAW AT THAT SPEED THOUGH...
IN THAT CASE, MAYBE I SHOULD START PREPARING ANOTHER STORY FOR HIM RIGHT NOW.
PCP, LOVETA, AND A THIRD STORY...
THAT'S IMPOSSIBLE! I'M NOT EVEN SURE IF I CAN MANAGE TWO YET!
I GUESS I CAN THINK OF LOVETA AS A TEST... SEE HOW WELL I CAN HANDLE TWO AT ONCE.
恋太&ピース
Loveta & Peace
A PURE-HEARTED FANTASY STORY!!
AND A DOG WITH A SPECIAL ABILITY.
STORY: TAKAAKI KIDO
HEY.
HMM?
LEAVING CHOPSTICKS IN YOUR MOUTH IS BAD MANNERS.
OH! SORRY.

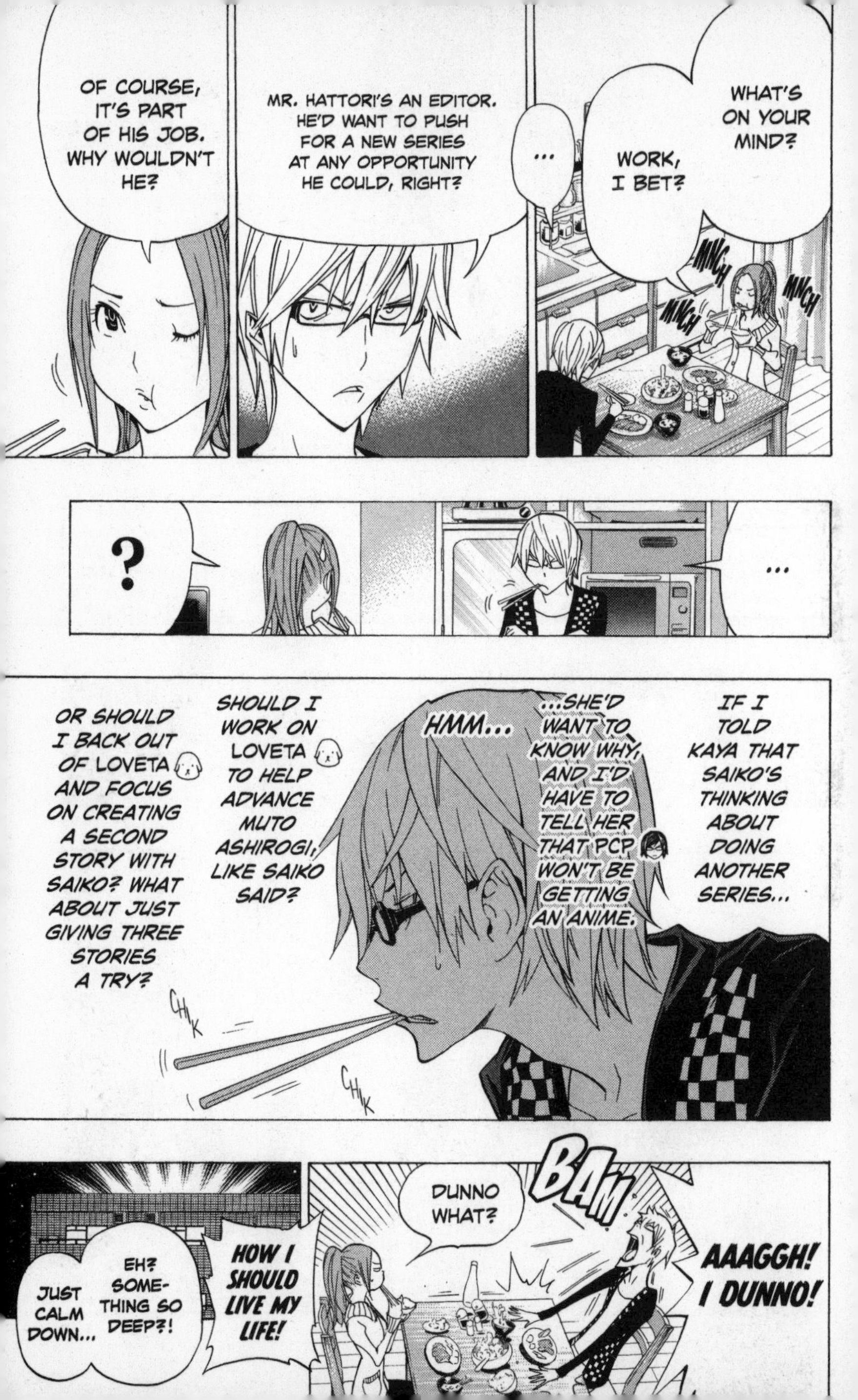
WHAT'S ON YOUR MIND?
WORK, I BET?
...
MNCH
MNCH
MNCH
MR. HATTORI'S AN EDITOR. HE'D WANT TO PUSH FOR A NEW SERIES AT ANY OPPORTUNITY HE COULD, RIGHT?
OF COURSE, IT'S PART OF HIS JOB. WHY WOULDN'T HE?
...
?
IF I TOLD KAYA THAT SAIKO'S THINKING ABOUT DOING ANOTHER SERIES...
...SHE'D WANT TO KNOW WHY, AND I'D HAVE TO TELL HER THAT PCP WON'T BE GETTING AN ANIME.
HMM...
SHOULD I WORK ON LOVETA TO HELP ADVANCE MUTO ASHIROGI, LIKE SAIKO SAID?
OR SHOULD I BACK OUT OF LOVETA AND FOCUS ON CREATING A SECOND STORY WITH SAIKO? WHAT ABOUT JUST GIVING THREE STORIES A TRY?
CHIK
CHIK
AAAGGH! I DUNNO!
BAM
DUNNO WHAT?
HOW I SHOULD LIVE MY LIFE!
EH? SOME-THING SO DEEP?!
JUST CALM DOWN...

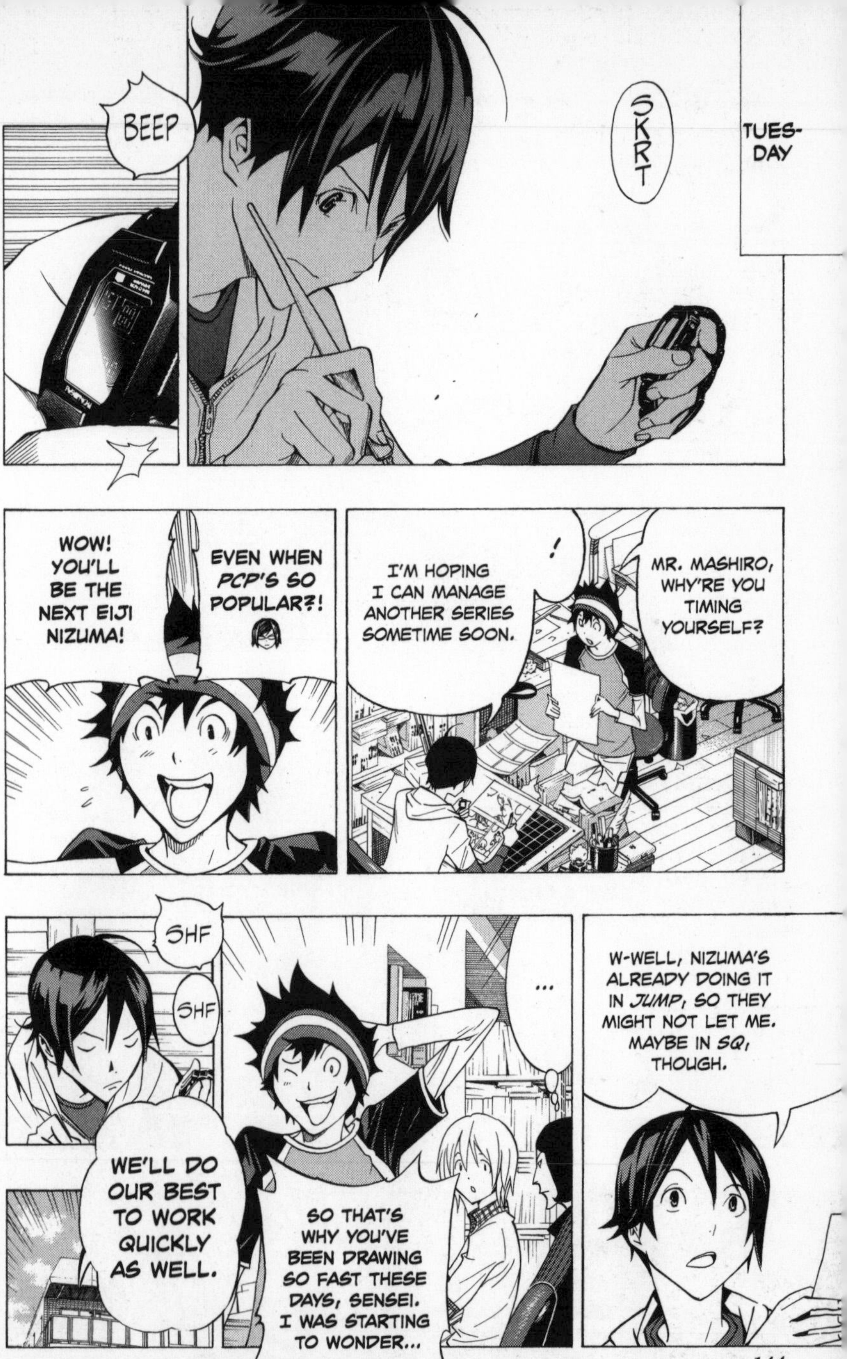
TUES-DAY
SKRT
BEEP
!
MR. MASHIRO, WHY'RE YOU TIMING YOURSELF?
I'M HOPING I CAN MANAGE ANOTHER SERIES SOMETIME SOON.
EVEN WHEN *PCP*'S SO POPULAR?!
WOW! YOU'LL BE THE NEXT EIJI NIZUMA!
W-WELL, NIZUMA'S ALREADY DOING IT IN *JUMP*, SO THEY MIGHT NOT LET ME. MAYBE IN *SQ*, THOUGH.
...
SO THAT'S WHY YOU'VE BEEN DRAWING SO FAST THESE DAYS, SENSEI. I WAS STARTING TO WONDER...
SHF
SHF
WE'LL DO OUR BEST TO WORK QUICKLY AS WELL.

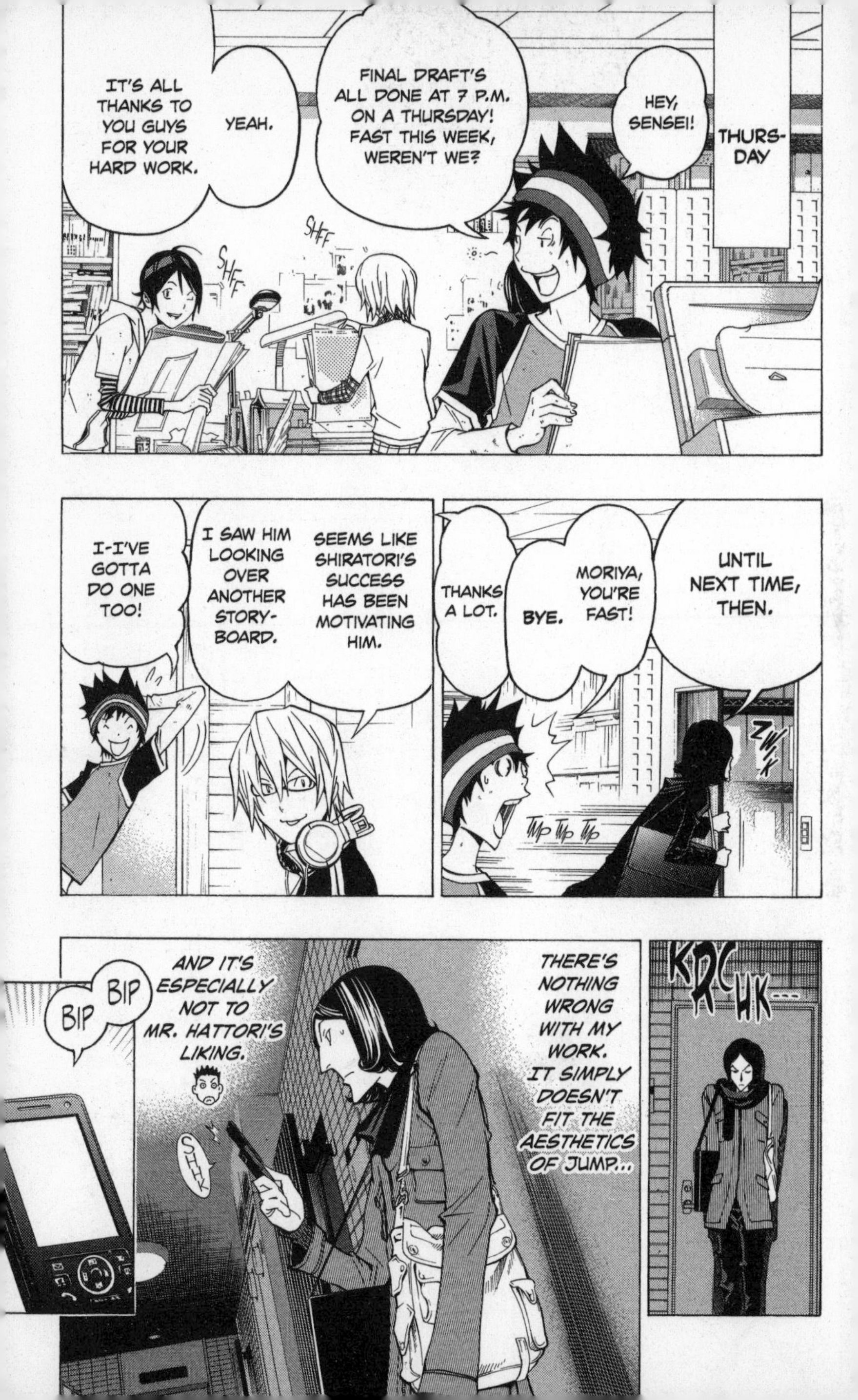
THURSDAY
HEY, SENSEI!
FINAL DRAFT'S ALL DONE AT 7 P.M. ON A THURSDAY! FAST THIS WEEK, WEREN'T WE?
YEAH.
IT'S ALL THANKS TO YOU GUYS FOR YOUR HARD WORK.
SHFF
SHFF
UNTIL NEXT TIME, THEN.
MORIYA, YOU'RE FAST!
BYE.
THANKS A LOT.
ZWIK
TMP TMP TMP
SEEMS LIKE SHIRATORI'S SUCCESS HAS BEEN MOTIVATING HIM.
I SAW HIM LOOKING OVER ANOTHER STORY-BOARD.
I-I'VE GOTTA DO ONE TOO!
KRCHK...
THERE'S NOTHING WRONG WITH MY WORK. IT SIMPLY DOESN'T FIT THE AESTHETICS OF JUMP...
AND IT'S ESPECIALLY NOT TO MR. HATTORI'S LIKING.
BIP
BIP
SHHK

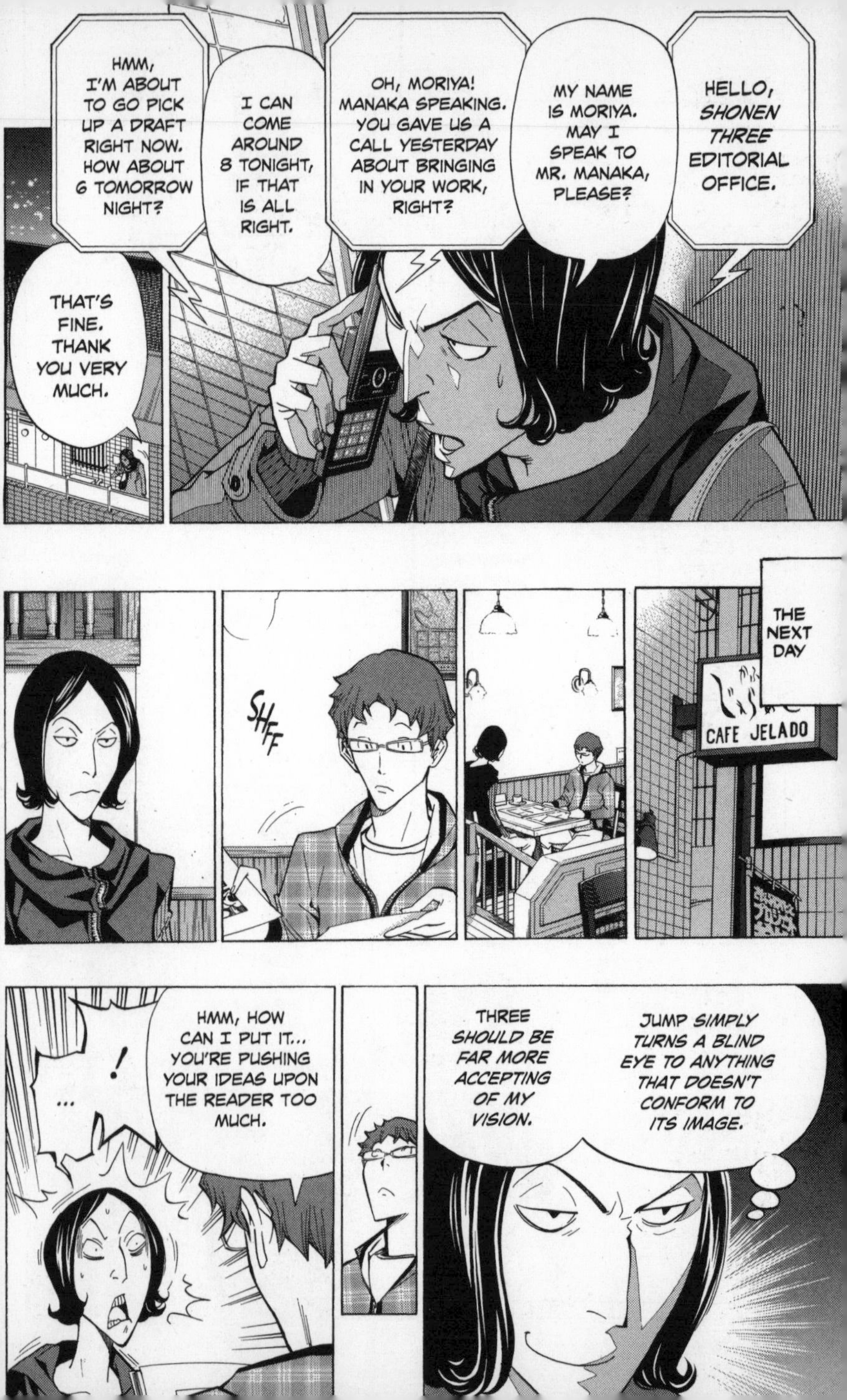
HELLO, SHONEN THREE EDITORIAL OFFICE.
MY NAME IS MORIYA. MAY I SPEAK TO MR. MANAKA, PLEASE?
OH, MORIYA! MANAKA SPEAKING. YOU GAVE US A CALL YESTERDAY ABOUT BRINGING IN YOUR WORK, RIGHT?
I CAN COME AROUND 8 TONIGHT, IF THAT IS ALL RIGHT.
HMM, I'M ABOUT TO GO PICK UP A DRAFT RIGHT NOW. HOW ABOUT 6 TOMORROW NIGHT?
THAT'S FINE. THANK YOU VERY MUCH.
THE NEXT DAY
CAFE JELADO
SHFF
JUMP SIMPLY TURNS A BLIND EYE TO ANYTHING THAT DOESN'T CONFORM TO ITS IMAGE.
THREE SHOULD BE FAR MORE ACCEPTING OF MY VISION.
HMM, HOW CAN I PUT IT... YOU'RE PUSHING YOUR IDEAS UPON THE READER TOO MUCH.
!
...

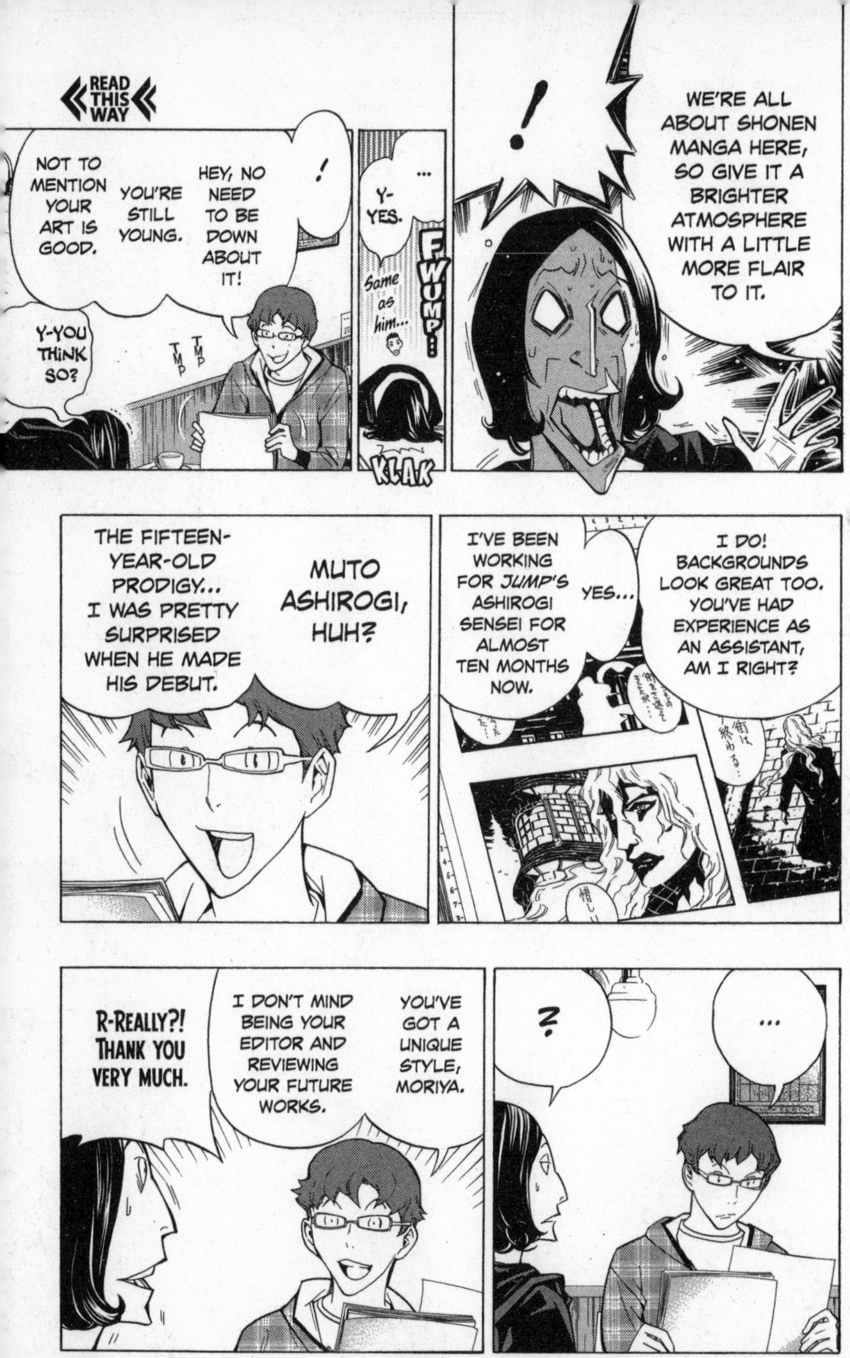
READ THIS WAY
WE'RE ALL ABOUT SHONEN MANGA HERE, SO GIVE IT A BRIGHTER ATMOSPHERE WITH A LITTLE MORE FLAIR TO IT.
!
...
Y-YES.
Same as him...
FWUMP...
KLAK
!
HEY, NO NEED TO BE DOWN ABOUT IT!
YOU'RE STILL YOUNG.
NOT TO MENTION YOUR ART IS GOOD.
Y-YOU THINK SO?
TMP TMP
I DO! BACKGROUNDS LOOK GREAT TOO. YOU'VE HAD EXPERIENCE AS AN ASSISTANT, AM I RIGHT?
YES...
I'VE BEEN WORKING FOR JUMP'S ASHIROGI SENSEI FOR ALMOST TEN MONTHS NOW.
MUTO ASHIROGI, HUH?
THE FIFTEEN-YEAR-OLD PRODIGY... I WAS PRETTY SURPRISED WHEN HE MADE HIS DEBUT.
...
?
YOU'VE GOT A UNIQUE STYLE, MORIYA.
I DON'T MIND BEING YOUR EDITOR AND REVIEWING YOUR FUTURE WORKS.
R-REALLY?! THANK YOU VERY MUCH.

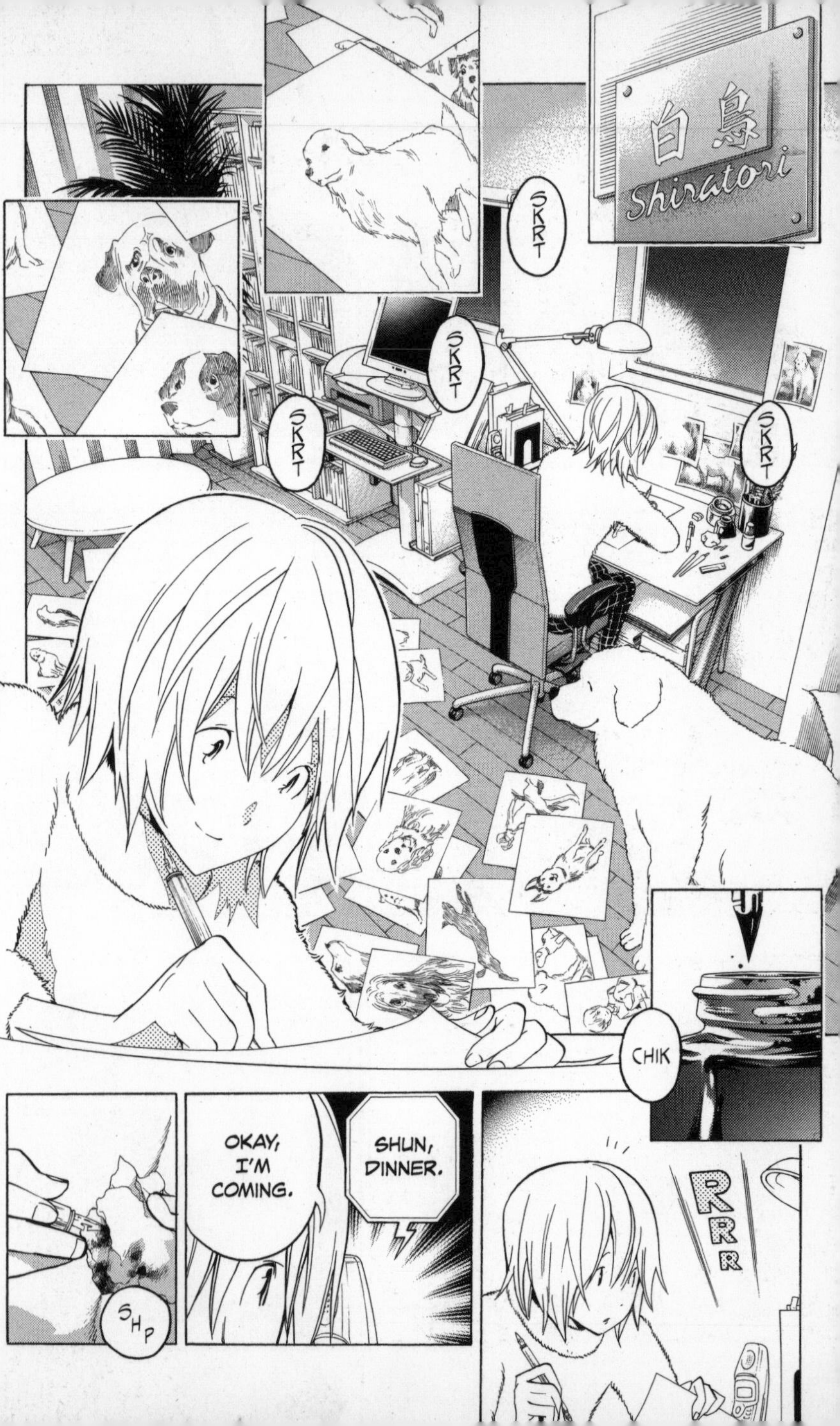

白鳥
Shiratori
SKRT
SKRT
SKRT
SKRT
CHIK
RRR
SHUN, DINNER.
OKAY, I'M COMING.
SHP

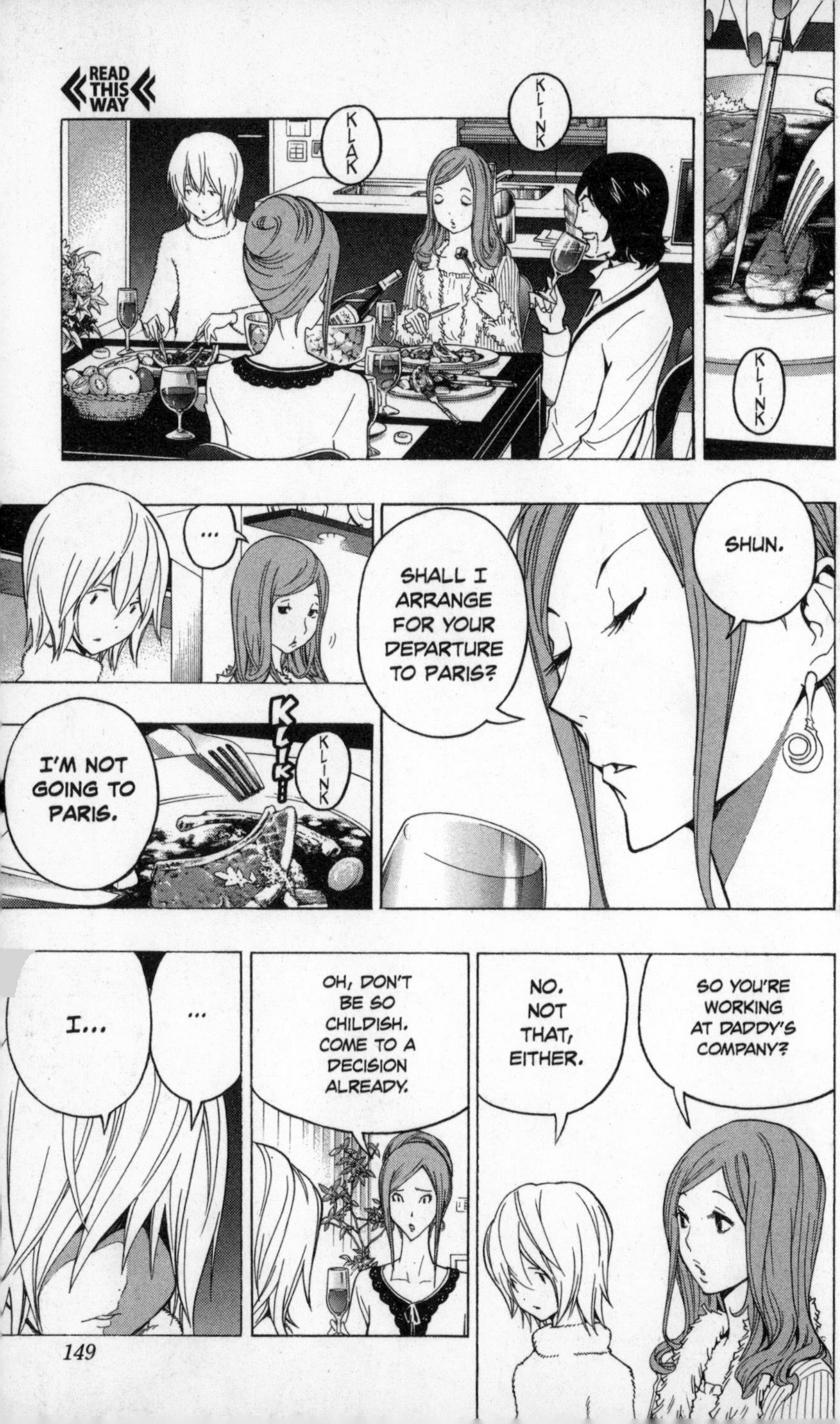
READ THIS WAY
KLINK
KLINK
KLAK
SHUN.
SHALL I ARRANGE FOR YOUR DEPARTURE TO PARIS?
...
KLINK
KLIK
I'M NOT GOING TO PARIS.
SO YOU'RE WORKING AT DADDY'S COMPANY?
NO. NOT THAT, EITHER.
OH, DON'T BE SO CHILDISH. COME TO A DECISION ALREADY.
...
I...

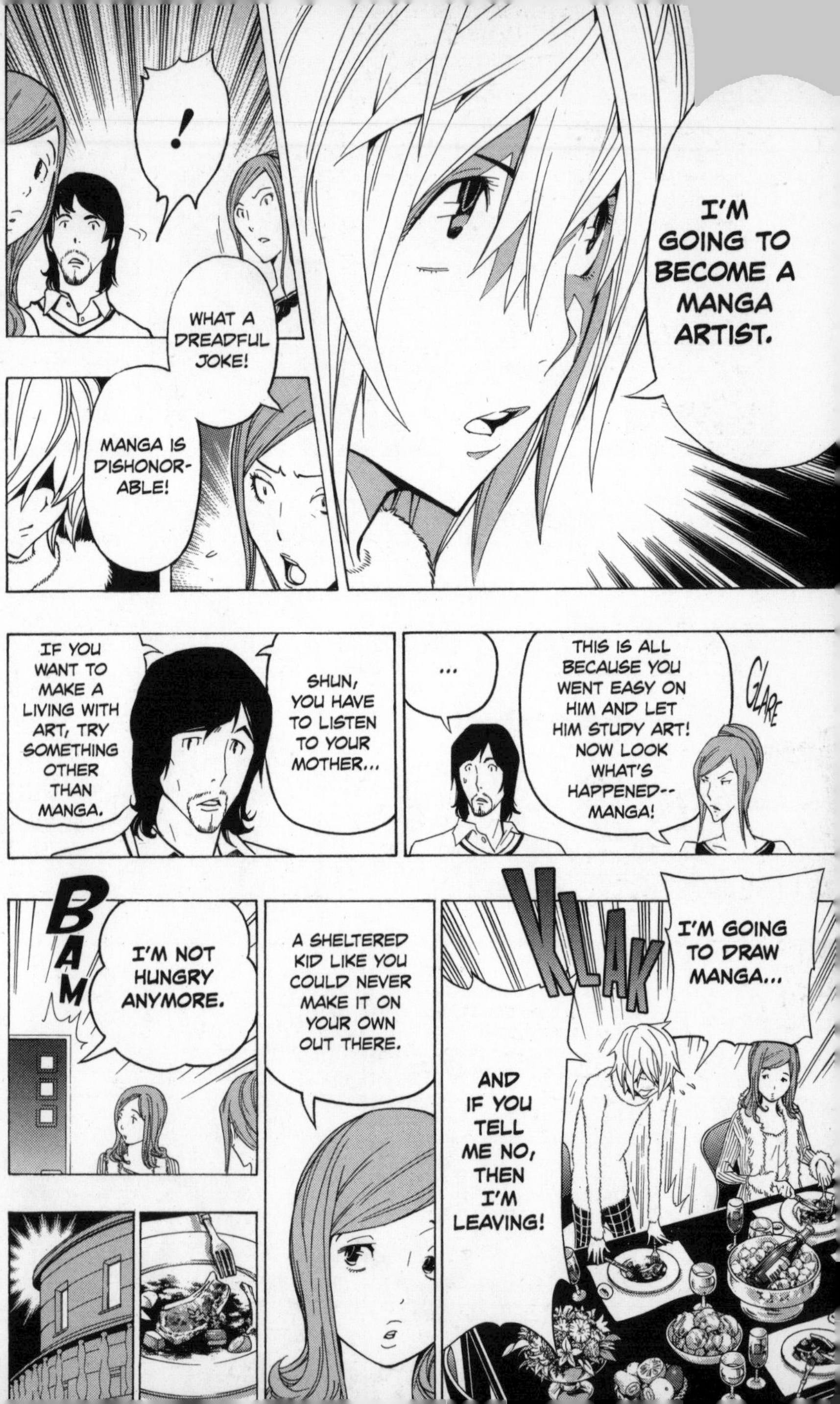
I'M GOING TO BECOME A MANGA ARTIST.
!
WHAT A DREADFUL JOKE!
MANGA IS DISHONOR-ABLE!
GLARE
THIS IS ALL BECAUSE YOU WENT EASY ON HIM AND LET HIM STUDY ART! NOW LOOK WHAT'S HAPPENED-- MANGA!
...
SHUN, YOU HAVE TO LISTEN TO YOUR MOTHER...
IF YOU WANT TO MAKE A LIVING WITH ART, TRY SOMETHING OTHER THAN MANGA.
I'M GOING TO DRAW MANGA...
KLAK
AND IF YOU TELL ME NO, THEN I'M LEAVING!
A SHELTERED KID LIKE YOU COULD NEVER MAKE IT ON YOUR OWN OUT THERE.
BAM
I'M NOT HUNGRY ANYMORE.

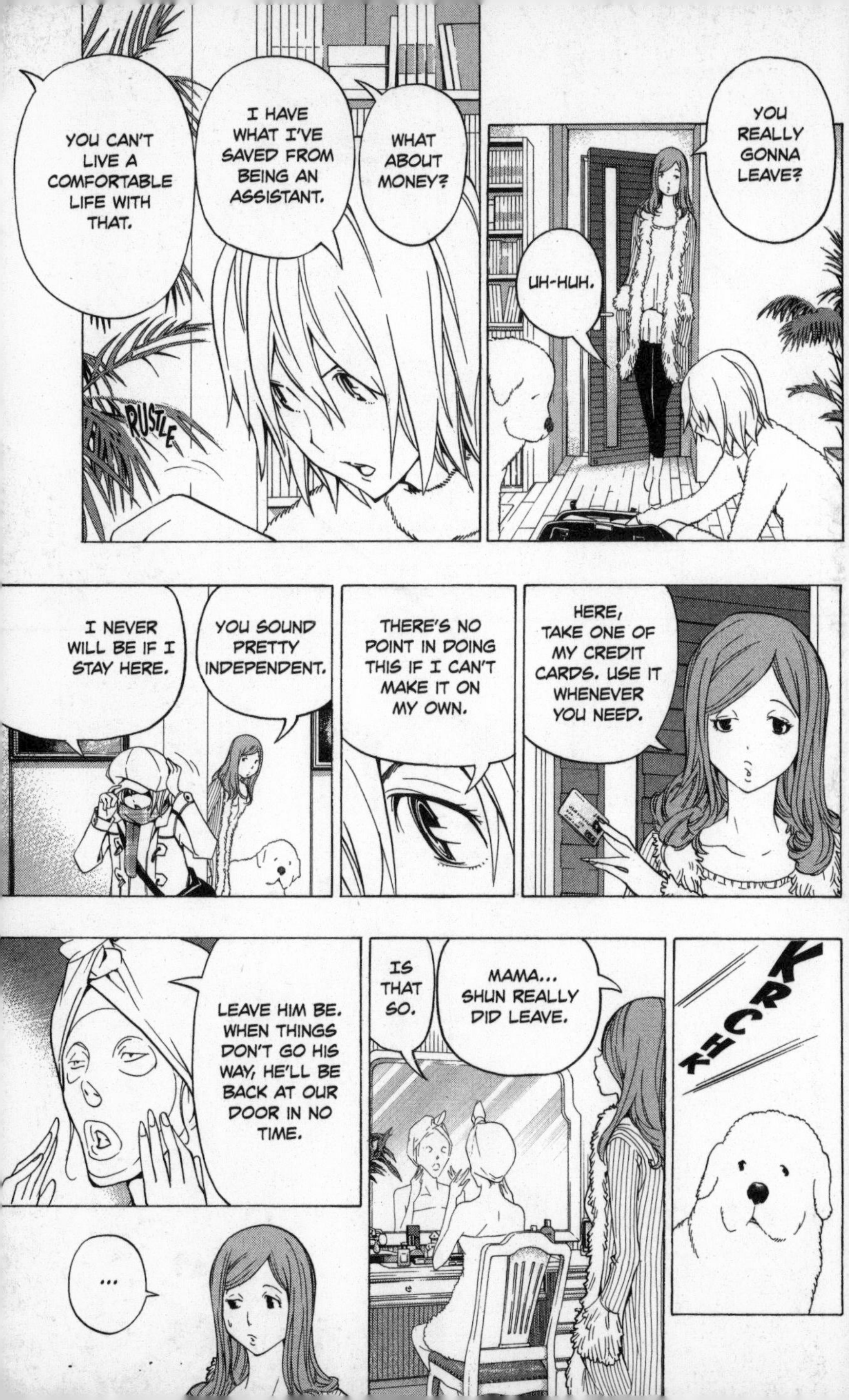
YOU REALLY GONNA LEAVE?
UH-HUH.
WHAT ABOUT MONEY?
I HAVE WHAT I'VE SAVED FROM BEING AN ASSISTANT.
YOU CAN'T LIVE A COMFORTABLE LIFE WITH THAT.
RUSTLE
HERE, TAKE ONE OF MY CREDIT CARDS. USE IT WHENEVER YOU NEED.
THERE'S NO POINT IN DOING THIS IF I CAN'T MAKE IT ON MY OWN.
YOU SOUND PRETTY INDEPENDENT.
I NEVER WILL BE IF I STAY HERE.
KRCHK
MAMA... SHUN REALLY DID LEAVE.
IS THAT SO.
LEAVE HIM BE. WHEN THINGS DON'T GO HIS WAY, HE'LL BE BACK AT OUR DOOR IN NO TIME.
...

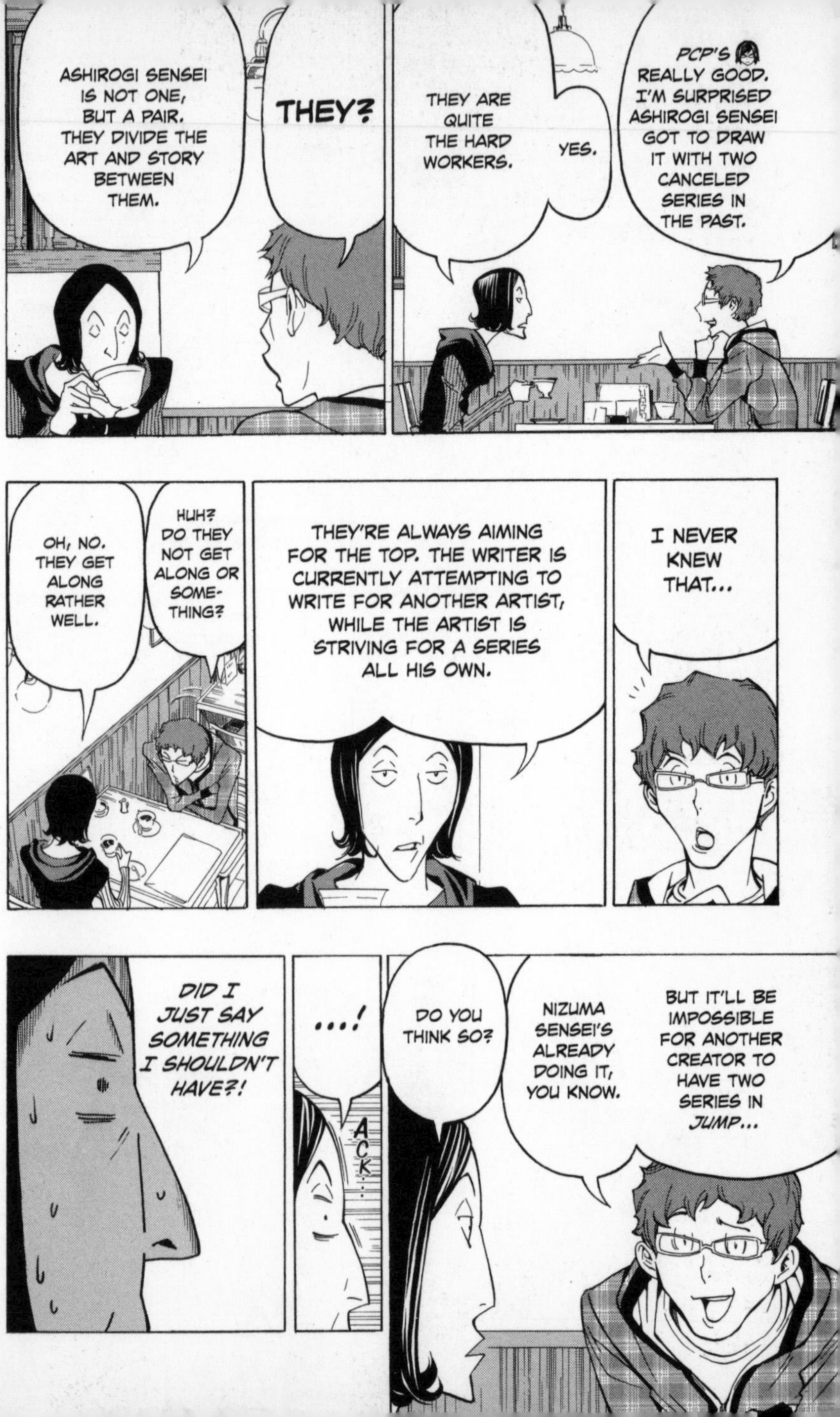
PCP'S REALLY GOOD. I'M SURPRISED ASHIROGI SENSEI GOT TO DRAW IT WITH TWO CANCELED SERIES IN THE PAST.
YES.
THEY ARE QUITE THE HARD WORKERS.
THEY?
ASHIROGI SENSEI IS NOT ONE, BUT A PAIR. THEY DIVIDE THE ART AND STORY BETWEEN THEM.
I NEVER KNEW THAT...
THEY'RE ALWAYS AIMING FOR THE TOP. THE WRITER IS CURRENTLY ATTEMPTING TO WRITE FOR ANOTHER ARTIST, WHILE THE ARTIST IS STRIVING FOR A SERIES ALL HIS OWN.
HUH? DO THEY NOT GET ALONG OR SOME-THING?
OH, NO. THEY GET ALONG RATHER WELL.
BUT IT'LL BE IMPOSSIBLE FOR ANOTHER CREATOR TO HAVE TWO SERIES IN JUMP...
NIZUMA SENSEI'S ALREADY DOING IT, YOU KNOW.
DO YOU THINK SO?
...!
ACK...
DID I JUST SAY SOMETHING I SHOULDN'T HAVE?!

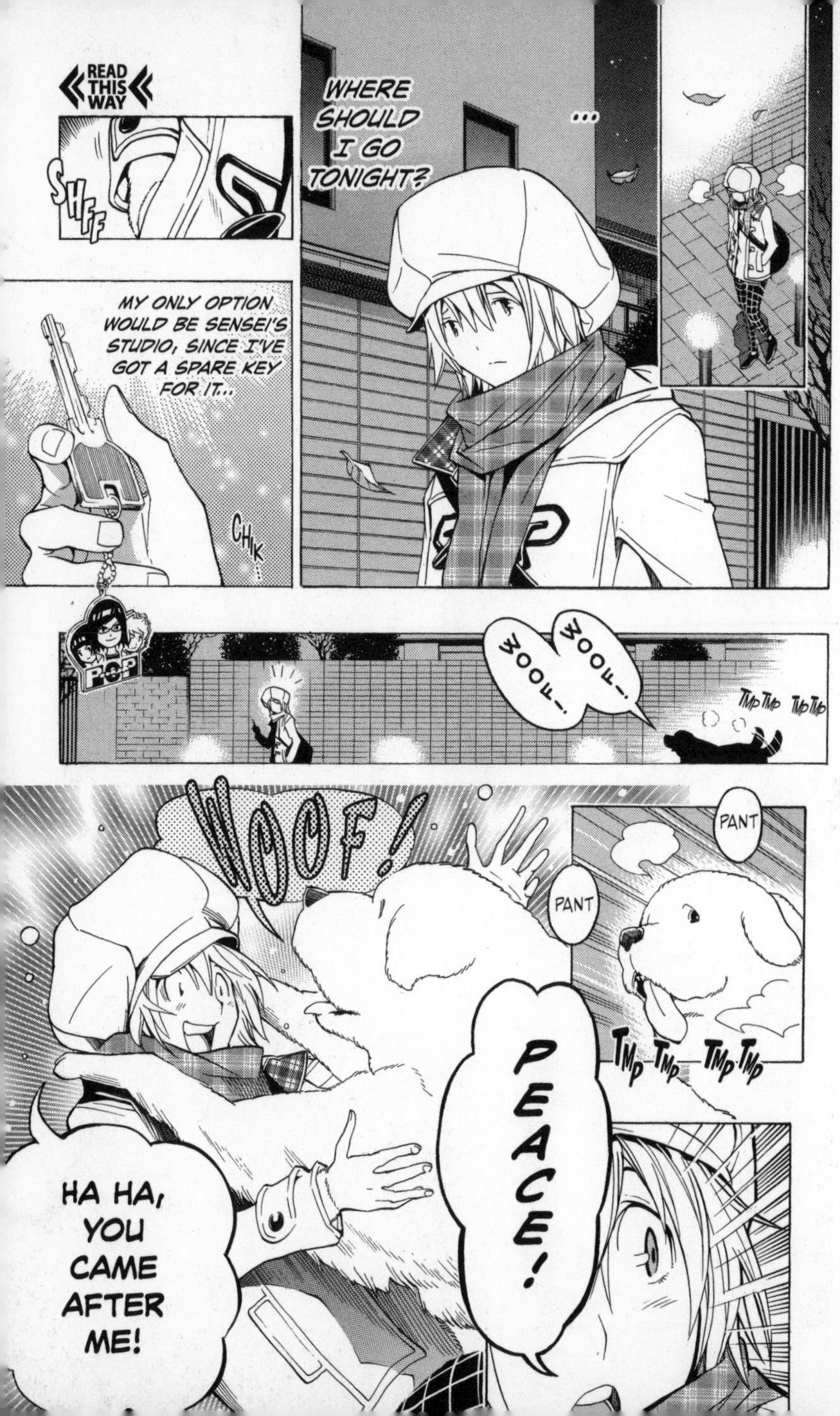
READ THIS WAY
...
WHERE SHOULD I GO TONIGHT?
SHFF
MY ONLY OPTION WOULD BE SENSEI'S STUDIO, SINCE I'VE GOT A SPARE KEY FOR IT...
CHIK
POP
WOOF...! WOOF...!
TMP TMP TMP TMP
PANT
PANT
TMP TMP TMP TMP
WOOF!
PEACE!
HA HA, YOU CAME AFTER ME!

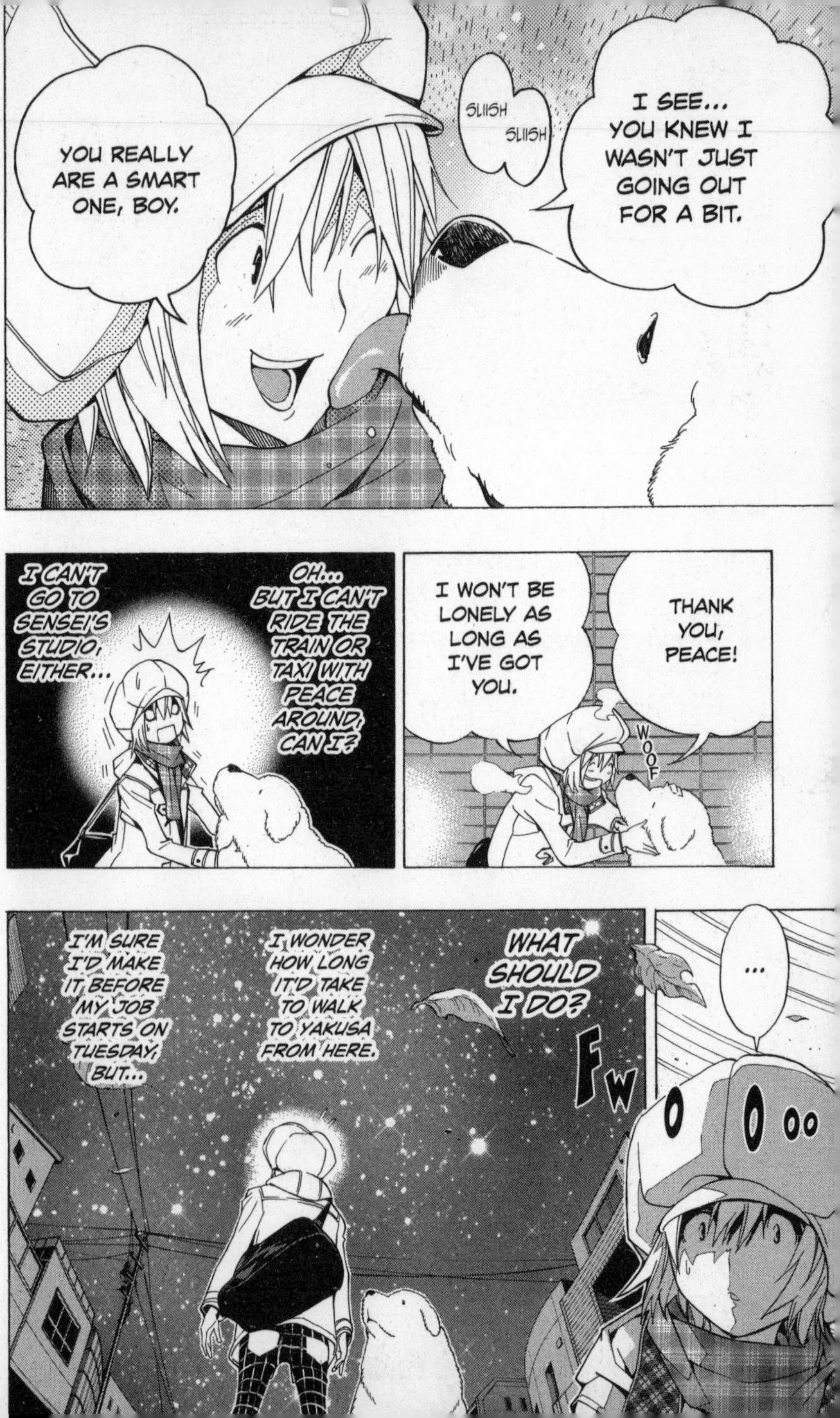
I SEE... YOU KNEW I WASN'T JUST GOING OUT FOR A BIT.
SLIISH
SLIISH
YOU REALLY ARE A SMART ONE, BOY.
THANK YOU, PEACE!
WOOF
I WON'T BE LONELY AS LONG AS I'VE GOT YOU.
OH... BUT I CAN'T RIDE THE TRAIN OR TAXI WITH PEACE AROUND, CAN I?
I CAN'T GO TO SENSEI'S STUDIO, EITHER...
...
WHAT SHOULD I DO?
FWW
I WONDER HOW LONG IT'D TAKE TO WALK TO YAKUSA FROM HERE.
I'M SURE I'D MAKE IT BEFORE MY JOB STARTS ON TUESDAY, BUT...

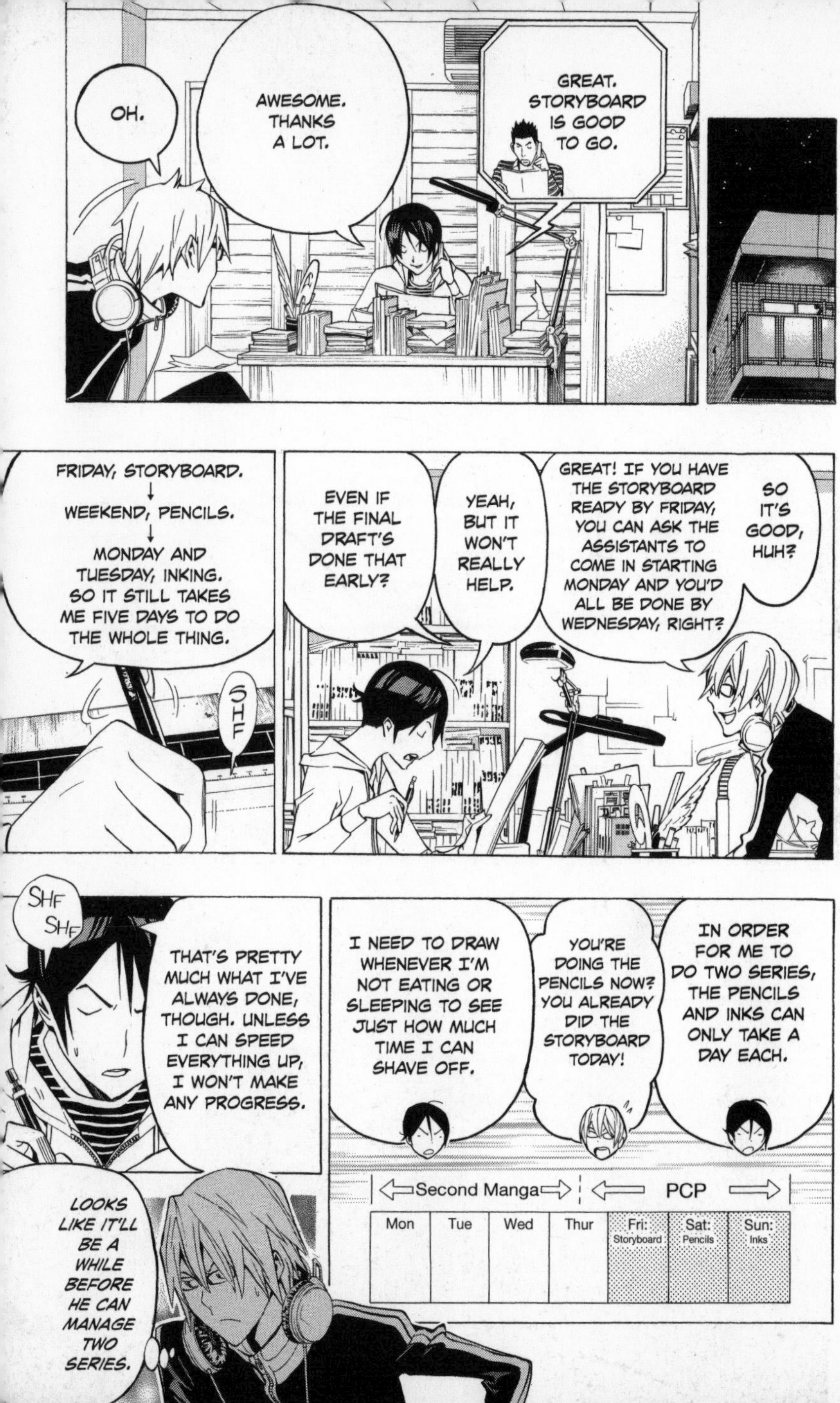
GREAT. STORYBOARD IS GOOD TO GO.
AWESOME. THANKS A LOT.
OH.
SO IT'S GOOD, HUH?
GREAT! IF YOU HAVE THE STORYBOARD READY BY FRIDAY, YOU CAN ASK THE ASSISTANTS TO COME IN STARTING MONDAY AND YOU'D ALL BE DONE BY WEDNESDAY, RIGHT?
YEAH, BUT IT WON'T REALLY HELP.
EVEN IF THE FINAL DRAFT'S DONE THAT EARLY?
FRIDAY, STORYBOARD. ↓ WEEKEND, PENCILS. ↓ MONDAY AND TUESDAY, INKING. SO IT STILL TAKES ME FIVE DAYS TO DO THE WHOLE THING.
SHF
IN ORDER FOR ME TO DO TWO SERIES, THE PENCILS AND INKS CAN ONLY TAKE A DAY EACH.
YOU'RE DOING THE PENCILS NOW? YOU ALREADY DID THE STORYBOARD TODAY!
I NEED TO DRAW WHENEVER I'M NOT EATING OR SLEEPING TO SEE JUST HOW MUCH TIME I CAN SHAVE OFF.
Second Manga
PCP
Mon
Tue
Wed
Thur
Fri: Storyboard
Sat: Pencils
Sun: Inks
SHF SHF
THAT'S PRETTY MUCH WHAT I'VE ALWAYS DONE, THOUGH. UNLESS I CAN SPEED EVERYTHING UP, I WON'T MAKE ANY PROGRESS.
LOOKS LIKE IT'LL BE A WHILE BEFORE HE CAN MANAGE TWO SERIES.

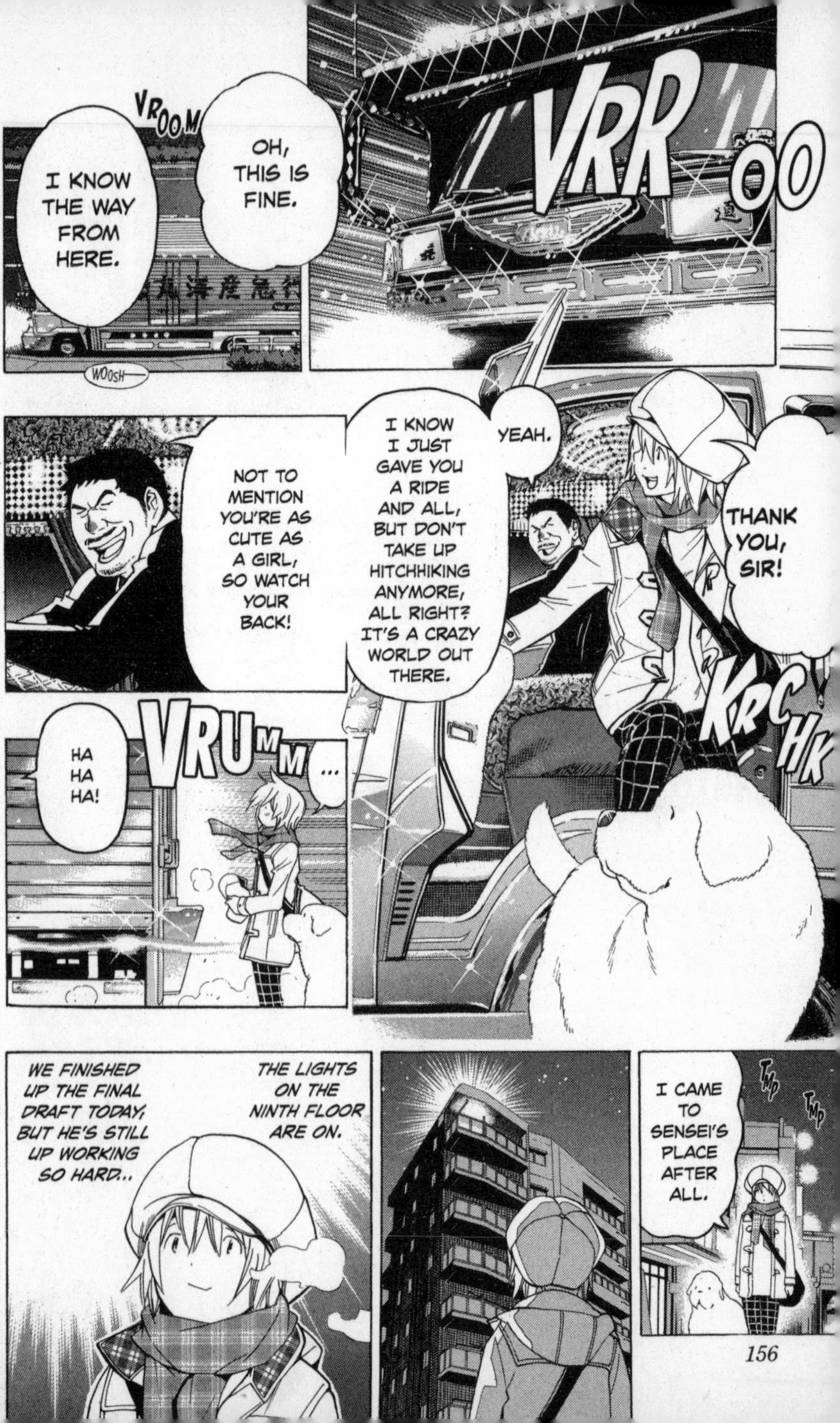
VRROO
VROOM
OH, THIS IS FINE.
I KNOW THE WAY FROM HERE.
WOOSH
THANK YOU, SIR!
YEAH.
I KNOW I JUST GAVE YOU A RIDE AND ALL, BUT DON'T TAKE UP HITCHHIKING ANYMORE, ALL RIGHT? IT'S A CRAZY WORLD OUT THERE.
KRCHK
NOT TO MENTION YOU'RE AS CUTE AS A GIRL, SO WATCH YOUR BACK!
VRUMM
HA HA HA!
...
TMP
TMP
I CAME TO SENSEI'S PLACE AFTER ALL.
THE LIGHTS ON THE NINTH FLOOR ARE ON.
WE FINISHED UP THE FINAL DRAFT TODAY, BUT HE'S STILL UP WORKING SO HARD...

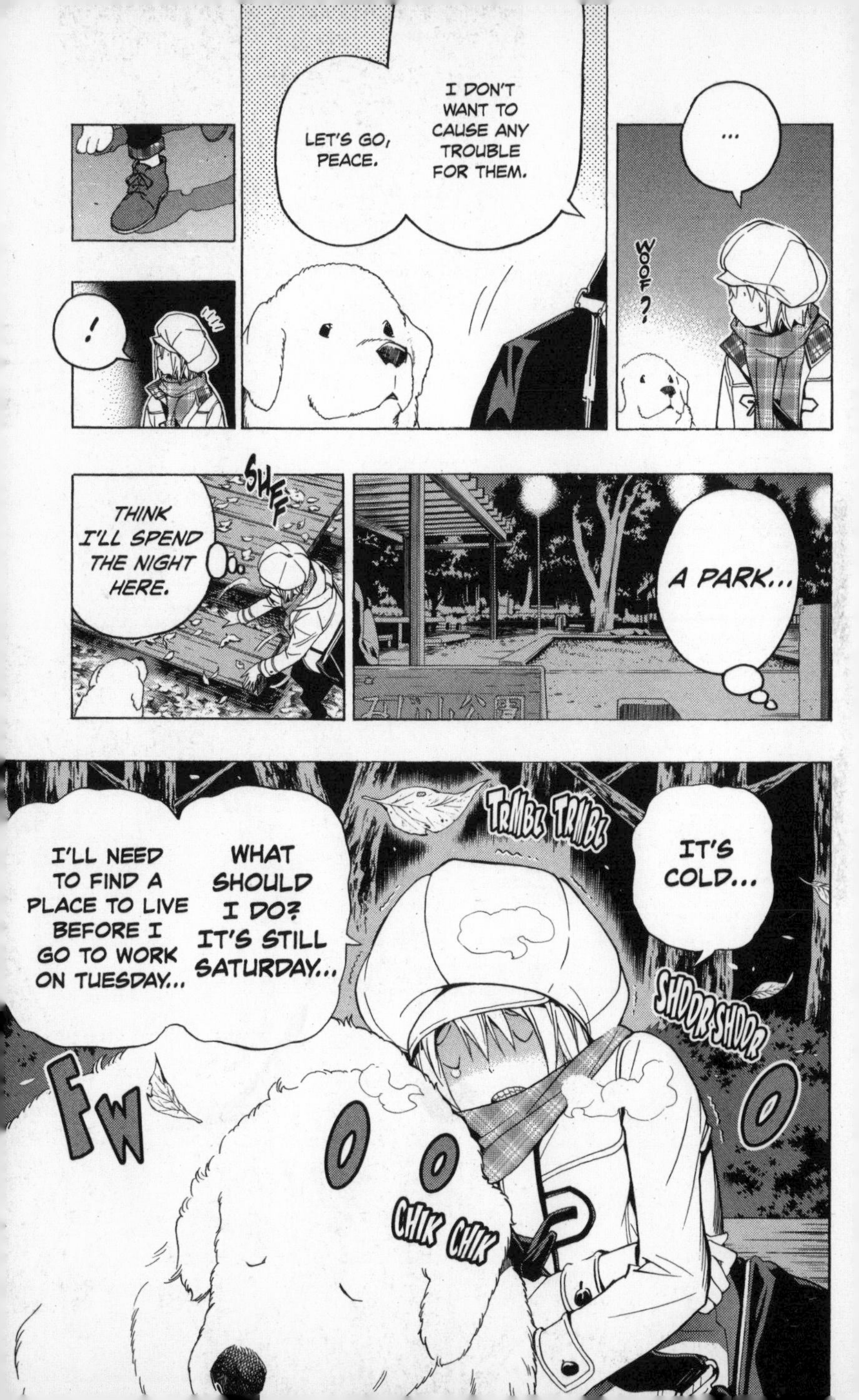
...
WOOF?
I DON'T WANT TO CAUSE ANY TROUBLE FOR THEM.
LET'S GO, PEACE.
!
A PARK...
SHFF
THINK I'LL SPEND THE NIGHT HERE.
IT'S COLD...
TRMBL TRMBL
WHAT SHOULD I DO? IT'S STILL SATURDAY...
I'LL NEED TO FIND A PLACE TO LIVE BEFORE I GO TO WORK ON TUESDAY...
SHOOR SHOOR
FWOOOO
CHIK CHIK

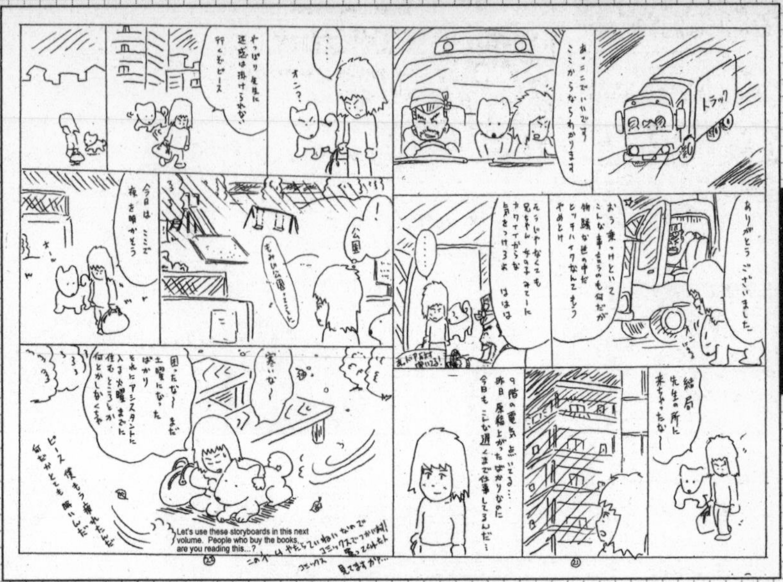
あっここでいいです ここからならわかります
トラック
ありがとうございました
おう乗っけといてこんな事言うのも何だが物騒な世の中だ ヒッチハイクなんてもうやめとけ
そうじゃなくても兄ちゃん女の子みてーにカワイイからな 気をつけろよ はははは
……
結局先生の所に来ちゃったな~
9階の電気点いてる… 昨日原稿上がったばかりなのに今日もこんな遅くまで仕事してるんだ…
……
オン?
やっぱり先生に迷惑は掛けらんない 行くぞピース
!
公園
もみじ公園…ここにしよ
今日はここで夜を明かそう
寒いな~
困ったな~ まだ土曜になったばかり それにアシスタントに入る火曜までに住むところを何とかしなくちゃ
ピース 僕もう疲れたよ 何だかとても眠いんだ
Let's use these storyboards in this next volume. People who buy the books, are you reading this...?

OHBA'S STORYBOARD

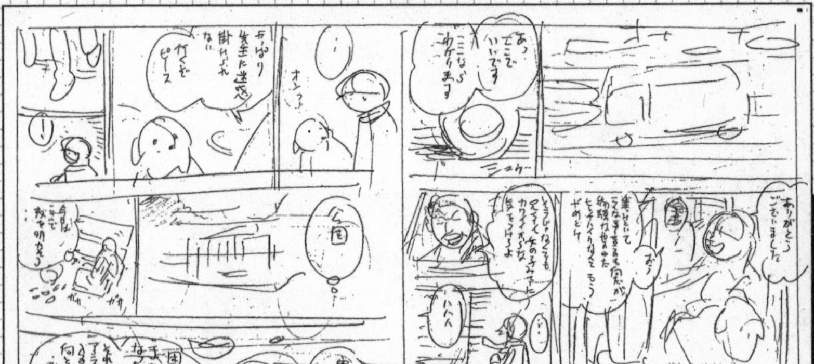

OBATA'S STORYBOARD

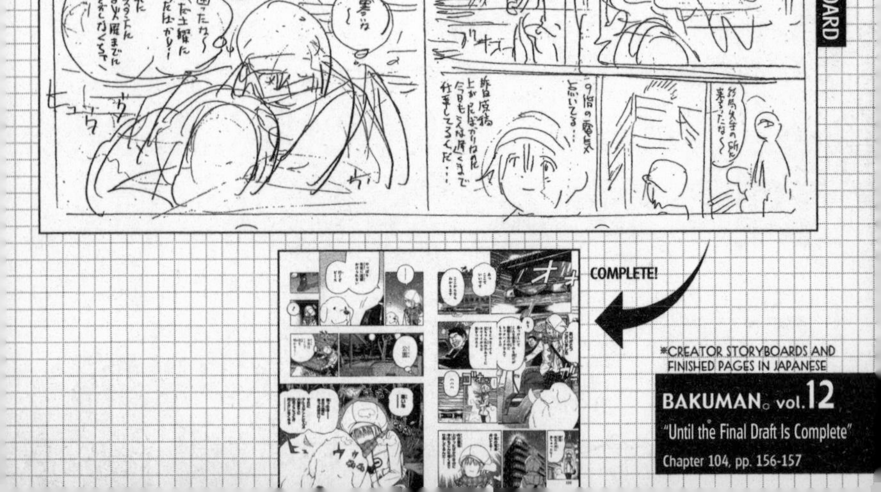

COMPLETE!

※CREATOR STORYBOARDS AND FINISHED PAGES IN JAPANESE

BAKUMAN。 vol. 12
"Until the Final Draft Is Complete"
Chapter 104, pp. 156-157

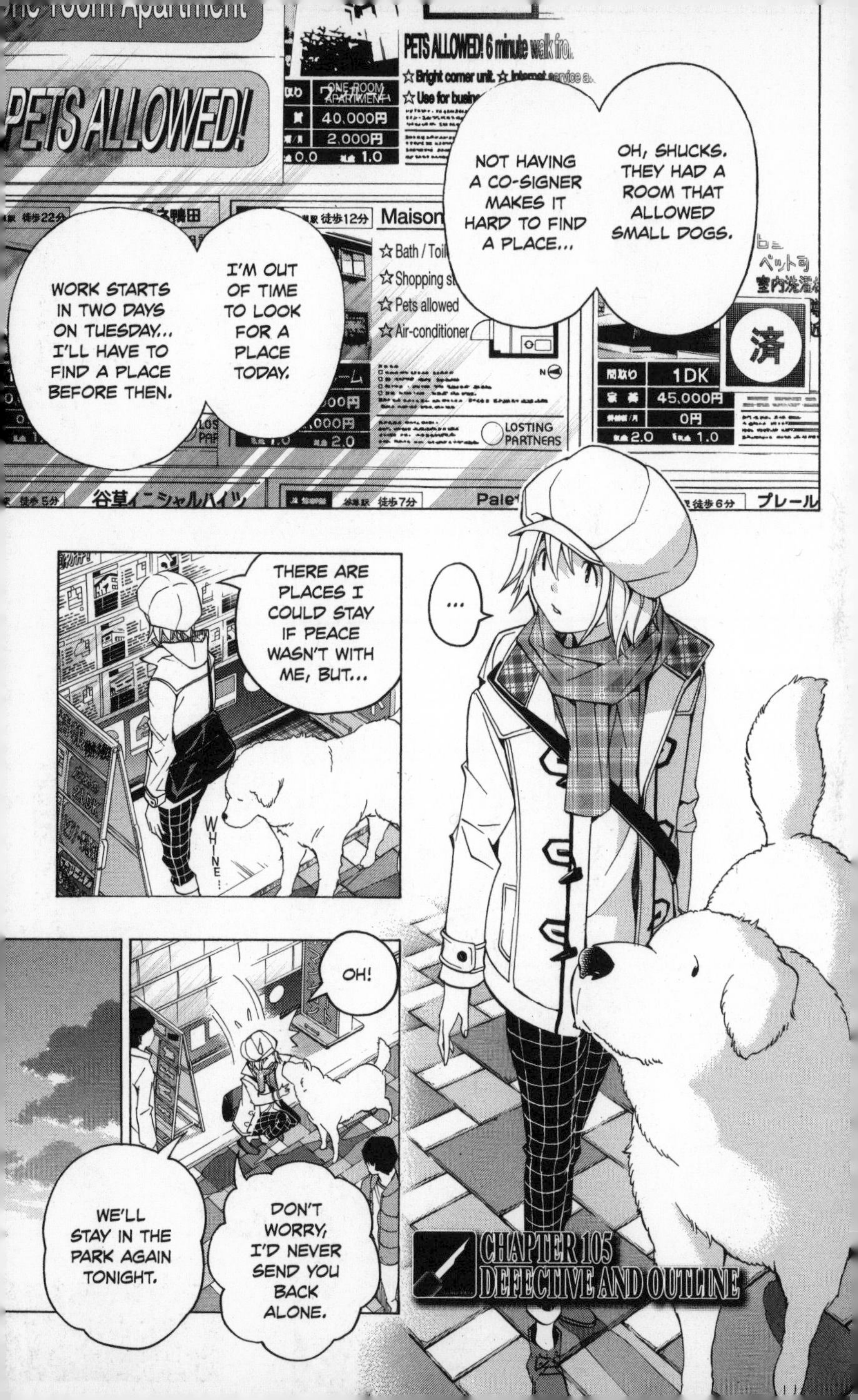
PETS ALLOWED!
☆Pets allowed
☆Air-conditioner
LOSTING PARTNERS
OH, SHUCKS. THEY HAD A ROOM THAT ALLOWED SMALL DOGS.
NOT HAVING A CO-SIGNER MAKES IT HARD TO FIND A PLACE...
I'M OUT OF TIME TO LOOK FOR A PLACE TODAY.
WORK STARTS IN TWO DAYS ON TUESDAY... I'LL HAVE TO FIND A PLACE BEFORE THEN.
...
CHAPTER 105
DEFECTIVE AND OUTLINE
THERE ARE PLACES I COULD STAY IF PEACE WASN'T WITH ME, BUT...
WHINE...
OH!
DON'T WORRY, I'D NEVER SEND YOU BACK ALONE.
WE'LL STAY IN THE PARK AGAIN TONIGHT.

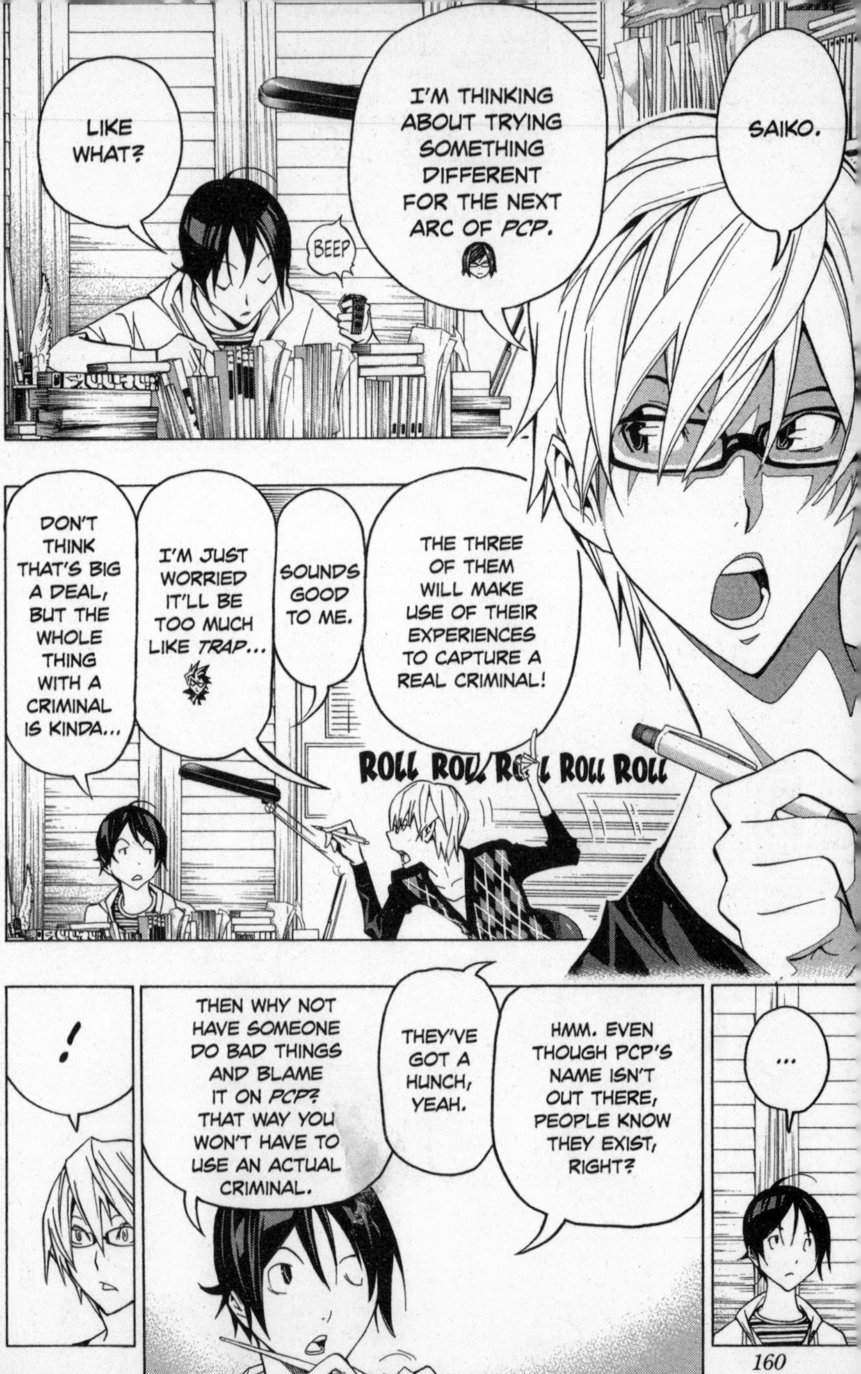
SAIKO.
I'M THINKING ABOUT TRYING SOMETHING DIFFERENT FOR THE NEXT ARC OF *PCP*.
BEEP
LIKE WHAT?
THE THREE OF THEM WILL MAKE USE OF THEIR EXPERIENCES TO CAPTURE A REAL CRIMINAL!
ROLL ROLL ROLL ROLL ROLL
SOUNDS GOOD TO ME.
I'M JUST WORRIED IT'LL BE TOO MUCH LIKE *TRAP*...
DON'T THINK THAT'S BIG A DEAL, BUT THE WHOLE THING WITH A CRIMINAL IS KINDA...
...
HMM. EVEN THOUGH PCP'S NAME ISN'T OUT THERE, PEOPLE KNOW THEY EXIST, RIGHT?
THEY'VE GOT A HUNCH, YEAH.
THEN WHY NOT HAVE SOMEONE DO BAD THINGS AND BLAME IT ON *PCP*? THAT WAY YOU WON'T HAVE TO USE AN ACTUAL CRIMINAL.
!

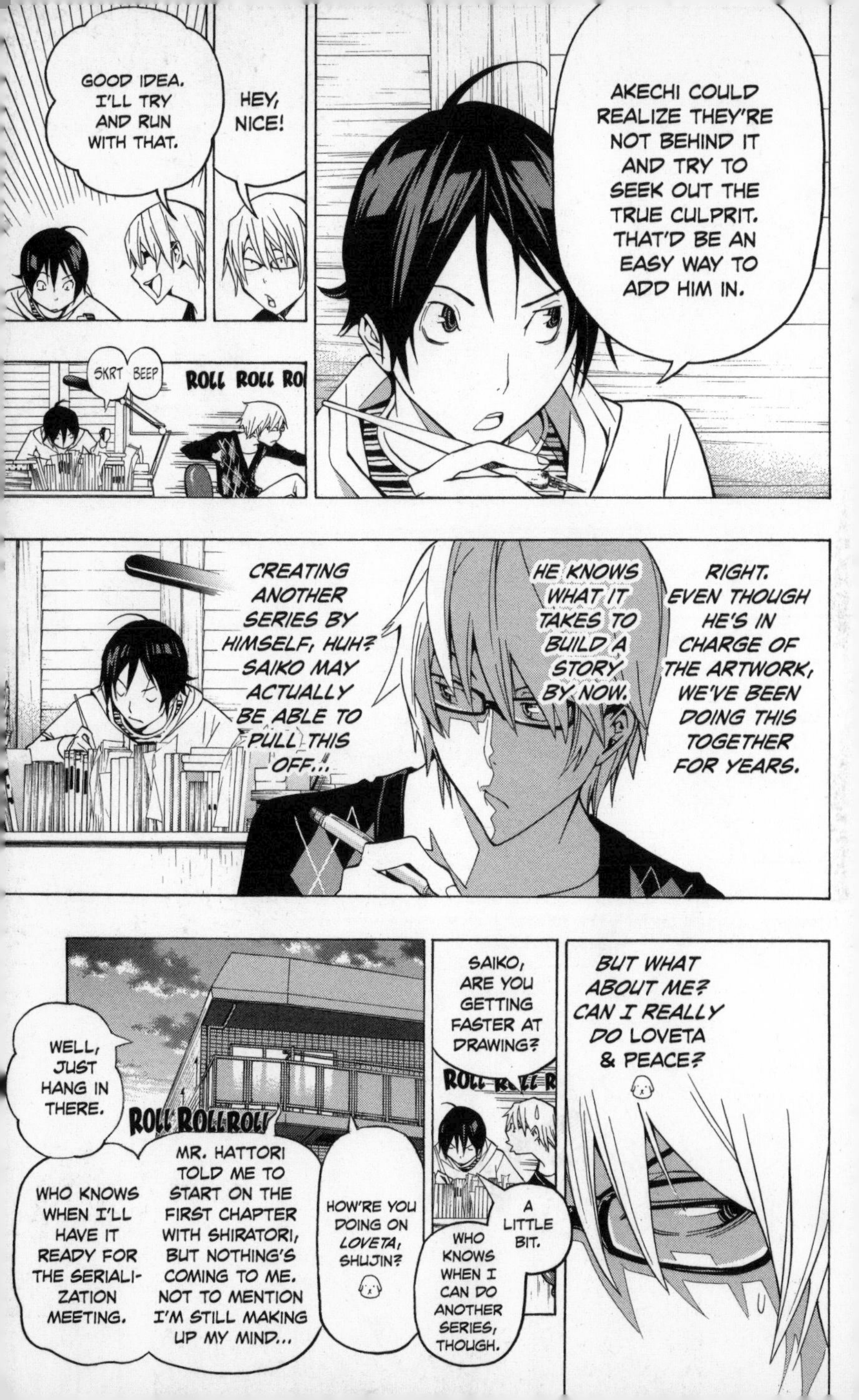
AKECHI COULD REALIZE THEY'RE NOT BEHIND IT AND TRY TO SEEK OUT THE TRUE CULPRIT. THAT'D BE AN EASY WAY TO ADD HIM IN.
HEY, NICE!
GOOD IDEA. I'LL TRY AND RUN WITH THAT.
ROLL ROLL RO
SKRT
BEEP
RIGHT. EVEN THOUGH HE'S IN CHARGE OF THE ARTWORK, WE'VE BEEN DOING THIS TOGETHER FOR YEARS.
HE KNOWS WHAT IT TAKES TO BUILD A STORY BY NOW.
CREATING ANOTHER SERIES BY HIMSELF, HUH? SAIKO MAY ACTUALLY BE ABLE TO PULL THIS OFF...
BUT WHAT ABOUT ME? CAN I REALLY DO LOVETA & PEACE?
SAIKO, ARE YOU GETTING FASTER AT DRAWING?
ROLL ROLL R
A LITTLE BIT.
WHO KNOWS WHEN I CAN DO ANOTHER SERIES, THOUGH.
HOW'RE YOU DOING ON LOVETA, SHUJIN?
MR. HATTORI TOLD ME TO START ON THE FIRST CHAPTER WITH SHIRATORI, BUT NOTHING'S COMING TO ME. NOT TO MENTION I'M STILL MAKING UP MY MIND...
WHO KNOWS WHEN I'LL HAVE IT READY FOR THE SERIALI-ZATION MEETING.
WELL, JUST HANG IN THERE.
ROLL ROLL ROLL

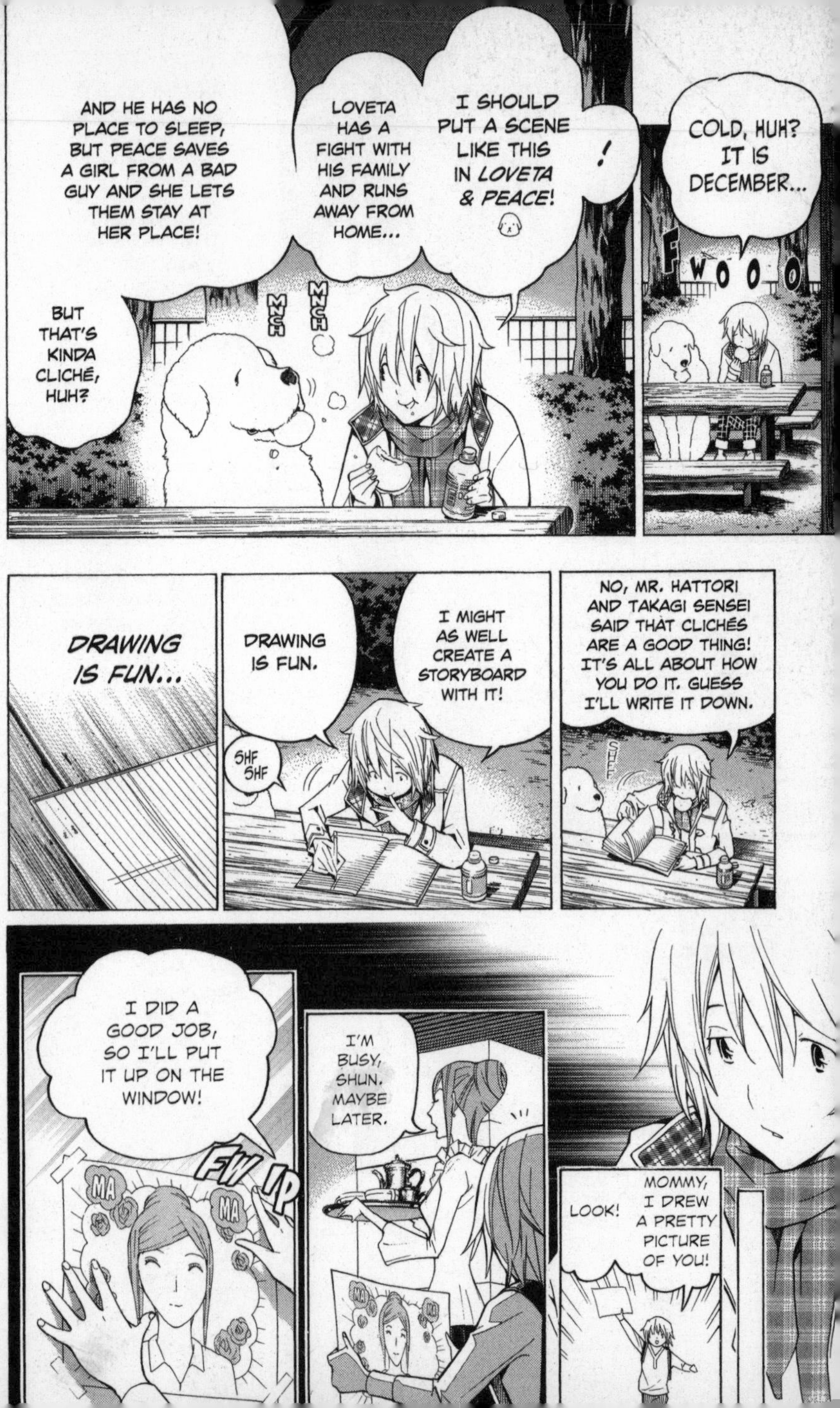
COLD, HUH? IT IS DECEMBER...
FWOOO
!
I SHOULD PUT A SCENE LIKE THIS IN *LOVETA & PEACE*!
LOVETA HAS A FIGHT WITH HIS FAMILY AND RUNS AWAY FROM HOME...
AND HE HAS NO PLACE TO SLEEP, BUT PEACE SAVES A GIRL FROM A BAD GUY AND SHE LETS THEM STAY AT HER PLACE!
MNCH
MNCH
BUT THAT'S KINDA CLICHÉ, HUH?
NO, MR. HATTORI AND TAKAGI SENSEI SAID THAT CLICHÉS ARE A GOOD THING! IT'S ALL ABOUT HOW YOU DO IT. GUESS I'LL WRITE IT DOWN.
SHFF
I MIGHT AS WELL CREATE A STORYBOARD WITH IT!
DRAWING IS FUN.
SHF SHF
DRAWING IS FUN...
MOMMY, I DREW A PRETTY PICTURE OF YOU!
LOOK!
I'M BUSY, SHUN. MAYBE LATER.
I DID A GOOD JOB, SO I'LL PUT IT UP ON THE WINDOW!
FWIP
MA
MA

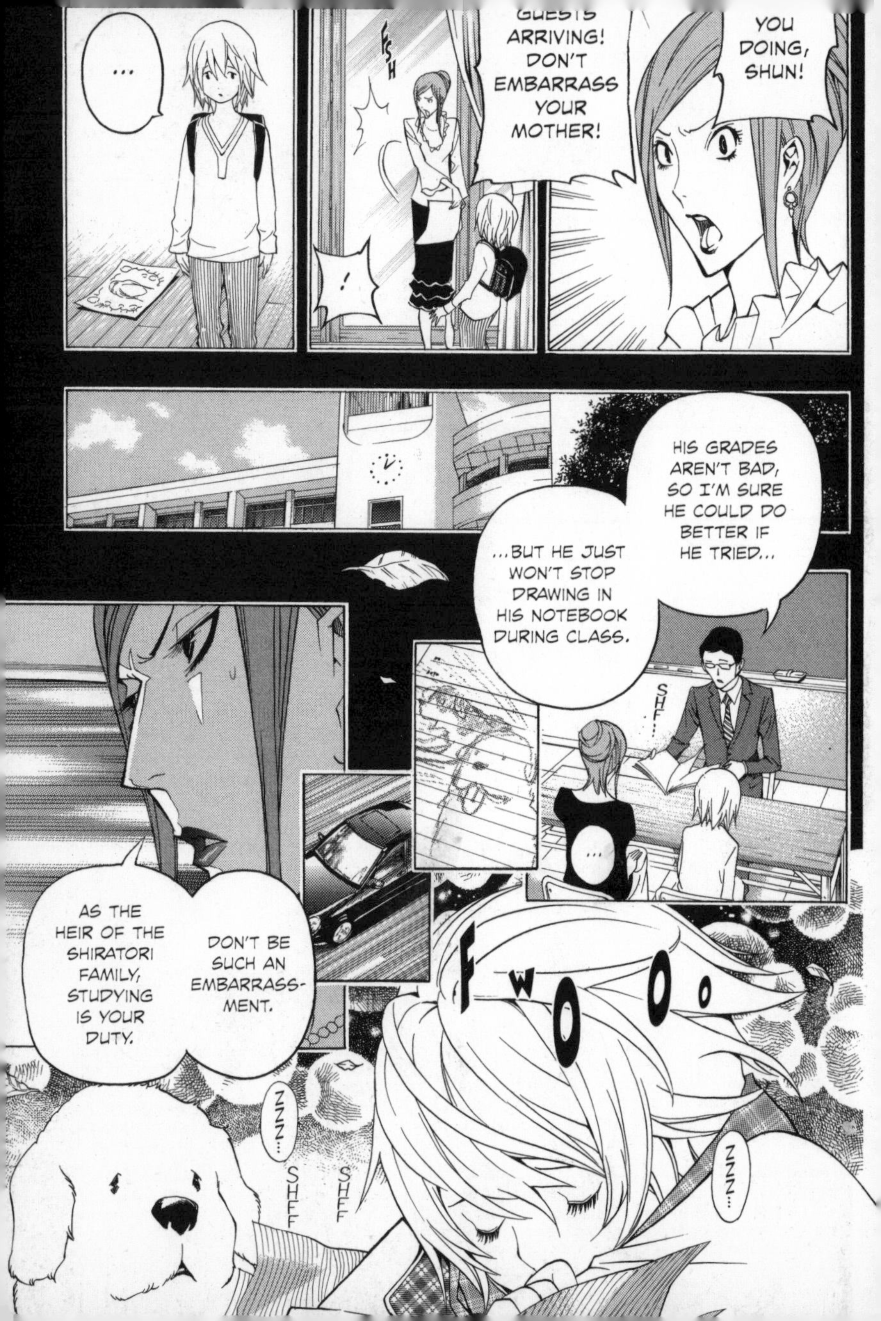
YOU DOING, SHUN!
GUESTS ARRIVING! DON'T EMBARRASS YOUR MOTHER!
FSH
!
...
HIS GRADES AREN'T BAD, SO I'M SURE HE COULD DO BETTER IF HE TRIED...
...BUT HE JUST WON'T STOP DRAWING IN HIS NOTEBOOK DURING CLASS.
SHF
...
DON'T BE SUCH AN EMBARRASS-MENT.
AS THE HEIR OF THE SHIRATORI FAMILY, STUDYING IS YOUR DUTY.
FWOOO
ZZZ...
SHFF
SHFF
ZZZ...

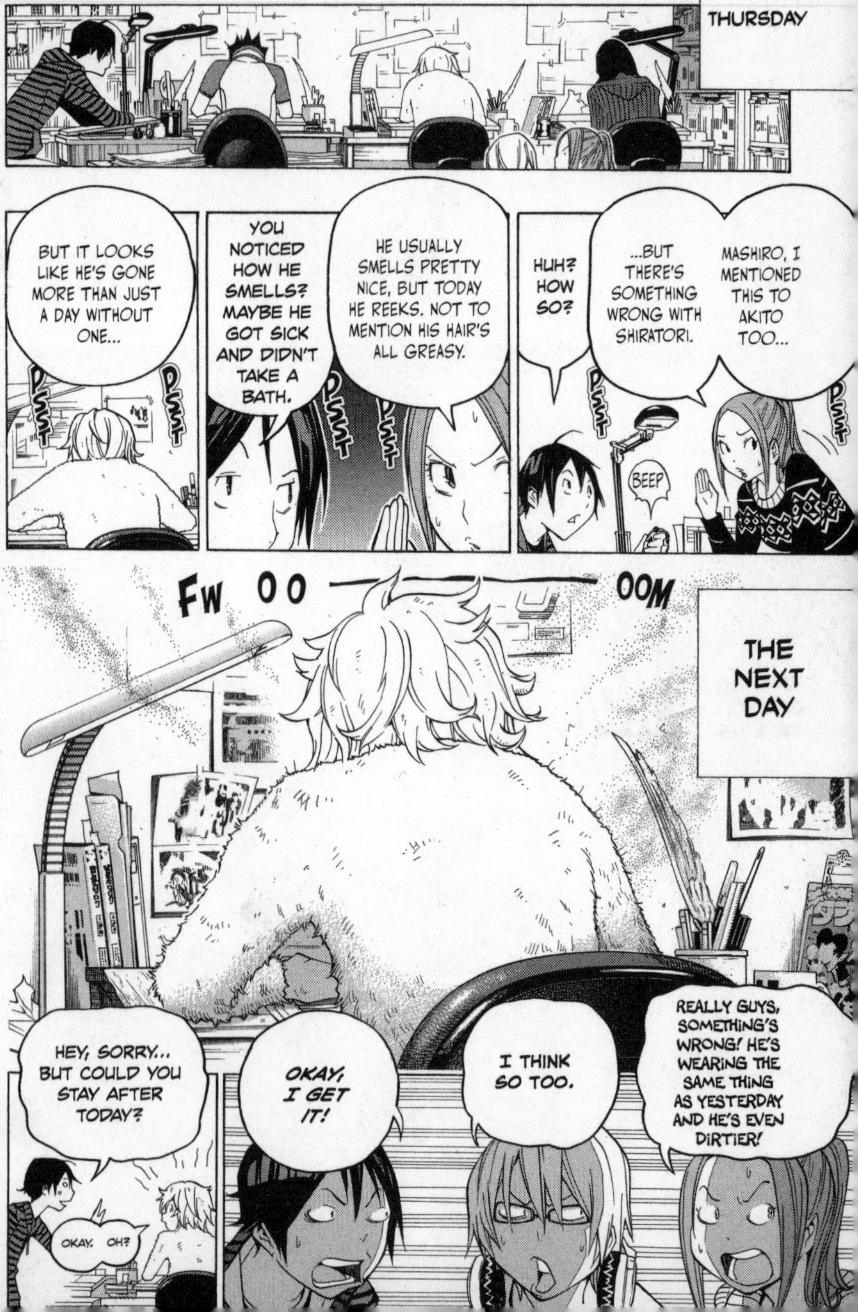
THURSDAY
MASHIRO, I MENTIONED THIS TO AKITO TOO...
...BUT THERE'S SOMETHING WRONG WITH SHIRATORI.
PSST
HUH? HOW SO?
PSST
BEEP
HE USUALLY SMELLS PRETTY NICE, BUT TODAY HE REEKS. NOT TO MENTION HIS HAIR'S ALL GREASY.
PSST
YOU NOTICED HOW HE SMELLS? MAYBE HE GOT SICK AND DIDN'T TAKE A BATH.
PSST
PSST
BUT IT LOOKS LIKE HE'S GONE MORE THAN JUST A DAY WITHOUT ONE...
PSST
THE NEXT DAY
FW OO —— OOM
REALLY GUYS, SOMETHING'S WRONG! HE'S WEARING THE SAME THING AS YESTERDAY AND HE'S EVEN DIRTIER!
I THINK SO TOO.
OKAY, I GET IT!
HEY, SORRY... BUT COULD YOU STAY AFTER TODAY?
OKAY. OH?

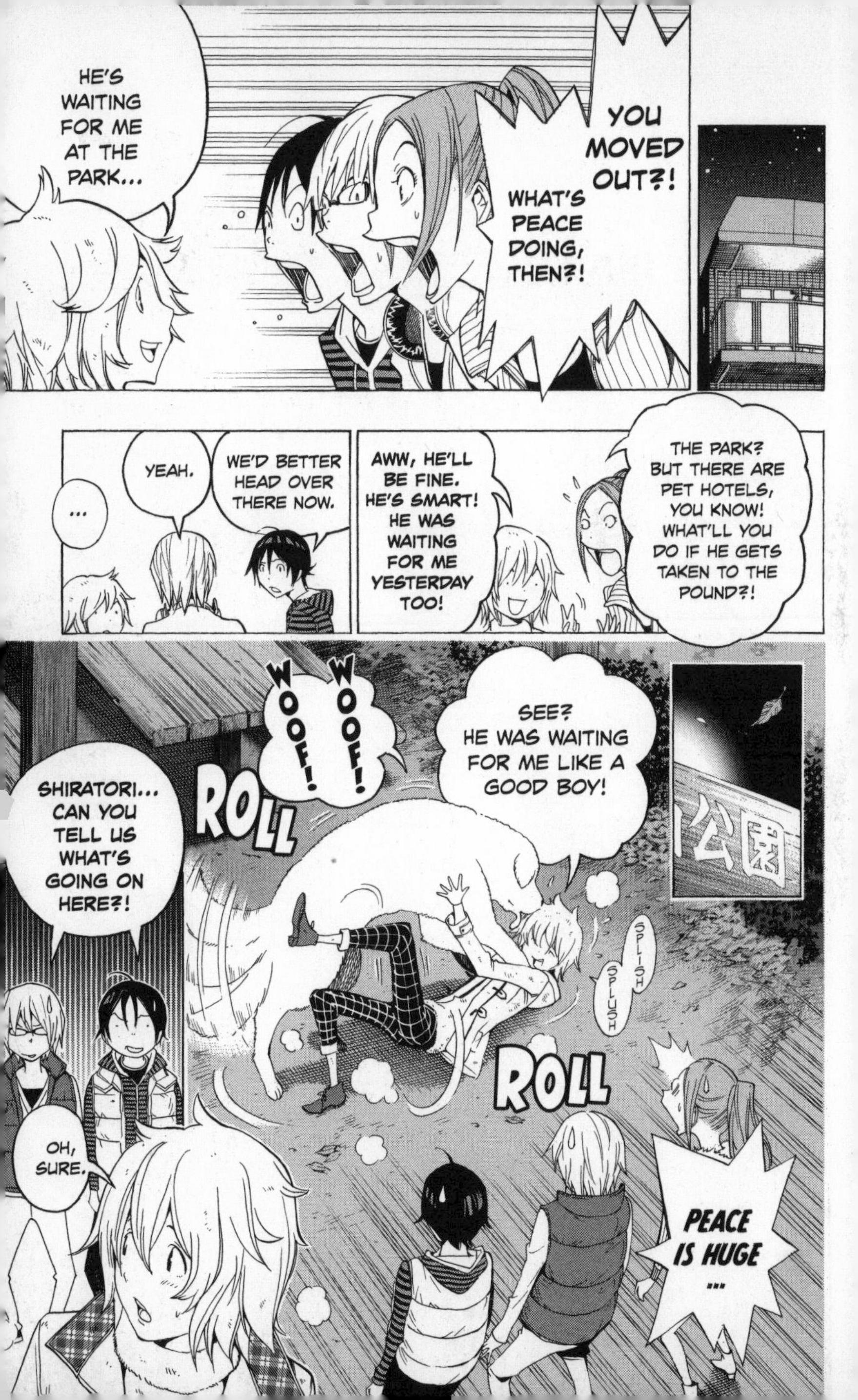
YOU MOVED OUT?!
WHAT'S PEACE DOING, THEN?!
HE'S WAITING FOR ME AT THE PARK...
THE PARK? BUT THERE ARE PET HOTELS, YOU KNOW! WHAT'LL YOU DO IF HE GETS TAKEN TO THE POUND?!
AWW, HE'LL BE FINE. HE'S SMART! HE WAS WAITING FOR ME YESTERDAY TOO!
WE'D BETTER HEAD OVER THERE NOW.
YEAH.
...
公園
SEE? HE WAS WAITING FOR ME LIKE A GOOD BOY!
WOOF! WOOF!
ROLL
SPLISH
SPLUSH
ROLL
SHIRATORI... CAN YOU TELL US WHAT'S GOING ON HERE?!
PEACE IS HUGE...
OH, SURE.

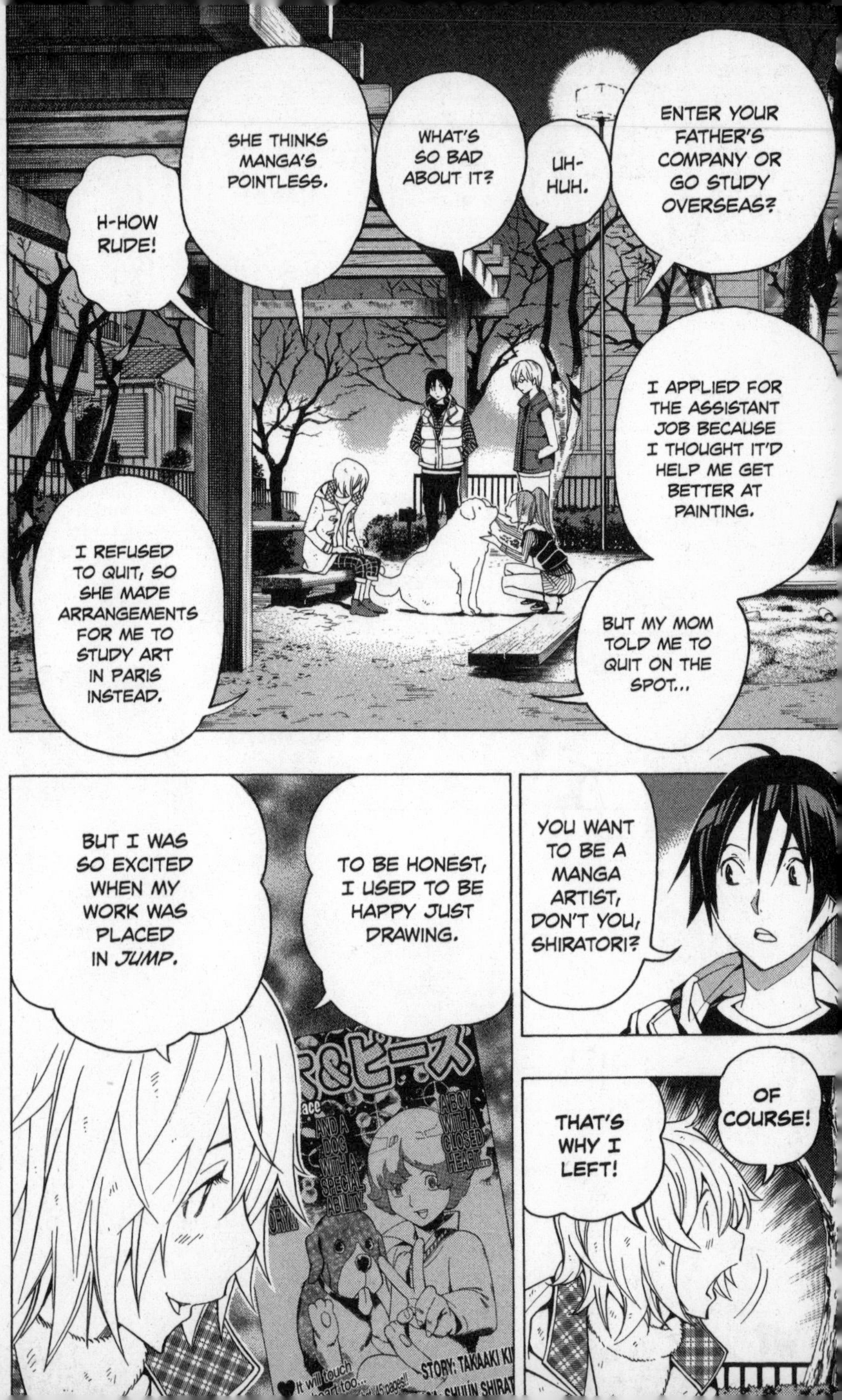
ENTER YOUR FATHER'S COMPANY OR GO STUDY OVERSEAS?
UH-HUH.
WHAT'S SO BAD ABOUT IT?
SHE THINKS MANGA'S POINTLESS.
H-HOW RUDE!
I APPLIED FOR THE ASSISTANT JOB BECAUSE I THOUGHT IT'D HELP ME GET BETTER AT PAINTING.
BUT MY MOM TOLD ME TO QUIT ON THE SPOT...
I REFUSED TO QUIT, SO SHE MADE ARRANGEMENTS FOR ME TO STUDY ART IN PARIS INSTEAD.
YOU WANT TO BE A MANGA ARTIST, DON'T YOU, SHIRATORI?
OF COURSE!
THAT'S WHY I LEFT!
TO BE HONEST, I USED TO BE HAPPY JUST DRAWING.
BUT I WAS SO EXCITED WHEN MY WORK WAS PLACED IN *JUMP*.
A BOY WITH A CLOSED HEART...
AND A DOG WITH A SPECIAL ABILITY.

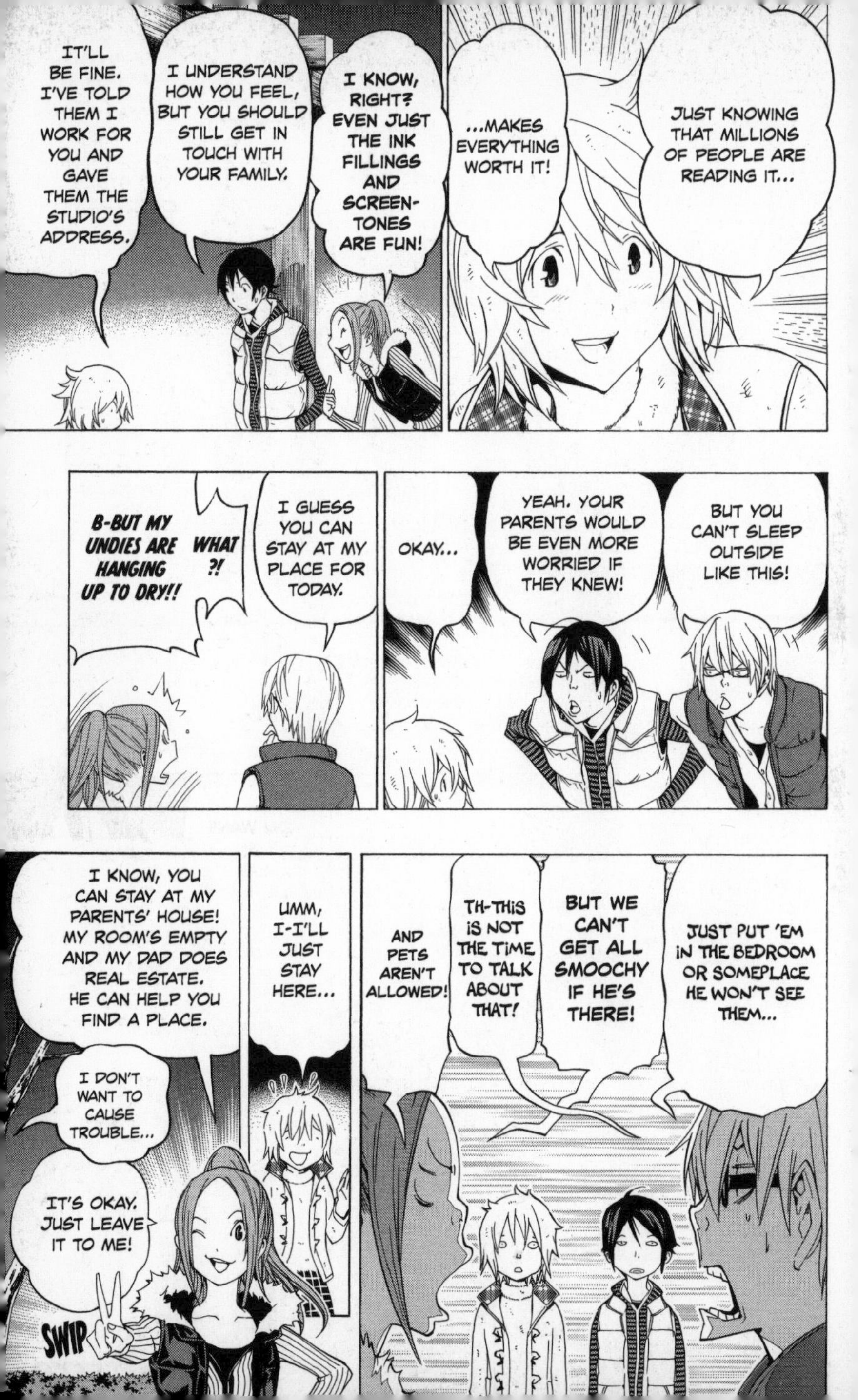
JUST KNOWING THAT MILLIONS OF PEOPLE ARE READING IT...
...MAKES EVERYTHING WORTH IT!
I KNOW, RIGHT? EVEN JUST THE INK FILLINGS AND SCREEN-TONES ARE FUN!
I UNDERSTAND HOW YOU FEEL, BUT YOU SHOULD STILL GET IN TOUCH WITH YOUR FAMILY.
IT'LL BE FINE. I'VE TOLD THEM I WORK FOR YOU AND GAVE THEM THE STUDIO'S ADDRESS.
BUT YOU CAN'T SLEEP OUTSIDE LIKE THIS!
YEAH. YOUR PARENTS WOULD BE EVEN MORE WORRIED IF THEY KNEW!
OKAY...
I GUESS YOU CAN STAY AT MY PLACE FOR TODAY.
WHAT?!
B-BUT MY UNDIES ARE HANGING UP TO DRY!!
JUST PUT 'EM IN THE BEDROOM OR SOMEPLACE HE WON'T SEE THEM...
BUT WE CAN'T GET ALL SMOOCHY IF HE'S THERE!
TH-THIS IS NOT THE TIME TO TALK ABOUT THAT!
AND PETS AREN'T ALLOWED!
UMM, I-I'LL JUST STAY HERE...
I KNOW, YOU CAN STAY AT MY PARENTS' HOUSE! MY ROOM'S EMPTY AND MY DAD DOES REAL ESTATE. HE CAN HELP YOU FIND A PLACE.
I DON'T WANT TO CAUSE TROUBLE...
IT'S OKAY. JUST LEAVE IT TO ME!
SWIP

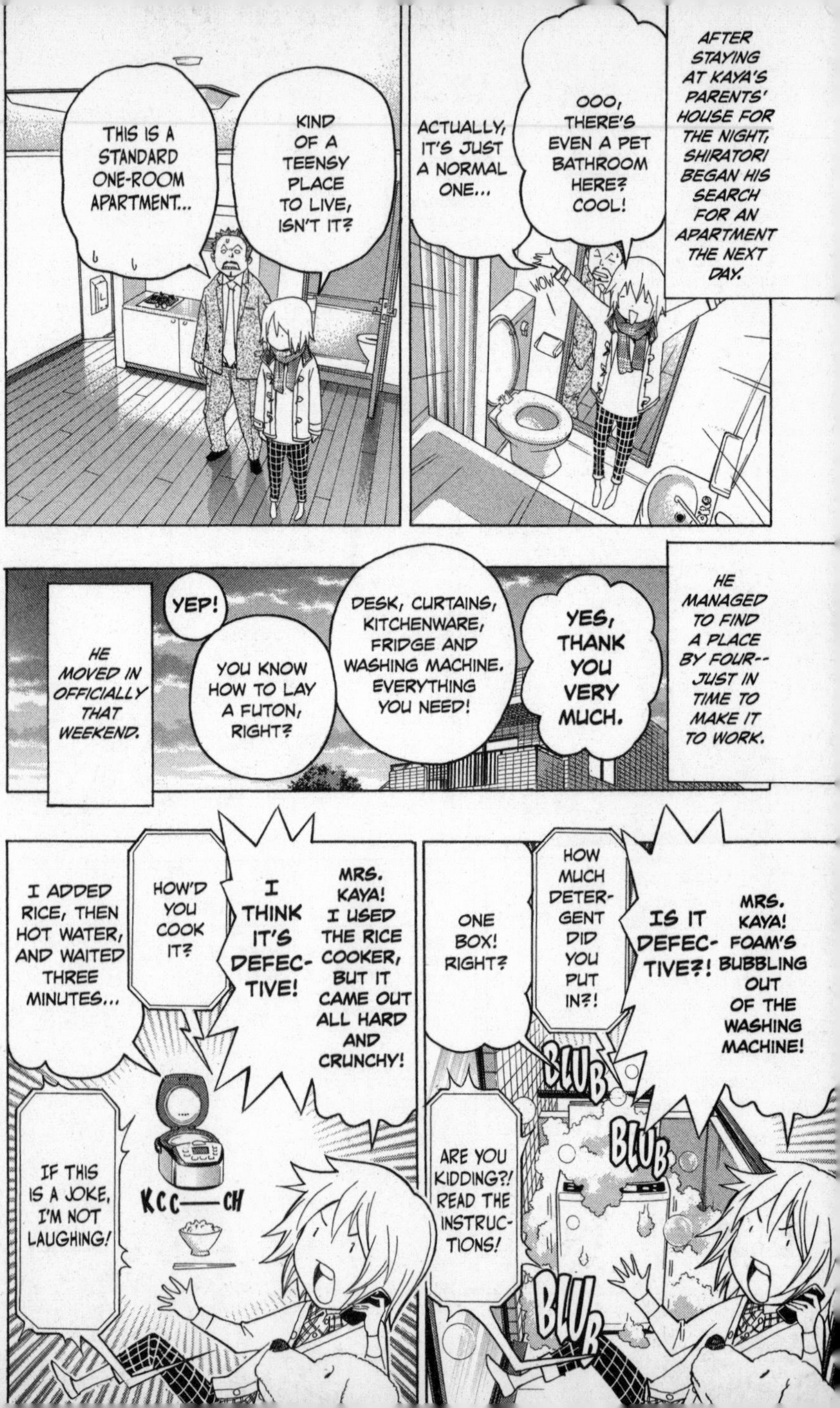
AFTER STAYING AT KAYA'S PARENTS' HOUSE FOR THE NIGHT, SHIRATORI BEGAN HIS SEARCH FOR AN APARTMENT THE NEXT DAY.
OOO, THERE'S EVEN A PET BATHROOM HERE? COOL!
WOW
ACTUALLY, IT'S JUST A NORMAL ONE...
KIND OF A TEENSY PLACE TO LIVE, ISN'T IT?
THIS IS A STANDARD ONE-ROOM APARTMENT...
HE MANAGED TO FIND A PLACE BY FOUR-- JUST IN TIME TO MAKE IT TO WORK.
YES, THANK YOU VERY MUCH.
DESK, CURTAINS, KITCHENWARE, FRIDGE AND WASHING MACHINE. EVERYTHING YOU NEED!
YOU KNOW HOW TO LAY A FUTON, RIGHT?
YEP!
HE MOVED IN OFFICIALLY THAT WEEKEND.
MRS. KAYA! FOAM'S BUBBLING OUT OF THE WASHING MACHINE!
IS IT DEFECTIVE?!
HOW MUCH DETERGENT DID YOU PUT IN?!
ONE BOX! RIGHT?
BLUB
BLUB
ARE YOU KIDDING?! READ THE INSTRUCTIONS!
BLUB
MRS. KAYA! I USED THE RICE COOKER, BUT IT CAME OUT ALL HARD AND CRUNCHY!
I THINK IT'S DEFECTIVE!
HOW'D YOU COOK IT?
I ADDED RICE, THEN HOT WATER, AND WAITED THREE MINUTES...
KCC—CH
IF THIS IS A JOKE, I'M NOT LAUGHING!

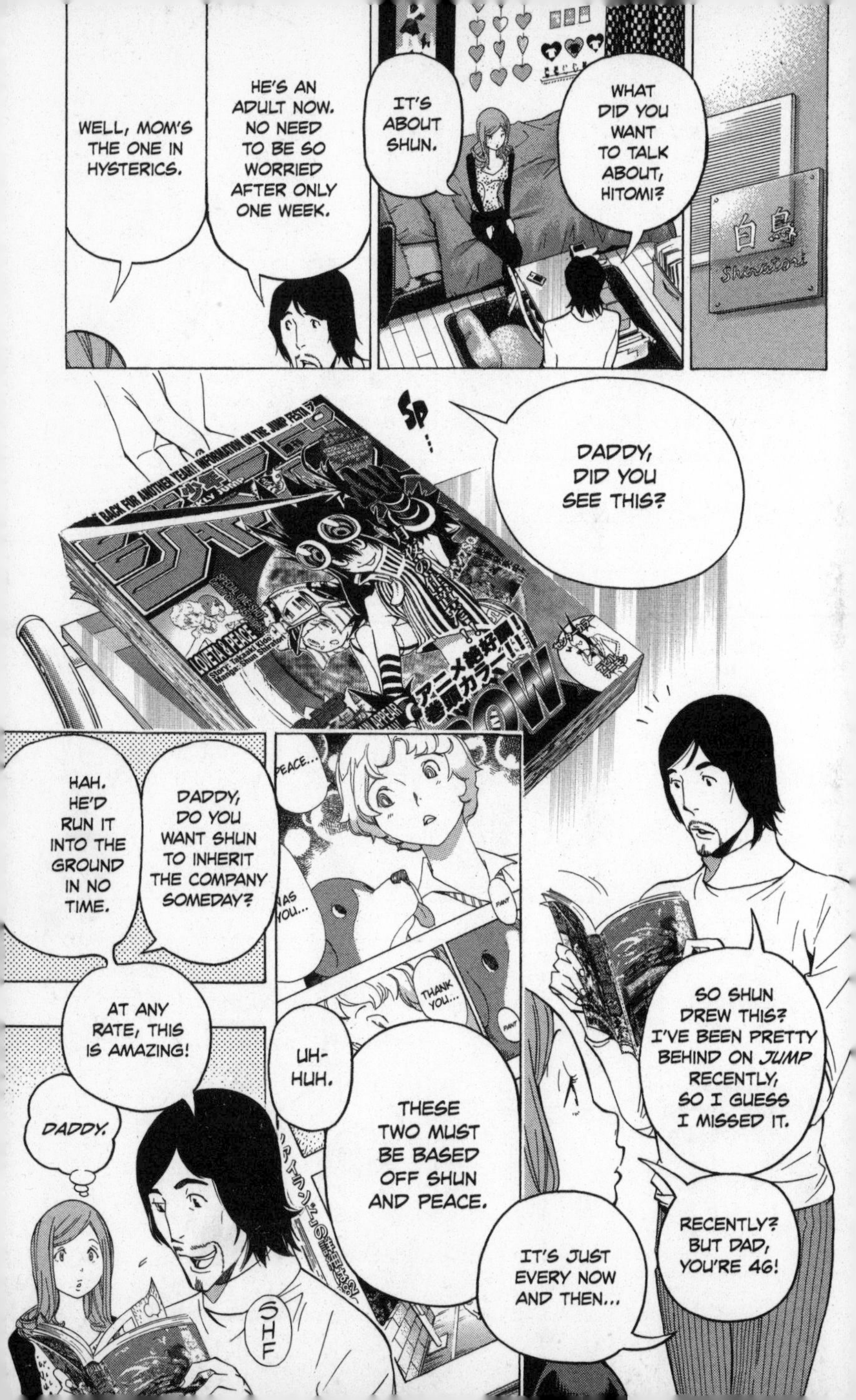

白鳥
Shiratori
WHAT DID YOU WANT TO TALK ABOUT, HITOMI?
IT'S ABOUT SHUN.
HE'S AN ADULT NOW. NO NEED TO BE SO WORRIED AFTER ONLY ONE WEEK.
WELL, MOM'S THE ONE IN HYSTERICS.
SP...
DADDY, DID YOU SEE THIS?
BACK FOR ANOTHER YEAR!! INFORMATION ON THE JUMP FESTA
SPECIAL ONE-SHOT
LOVETA & PEACE
Story: Takaaki Kido
Manga: Shun Shiratori
アニメ絶好調！巻頭カラー！！
SO SHUN DREW THIS? I'VE BEEN PRETTY BEHIND ON *JUMP* RECENTLY, SO I GUESS I MISSED IT.
RECENTLY? BUT DAD, YOU'RE 46!
IT'S JUST EVERY NOW AND THEN...
PEACE...
PANT
THANK YOU...
PANT
DADDY, DO YOU WANT SHUN TO INHERIT THE COMPANY SOMEDAY?
HAH. HE'D RUN IT INTO THE GROUND IN NO TIME.
AT ANY RATE, THIS IS AMAZING!
UH-HUH.
THESE TWO MUST BE BASED OFF SHUN AND PEACE.
DADDY.
SHF

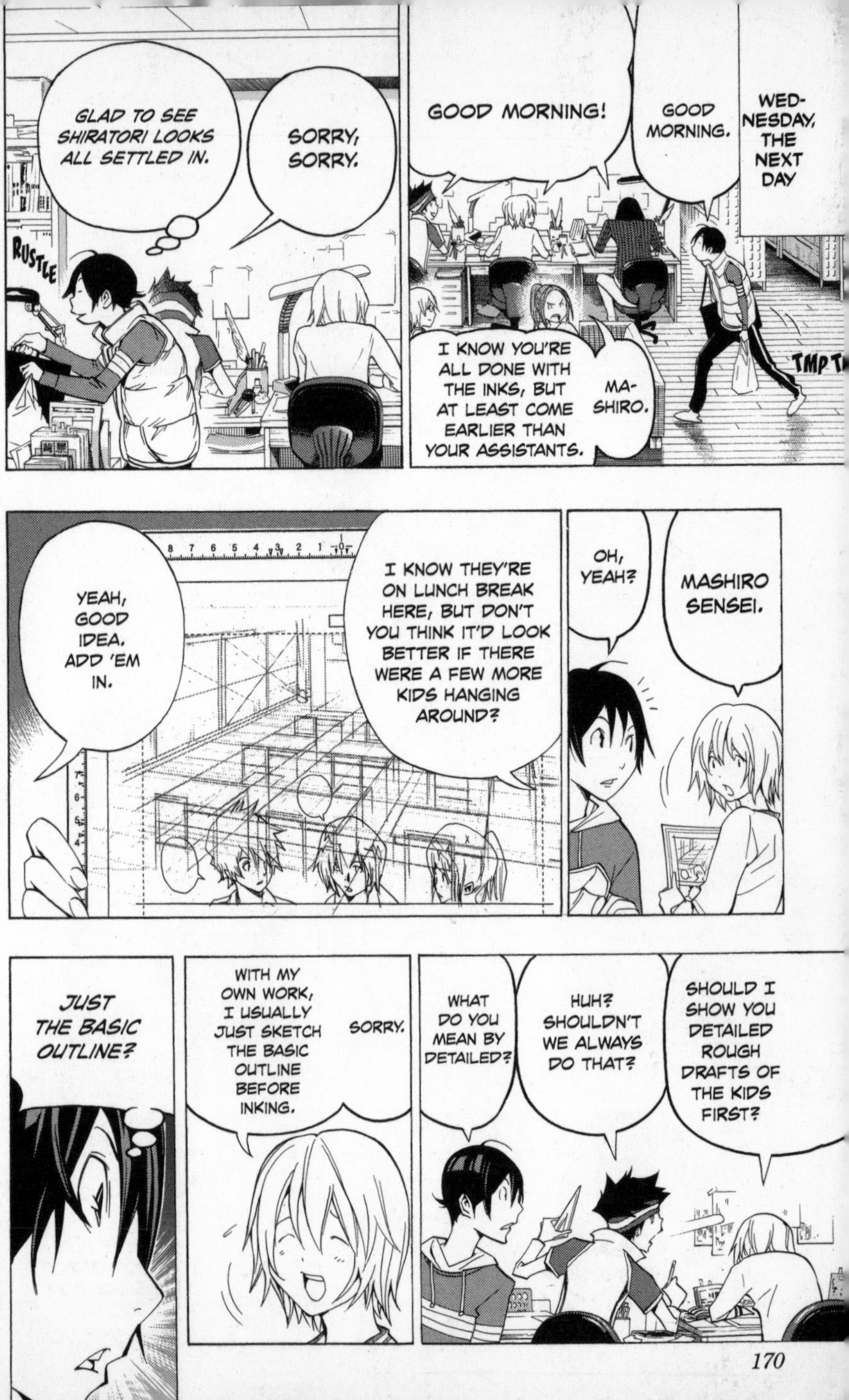
WEDNESDAY, THE NEXT DAY
GOOD MORNING.
GOOD MORNING!
MASHIRO.
I KNOW YOU'RE ALL DONE WITH THE INKS, BUT AT LEAST COME EARLIER THAN YOUR ASSISTANTS.
TMP T
SORRY, SORRY.
GLAD TO SEE SHIRATORI LOOKS ALL SETTLED IN.
RUSTLE
MASHIRO SENSEI.
OH, YEAH?
I KNOW THEY'RE ON LUNCH BREAK HERE, BUT DON'T YOU THINK IT'D LOOK BETTER IF THERE WERE A FEW MORE KIDS HANGING AROUND?
YEAH, GOOD IDEA. ADD 'EM IN.
SHOULD I SHOW YOU DETAILED ROUGH DRAFTS OF THE KIDS FIRST?
HUH? SHOULDN'T WE ALWAYS DO THAT?
WHAT DO YOU MEAN BY DETAILED?
SORRY.
WITH MY OWN WORK, I USUALLY JUST SKETCH THE BASIC OUTLINE BEFORE INKING.
JUST THE BASIC OUTLINE?

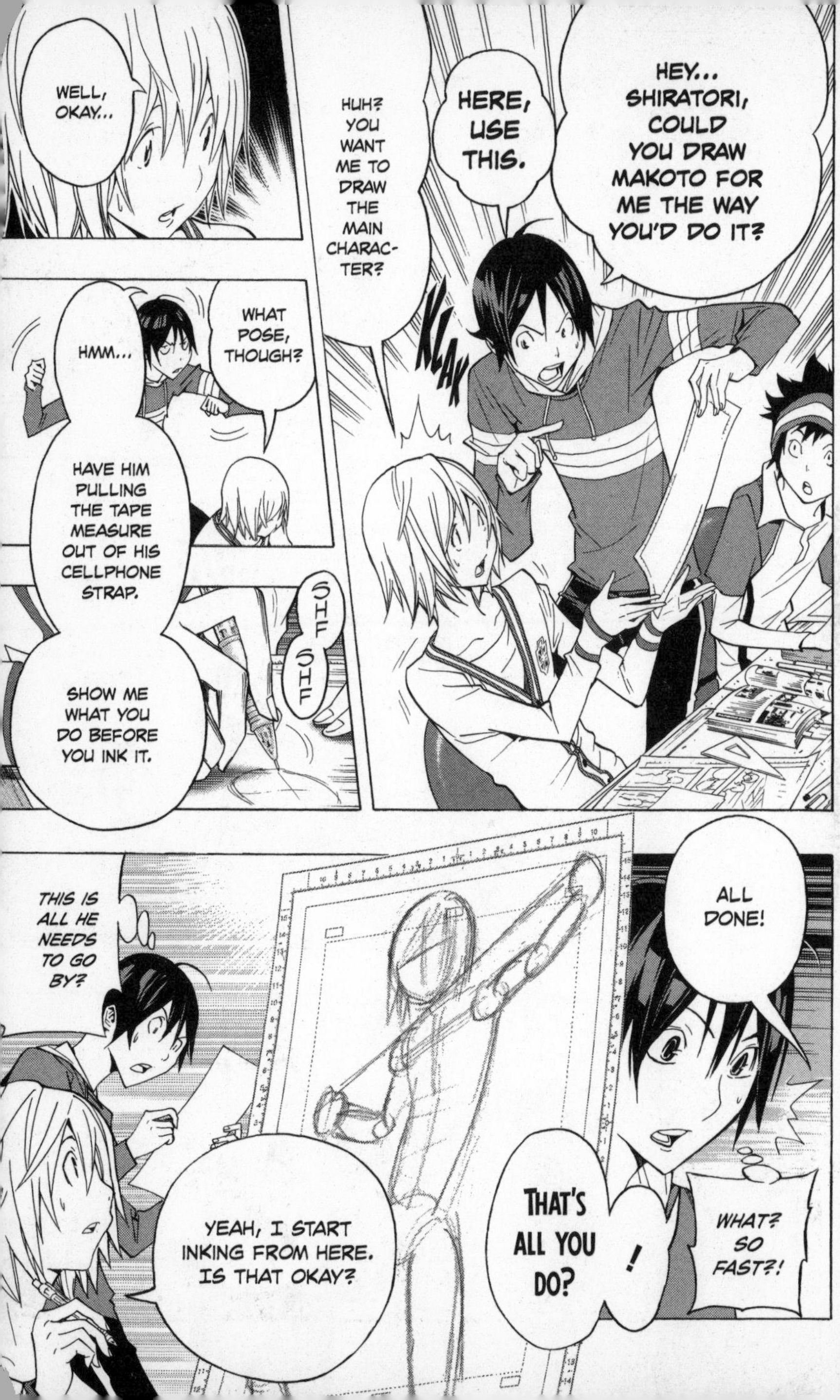
HEY... SHIRATORI, COULD YOU DRAW MAKOTO FOR ME THE WAY YOU'D DO IT?
HERE, USE THIS.
HUH? YOU WANT ME TO DRAW THE MAIN CHARACTER?
KLAK
WELL, OKAY...
WHAT POSE, THOUGH?
HMM...
HAVE HIM PULLING THE TAPE MEASURE OUT OF HIS CELLPHONE STRAP.
SHOW ME WHAT YOU DO BEFORE YOU INK IT.
SHF SHF
ALL DONE!
WHAT? SO FAST?!
!
THAT'S ALL YOU DO?
YEAH, I START INKING FROM HERE. IS THAT OKAY?
THIS IS ALL HE NEEDS TO GO BY?

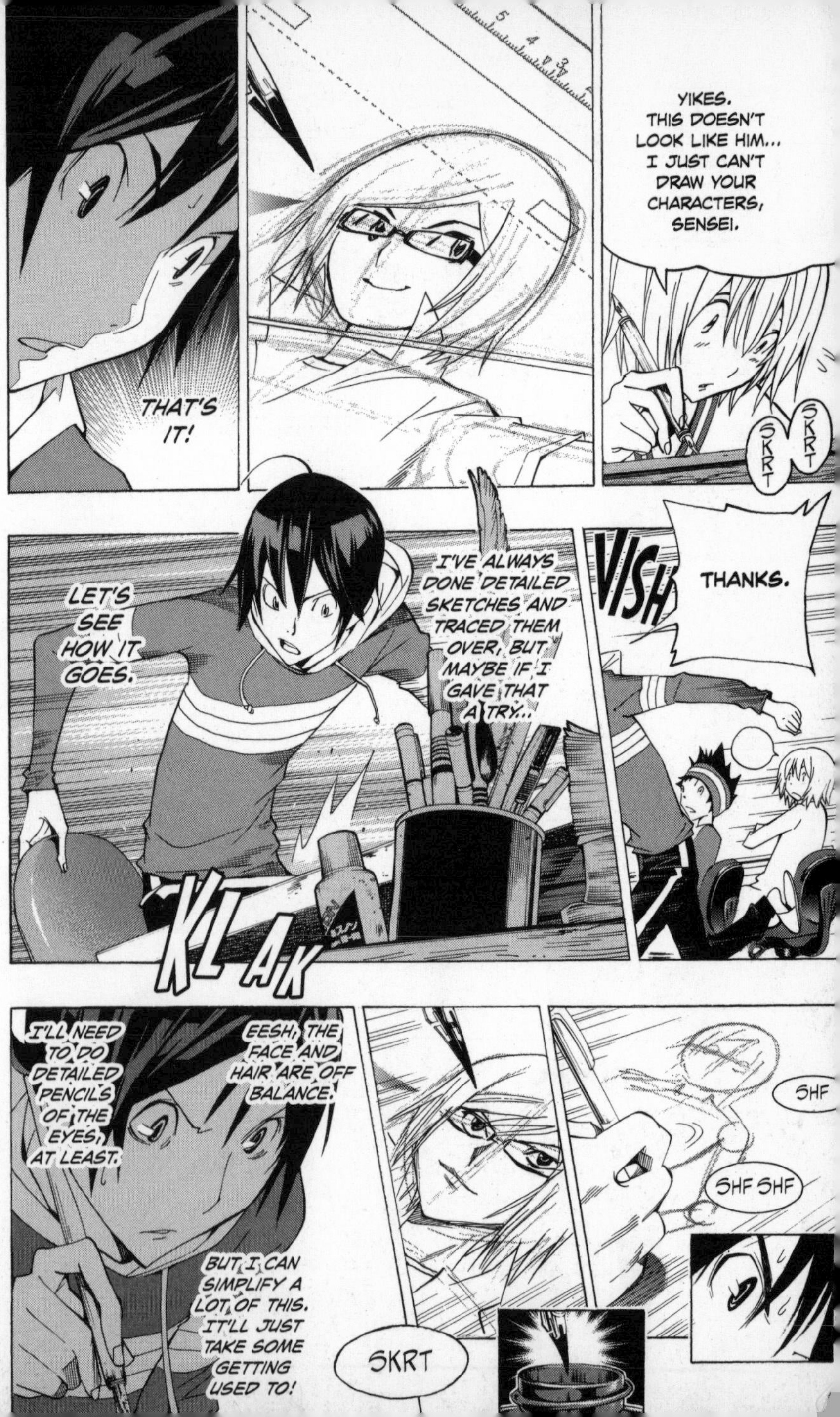
YIKES. THIS DOESN'T LOOK LIKE HIM... I JUST CAN'T DRAW YOUR CHARACTERS, SENSEI.
SKRT SKRT
SKRT
THAT'S IT!
VISH
THANKS.
I'VE ALWAYS DONE DETAILED SKETCHES AND TRACED THEM OVER, BUT MAYBE IF I GAVE THAT A TRY...
LET'S SEE HOW IT GOES.
KLAK
SHF
SHF SHF
SKRT
EESH, THE FACE AND HAIR ARE OFF BALANCE.
I'LL NEED TO DO DETAILED PENCILS OF THE EYES, AT LEAST.
BUT I CAN SIMPLIFY A LOT OF THIS. IT'LL JUST TAKE SOME GETTING USED TO!

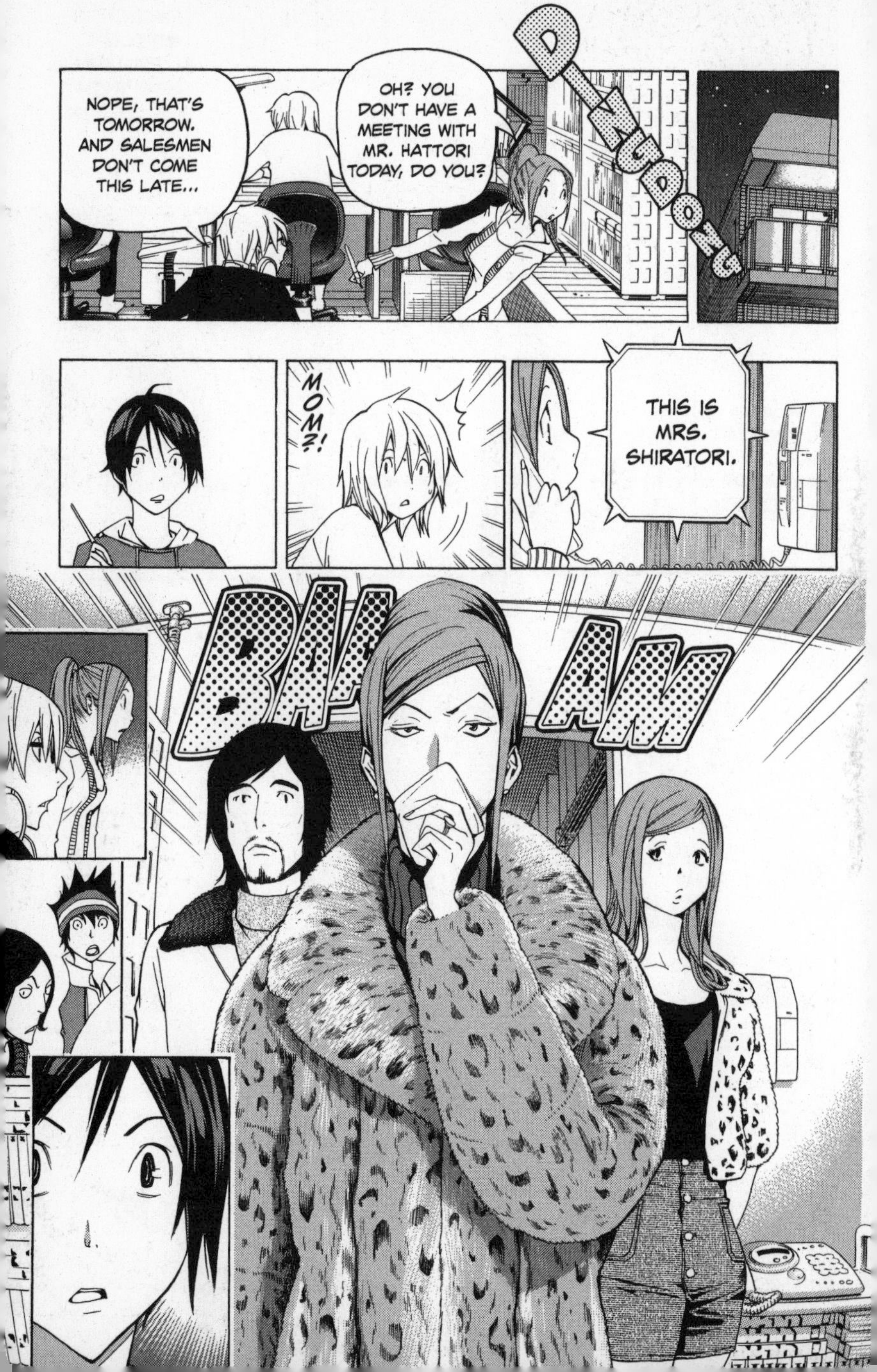
DINGDONG
OH? YOU DON'T HAVE A MEETING WITH MR. HATTORI TODAY, DO YOU?
NOPE, THAT'S TOMORROW. AND SALESMEN DON'T COME THIS LATE...
THIS IS MRS. SHIRATORI.
MOM?!
BA AM

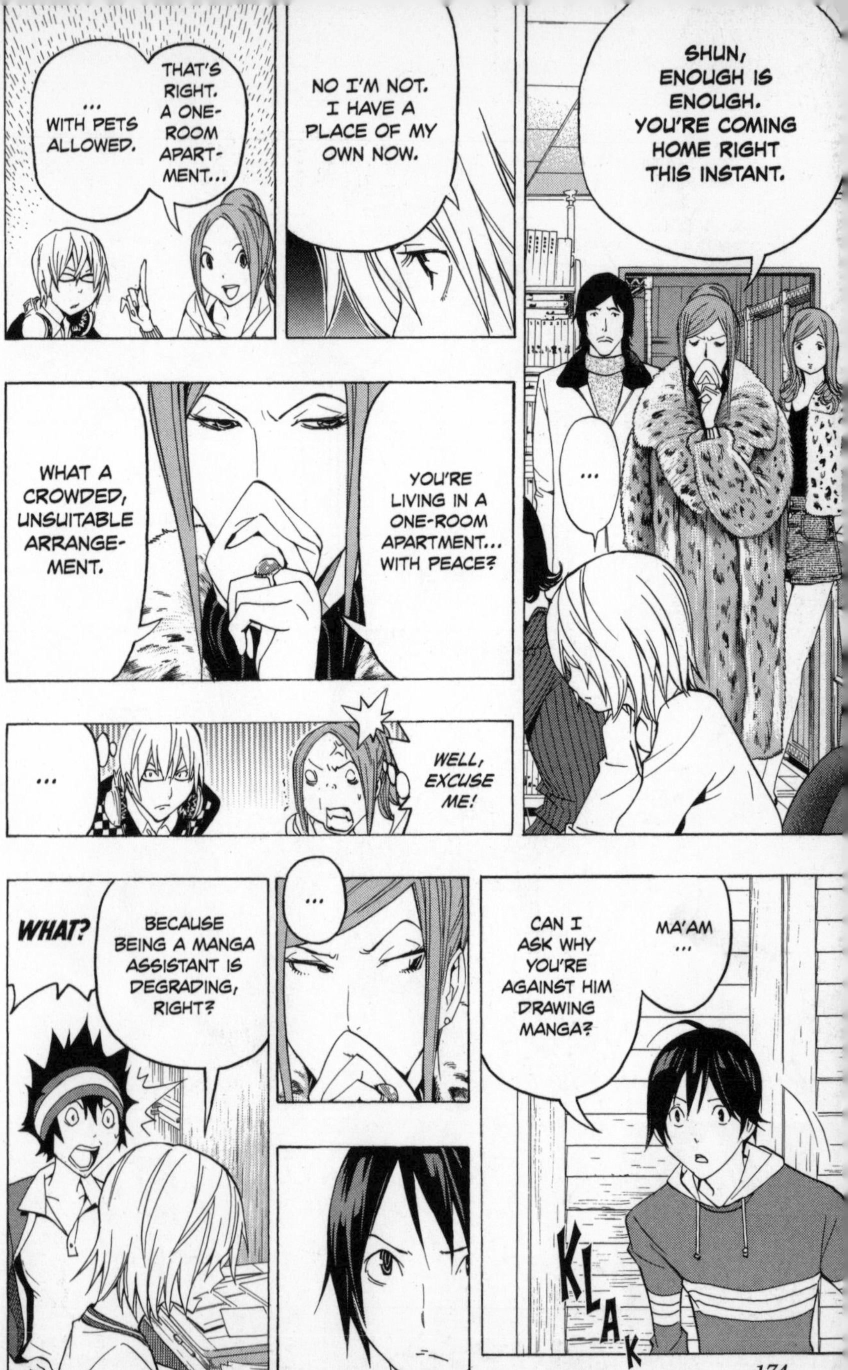
SHUN, ENOUGH IS ENOUGH. YOU'RE COMING HOME RIGHT THIS INSTANT.
...
NO I'M NOT. I HAVE A PLACE OF MY OWN NOW.
THAT'S RIGHT. A ONE-ROOM APARTMENT...
... WITH PETS ALLOWED.
YOU'RE LIVING IN A ONE-ROOM APARTMENT... WITH PEACE?
WHAT A CROWDED, UNSUITABLE ARRANGEMENT.
WELL, EXCUSE ME!
...
MA'AM ...
CAN I ASK WHY YOU'RE AGAINST HIM DRAWING MANGA?
KLAK
...
BECAUSE BEING A MANGA ASSISTANT IS DEGRADING, RIGHT?
WHAT?

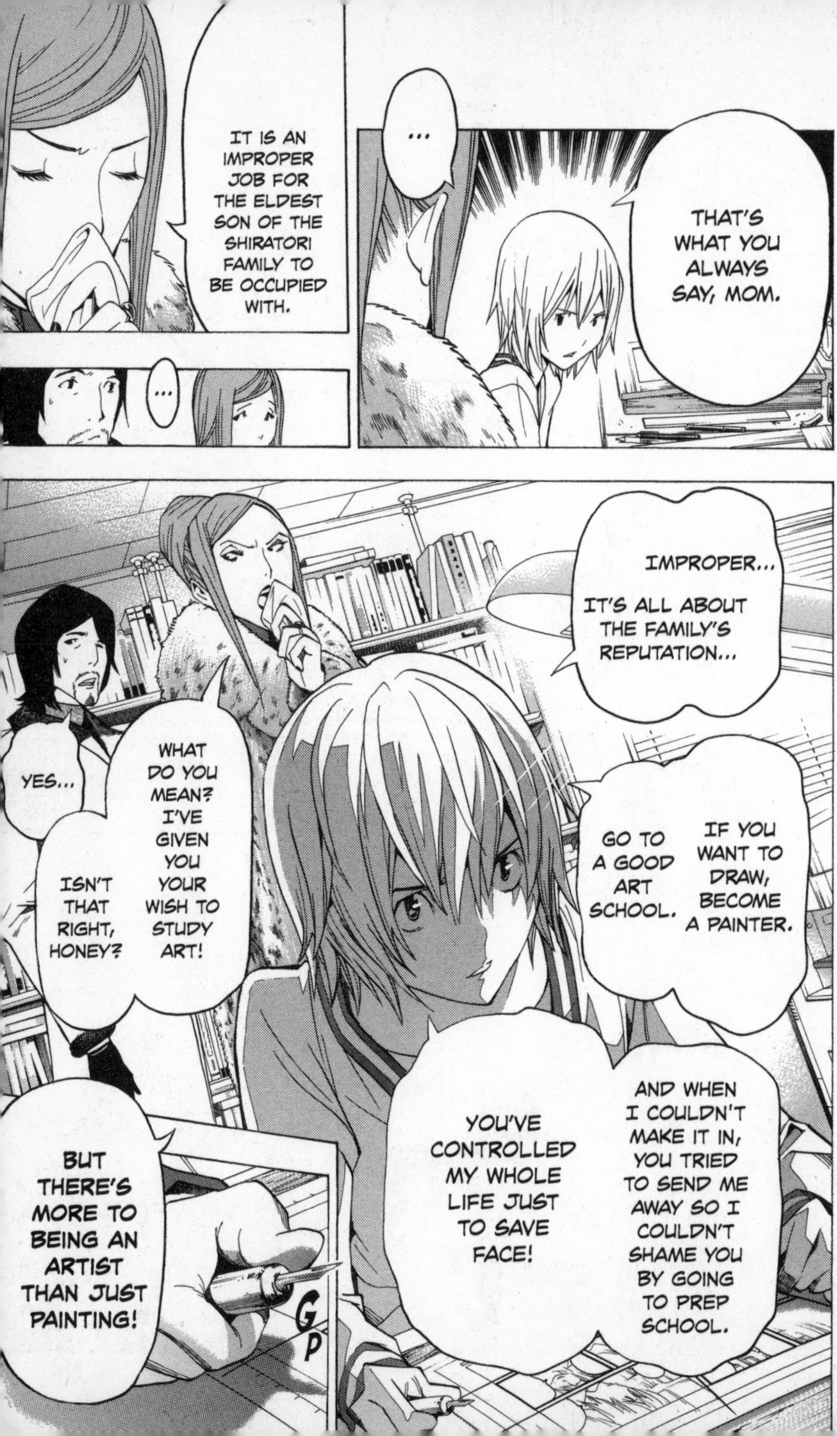
...
THAT'S WHAT YOU ALWAYS SAY, MOM.
IT IS AN IMPROPER JOB FOR THE ELDEST SON OF THE SHIRATORI FAMILY TO BE OCCUPIED WITH.
...
IMPROPER...
IT'S ALL ABOUT THE FAMILY'S REPUTATION...
IF YOU WANT TO DRAW, BECOME A PAINTER.
GO TO A GOOD ART SCHOOL.
WHAT DO YOU MEAN? I'VE GIVEN YOU YOUR WISH TO STUDY ART!
ISN'T THAT RIGHT, HONEY?
YES...
AND WHEN I COULDN'T MAKE IT IN, YOU TRIED TO SEND ME AWAY SO I COULDN'T SHAME YOU BY GOING TO PREP SCHOOL.
YOU'VE CONTROLLED MY WHOLE LIFE JUST TO SAVE FACE!
BUT THERE'S MORE TO BEING AN ARTIST THAN JUST PAINTING!
GP

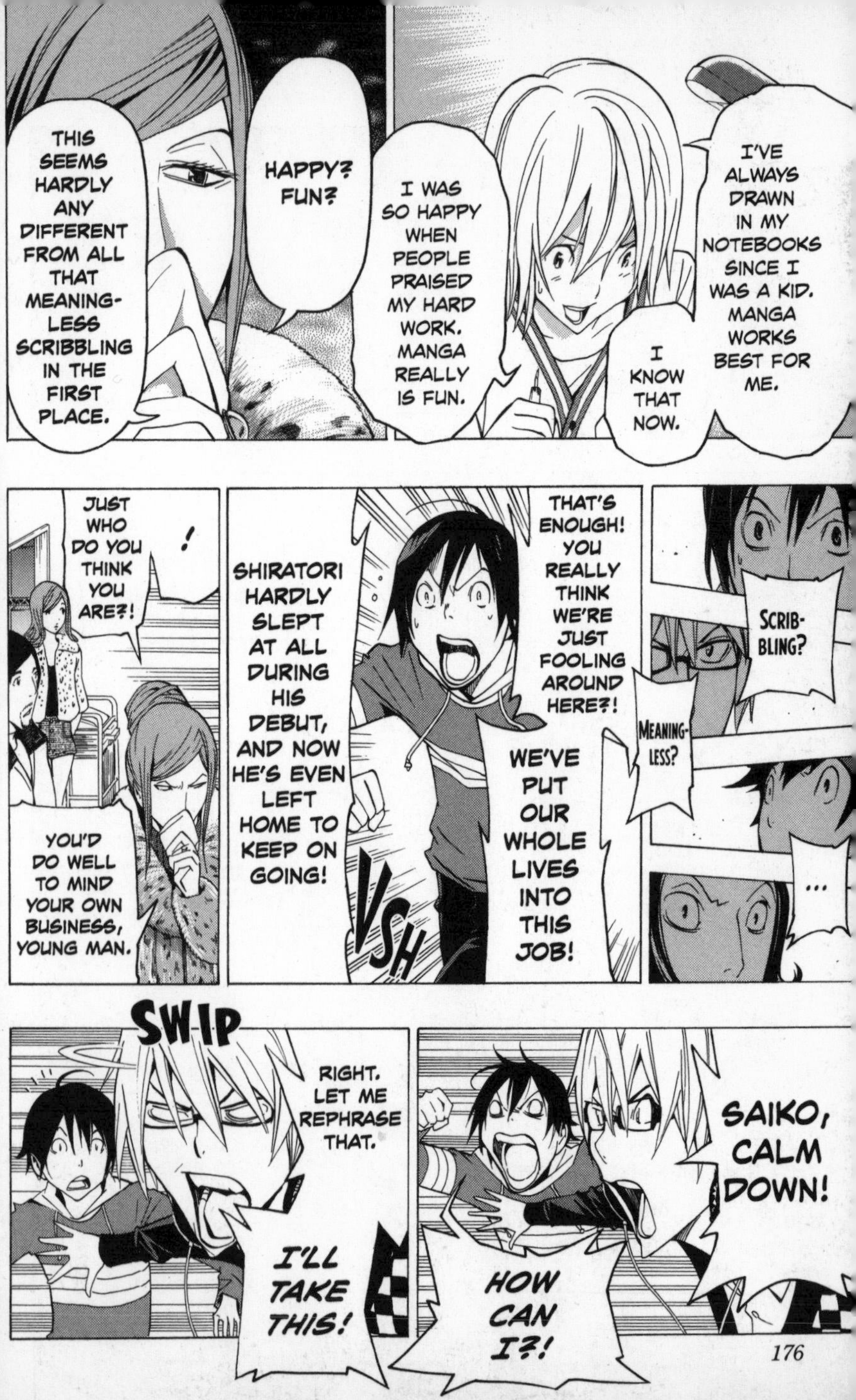
I'VE ALWAYS DRAWN IN MY NOTEBOOKS SINCE I WAS A KID. MANGA WORKS BEST FOR ME.
I KNOW THAT NOW.
I WAS SO HAPPY WHEN PEOPLE PRAISED MY HARD WORK. MANGA REALLY IS FUN.
HAPPY? FUN?
THIS SEEMS HARDLY ANY DIFFERENT FROM ALL THAT MEANING-LESS SCRIBBLING IN THE FIRST PLACE.
SCRIB-BLING?
MEANING-LESS?
...
THAT'S ENOUGH! YOU REALLY THINK WE'RE JUST FOOLING AROUND HERE?!
SHIRATORI HARDLY SLEPT AT ALL DURING HIS DEBUT, AND NOW HE'S EVEN LEFT HOME TO KEEP ON GOING!
WE'VE PUT OUR WHOLE LIVES INTO THIS JOB!
VSH
!
JUST WHO DO YOU THINK YOU ARE?!
YOU'D DO WELL TO MIND YOUR OWN BUSINESS, YOUNG MAN.
SAIKO, CALM DOWN!
HOW CAN I?!
SWIP
RIGHT. LET ME REPHRASE THAT.
I'LL TAKE THIS!

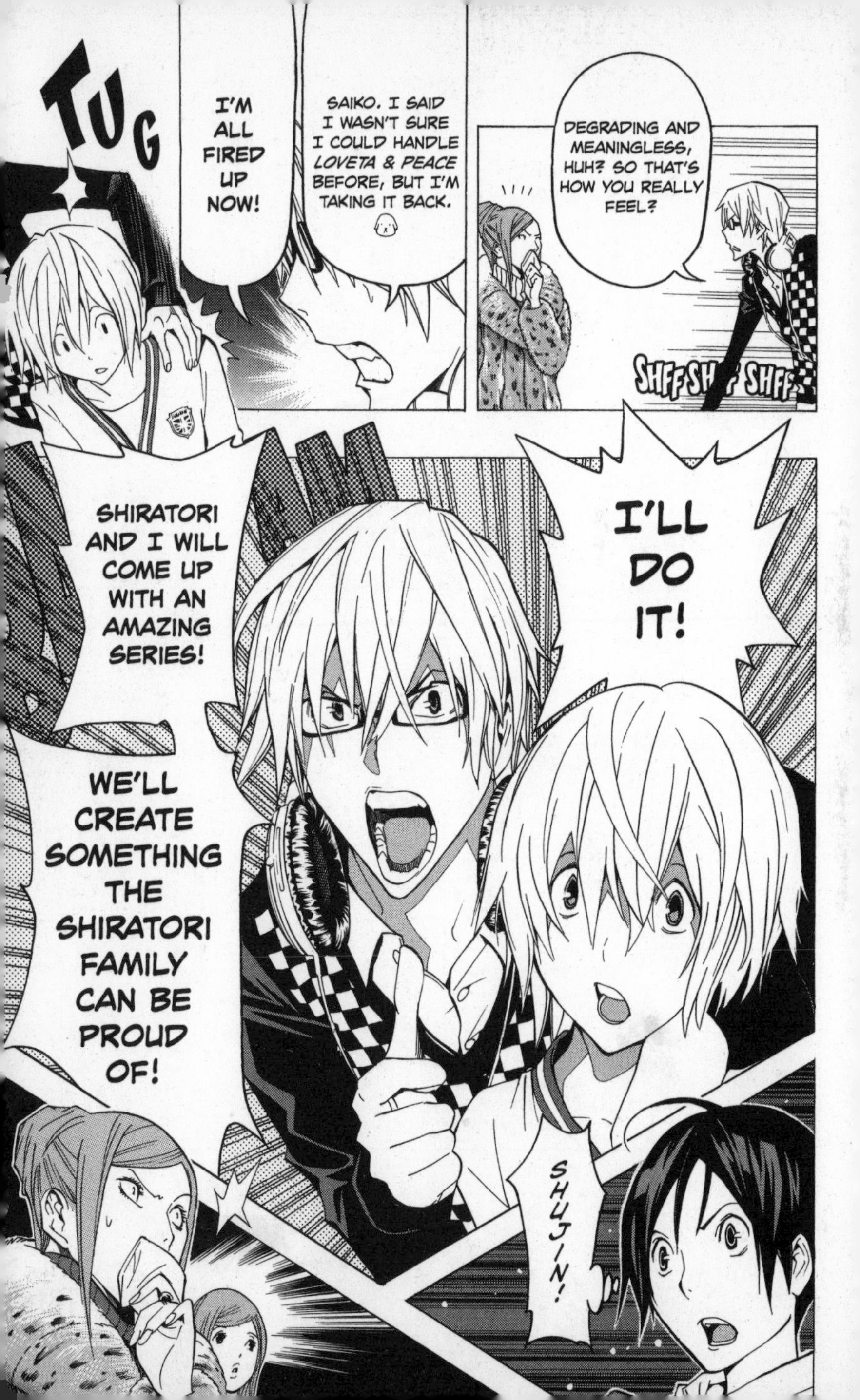
DEGRADING AND MEANINGLESS, HUH? SO THAT'S HOW YOU REALLY FEEL?
SHFF SHFF SHFF
SAIKO. I SAID I WASN'T SURE I COULD HANDLE LOVETA & PEACE BEFORE, BUT I'M TAKING IT BACK.
I'M ALL FIRED UP NOW!
TUG
I'LL DO IT!
SHIRATORI AND I WILL COME UP WITH AN AMAZING SERIES!
WE'LL CREATE SOMETHING THE SHIRATORI FAMILY CAN BE PROUD OF!
SHUJIN!

OHBA'S STORYBOARD

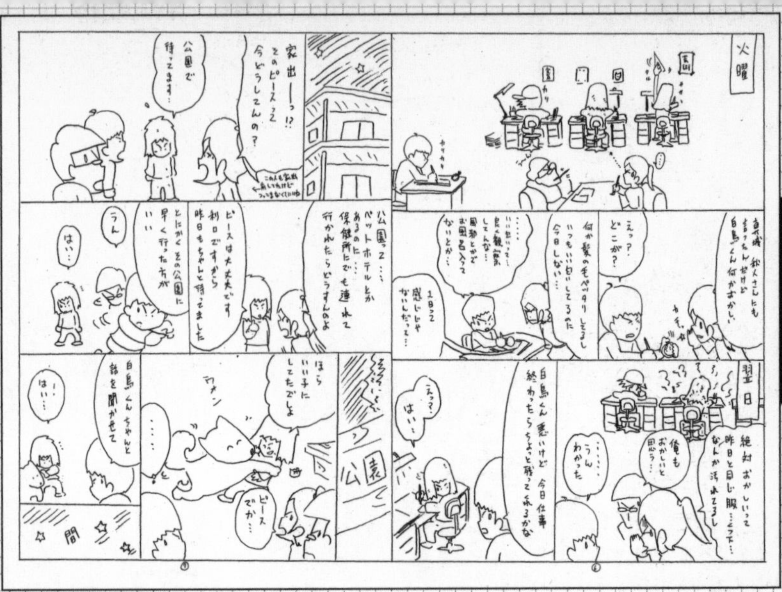
火曜
東城秋人さんにも言ってたんだけど白鳥くん何かおかしい
えっ？どこが？
何か髪の毛ペッタリしてるし いつもいい匂いしてるのに今日しない…
いい匂いって… 良く観察してんな… 風邪とかでお風呂入ってないとか…
1日って感じじゃないんだって…
翌日
絶対おかしいって 昨日と同じ服… なんか汚れてるし
俺もおかしいと思う…
…うん わかった
白鳥くん 悪いけど 今日仕事終わったらちょっと残ってくれるかな
えっ？ はい…
家出ーっ!? そのピースってのは今どうしてんの？
公園で待ってます…
公園って… ペットホテルとかあるのに… 保健所にでも連れて行かれたらどうすんのよ
ピースは大丈夫です 利口ですから 昨日もちゃんと待ってました
とにかくその公園に早く行った方がいい
うん
はい…
公園
ほら いい子にしてたでしょ
ワン
ピースでか…
……
白鳥くん ちゃんと話を聞かせて
…はい…
間

OBATA'S STORYBOARD

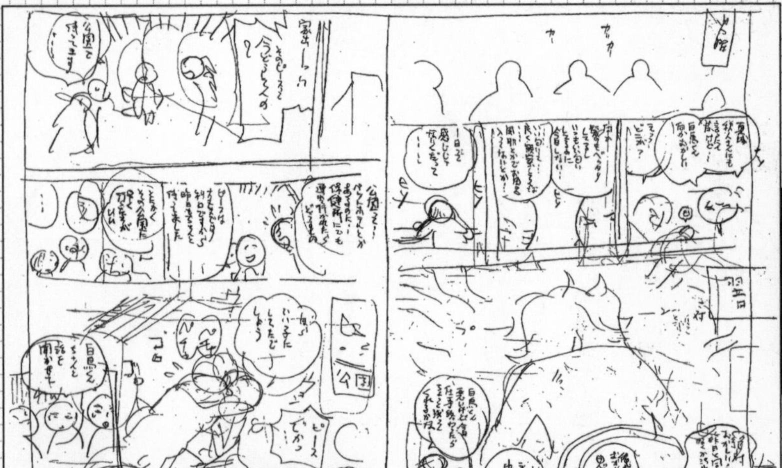

COMPLETE!

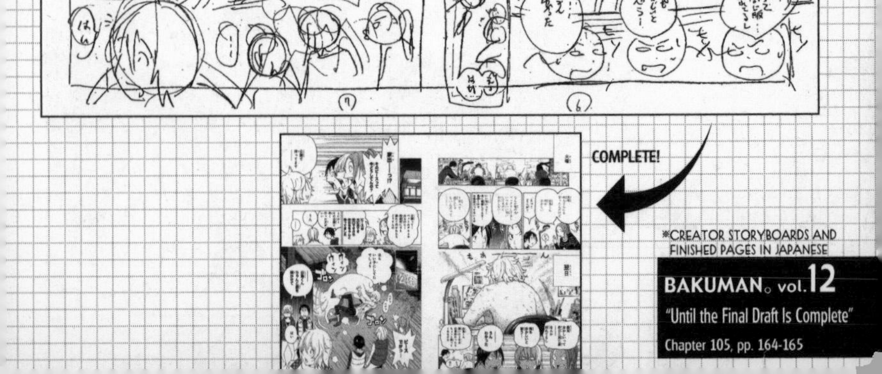

※CREATOR STORYBOARDS AND FINISHED PAGES IN JAPANESE

BAKUMAN。 vol.12

"Until the Final Draft Is Complete"

Chapter 105, pp. 164-165

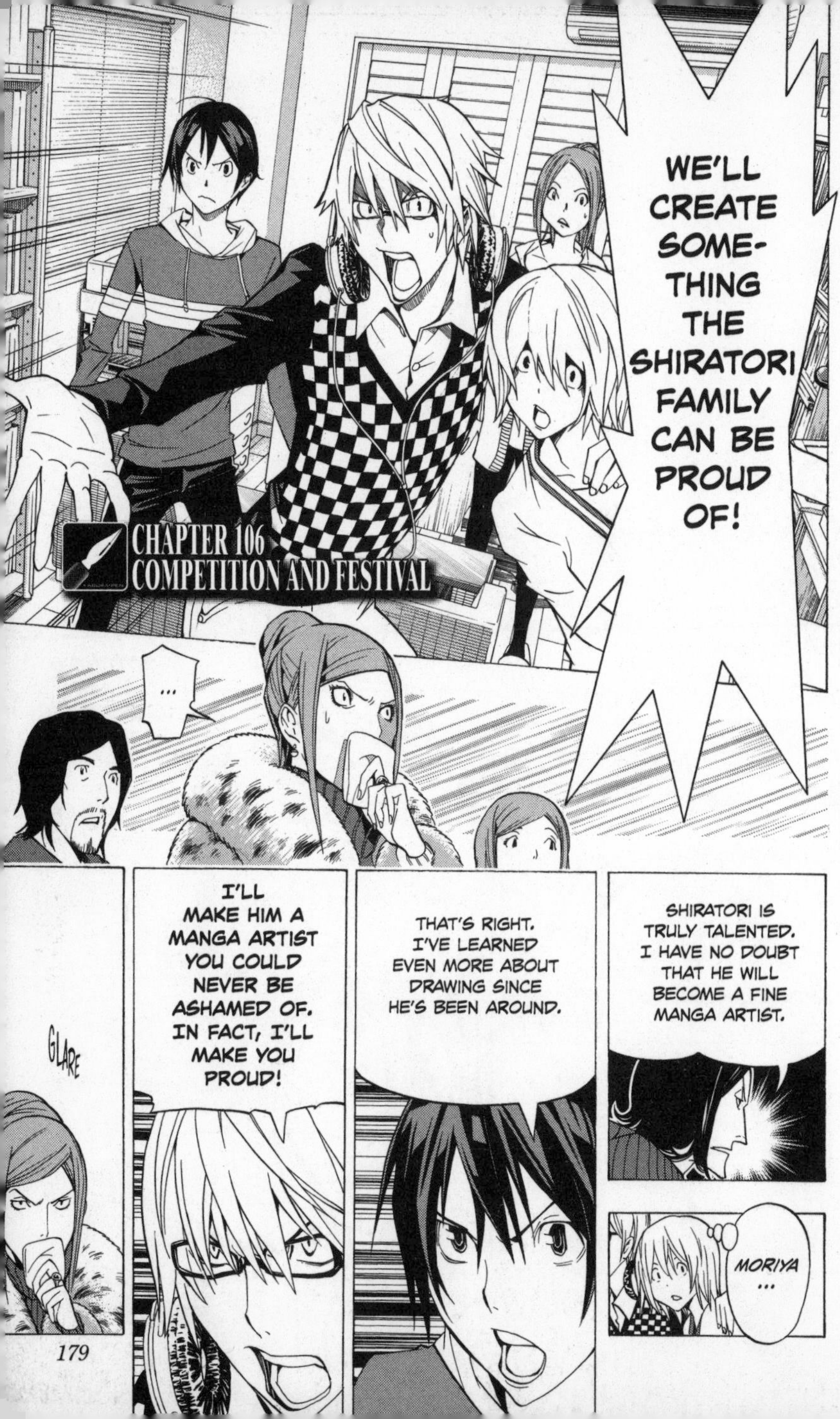
WE'LL CREATE SOMETHING THE SHIRATORI FAMILY CAN BE PROUD OF!
CHAPTER 106
COMPETITION AND FESTIVAL
...
SHIRATORI IS TRULY TALENTED. I HAVE NO DOUBT THAT HE WILL BECOME A FINE MANGA ARTIST.
MORIYA ...
THAT'S RIGHT. I'VE LEARNED EVEN MORE ABOUT DRAWING SINCE HE'S BEEN AROUND.
I'LL MAKE HIM A MANGA ARTIST YOU COULD NEVER BE ASHAMED OF. IN FACT, I'LL MAKE YOU PROUD!
GLARE

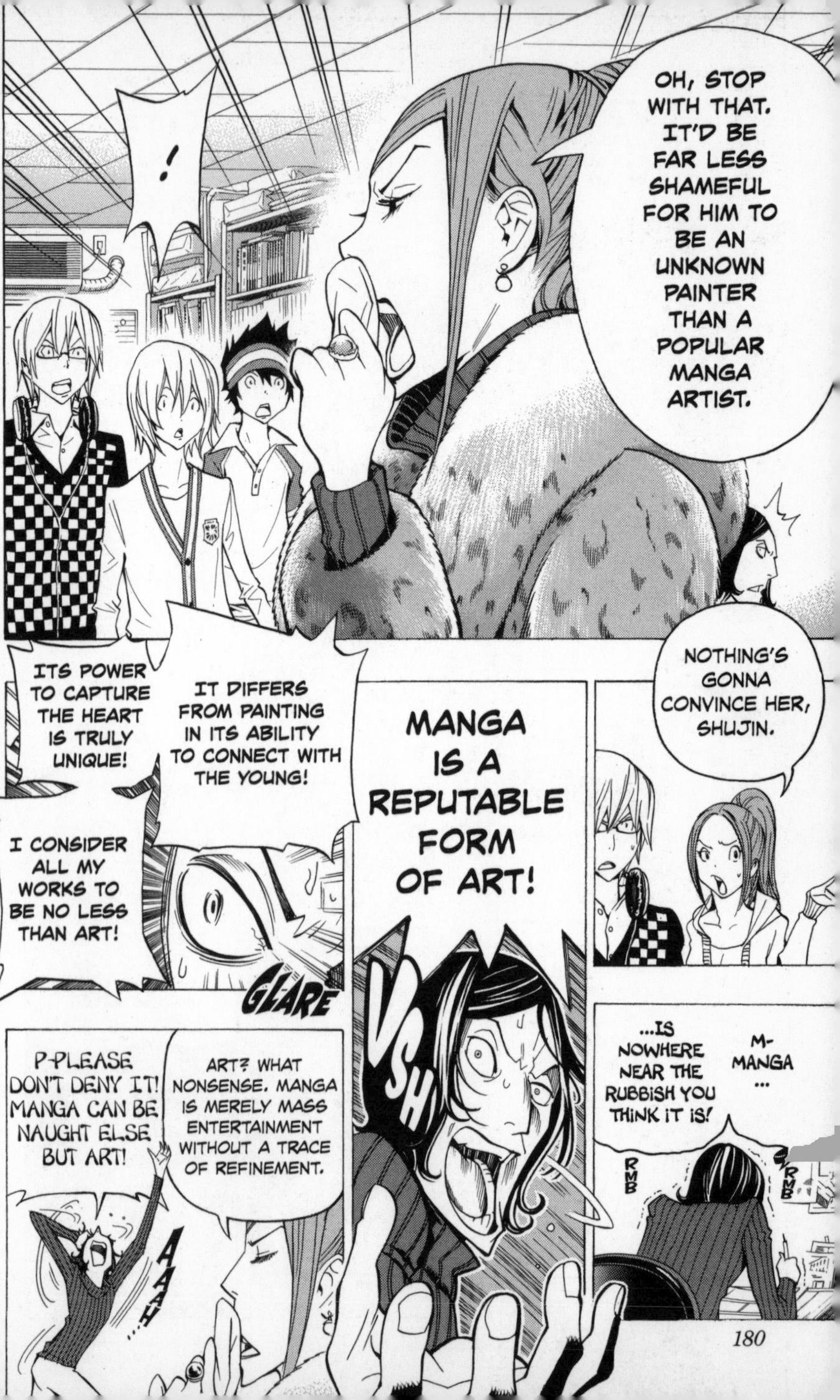
OH, STOP WITH THAT. IT'D BE FAR LESS SHAMEFUL FOR HIM TO BE AN UNKNOWN PAINTER THAN A POPULAR MANGA ARTIST.
!
NOTHING'S GONNA CONVINCE HER, SHUJIN.
MANGA IS A REPUTABLE FORM OF ART!
IT DIFFERS FROM PAINTING IN ITS ABILITY TO CONNECT WITH THE YOUNG!
ITS POWER TO CAPTURE THE HEART IS TRULY UNIQUE!
I CONSIDER ALL MY WORKS TO BE NO LESS THAN ART!
GLARE
M-MANGA ...
...IS NOWHERE NEAR THE RUBBISH YOU THINK IT IS!
RMB
RMB
VSH
ART? WHAT NONSENSE. MANGA IS MERELY MASS ENTERTAINMENT WITHOUT A TRACE OF REFINEMENT.
P-PLEASE DON'T DENY IT! MANGA CAN BE NAUGHT ELSE BUT ART!
AAAH...

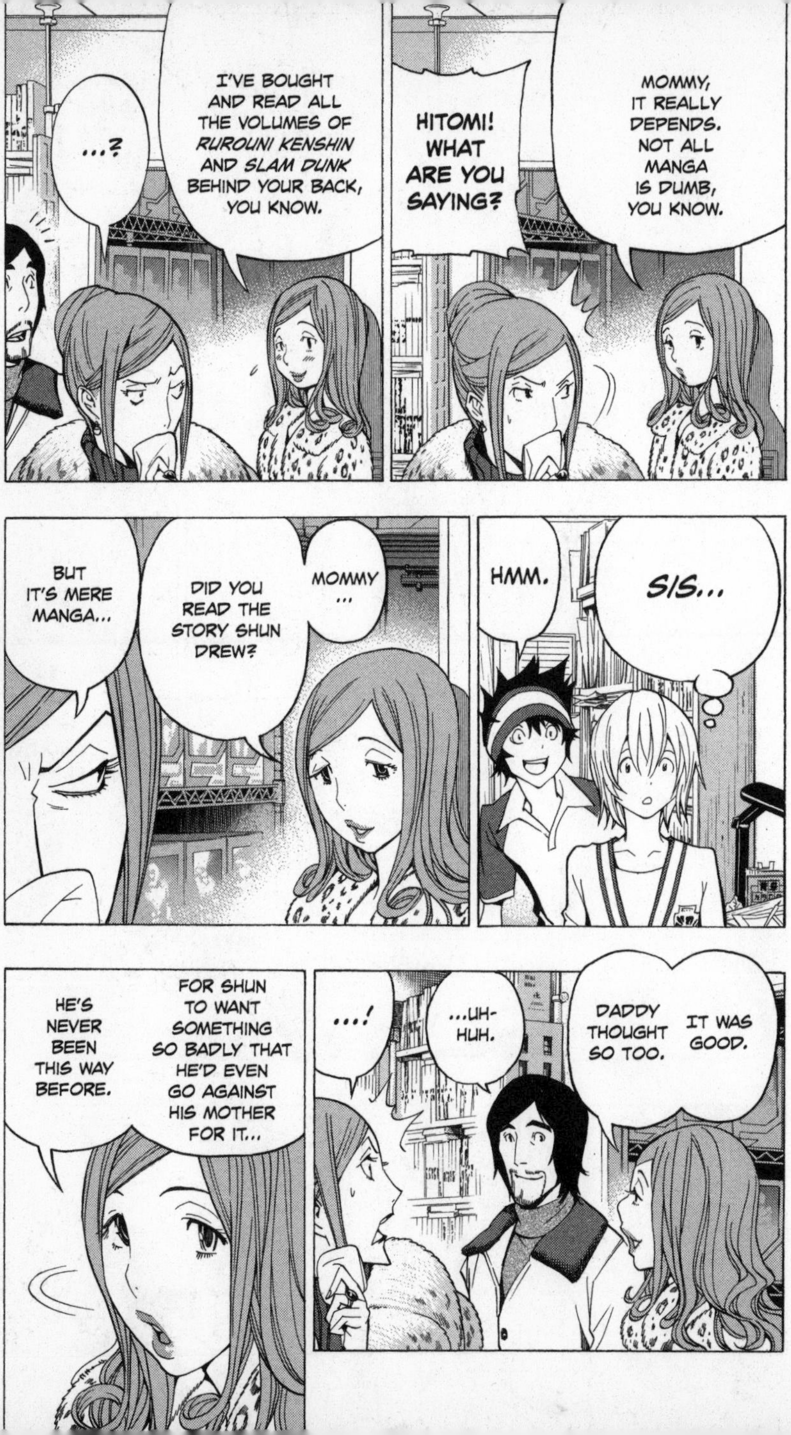
MOMMY, IT REALLY DEPENDS. NOT ALL MANGA IS DUMB, YOU KNOW.
HITOMI! WHAT ARE YOU SAYING?
I'VE BOUGHT AND READ ALL THE VOLUMES OF *RUROUNI KENSHIN* AND *SLAM DUNK* BEHIND YOUR BACK, YOU KNOW.
...?
SIS...
HMM.
MOMMY...
DID YOU READ THE STORY SHUN DREW?
BUT IT'S MERE MANGA...
IT WAS GOOD.
DADDY THOUGHT SO TOO.
...UH-HUH.
...!
FOR SHUN TO WANT SOMETHING SO BADLY THAT HE'D EVEN GO AGAINST HIS MOTHER FOR IT...
HE'S NEVER BEEN THIS WAY BEFORE.

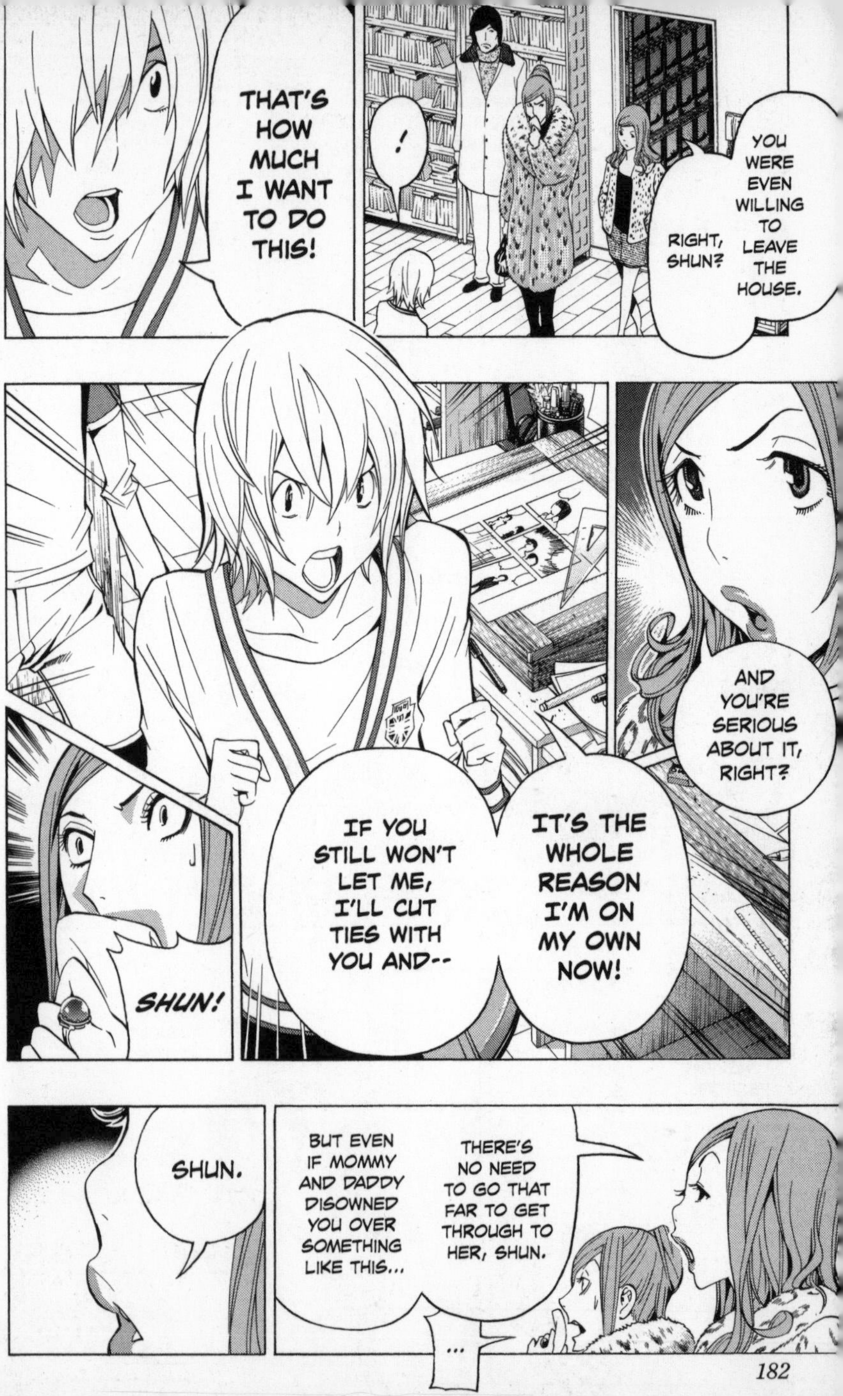
YOU WERE EVEN WILLING TO LEAVE THE HOUSE.
RIGHT, SHUN?
!
THAT'S HOW MUCH I WANT TO DO THIS!
AND YOU'RE SERIOUS ABOUT IT, RIGHT?
IT'S THE WHOLE REASON I'M ON MY OWN NOW!
IF YOU STILL WON'T LET ME, I'LL CUT TIES WITH YOU AND--
SHUN!
THERE'S NO NEED TO GO THAT FAR TO GET THROUGH TO HER, SHUN.
BUT EVEN IF MOMMY AND DADDY DISOWNED YOU OVER SOMETHING LIKE THIS...
...
SHUN.

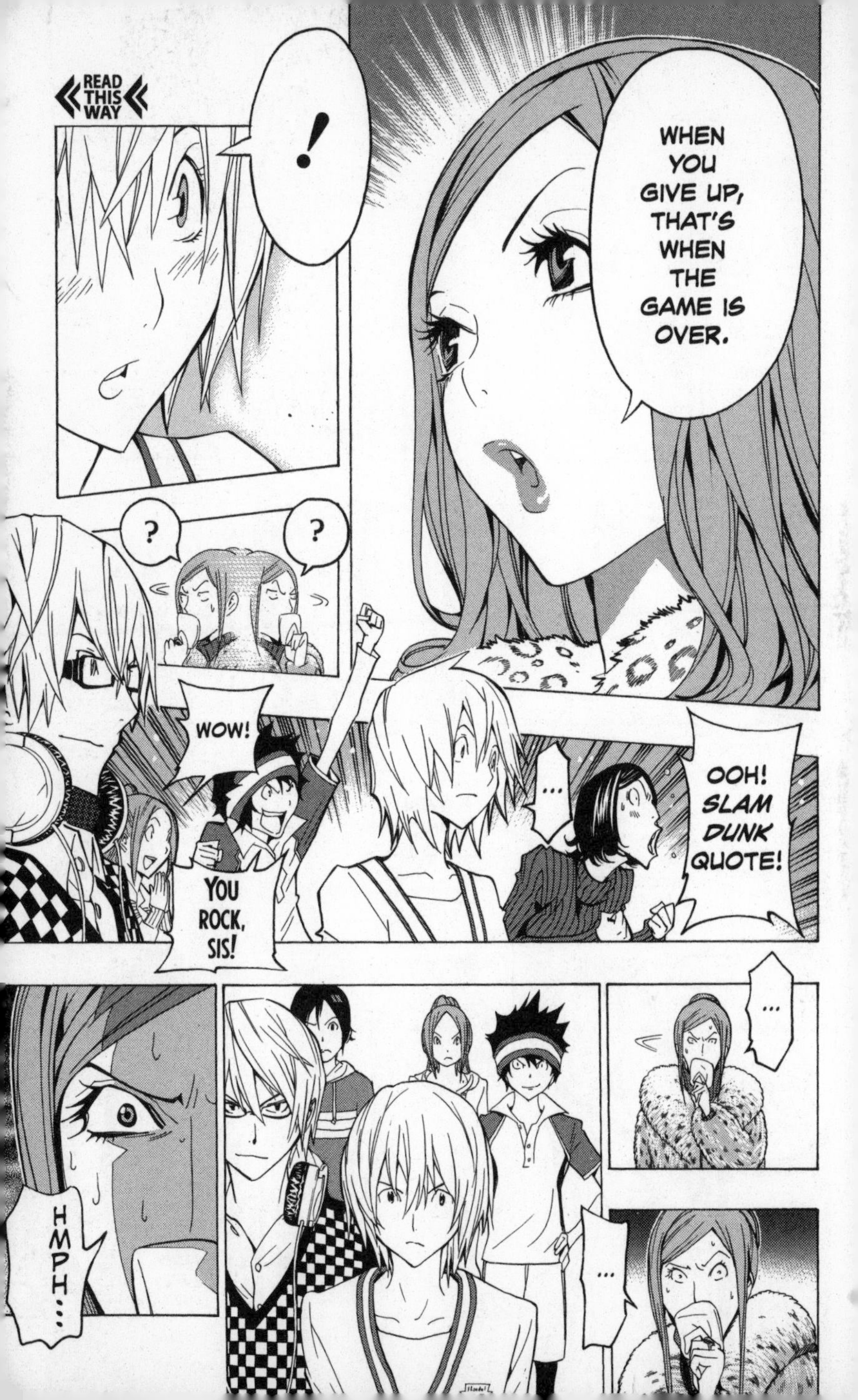
READ THIS WAY
WHEN YOU GIVE UP, THAT'S WHEN THE GAME IS OVER.
!
?
?
OOH! SLAM DUNK QUOTE!
...
WOW!
YOU ROCK, SIS!
...
...
HMPH...

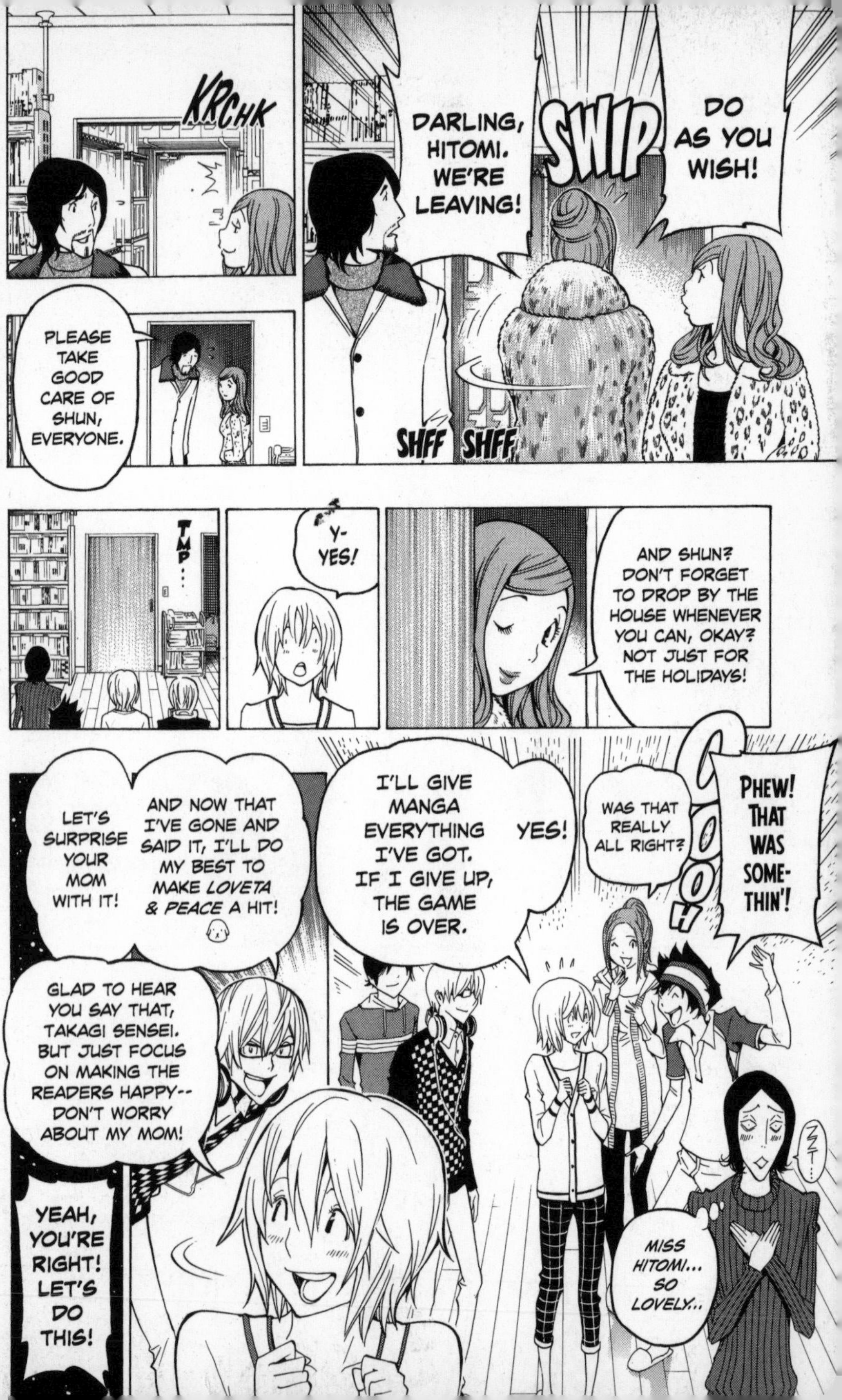
DO AS YOU WISH!
SWIP
DARLING, HITOMI. WE'RE LEAVING!
SHFF SHFF
KRCHK
PLEASE TAKE GOOD CARE OF SHUN, EVERYONE.
AND SHUN? DON'T FORGET TO DROP BY THE HOUSE WHENEVER YOU CAN, OKAY? NOT JUST FOR THE HOLIDAYS!
Y- YES!
TMP...
PHEW! THAT WAS SOME-THIN'!
GOOOH
WAS THAT REALLY ALL RIGHT?
I'LL GIVE MANGA EVERYTHING I'VE GOT. IF I GIVE UP, THE GAME IS OVER.
YES!
AND NOW THAT I'VE GONE AND SAID IT, I'LL DO MY BEST TO MAKE *LOVETA & PEACE* A HIT!
LET'S SURPRISE YOUR MOM WITH IT!
GLAD TO HEAR YOU SAY THAT, TAKAGI SENSEI. BUT JUST FOCUS ON MAKING THE READERS HAPPY-- DON'T WORRY ABOUT MY MOM!
ZZT...
MISS HITOMI... SO LOVELY...
YEAH, YOU'RE RIGHT! LET'S DO THIS!

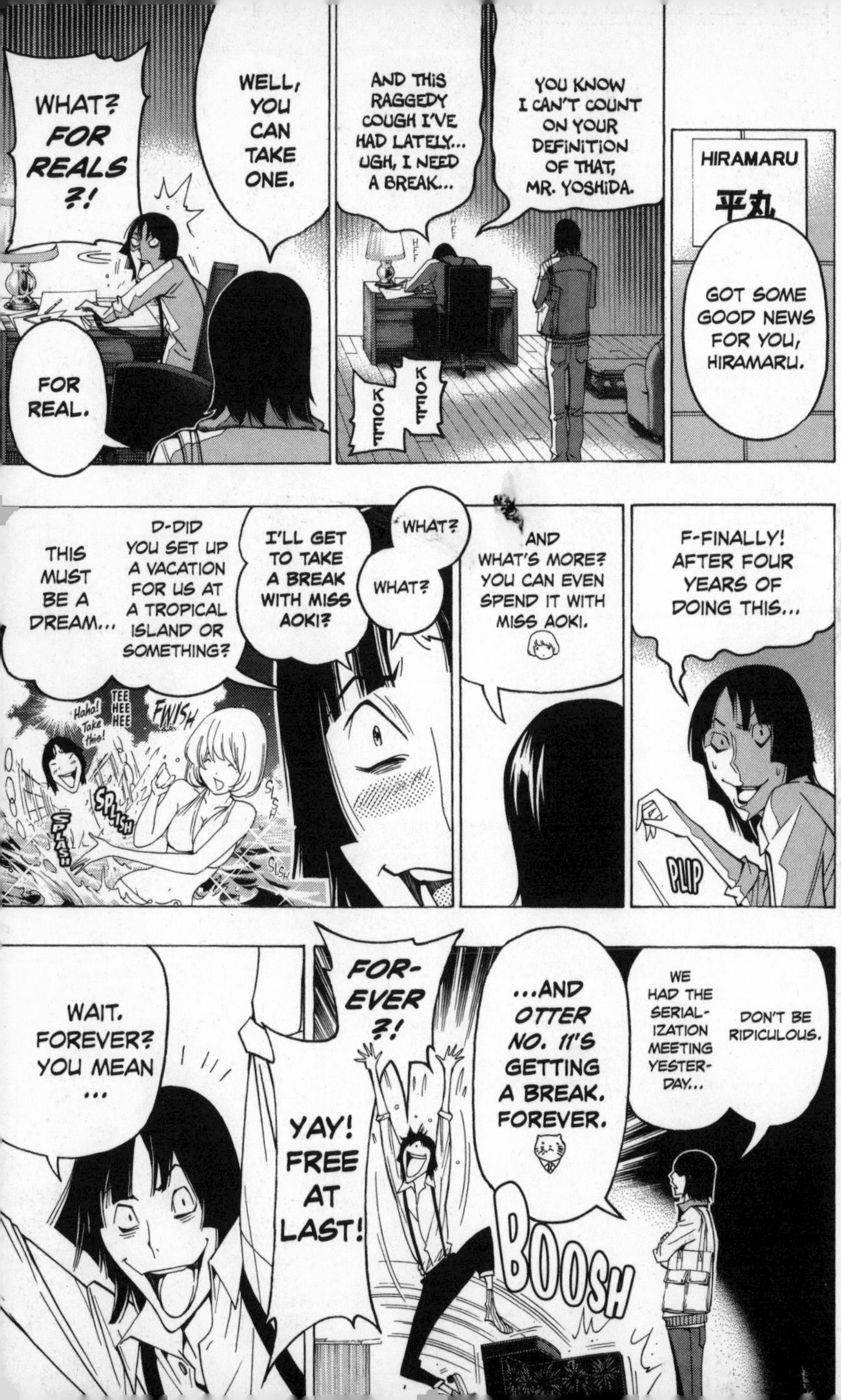
HIRAMARU
平丸
GOT SOME GOOD NEWS FOR YOU, HIRAMARU.
YOU KNOW I CAN'T COUNT ON YOUR DEFINITION OF THAT, MR. YOSHIDA.
AND THIS RAGGEDY COUGH I'VE HAD LATELY... UGH, I NEED A BREAK...
HFF
HFF
KOFF
KOFF
WELL, YOU CAN TAKE ONE.
WHAT? FOR REALS?!
FOR REAL.
F-FINALLY! AFTER FOUR YEARS OF DOING THIS...
PLIP
AND WHAT'S MORE? YOU CAN EVEN SPEND IT WITH MISS AOKI.
WHAT?
WHAT?
I'LL GET TO TAKE A BREAK WITH MISS AOKI?
D-DID YOU SET UP A VACATION FOR US AT A TROPICAL ISLAND OR SOMETHING?
THIS MUST BE A DREAM...
FWISH
TEE HEE HEE
Haha! Take this!
SLSH
SPLISH
SPLASH
SLSH
DON'T BE RIDICULOUS.
WE HAD THE SERIAL-IZATION MEETING YESTER-DAY...
...AND OTTER NO. 11'S GETTING A BREAK. FOREVER.
BOOSH
FOR-EVER?!
YAY! FREE AT LAST!
WAIT. FOREVER? YOU MEAN ...

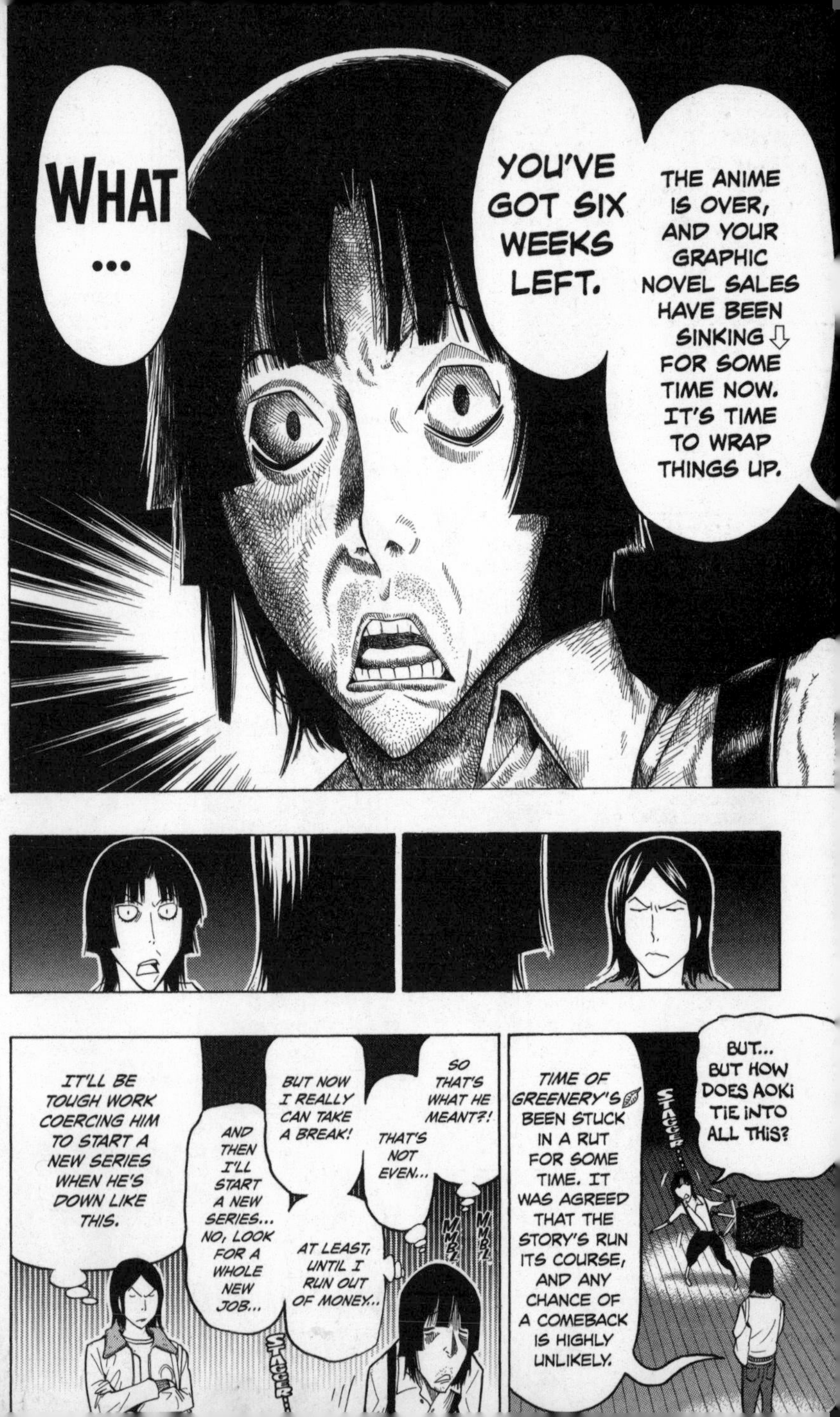
THE ANIME IS OVER, AND YOUR GRAPHIC NOVEL SALES HAVE BEEN SINKING⇩ FOR SOME TIME NOW. IT'S TIME TO WRAP THINGS UP.
YOU'VE GOT SIX WEEKS LEFT.
WHAT ...
BUT... BUT HOW DOES AOKI TIE INTO ALL THIS?
STAGGER...
TIME OF GREENERY'S BEEN STUCK IN A RUT FOR SOME TIME. IT WAS AGREED THAT THE STORY'S RUN ITS COURSE, AND ANY CHANCE OF A COMEBACK IS HIGHLY UNLIKELY.
SO THAT'S WHAT HE MEANT?!
THAT'S NOT EVEN...
BUT NOW I REALLY CAN TAKE A BREAK!
MMBL
MMBL
AT LEAST, UNTIL I RUN OUT OF MONEY...
AND THEN I'LL START A NEW SERIES... NO, LOOK FOR A WHOLE NEW JOB...
STAGGER...
IT'LL BE TOUGH WORK COERCING HIM TO START A NEW SERIES WHEN HE'S DOWN LIKE THIS.

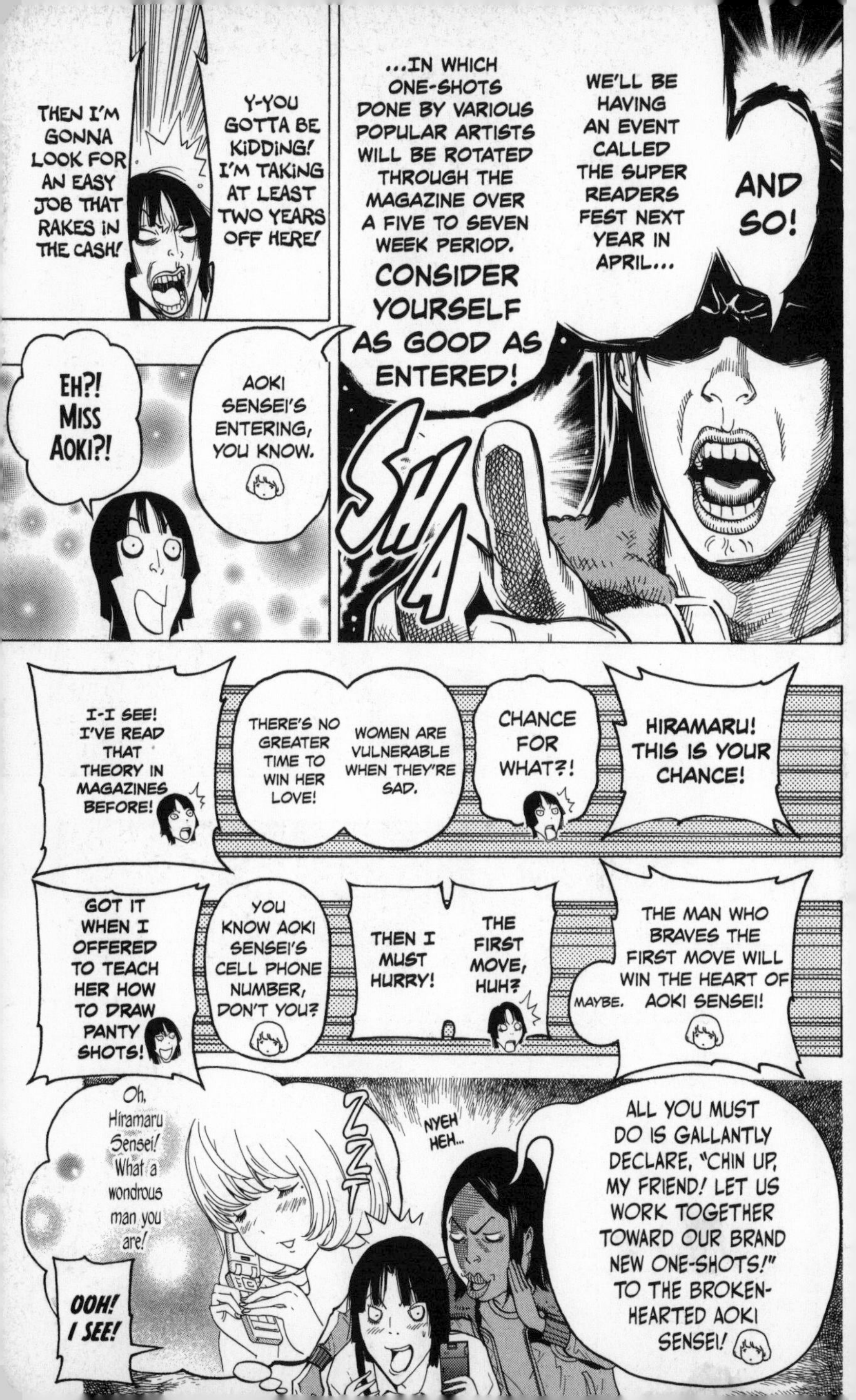
AND SO!
WE'LL BE HAVING AN EVENT CALLED THE SUPER READERS FEST NEXT YEAR IN APRIL...
...IN WHICH ONE-SHOTS DONE BY VARIOUS POPULAR ARTISTS WILL BE ROTATED THROUGH THE MAGAZINE OVER A FIVE TO SEVEN WEEK PERIOD.
CONSIDER YOURSELF AS GOOD AS ENTERED!
SHA
Y-YOU GOTTA BE KIDDING! I'M TAKING AT LEAST TWO YEARS OFF HERE!
THEN I'M GONNA LOOK FOR AN EASY JOB THAT RAKES IN THE CASH!
AOKI SENSEI'S ENTERING, YOU KNOW.
EH?! MISS AOKI?!
HIRAMARU! THIS IS YOUR CHANCE!
CHANCE FOR WHAT?!
WOMEN ARE VULNERABLE WHEN THEY'RE SAD.
THERE'S NO GREATER TIME TO WIN HER LOVE!
I-I SEE! I'VE READ THAT THEORY IN MAGAZINES BEFORE!
THE MAN WHO BRAVES THE FIRST MOVE WILL WIN THE HEART OF AOKI SENSEI!
MAYBE.
THE FIRST MOVE, HUH?
THEN I MUST HURRY!
YOU KNOW AOKI SENSEI'S CELL PHONE NUMBER, DON'T YOU?
GOT IT WHEN I OFFERED TO TEACH HER HOW TO DRAW PANTY SHOTS!
ALL YOU MUST DO IS GALLANTLY DECLARE, "CHIN UP, MY FRIEND! LET US WORK TOGETHER TOWARD OUR BRAND NEW ONE-SHOTS!" TO THE BROKEN-HEARTED AOKI SENSEI!
NYEH HEH...
Oh, Hiramaru Sensei! What a wondrous man you are!
OOH! I SEE!

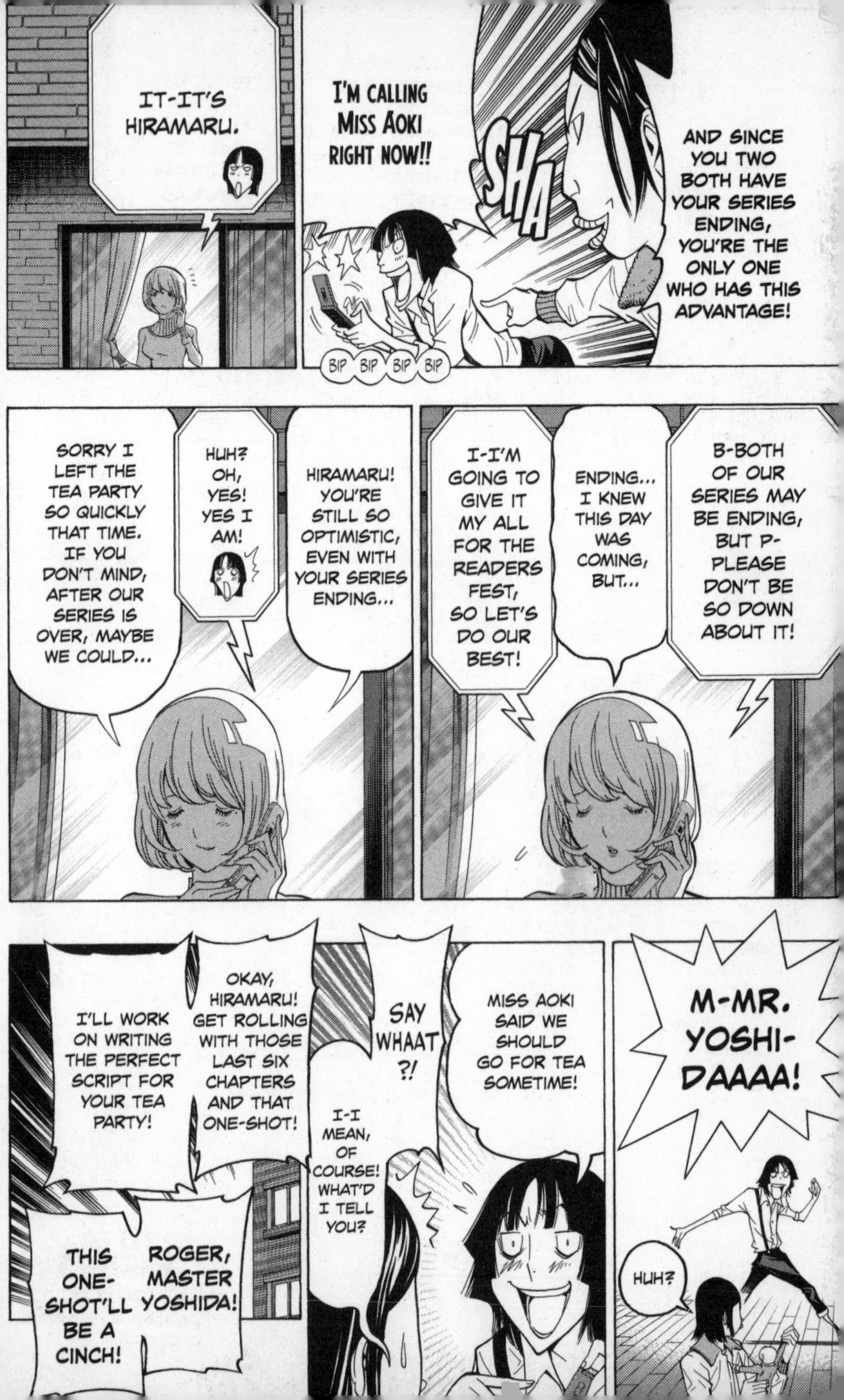
AND SINCE YOU TWO BOTH HAVE YOUR SERIES ENDING, YOU'RE THE ONLY ONE WHO HAS THIS ADVANTAGE!
SHA
I'M CALLING MISS AOKI RIGHT NOW!!
BIP BIP BIP BIP
IT-IT'S HIRAMARU.
B-BOTH OF OUR SERIES MAY BE ENDING, BUT P-PLEASE DON'T BE SO DOWN ABOUT IT!
ENDING... I KNEW THIS DAY WAS COMING, BUT...
I-I'M GOING TO GIVE IT MY ALL FOR THE READERS FEST, SO LET'S DO OUR BEST!
HIRAMARU! YOU'RE STILL SO OPTIMISTIC, EVEN WITH YOUR SERIES ENDING...
HUH? OH, YES! YES I AM!
SORRY I LEFT THE TEA PARTY SO QUICKLY THAT TIME. IF YOU DON'T MIND, AFTER OUR SERIES IS OVER, MAYBE WE COULD...
M-MR. YOSHI-DAAAA!
HUH?
MISS AOKI SAID WE SHOULD GO FOR TEA SOMETIME!
SAY WHAAT?!
I-I MEAN, OF COURSE! WHAT'D I TELL YOU?
OKAY, HIRAMARU! GET ROLLING WITH THOSE LAST SIX CHAPTERS AND THAT ONE-SHOT!
I'LL WORK ON WRITING THE PERFECT SCRIPT FOR YOUR TEA PARTY!
ROGER, MASTER YOSHIDA!
THIS ONE-SHOT'LL BE A CINCH!

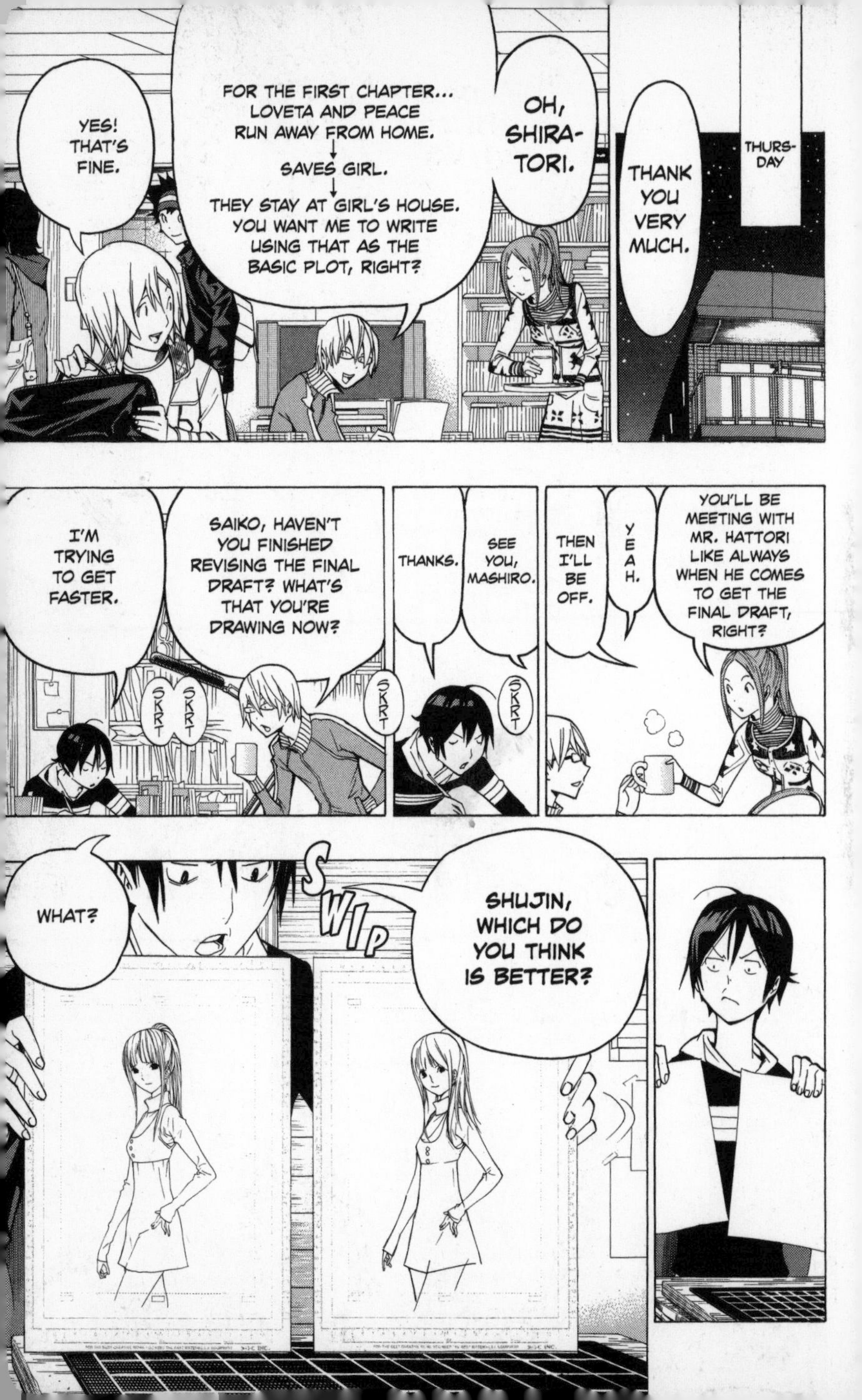
THURSDAY
THANK YOU VERY MUCH.
OH, SHIRATORI.
FOR THE FIRST CHAPTER... LOVETA AND PEACE RUN AWAY FROM HOME. ↓ SAVES GIRL. ↓ THEY STAY AT GIRL'S HOUSE. YOU WANT ME TO WRITE USING THAT AS THE BASIC PLOT, RIGHT?
YES! THAT'S FINE.
YOU'LL BE MEETING WITH MR. HATTORI LIKE ALWAYS WHEN HE COMES TO GET THE FINAL DRAFT, RIGHT?
YEAH.
THEN I'LL BE OFF.
SEE YOU, MASHIRO.
THANKS.
SKRT
SKRT
SAIKO, HAVEN'T YOU FINISHED REVISING THE FINAL DRAFT? WHAT'S THAT YOU'RE DRAWING NOW?
I'M TRYING TO GET FASTER.
SKRT SKRT
SHUJIN, WHICH DO YOU THINK IS BETTER?
SWIP
WHAT?

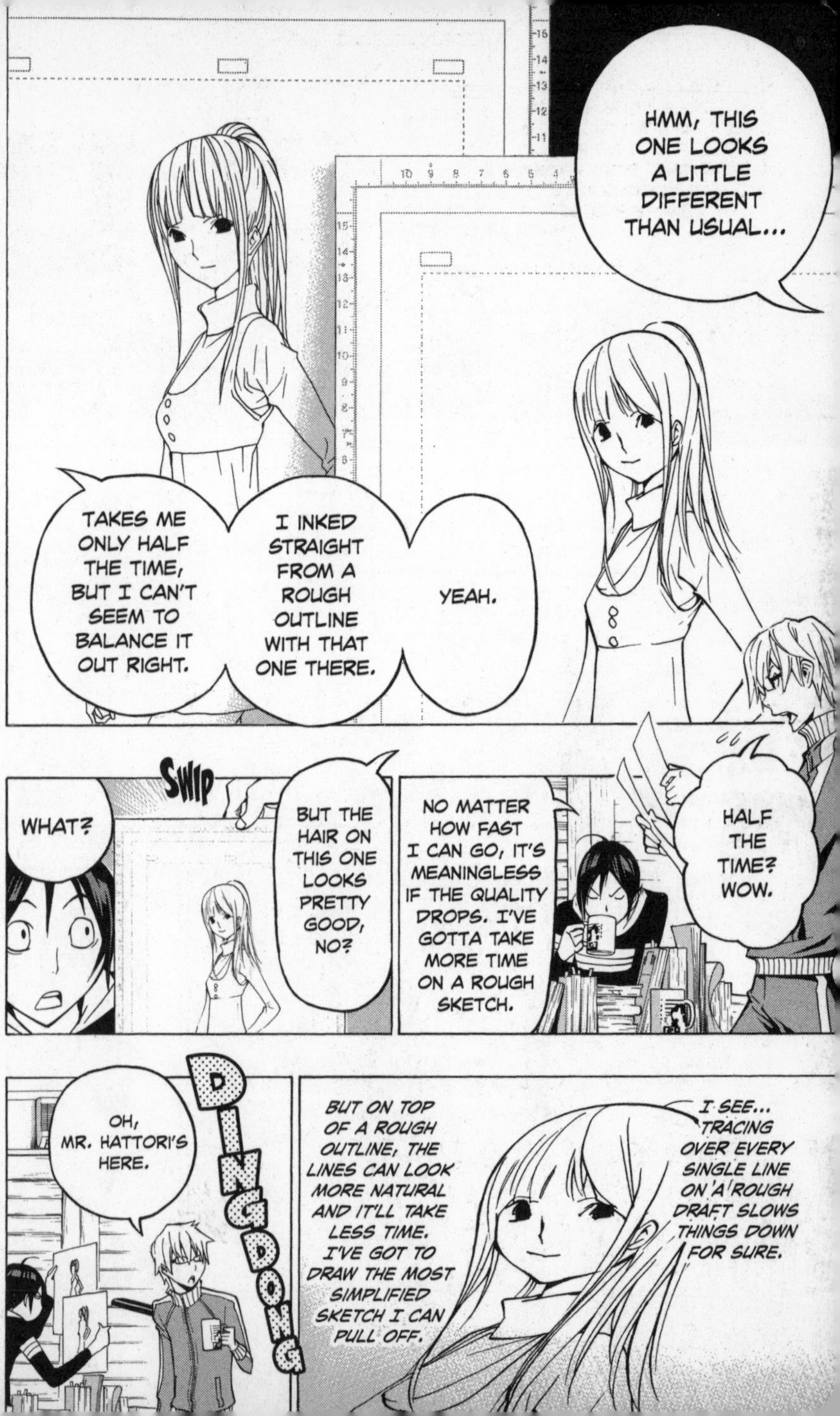
HMM, THIS ONE LOOKS A LITTLE DIFFERENT THAN USUAL...
YEAH.
I INKED STRAIGHT FROM A ROUGH OUTLINE WITH THAT ONE THERE.
TAKES ME ONLY HALF THE TIME, BUT I CAN'T SEEM TO BALANCE IT OUT RIGHT.
HALF THE TIME? WOW.
NO MATTER HOW FAST I CAN GO, IT'S MEANINGLESS IF THE QUALITY DROPS. I'VE GOTTA TAKE MORE TIME ON A ROUGH SKETCH.
SWIP
BUT THE HAIR ON THIS ONE LOOKS PRETTY GOOD, NO?
WHAT?
I SEE... TRACING OVER EVERY SINGLE LINE ON A ROUGH DRAFT SLOWS THINGS DOWN FOR SURE.
BUT ON TOP OF A ROUGH OUTLINE, THE LINES CAN LOOK MORE NATURAL AND IT'LL TAKE LESS TIME. I'VE GOT TO DRAW THE MOST SIMPLIFIED SKETCH I CAN PULL OFF.
DINGDONG
OH, MR. HATTORI'S HERE.

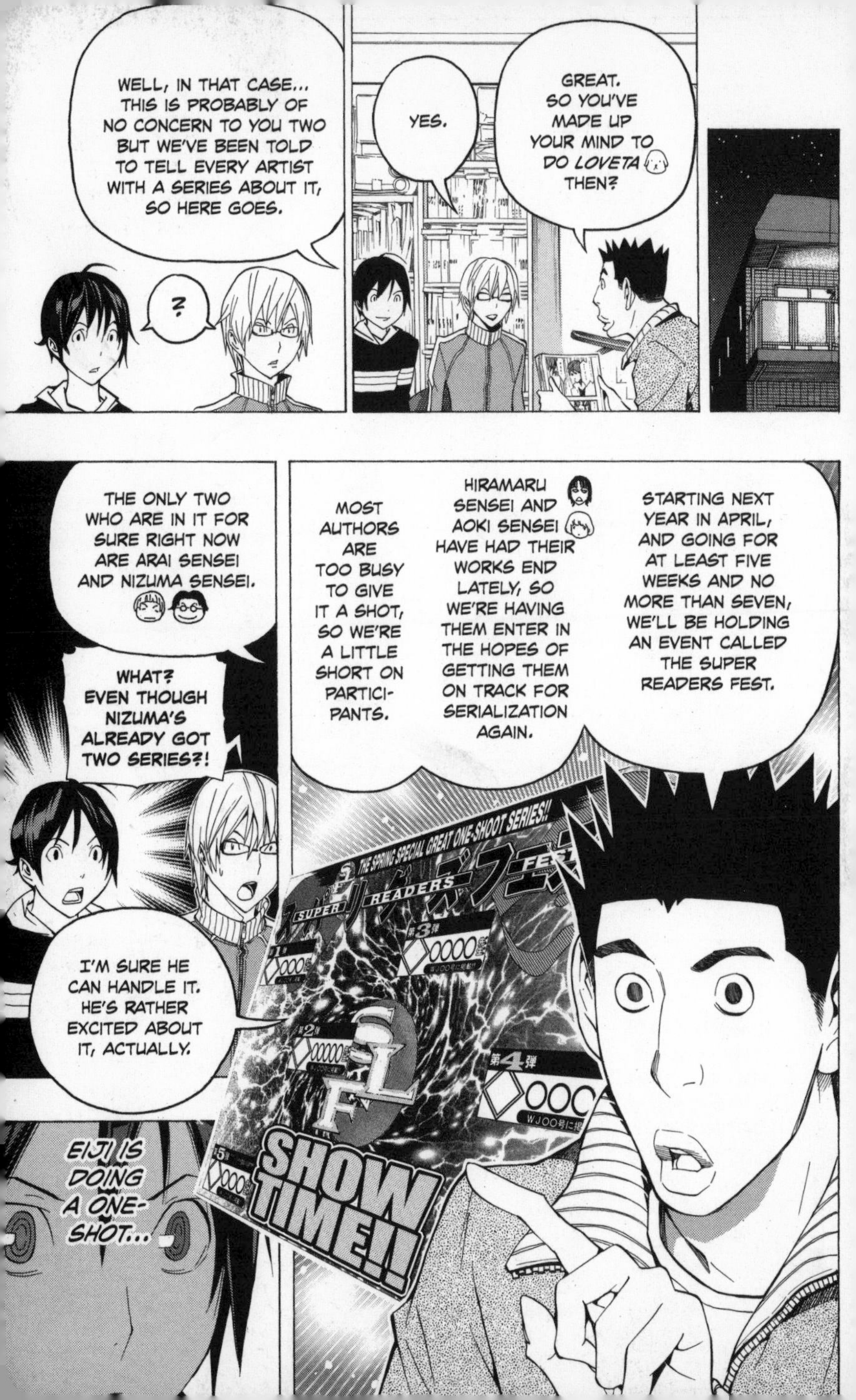
GREAT. SO YOU'VE MADE UP YOUR MIND TO DO LOVETA THEN?
YES.
WELL, IN THAT CASE... THIS IS PROBABLY OF NO CONCERN TO YOU TWO BUT WE'VE BEEN TOLD TO TELL EVERY ARTIST WITH A SERIES ABOUT IT, SO HERE GOES.
?
STARTING NEXT YEAR IN APRIL, AND GOING FOR AT LEAST FIVE WEEKS AND NO MORE THAN SEVEN, WE'LL BE HOLDING AN EVENT CALLED THE SUPER READERS FEST.
HIRAMARU SENSEI AND AOKI SENSEI HAVE HAD THEIR WORKS END LATELY, SO WE'RE HAVING THEM ENTER IN THE HOPES OF GETTING THEM ON TRACK FOR SERIALIZATION AGAIN.
MOST AUTHORS ARE TOO BUSY TO GIVE IT A SHOT, SO WE'RE A LITTLE SHORT ON PARTICIPANTS.
THE SPRING SPECIAL GREAT ONE-SHOOT SERIES!!
SUPER READERS FEST
SHOW TIME!!
THE ONLY TWO WHO ARE IN IT FOR SURE RIGHT NOW ARE ARAI SENSEI AND NIZUMA SENSEI.
WHAT? EVEN THOUGH NIZUMA'S ALREADY GOT TWO SERIES?!
I'M SURE HE CAN HANDLE IT. HE'S RATHER EXCITED ABOUT IT, ACTUALLY.
EIJI IS DOING A ONE-SHOT...

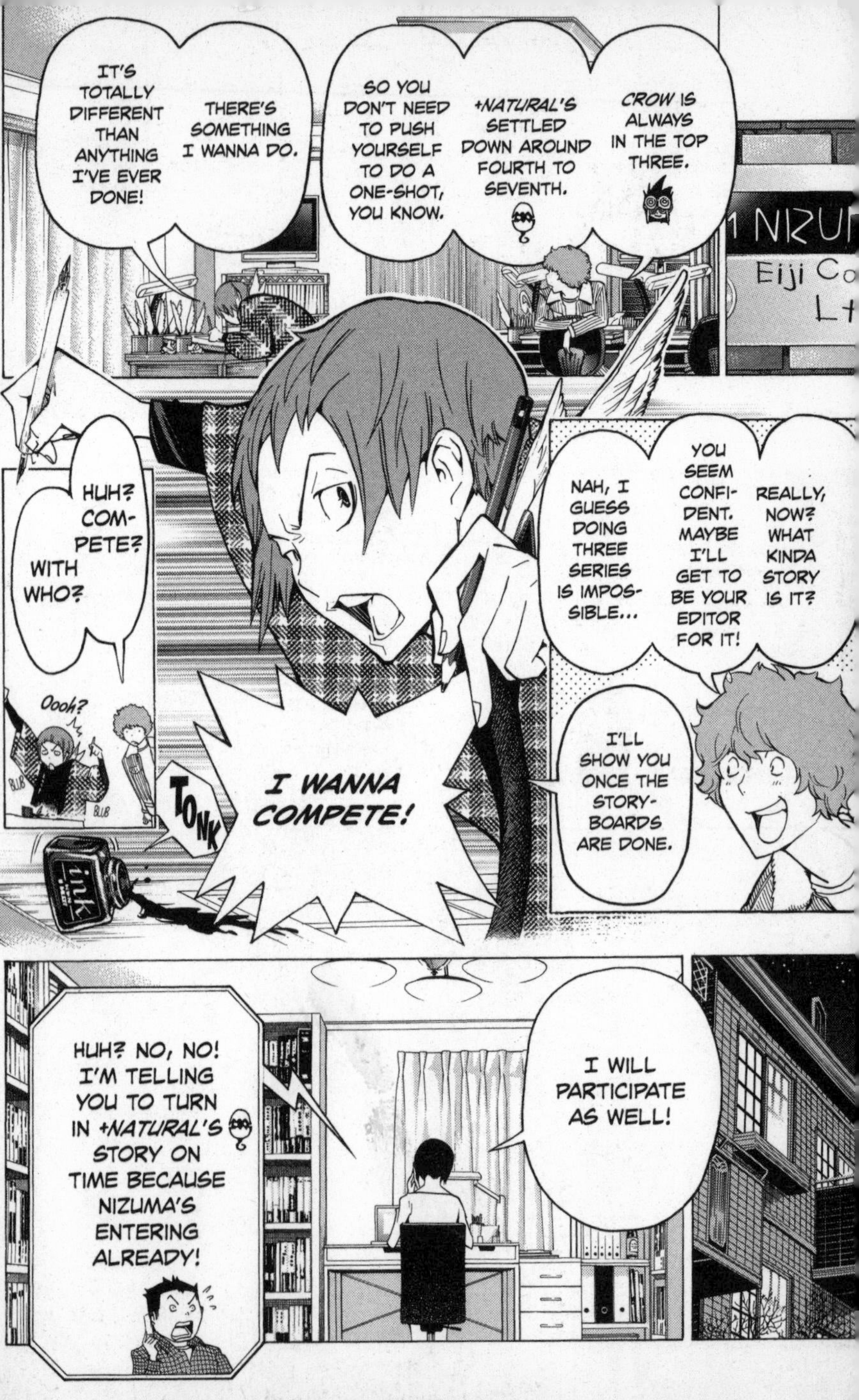
CROW IS ALWAYS IN THE TOP THREE.
+NATURAL'S SETTLED DOWN AROUND FOURTH TO SEVENTH.
SO YOU DON'T NEED TO PUSH YOURSELF TO DO A ONE-SHOT, YOU KNOW.
THERE'S SOMETHING I WANNA DO.
IT'S TOTALLY DIFFERENT THAN ANYTHING I'VE EVER DONE!
REALLY, NOW? WHAT KINDA STORY IS IT?
YOU SEEM CONFI-DENT. MAYBE I'LL GET TO BE YOUR EDITOR FOR IT!
NAH, I GUESS DOING THREE SERIES IS IMPOS-SIBLE...
I'LL SHOW YOU ONCE THE STORY-BOARDS ARE DONE.
I WANNA COMPETE!
TONK
ink
HUH? COM-PETE? WITH WHO?
Oooh?
BLUB
BLUB
I WILL PARTICIPATE AS WELL!
HUH? NO, NO! I'M TELLING YOU TO TURN IN +NATURAL'S STORY ON TIME BECAUSE NIZUMA'S ENTERING ALREADY!

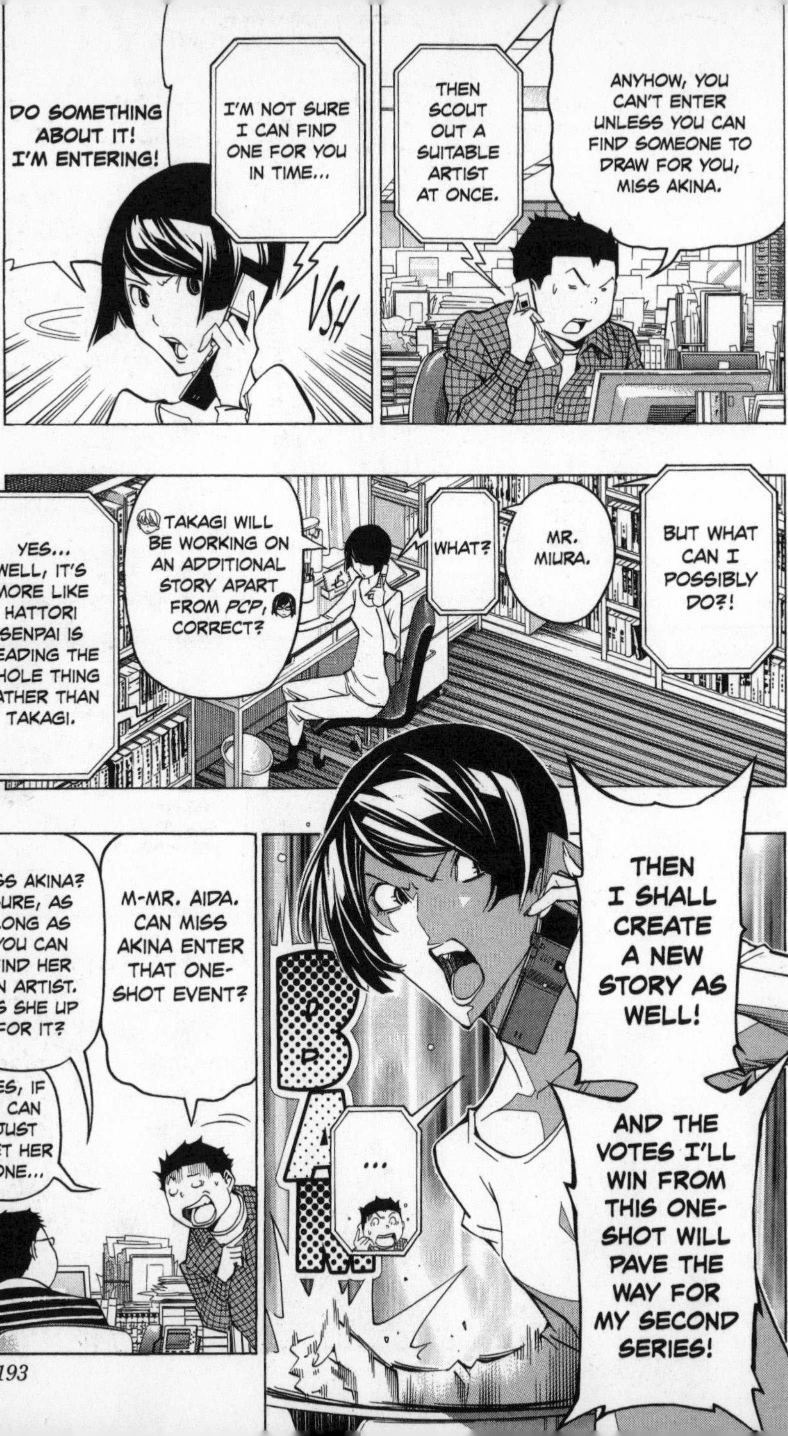
ANYHOW, YOU CAN'T ENTER UNLESS YOU CAN FIND SOMEONE TO DRAW FOR YOU, MISS AKINA.
THEN SCOUT OUT A SUITABLE ARTIST AT ONCE.
I'M NOT SURE I CAN FIND ONE FOR YOU IN TIME...
DO SOMETHING ABOUT IT! I'M ENTERING!
VSH
BUT WHAT CAN I POSSIBLY DO?!
MR. MIURA.
WHAT?
TAKAGI WILL BE WORKING ON AN ADDITIONAL STORY APART FROM *PCP*, CORRECT?
YES... WELL, IT'S MORE LIKE HATTORI SENPAI IS LEADING THE WHOLE THING RATHER THAN TAKAGI.
THEN I SHALL CREATE A NEW STORY AS WELL!
AND THE VOTES I'LL WIN FROM THIS ONE-SHOT WILL PAVE THE WAY FOR MY SECOND SERIES!
...
M-MR. AIDA. CAN MISS AKINA ENTER THAT ONE-SHOT EVENT?
MISS AKINA? SURE, AS LONG AS YOU CAN FIND HER AN ARTIST. IS SHE UP FOR IT?
YES, IF I CAN JUST GET HER ONE...

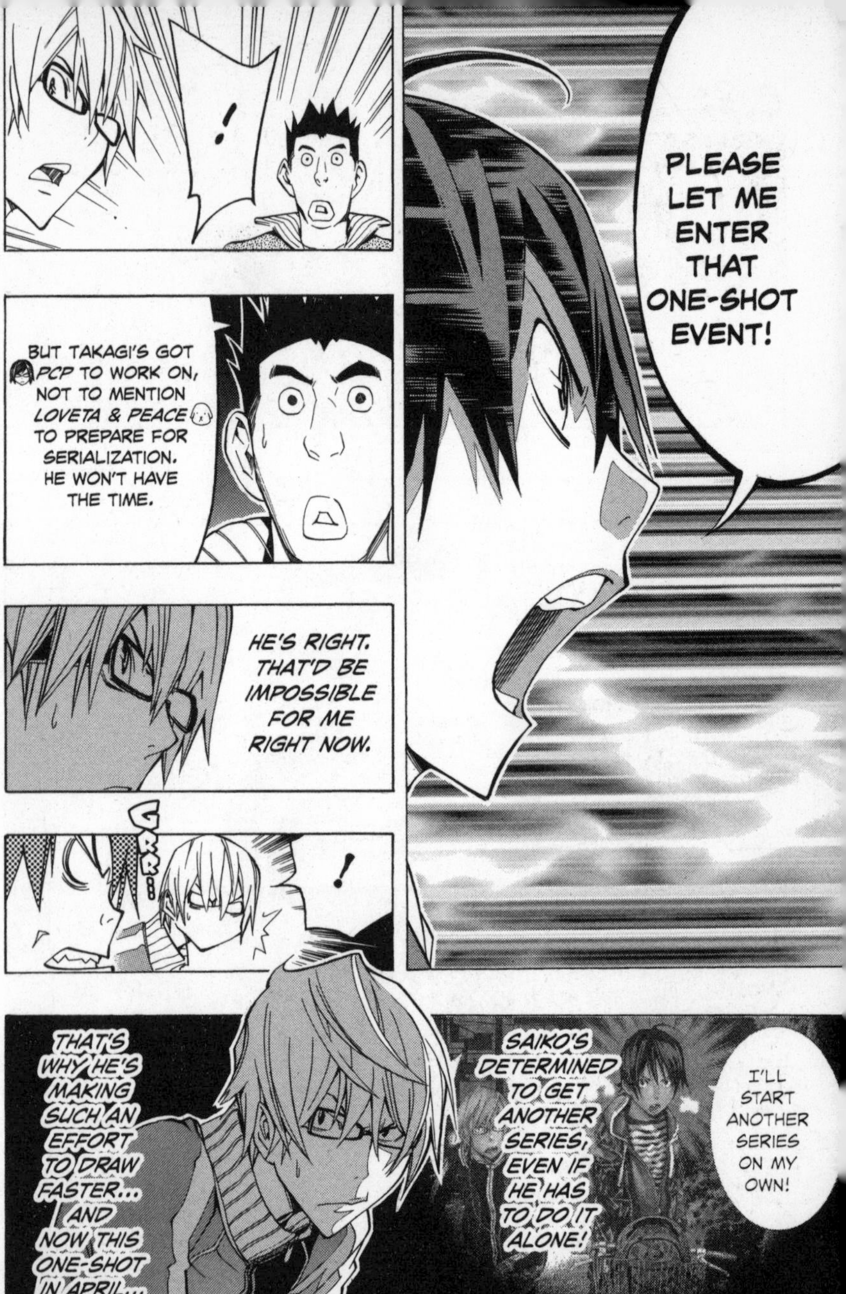
PLEASE LET ME ENTER THAT ONE-SHOT EVENT!
!
BUT TAKAGI'S GOT *PCP* TO WORK ON, NOT TO MENTION *LOVETA & PEACE* TO PREPARE FOR SERIALIZATION. HE WON'T HAVE THE TIME.
HE'S RIGHT. THAT'D BE IMPOSSIBLE FOR ME RIGHT NOW.
GRR...
!
I'LL START ANOTHER SERIES ON MY OWN!
SAIKO'S DETERMINED TO GET ANOTHER SERIES, EVEN IF HE HAS TO DO IT ALONE!
THAT'S WHY HE'S MAKING SUCH AN EFFORT TO DRAW FASTER... AND NOW THIS ONE-SHOT IN APRIL...

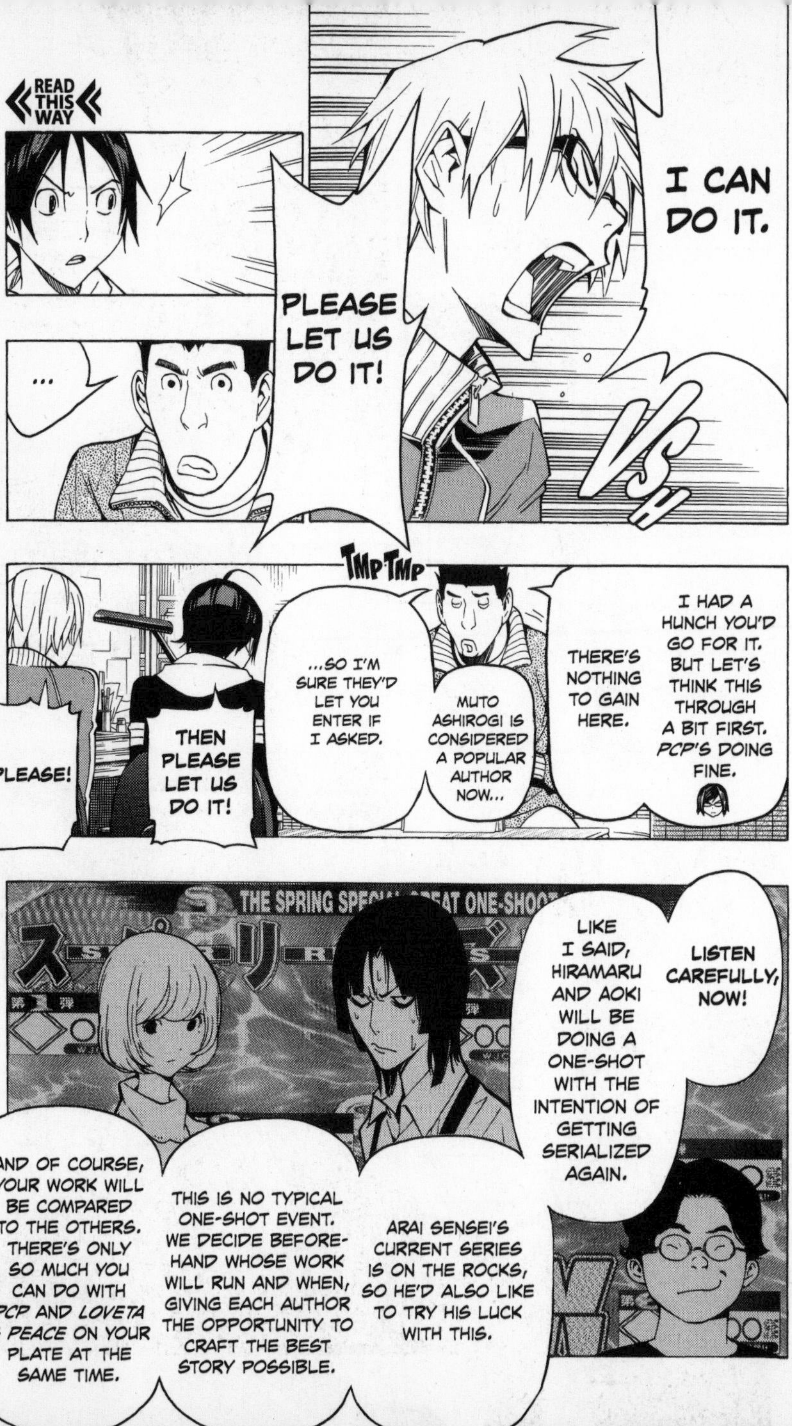
READ THIS WAY
I CAN DO IT.
PLEASE LET US DO IT!
VSH
...
I HAD A HUNCH YOU'D GO FOR IT. BUT LET'S THINK THIS THROUGH A BIT FIRST. PCP'S DOING FINE.
THERE'S NOTHING TO GAIN HERE.
MUTO ASHIROGI IS CONSIDERED A POPULAR AUTHOR NOW...
...SO I'M SURE THEY'D LET YOU ENTER IF I ASKED.
TMP TMP
THEN PLEASE LET US DO IT!
PLEASE!
LISTEN CAREFULLY, NOW!
LIKE I SAID, HIRAMARU AND AOKI WILL BE DOING A ONE-SHOT WITH THE INTENTION OF GETTING SERIALIZED AGAIN.
ARAI SENSEI'S CURRENT SERIES IS ON THE ROCKS, SO HE'D ALSO LIKE TO TRY HIS LUCK WITH THIS.
THIS IS NO TYPICAL ONE-SHOT EVENT. WE DECIDE BEFORE-HAND WHOSE WORK WILL RUN AND WHEN, GIVING EACH AUTHOR THE OPPORTUNITY TO CRAFT THE BEST STORY POSSIBLE.
AND OF COURSE, YOUR WORK WILL BE COMPARED TO THE OTHERS. THERE'S ONLY SO MUCH YOU CAN DO WITH PCP AND LOVETA & PEACE ON YOUR PLATE AT THE SAME TIME.

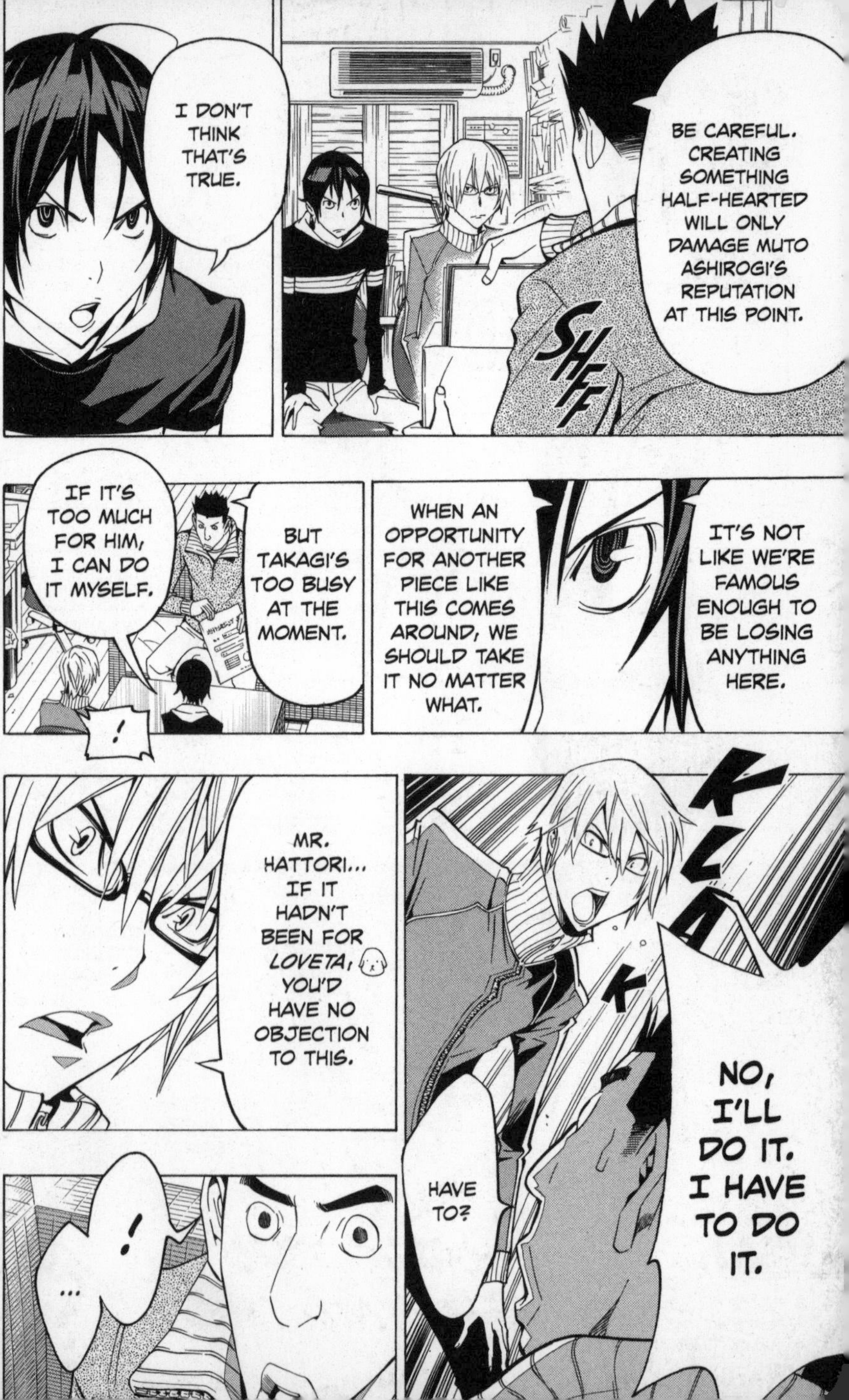
BE CAREFUL. CREATING SOMETHING HALF-HEARTED WILL ONLY DAMAGE MUTO ASHIROGI'S REPUTATION AT THIS POINT.
SHFF
I DON'T THINK THAT'S TRUE.
IT'S NOT LIKE WE'RE FAMOUS ENOUGH TO BE LOSING ANYTHING HERE.
WHEN AN OPPORTUNITY FOR ANOTHER PIECE LIKE THIS COMES AROUND, WE SHOULD TAKE IT NO MATTER WHAT.
BUT TAKAGI'S TOO BUSY AT THE MOMENT.
IF IT'S TOO MUCH FOR HIM, I CAN DO IT MYSELF.
!
KLAK
NO, I'LL DO IT. I HAVE TO DO IT.
HAVE TO?
MR. HATTORI... IF IT HADN'T BEEN FOR LOVETA, YOU'D HAVE NO OBJECTION TO THIS.
!
...

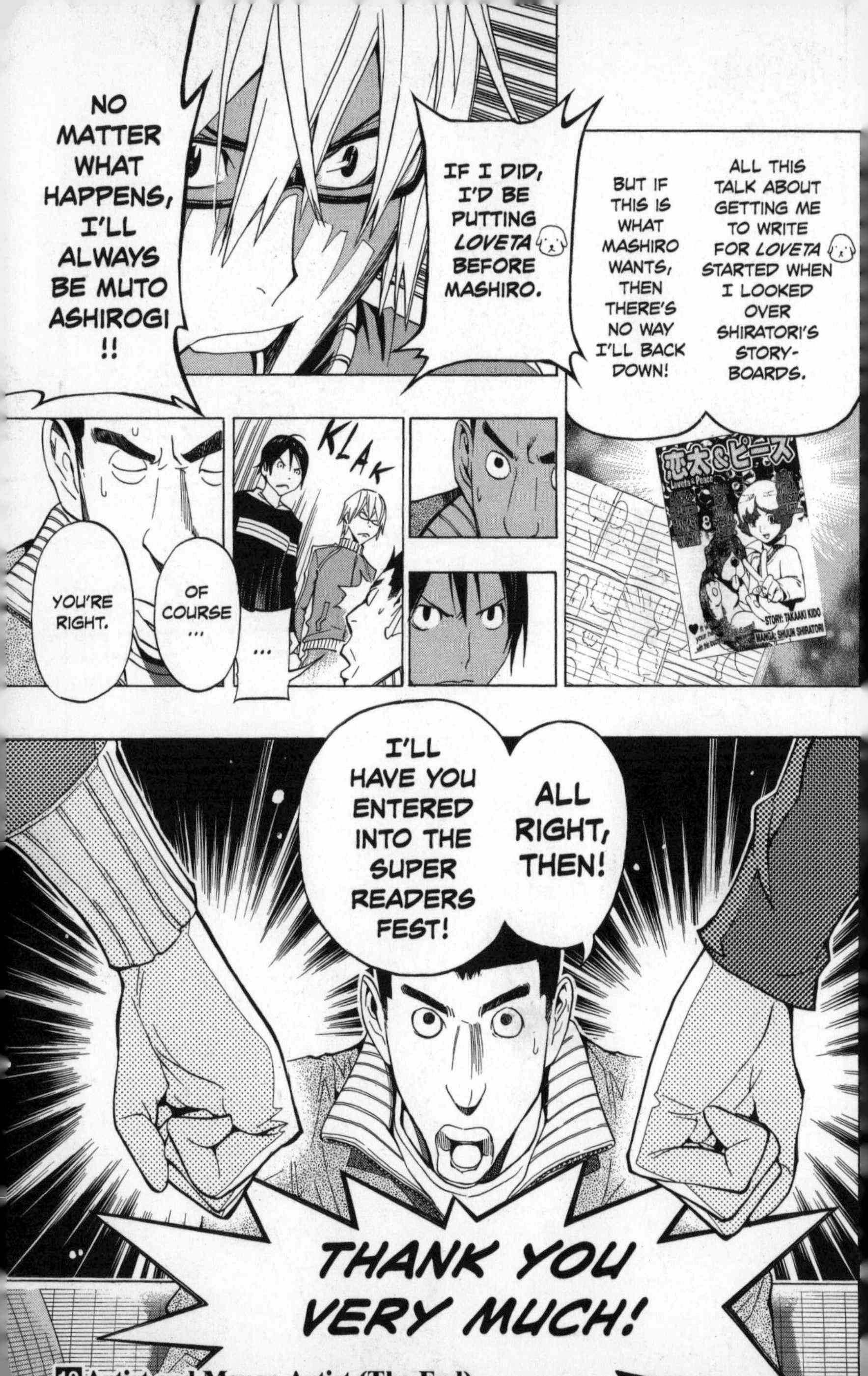
ALL THIS TALK ABOUT GETTING ME TO WRITE FOR *LOVETA* STARTED WHEN I LOOKED OVER SHIRATORI'S STORY-BOARDS.
BUT IF THIS IS WHAT MASHIRO WANTS, THEN THERE'S NO WAY I'LL BACK DOWN!
IF I DID, I'D BE PUTTING *LOVETA* BEFORE MASHIRO.
NO MATTER WHAT HAPPENS, I'LL ALWAYS BE MUTO ASHIROGI !!
恋太&ピース
Loveta & Peace
STORY: TAKAAKI KIDO
MANGA: SHUJIN SHIRATORI
KLAK
...
OF COURSE ...
YOU'RE RIGHT.
ALL RIGHT, THEN!
I'LL HAVE YOU ENTERED INTO THE SUPER READERS FEST!
THANK YOU VERY MUCH!

12 Artist and Manga Artist (The End)

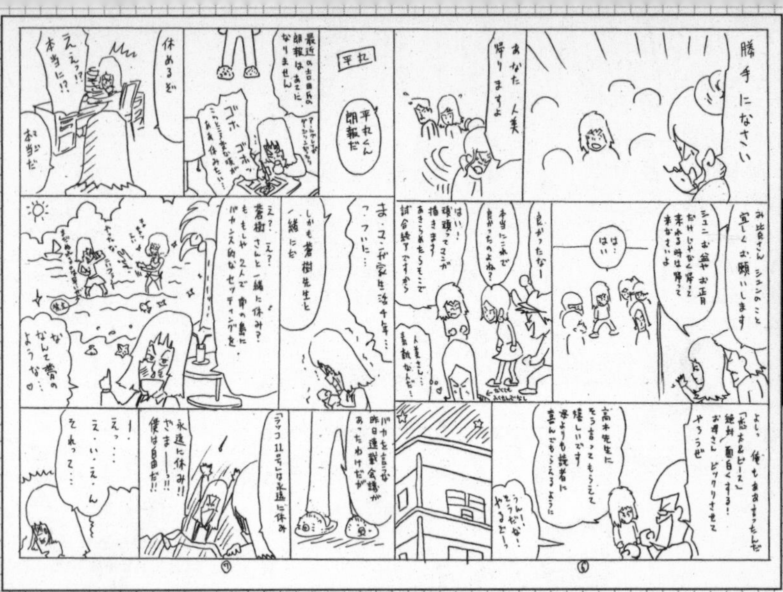

勝手になさい
あなた 人美 帰りますよ
み岩さん シュンのこと 宜しくお願いします
シュニお盆や お正月 だけじゃなく帰って 来れる時は帰って 来なさいよ
は…はい
良かったなー
本当にこれで良かったのよね?
はい! 頑張ってマンガ描きます あきらめたらそこで試合終了ですから
人美さん…素敵なんだ…
よし、俺もあきまったんだ 「恋太&ピース」絶対面白くする! お母さん ビックリさせてやろうぜ
高木先生にそう言ってもらえて嬉しいです 母よりも読者に喜んでもらえるように
うん! そうだな! やるぞ!
平丸
平丸くん 朗報だ
最近の吉田氏の朗報はあてになりません
ゴホ ゴホッ
休めるぞ
ええっ!? 本当に!?
本当だ
ま・ユージ家生活4年… つ・ついに…
しかも蒼樹先生と一緒にだ
え? え? 蒼樹さんと一緒に休み? もしや 2人で 南の島に バカンス的なセッティングを
な なんて夢のような…
バカを言うな 昨日連載会議があったわけだが 「ラッコ11号」は永遠に休み
永遠に休み!! やまー…っ!! 僕は自由だ!!
え…え・い・え・ん それって…

OHBA'S STORYBOARD

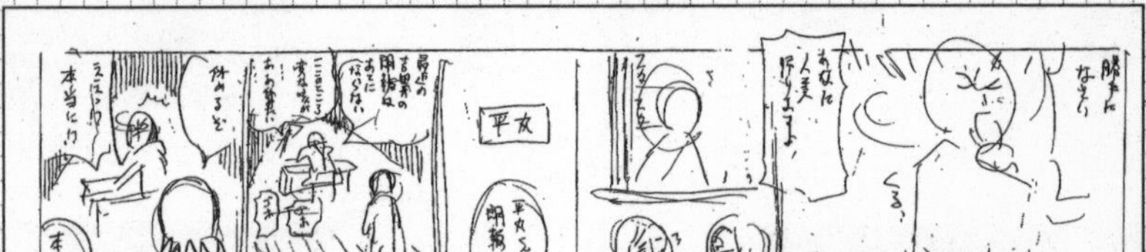

OBATA'S STORYBOARD

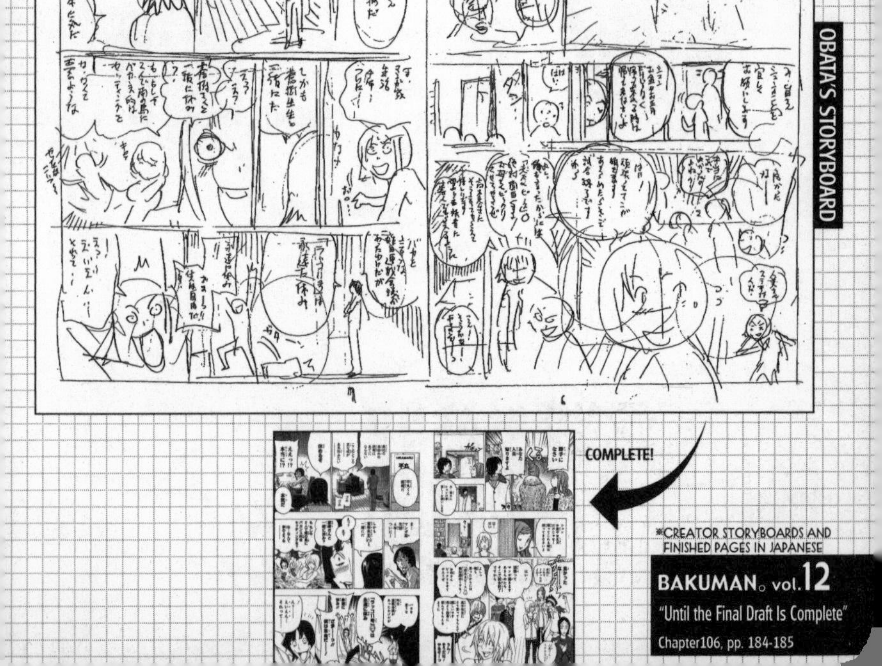

COMPLETE!

※CREATOR STORYBOARDS AND FINISHED PAGES IN JAPANESE

BAKUMAN。 vol.12

"Until the Final Draft Is Complete"

Chapter106, pp. 184-185